List of
FREE AFRICAN AMERICANS
in the
AMERICAN REVOLUTION:
Virginia, North Carolina, South Carolina,
Maryland, and Delaware
(Followed by the French and Indian War
and Colonial Militias)

By
Paul Heinegg

CLEARFIELD

Published for Clearfield Company by
Genealogical Publishing Company
Baltimore, Maryland
2021

ISBN 9780806359342

CONTENTS

ABBREVIATIONS AND NOTES ON THE TEXT

CR	North Carolina State Archives stack file number
DB, DW	Deeds, Orders, Wills, etc.
DHS	Delaware Historical Society
DSA	Delaware State Archives
G.A.	North Carolina Archives General Assembly Papers
LVA	The Library of Virginia
M804, 805	National Archives Revolutionary War pension files
MSA	Maryland State Archives
PPTL	Personal Property Tax Lists on microfilm at the Library of Virginia and http://familysearch.org
NCGSJ	North Carolina Genealogical Society Journal
Orders	Order books for the county court of pleas and quarter sessions
OW	Orders, Wills
SS	N.C. Archives Secretary of State records
T&C	N.C. Archives Treasurer and Controller's files
T.R.	North Carolina Archives Military Troop Returns
VA:, NC:, etc.	Federal census records for the state. Page number is for the printed version in 1790 and the microfilm of the original for all other years.
WB	Will Book

Sources are referenced in square brackets within the text in abbreviated format. The full citations are in the list of sources at the end of the book. Free African Americans, other than the soldier described, are in bold letters.

INTRODUCTION

Over 420 African Americans who were born free during the colonial period served in the Revolution from Virginia. Another 400 who descended from free-born colonial families served from North Carolina, 40 from South Carolina, 60 from Maryland, and 17 from Delaware. At least 24 from Virginia and 41 from North Carolina died in the service.

Over 75 free African Americans were in colonial militias and the French and Indian Wars in Virginia, North and South Carolina.

See *Free African Americans of North Carolina, Virginia and South Carolina* and *Free African Americans of Maryland and Delaware* by this author for the family history of these soldiers.

Note that some slaves fought to gain their freedom as substitutes for their masters, but they were relatively few in number. Those who were not serving under their own free will are not included in this list. It was simply not their fight. For example, when slave Harry deserted from the galley *Norfolk Revenge*, Captain Calvert advertised in the *Virginia Gazette* on 21 November 1777 for the return of his property, not a member of the crew. Likewise, when two Negro men Pass and Cambridge deserted from the galley *Manly*, they were described in the *Virginia Gazette* on 14 November 1777 as the property of Mr. Willis Cowper of Suffolk, not as seamen [Purdie edition, p. 3, col. 2].

VIRGINIA

Absalom Ailstock, born in Louisa County, a "free born Mulatto," appeared in Rockbridge County, Virginia court to make a declaration to obtain a pension for his services in the Revolution. He served in the militia for two tours. On his first tour he marched from Louisa County courthouse to Hanover County courthouse where he joined the 2nd Regiment under Colonel Richardson (Holt Richeson) and Major Armistead. Colonel Richeson then marched to "Marben Hills" (Malvern Hill) where there was a skirmish and they took two of the British gunboats which had come to plunder the area. On his second tour he was involved in the siege of York where he was engaged in digging entrenchments and making sand baskets and fascines for the entrenchments [NARA, S.6475, M804, roll 21, frame 519; http://fold3.com/image/11056431]. He was taxable in Louisa County from 1785 to 1799 and in a "list of "free Negroes & Mulattoes in 1813 [PPTL, 1782-184]. He was head of a Botetourt County household of 9 "other free" in 1810.

Charles Ailstock was said to have been a son of Michael Ailstock, Sr., and served in the 3rd Virginia Regiment. On 3 August 1832 Abraham H. Davis, a pensioner in Louisa County, testified that he had enlisted in 1776 in the 3rd Virginia Regiment in the company commanded by Thomas Johnson and that James and Charles Ailstock enlisted with him and were with him in the engagements which took place at Harlem Heights in New York as well as the Battles of Trenton and Princeton. They did not return to Louisa County, and he had no idea what had become of them. John Thomason of Louisa County certified that two sons of Michael Alesocke, whose Christian names he could not recollect, enlisted with him in the company commanded by Captain Thomas Johnson [Revolutionary War Rejected Claims, Louisa County, 1834, Ailstock, Charles, Digital Collections, LVA]. Charles Ailstock was head of a King George County household of 2 "other free" in 1810 [VA:203].

James Ailstock, said to have been a son of Michael Ailstock, Sr., served in the 3rd Virginia Regiment and failed to return to Louisa County [Revolutionary War Rejected Claims, Louisa County, 1834, Ailstock, Charles, Digital Collections, LVA]. Michael Ailstock, Sr.'s race was never indicated in the records, but his widow Rebecca was in a list of free "mulattoes" in Louisa County about 1802 [Abercrombie, *Free Blacks of Louisa County*, 21].

Lewis Ailstock was living in Caroline County on 12 August 1756 when the court ordered the churchwardens of St. Mary's Parish to bind him to Thomas Roy, Gentleman [Orders 1755-8, 191]. He enlisted for three years, was in Captain Richard Stephens's Company of the 10th Virginia Regiment from March 1777 to August 1778, at Valley Forge from May to June 1778, and in Lieutenant Colonel Hawes's Company of the 6th Regiment from June 1779 to November 1779 [NARA, M246, Roll 103, frames 591, 632, 638, 642 of 756; Roll 104, frame 316; Roll 108, frames 761, 782, 787, 789; M881, http://fold3.com/image/22954787].

Michael Ailstock, Jr., was living in Louisa County on 9 March 1773 when his suit against William Johnson, Gent., was dismissed by the Louisa County court [Orders 1766-74, 92, 97, 115, 177]. He was a drummer in Hazen's Regiment in a list of men considered as part of the quota of the state and settled for depreciation in Richmond on 28 May 1785 [New-York Historical Society, Muster and pay rolls of the War of the Revolution, 1775-1783, II:628-9; http://babel.hathitrust.org]. He was taxable in Amherst County in 1782 [PPTL 1782-1803, frame 9], taxable in Louisa County from 1783 to 1794 [PPTL, 1782-1814] and was taxable in Albemarle County from 1795 to 1807, probably related to Patience Alstock who was counted in a "list of Free Negroes & Mulattoes" in Albemarle County in 1813 [PPTL, 1782-1799, frames 445, 477, 584; 1800-1813, frames 22, 66, 111, 135, 154, 200, 290, 337, 553]. On 6 January 1800 he was ordered to remain in the Albemarle County jail for a breach of the peace until he posted bond of $100 and his securities James **Going** and Shadrack **Battles** posted bond of $50 each for his good behavior.

William Ailstock was a "free" taxable in Richmond City in 1784 [PPTL 1787-99]. He received approval for bounty land on 29 May 1783 for serving three years in the Virginia State

Artillery commanded by Colonel Thomas Marshall. He was discharged on 22 August 1780 [Revolutionary War Bounty Warrants, Ailstock, William, 1783, Digital Collection, LVA].

Emmanuel Alvis was a soldier serving in the Revolution on 15 June 1778 and 21 June 1779 when the York County court allowed his wife Mildred Alvis pay for her subsistence [Orders 1774-84, 163, 219]. He was called Emanuel Olvis on his discharge which stated that he enlisted on 25 September 1777 under Captain Samuel Timson, decd., to serve in the State Regiment of Artillery for three years and he served that time [Revolutionary War Bounty Warrants, Olvis, Emanuel, Digital Collections, LVA]. He was taxable in York County on 4 cattle in 1785, taxable on 2 tithes in 1797, 1798, 1802, 1803, 1805, and a tithe in 1806 and 1807. Milly Alvis was head of a household of 1 "free Negro & mulattoes over 16" in 1813 [PPTL, 1782-1841, frames 106, 180, 199, 209, 227, 235, 284 , 314, 325, 384].

William Ampey was in the list of men in the service of the Amherst County Militia with John Redcross in 1781 [William & Mary Digital Archives, Swem Library's Special Collections, Cabell Papers Box 2, Folder11.pdf]. Colonel Hugh Rose received his final pay of £16 on 24 January 1786 [NARA, M881, Roll 1090, frame 228 of 2028]. He was head of an Amherst County household of 5 persons in 1783 [VA:48]. In October 1782 John Redcross sued him in Amherst County court for slander, and William countersued Redcross for trespass. Both cases were dismissed because they failed to appear. He and John Redcross were sued for a debt of £40 on 3 May 1786 [Orders 1782-4, 49-50; 1784-7, 510]. He was taxable in Amherst County from 1782 to 1786 [PPTL 1782-1803, 9, 43, 70] and taxable in Rockbridge County from 1788 to 1795: called William Empy in 1788, William Aimpty (Negroe) in 1790, William Ampey in 1791 and 1792, William Ampy (Negro) in 1793 and taxable in 1800, 1803, 1805, 1806 and from 1809 to 1818 [PPTL 1787-1810, frames 33, 87, 100, 120, 147, 178, 202, 347, 437, 464, 491, 515, 593, 606; 1811-1822, frames 22, 46, 183, 332, 375, 486, 535].

Nathaniel Anderson was a "free negro" ordered bound as an apprentice by the churchwardens of Elizabeth River Parish to John Dennis in Norfolk County on 16 January 1755 [Orders 1753-5, 105]. He was a resident of Princess Anne County when he enlisted in the Revolution and was sized in 1780: *age 39, 5'4-1/2" high, a carpenter, born in Norfolk County, black complexion, deserted* [Register & description of Noncommissioned officers & Privates, LVA accession no. 24296, by http://revwarapps.org/b69.pdf (p.33)].

Francis Arbado was a "black Frenchman" who deserted the Manley Galley according to the 16 May 1777 issue of the *Virginia Gazette* [Dixon & Hunter edition, p. 2, col. 1].

Evans Archer was a soldier born in Hertford County, North Carolina, and living in Norfolk County on 23 September 1780 when he enlisted in the Revolution for 1-1/2 years: *age 25, yellow complexion, 5'4-1/4" high, marched to join Colonel Green* [Register & description of Noncommissioned officers & Privates, LVA accession no. 24296, by http://revwarapps.org/b69.pdf (p.70)]. He was taxable in Norfolk County in 1786 and 1787 [PPTL, 1782-91, frames 525, 558] and head of a Hertford County household of 3 "other free" in 1790 [NC:25], 3 in 1800, and 3 "free colored" in 1820 [NC:186]. He applied for a Revolutionary War pension in Hertford County court, stating that he enlisted in Portsmouth, Virginia, for 18 months until January 1782. He was in the Battle of Eutaw Springs and the Siege of Ninety-Six. Martin Bizzell testified that Evans was away from the neighborhood during his time of enlistment and James Smith testified that he met Evans in the service in Eutaw and Santee, South Carolina [NARA, S.41415, M805, Roll 25, frames 0113-8; http://fold3.com/image/11131047].

Adam Armstrong, the "Mulatto" son of Frances Armstrong, was bound out as an apprentice in Henrico County on 3 May 1762 [Orders 1755-62, 585]. He served in the infantry during the Revolution in Virginia. General Morgan received his pay of £102 on 7 April 1783, and William Reynolds received his pay of £5 on 24 January 1784 [NARA, M881, Roll 1090, frames 327-30 of 2028; http://fold3.com/image/23344857]. He received bounty land based on his discharge on 1 March 1780 by Colonel Porterfield after three years service [Revolutionary War Bounty Warrants, Armstrong, Adam, Digital Collections, LVA]. He was

7

taxable in the lower district of Henrico County from 1787 to 1788 and from 1807 to 1809 [PPTL 1782-1814, frames 119, 137, 508, 549, 571], taxable in Richmond City from 1791 to 1797 [PPTL 1787-1799].

Tobias Armstrong, the "Mulatto" son of Frances Armstrong, was bound out as an apprentice in Henrico County on 3 May 1762 [Orders 1755-62, 585]. He and Bennett **McGuy** were in the Light Infantry Muster of Lieutenant Colonel Thomas Posey's Detachment of Virginia Troops from 1 January to 1 April 1782. They were on command in Georgia in May 1783 [NARA, M246, Roll 113, frame 683 of 752; http://fold3.com/image/9649148], enlisted in the Revolution in Virginia in May 1779 and served for the war according to an affidavit from Lieutenant N. Darby of the 1st Virginia Regiment on 30 June 1783 [Revolutionary War Bounty Warrants, Armstrong, Tobias, Digital Collections, LVA].

Burrell Artis was born in Southampton County and was living there in September 1780 when he enlisted: *planter, black complexion* [Register & description of Noncommissioned officers & Privates, LVA accession no. 24296, by http://revwarapps.org/b69.pdf (p.70)]. John Taylor received his final pay of £36 for service in the infantry on 13 May 1783 [NARA, M881, Roll 1090, frame 355 of 2028; http://fold3.com/image/23344935].

James Ash, "orphan of Rachel," was bound apprentice in Norfolk County on 4 April 1764 [Orders 1764-68, 11]. He was a soldier born in Isle of Wight County and residing there on 28 September 1780 when he enlisted in the Revolution for 1-1/2 years: *age 18, black complexion, 4'9-3/4" high, a farmer by trade* [Register & description of Noncommissioned officers & Privates, LVA accession no. 24296, by http://revwarapps.org/b69.pdf (p.70)]. He was a "Mulatto" head of a Nansemond County household in Buxton's list for 1784 [VA:74]. In 1784 he was called James Ash of Isle of Wight County when he petitioned the Virginia Legislature for payment due him for 18 months service as a Continental soldier in one of the Isle of Wight County divisions [LVA, State Legislative Petitions, 23 November 1784].

John Ashby was married to Sarah Ashby, "Free Mulattoes," in 1765 when the birth and baptism of their children Matthew and Philemon were recorded in Bruton Parish, James City and York counties [Bruton Parish Register, 26, 32]. He died before 21 October 1776 when the York County court ordered the churchwardens of Bruton Parish to bind out his unnamed orphans and also (his son) Matt Ashby. On 15 June 1778 the court allowed (his widow) Sally Ashby, "wife of ___ Ashby" £12 for the subsistence allowed wives, children and aged parents of poor soldiers serving in the Revolution. She was called the mother of a soldier when she received an allowance on 21 June 1779 and 17 July 1780 [Orders 1774-84, 127, 163, 219, 273].

Humphrey Baine was presented by the grand jury in York County on 21 December 1772 for not listing himself as a tithable [Judgments & Orders 1772-4, 172]. He received bounty land based on his discharge by Lieutenant D. Mann which stated that he enlisted in the State Garrison Regiment on 23 September 1778 and served until 23 September 1781 [Revolutionary War Bounty Warrants, Bane, Humphrey, 1783, Digital Collections, LVA]. P. Humphrey Baine was with a group of "Free mulattoes or negroes" with Nancy Baine and a horse, tenants to Mr. Borum, living in a lot or rear of a residence in Richmond City in 1782 [VA:112]. Nancy Baine was head of a Richmond City household of 3 "other free" in 1810 [VA:361].

John Baker was called "a Mulatto by a White Woman" when the York County court ordered the churchwardens of Yorkhampton Parish to bind him out as an apprentice on 21 February 1763. James Hubbard of Yorktown certified on 26 September 1833 that he was acquainted with John Baker, a "coloured man" who lived with his father in Warwick County, and enlisted in the Revolution for three years in the Continental Service, remained in service until the end of the war and returned to his father's for many years after [Baker, John: Revolutionary War Bounty Warrants, Digital Collection, LVA]. John was taxable in New Kent County from 1787 to 1814: called a "molatto" from 1791 to 1796 and from 1805 to 1814 [PPTL 1782-1800, frames 93, 109, 159, 202; 1791-1828, frames 264, 293, 317, 341, 367, 417, 441, 462, 503].

He was head of a New Kent County household of 8 "other free" in 1810 [VA:745].

Jacob Banks registered as a "free Negro" in Goochland County on 21 September 1818: *a free man of color aged 64 years about five feet Six inches high* [Register of Free Negroes, p.106, no.221]. He was a "free man of color" of Goochland County who served 18 months as a wagoner at the Albemarle barracks [NARA, M804, S.8056, roll 134, frame 271; http://fold3.com/image/10996056].

John Banks registered as a free Negro in Goochland County on 3 September 1823: *a man of colour, was 74 years of age the 25th day of last February, about six feet high* [Register of Free Negroes, p.152]. He enlisted in Goochland County in 1779 under Captain Holman Rice and was discharged at the barracks in Albemarle in May 1781 [NARA, W.5763, M804, roll 134, frame 329; http://fold3.com/image/10996332].

Matthew Banks was the son of John Banks who was indicted by the Surry County court on 21 November 1758 for not listing his "Mulatto" wife as a tithable [Orders 1757-64, 135]. John left Matthew land by his 3 September 1780 Surry County will, proved 26 December the same year [Unrecorded Wills, 1767-1828, frames 10-1, http://familysearch.org/search/catalog/1908507, film 4121861]. James Kee, Esquire, received his final pay of £22 for service as a soldier in the artillery [NARA, M881, Roll 1090, frame 575 of 2028; http://fold3.com/image/286702693].[1] Matthew was head of a Surry County household of 1 free person in 1784 [VA:78], and in 1787 he was taxable on the 100 acres he inherited from his father. He sold this land to William Kea in 1795 and purchased 75 acres in Surry County on 1 February 1795 from Sampson **Walden** [Property Tax Alterations, 1796; Deeds 1792-99, 296-7]. He was taxable on his personal property from 1783 to 1794 [PPTL, 1782-90, frames 369, 399, 490, 565; 1791-1816, frames 75, 176]. He died before 22 February 1796 when his heirs (brother and sisters: John Banks, Judy **Charity**, Susanna **Howell**, and Hannah **Roberts**) sold this 75 acres to Howell **Deberix** [Deeds, 1792-99, 344-6].

William Barber, born on 17 May 1745 in Dinwiddie County, was living in Surry County, North Carolina, on 2 January 1833 when he made a declaration in court to obtain a Revolutionary War pension. He stated that he was living in Halifax County, Virginia, when called into the service in the militia under Captain Fleming Bates for three months in January 1781 and three months in September 1781 under Captain John Fortner during which he participated in the Siege of Yorktown. He moved to Surry County about 1805 [NARA, S.6572, M805, roll 48; M804, roll 138, frame 602 of 670; http://fold3.com/image/12783624]. He was taxable in the southern district of Halifax County, Virginia, from 1782 to 1803: called a "Mulatto" starting in 1792, listed with 2 tithables in 1795 and 1796; 3 in 1798, 3 in 1800 when he was called "Senr." [PPTL, 1782-1799, frames 5, 127, 185, 259, 412, 434, 533, 598, 671, 808; 1800-12, 49, 175, 304]. He was head of a Surry County, North Carolina household of 8 "other free" in 1810 [NC:697] and 6 "free colored" in 1820 [NC:670].

Charles Barnett, born in Albemarle County, enlisted in the Revolution in Charlottesville for 1-1/2 years from Albemarle County on 18 September 1780 and was sized at Chesterfield County court house about the same time: *age 18, 5'5" high, yellow complexion, a farmer, born in Albemarle County* [Register & description of Noncommissioned officers & Privates, LVA accession no. 24296, by http://revwarapps.org/b69.pdf (p.61)]. According to his pension application, he was a "mulatto" who enlisted as a private in Charlottesville in the 7th Virginia Regiment under Captain John Marks in Colonel William Davies' Regiment and was in the Siege of Yorktown. He was later sent with some baggage wagons to Philadelphia where he was discharged by General Steuben. He lived in Albemarle County until 1800, moved to Carter County, Tennessee, then Georgia, and then stayed in Granville County from about 1808 to 1833 when he applied. He was a "man of couller" who moved back to Albemarle County about 1839. In 1849 the Granville County authorities complained that he had left "a widow and a parcel of children" in Granville County. Sharod **Going** testified that he was with him

---

[1] James Kee was the tax commissioner for Surry County in 1784 [VA:78].

9

at Chesterfield courthouse [NARA, S.8048, M804, Roll 150, frame 457 of 664; http://fold3.com/image/11000781].

Benjamin Bartlett, born about 1755, was a "poor child" bound apprentice in Southampton County to John **Byrd** on 14 May 1772 [Orders 1768-72, 470, 532]. He was in the 10th Virginia Regiment on 7 December 1780 when he was sized at Chesterfield: *age 23, residing in Southampton County, entered service in September, drafted for 1 year, 6 months* [New-York Historical Society, Muster and pay rolls of the War of the Revolution, 1775-1783, II:600-1, 604; http://babel.hathitrust.org]. He registered as a free Negro in Southampton County on 12 June 1794: *Age 39, Colour Black, born of free parents in Southampton* [Register of Free Negroes 1794-1832, no. 27]. He was living in Prince Edward County on 16 April 1796 when he sold Aaron Smith his bounty land due him for serving for three years as a soldier in Lieutenant David Walker's Company of Colonel Febiger's Regiment and recorded the sale in Richmond [Revolutionary Bounty Warrants, Bartlett, Benjamin, Digital Collections, LVA].

Godfrey Bartley, born 29 November 1764, was the son of David Bartley and his wife Lucretia, "free mulattoes," who registered his birth in Bruton Parish, James City and York counties [Bruton Parish Register, 27]. Godfrey Bartlett was a soldier born in York County and residing there in September 1780 when he enlisted in the Revolution: *age 15, 5'3-1/4" high, Mulattoe complexion, a farmer* [Register & description of Noncommissioned officers & Privates, LVA accession no. 24296, by http://revwarapps.org/b69.pdf (p.56)].

Joseph Barkley, a "Mulatto," was indicted by the Surry County court on 21 November 1758 for not listing his wife as a tithable [Orders 1757-64, 135]. The following year on 19 November 1759 the York County court presented him for not listing himself as a tithable, but the case was dismissed when he paid his tax. He was called Joseph Bartlett on 20 August 1764 when he sued Christiana Kemp for debt in York County court in a case that was dismissed on agreement of the parties. On 17 December 1764 he was called Joseph Bartley when the court ordered him to pay the parish of Bruton £500 of tobacco for not listing his wife as a tithable [Judgments & Orders 1759-63, 281, 308, 320, 90]. He and his wife Elizabeth, "Boath free mulattoes," registered the birth of their son James in Bruton Parish, James City and York counties in 1768 [Bruton Parish Register, 33]. He was called Joseph Barclay on 15 July 1771 when the York County grand jury presented him for failing to list himself as a tithable [Orders 1768-70, 508; 1770-2, 25, 336]. He was called Joseph Barkly in the muster of Captain Nathan Reed's Company of the 14th Virginia Regiment for the month of June 1778: sick at Valley Forge and called Joseph Bartly in the June 1779 muster [NARA, M246, Roll 112, frame 679; http://fold3.com/image/10068412; http://fold3.com/image/10104087]. Joseph Bartlet was a "M"(ulatto) tavern keeper with Mary Bartlet on Tanner's Creek in Norfolk County from 1800 to 1802 [PPTL, 1791-1812, frames 351, 371, 383, 427].

James Bartlett was listed in muster of Lieutenant Gibbs of the 15th Virginia Regiment on 3 February 1778 in the same list as Benjamin Bartlett, both enlisted for 3 years. Benjamin enlisted on 14 July 1777. James enlisted on 26 March 1776 and deserted on 15 February 1778 [NARA, M246, Roll 113, frames 291, 300, 303 of 752; Roll 106, frame 168 of 847; http://fold3.com/image/9641502].

James Bass was taxable on a free tithe in Norfolk County in 1787 and from 1798 to 1810: a labourer in a "List of Free Negroes and Mulattoes" on Deep Creek in 1801 [PPTL, 1782-90, frame 562; 1791-1812, frames 243, 295, 351, 427, 461, 479, 555, 572, 674, 720]. He appeared in Bedford County, Tennessee court in November 1832 to apply for a pension for his services as a private in the Virginia Militia. He stated that he was born in Norfolk County, Virginia, enlisted in 1778 in Captain Moody's Company of Colonel James Matthews's Virginia Regiment and was in the Battle of Great Bridge on the Elizabeth River. He enlisted again in Captain Green's Company of Colonel Hutson's Virginia Regiment and enlisted a third time in Captain Cormack's Virginia Company. He had moved to Bedford County 13 years previous [NARA, S1745, M804, roll 169, frame 102; http://fold3.com/image/11695258]. He was head of a Bedford County household of 9 "free colored " in 1820.

Shadrack Battles enlisted in the Revolution in Louisa County on 14 December 1781, and was sized the following day: *age 26, 5'10-1/2" high, yellow complexion, a planter* [The Chesterfield Supplement or Size Roll of Troops at Chesterfield Court House, LVA accession no. 23816, by http://revwarapps.org/b81.pdf (p.99)]. He registered in Albemarle County on 10 March 1810: *a man of Colour, a black man, aged about fifty seven years, five feet 10-1/2 inches high* [Orders 1810-11, 62]. He was "a man of Color," a carpenter, who appeared in Albemarle County court on 14 May 1818 and testified that he enlisted while resident in Amherst County in 1777 or 1778 in Captain James Franklin's 10th Virginia Regiment and served for three years. He stated that he was in the Battles of Brandywine, Germantown, and Monmouth as well as the Siege of Augusta, Georgia, where he was discharged [NARA, S.37713, M805, Roll 63, frames 183-9; http://fold3.com/image/11069584].

George Beckett was sued in Northampton County court for a £4.8 debt on 13 April 1774 [Minutes 1771-5, 247]. He was listed as one of the men aboard the *Accomac* who was entitled to bounty land for 3 years service in the Revolution [Brumbaugh, *Revolutionary War Records*, 5, 67, 407]. He was a seaman from Accomack County who served in the Revolution and died intestate leaving no children. His estate was divided in Accomack County among his four sisters: Nancy, Betty, Rebecca, and Mason [Orders 1832-36, 251]. Their claim for his service aboard the galley *Accomac* was allowed on 9 December 1833 [Revolutionary War Bounty Warrants, Tunnel, William, Digital Collections, LVA]. Rebecca Beckett registered as a "free Negro" in Northampton County on 12 June 1794 [Orders 1789-95, 358]. Mason Beckett was head of an Accomack County household of 2 "other free" in 1800 [*Virginia Genealogist* 2:129].

James Berry was one of the members of Captain Joseph Spencer's 7th Virginia Regiment who did not return from furlough in Gloucester Town. Spencer advertised a reward for their return in the 8 August 1777 issue of the *Virginia Gazette*, describing James as a mulatto fellow, about 30 years old, 5 feet 8 or 9 inches high; enlisted in Fredericksburg but served his time with Mr. Thomas Bell of Orange County [Purdie edition, p.4, col. 3].

Charles Beverly was listed as deceased in the 12 November 1777 muster of Captain John Nicholas's 1st Virginia Regiment, in the same list with Silvester Beverly and Abraham **Goff** [NARA, M246, Roll 94, frame 43 of 742; http://fold3.com/image/10068453]. On 7 May 1784 the clerk of Buckingham County court certified that Priscilla and Jane Beverly were his only heirs. The affidavit was filed with the bounty land warrant for his services in the Revolution [Revolutionary War Bounty Warrants, Beverly, Charles, Digital Collections, LVA]. Priscilla and Jane were "Mulatto" taxables in Buckingham County from 1783 to 1788 [PPTL, 1782-1797]. Priscilla was head of a Buckingham County household of 1 "other free" in 1810 and Jane was head of a Buckingham County household of 12 "other free" in 1810 [VA:776].

Sylvester Beverly was listed in the payroll of the 1st Virginia Regiment from November 1777 to December 1779 [NARA, M246, roll 94, frames 43, 59, 91, 113, 121, 725 of 742; http://fold3.com/image/10068722]. He was a Revolutionary War soldier from Franklin County, Virginia, who enlisted in 1776 and served until the end of the War. He was 80 years old and owned 126 acres of land in 1822 when he petitioned the Legislature for a state pension [LVA receipt for petition dated 25 February 1823; petition on reel 235, box 296, folder 103 cited by Jackson, *Virginia Negro Soldiers*, 30]. He was a "Mulatto" taxable in Buckingham County in 1783 and 1784 [PPTL 1782-97] and was head of a Fluvanna County household of 7 "other free" in 1810 [VA:493]. He and his wife Nancy registered in Franklin County on 1 May 1809: *a Black Man, aged Sixty, of low Stature. Nancy Beverley wife of Silvester Beverley a Black woman aged forty three year of low Stature* [Minutes 1806-9, 270, 273]. He was on a list of soldiers in the Revolution who had not yet received bounty land by 25 November 1834 [Brumbaugh, *Revolutionary War Records*, 199].

11

John Bird was in the size roll of Captain Tarpley White's Company of the 6th Virginia Regiment on 13 December 1780: *age 16, 5'11", planter, born Southampton County, residing Southampton County, Eyes· Black, Hair: Black, Complexion· Yellow* [New-York Historical Society, Muster and pay rolls of the War of the Revolution, 1775-1783, II:600-1, 604; http://babel.hathitrust.org].

Peter Blizzard was called a "poor Mulatto" on 21 January 1772 when the Surry County court ordered him bound out as an apprentice [Orders 1764-74, 81, 276; 1775-85, 80]. He was called Peter Blizzard of Surry County on 29 October 1788 when he sold 100 acres in Prince George County which Edward Newell had sold to him in the year 1782 for serving as a soldier in the Continental Service for 18 months in place of John Newell [DB 1787-92, 232]. He was taxable in Surry County from 1788 to 1816: listed with 4 "free Negroes & Mulattoes above the age of 16" in 1813; taxable on 2 free tithes in 1812 and 1813, 3 in 1815, and 2 in 1816 [PPTL, 1782-90, frames 469, 594; 1791-1816, 105, 232, 282, 361, 439, 514, 588, 628, 666, 704, 726, 847]. He was head of a Surry County household of 2 "free colored" in 1830.

Jacob Boon was a yellow complexioned soldier, 5'5-1/2" high, a farmer born in Isle of Wight and living in Nansemond County when he enlisted in the Revolution for 1-1/2 years on 28 September 1780 [Register & description of Noncommissioned officers & Privates, LVA accession no. 24296, by http://revwarapps.org/b69.pdf (p.61)]. He was in a list of soldiers who had served but had not received bounty land by 7 January 1835 [Brumbaugh, *Revolutionary War Records, Virginia*, 221, 613].

Giles Bowers was living in Southampton County in 1766 when he and William **Kersey** were presented by the court for failing to list themselves as tithables [Judgment Papers 1765-6, 1026]. He was called Giels Bowry when he received a discharge from Captain Henry Pitt that he enlisted in the Revolution on 26 November 1776 for three years and faithfully served [Bowry, Giels: Revolutionary War Bounty Warrants, Digital Collection, LVA]. He was called Giles Bourey when he was listed in the muster of the 15th Regiment in Morristown on 9 December 1779 with James Casey and Charles Broadfield [NARA, M246, roll 102, frame 651 of 774; http://fold3.com/image/9946566]. He was taxable in Isle of Wight County from 1782 to 1809: listed as a "F.N." in 1792 and thereafter, called Jiles **Bowser** from 1804 to 1806 [PPTL 1782-1810, frames 4, 27, 45, 60, 74, 89, 242, 271, 346, 390, 428, 473, 491, 652, 673, 715, 771, 791]. James Casey made an affidavit in Isle of Wight County on 26 July 1833 that he and 7 other soldiers from Isle of Wight County, including Giles Bowery, enlisted in the 15th Virginia Regiment under Captain Henry Pitt in the regiment commanded by Colonel David Mason, went north with him, and served for three years [Broadfield, Charles: Revolutionary War Bounty Warrants, Digital Collection, LVA]. Daniel **Goff**, Burwell **Flood**, William **Clark**, Raymond **Reed** and Joshua **Perkins** were in the same muster as Giles. Thomas **Tann**, Dennis **Garner**, John **Goff** and Abraham **Goff** were in some of the previous musters of the 15th Virginia Regiment [NARA, M246, roll 113, frames 189, 224, 291 of 752; roll 110, frames 242, 484 of 768; http://fold3.com/image/9639784].

James Bowman was a soldier who enlisted in the 2nd Virginia Regiment on 1 July 1778 and served with Captain Thomas Parker until his death on 25 September 1782 [Bowman, James: Revolutionary War Bounty Warrants, Digital Collection, LVA]. On 6 October 1783 an affidavit by Betty **Morris**, a "free Mulatto woman," that William Bowman was his brother and only surviving heir was certified by the Henrico County court [Orders 1781-4, 439].

William Bowman, a "Mulatto," was charged with felony in Chesterfield County on 10 October 1767. His case was referred to the General Court [Orders 4:146]. He enlisted in the 2nd Virginia Regiment on 2 September 1780 for 18 months and was sized: *age 30, 5'6-1/4 inches, sawer, born Chesterfield County, residence Cumberland County, hair Black, Eyes Black, Complexion Swathy* [Register & description of Noncommissioned officers & Privates, LVA accession no. 24296, by http://revwarapps.org/b69.pdf (p.25)].

James Bowser was born in Nansemond County and enlisted in the Revolution there for 1-1/2 years on 28 September 1780: *50 years of age, 5'6-3/4" high, a farmer, yellow complexion*

[Register & description of Noncommissioned officers & Privates, LVA accession no. 24296, by http://revwarapps.org/b69.pdf (p.61)]. He was taxable in Isle of Wight County from 1782 to 1800: a "free Mulatto" in 1782, a "F.N." from 1793 to 1795 [PPTL 1782-1810, frames 4, 61, 89, 135, 181, 241, 331, 346, 418, 428, 491]. He received a certificate in Richmond on 28 May 1783 that he was a Continental soldier for the war and had served four years successively and was then in service [Bowser, James: Revolutionary War Bounty Warrants, Digital Collection, LVA]. He was eligible for military bounty land in 1803 [NARA, M246, roll 114, frame 448 of 492; http://fold3.com/image/9947440]. He was a "Free Negro" over the age of 45 in 1815 when he was taxable on a slave over the age of 16, 2 cattle, and 17 horses in "S. Hole" in Nansemond County in 1815 and 1816 [PPTL 1815-1837, frames 10, 51].

James Bowser was a native and resident of Nansemond County on 1 January 1782 when he enlisted in the Revolution for the duration of the war. He was sized in June 1782: *age 19, 5'1-3/4" high, yellow complexion, marked from pox* [The Chesterfield Supplement or Size Roll of Troops at Chesterfield Court House, LVA accession no. 23816, by http://revwarapps.org/b81.pdf (p.81)]. Nathaniel Bowser, Sr., and Thomas Bowser, heir at law of James Bowser, testified on 17 October 1833 that Nathaniel Bowser, Thomas Bowser, and Betsy Bowser, Moses **Ash**, Caroline **Ash**, Lydia **Ash**, Thomas **Ash**, and Curtis **Ash** were the only heirs of James Bowser who had served in the Revolution in 1782. In 1835 they received bounty land scrip for his service [NARA, BLWt. 2001-100, M804, Roll 306, frame 0123; frame 138 of 809; http://fold3.com/image/11409941].

Randal Bowser was in the payroll of the 3rd South Carolina Regiment in July and August 1779 [NARA, M246, roll 89, frame 171; http://fold3.com/image/9679437]. He was head of a Hertford County household of 6 "other free" in Moore's District in 1800 [NC:133].

Augustine Boyd was among a group of Revolutionary War seamen who deserted from the ship *Tartar* and for each of whom a $100 reward was offered by Thomas Grant of the Chickahominy Shipyard in the 11 September 1779 issue of the *Virginia Gazette*: *...George Day, and Augustine Boyd, all of Wicomico parish, Northumberland county* [Dixon and Nicholson edition, p. 3, col. 2]. He was a "Mulatto" sailor, born in Northumberland County, drafted there on 21 March 1781 and sized in 1781: *yellow complexion, Mulatto, age 25, 5'11-1/4" high* [The Chesterfield Supplement or Size Roll of Troops at Chesterfield Court House, LVA accession no. 23816, by http://revwarapps.org/b81.pdf (p.47)]. He appeared on the muster rolls of Col. Thomas Posey's 2nd Virginia Regiment from January 1 to April 1, 1782. Captain Blackwell received his final pay of £15 on 23 October 1783 [NARA, M881, Roll 1089, frames 192-194 of 1808; http://fold3.com/image/23297652]. He was a "free mulatto" head of a Northumberland County household of 7 "other free" in 1810 [VA:973]. He was entitled to bounty land for his service as a seaman [Brumbaugh, *Revolutionary War Records, Virginia*, 215].

James Brandom was a soldier born in Goochland County and living there in June 1779 when he enlisted in the Revolution. He was sized on 4 April 1781: *yellow Negro, age 23, 5'5-1/4" high, a planter, made his escape from Ch'stown* [Register & description of Noncommissioned officers & Privates, LVA accession no. 24296, by http://revwarapps.org/b69.pdf (p.90)].

John Brandom, son of Mary Brandom, was born 4 October 1760. He and Rhode Brandom were on the payroll of Captain Dudley's Company of the 2nd Virginia Regiment from 1 May to September 1778 [NARA, M246, roll 96, frames 326, 530, 536, 541 of 736; http://fold3.com/image/10081813].

Rhode Brandom was called the son of Mary Brandom when he was bound out as an apprentice by the churchwardens of Mecklenburg County, Virginia, on 11 August 1766 and called a "Molotto Boy" on 12 October 1772 when the court ordered him bound to someone else. He was listed in the payroll of Captain Dudley's 2nd Virginia State Regiment commanded by Colonel Gregory Smith from July to December 1778 [NARA, M246, Roll 96, frames 530, 538, 558, 581 of 736; http://fold3.com/image/10081826, 10081833, 10081873]. He was on a list of soldiers in the Revolution who had not yet received bounty land by 25

November 1834 [Brumbaugh, *Revolutionary War Records*, 199].

Thomas Brannum/ Brandom/ Brandon, "Son of Elenor Brandon, was bound as an apprentice to Jacob **Chavis** in Mecklenburg County, Virginia, on 13 July 1764 [Orders 1763-4, 35, 91; 1764-5, 108]. He was head of a Mecklenburg County household of 6 "free colored" in 1820. He was living in Mecklenburg County when he applied for a pension for his services in the Revolution, stating that he was born in Hanover County in 1746 and moved to Mecklenburg County before the Revolution. He entered the service in June 1780 under Captain Richard Swepson, marched south, first to Hillsbororough, and then under General Stevens marched to South Carolina where they joined General Gates in the Battle of Camden. They returned to Caswell County, North Carolina, where he was discharged. He was drafted again in August 1781 in Colonel Lewis Burwell's Regiment, marched to Hog Island, crossed the James River to Williamsburg, then to Gloucester County where he was discharged after Cornwallis's surrender [NARA, W.4643, M804, roll 323, frame 507 of 1136; http://fold3.com/image/13730023].

William Brandum was in the list of men from Mecklenburg County under the command of Captain Reuben Vaughan who were on a detachment to the southward under immediate command of Colonel David Mason in 1779 [Elliott, Katherine, *Revolutionary War Records, Mecklenburg County, Virginia* (1964), 162-3, citing Edmund W. Hubbard Papers, Southern Historical Collection, UNC Chapel Hill, NC]. He was head of a Mecklenburg County, Virginia household of 5 persons in 1782 [VA:34] and was a "melatto" taxable in the northern district of Campbell County in 1789 [PPTL, 1785-1814, frame 123].

Benjamin Brown was in a list of deserters advertised in the 28 November 1777 issue of the *Virginia Gazette* by Lieutenant John Dudley as one of the drafts from Charles City County who were lurking about the county. A reward was offered for their delivery to the commanding officer in Williamsburg [Purdie edition, p.3, col.2]. He was taxable on his own tithe and a horse in Waynoke Precinct of Charles City County from 1784 to 1814, listed as a "Mulattoe" in 1813 and 1814 [PPTL, 1784-1814] and head of a household of 3 "other free" in 1810 [VA:958].

Edward Brown, Sr., was taxable in Charles City County from 1784 to 1794 [PPTL 1783-7; 1788-1814] and taxable on 200 acres from 1782 to 1793 [Land Tax List, 1782-1830]. He was probably the Edward Brown who was drafted out of Charles City County but had not yet reported for duty in Williamsburg on 28 November 1777 when Lieutenant John Dudley placed an ad in the *Virginia Gazette* warning him and John Major, Jr., that they had until 10 December to report [Purdie edition, p.3, col.2].

Edward Brown, Jr., was taxable in the Charles City County household of Edward Brown in 1784 and called "son of Ned" in 1809 when he was taxable on 2 tithes [PPTL, 1783-7; 1788-1814]. He was head of a Charles City County household of 8 "other free" in 1810 [VA:957]. He received pay for service in the Revolution [Eckenrode, *Virginia Soldiers of the American Revolution*, I:68, citing Auditors' Account XVIII:558].

Freeman Brown(e) was head of a Charles City County household of 5 "other free" in 1810 [VA:959]. He received payment for service in the Revolution [Eckenrode, *Virginia Soldiers of the American Revolution*, I:68, citing Auditors' Account XVIII:558-9, LVA].

Isaac Brown was born in Charles City County and enlisted there in the Revolution for 1-1/2 years on 12 September 1780: *complexion black, 5'2-1/2" high, a farmer* [Register & description of Noncommissioned officers & Privates, LVA accession no. 24296, by http://revwarapps.org/b69.pdf(p.45)]. He was taxable in Lower Westover Precinct of Charles City County in 1786 [PPTL, 1783-7], head of a Charles City County household of 10 "other free" in 1810 [VA:959] and 4 "free colored" in 1820 [VA:13]. He applied for a pension in Charles City County at the age of 69 on 19 May 1829, stating that he enlisted in Charles City County in the fall of the year 1780 and served in Captain Sanford's Company in Colonel Campbell's Regiment for 18 months. He was in the Battle of Guildford Courthouse, the Siege of Ninety Six, and the Battle of Eutaw Springs. He owned 70 acres in Charles City County [NARA, S.39,214, M804, Roll 366, frame 240 of 893; http://fold3.com/image/11713004].

James Brown was a native and resident of Dinwiddie County on 6 June 1782 when he enlisted in the Revolution and was sized the same month: *age 18, 5'6" high, yellow complexion* [The Chesterfield Supplement or Size Roll of Troops at Chesterfield Court House, LVA accession no. 23816, by http://revwarapps.org/b81.pdf (p.99)].

William B[rown] was in the size roll of Captain T. White's 6th Virginia Regiment in 1780: *William B[rown], Age 22, Black Eyes, Black Hair, Yellow Complexion, enlisted 1 August 1780, Southampton* [New-York Historical Society, Muster and pay rolls of the War of the Revolution, 1775-1783, II:602, 606; http://babel.hathitrust.org].

George Bruma enlisted in the Revolution as a substitute in Fairfax County on 16 March 1781: *Brumma, Geo., age 23, 5'8-1/2" high, yellow complexion, a tailor, born in Austatia* [The Chesterfield Supplement or Size Roll of Troops at Chesterfield Court House, LVA accession no. 23816, by http://revwarapps.org/b81.pdf (p. 55)].

George Burk enlisted in the Revolution in Shenandoah County for two years in 1779 in Captain Abraham Tipton's Company of Colonel Joseph Crockett Virginia Regiment. He applied for a pension in Jefferson County, Indiana, in 1831. He spent his time in the service guarding British prisoners at Albemarle Barracks and repulsing the Indians in Kentucky [NARA, S.32152, M804, roll 413, frame 436 of 548; http://fold3.com/image/12033024]. He was head of a Ripley Township, Johnson County, Indiana household of 5 "free colored" in 1820 and 7 "free colored" in 1830.

Francis Bunday was a soldier born in Caroline County and living there on 30 March 1781 when he enlisted in the Revolution: *age 18, 5'2-1/2" high, Negro* [Register & description of Noncommissioned officers & Privates, LVA accession no. 24296, by http://revwarapps.org/b69.pdf (p.90)]. On 9 July 1783 he received his discharge papers and a certificate from the War Office that he had only received four months pay since 1 January 1782 [Revolutionary War Bounty Warrants, Bundy, Francis, Digital Collections, LVA]. He was a "Free Negro" head of a Culpeper County household of 5 "other free" in 1810 [VA:7]. He was a resident of Culpeper County when he applied for a pension for his services in the Revolution. He stated that he enlisted in Caroline County under Captain Kirkpatrick in the Regiment of Colonel Thomas Gaskins, was in the Siege of Yorktown and was discharged in 1782 [NARA, S.37719, M805, Roll 139, frames 554-7; http://fold3.com/image/12026831].

Thomas Bunday was a "Mulatto Man" with between 12 and 13 years to serve on 18 March 1763 when he was listed in the Culpeper County estate of Humphrey Brooke, decd [WB A:394]. He received payment for military service in the Revolution [Eckenrode, *List of the Revolutionary Soldiers of Virginia (Supplement)*, 50, citing Auditors Accounts XXXI:219]. Thomas Bunda was a "Free Negro" head of a Culpeper County household of 1 "other free" in 1810 [VA:14].

William Bunday was taxable in Culpeper County in Reuben Zimmerman's household in 1787 and a "Mulatto" taxable in 1793, 1796 and 1797 [PPTL 1782-1802, frames 200, 490, 598, 640]. He was listed among the soldiers who had served three years in the Revolution and had not yet drawn bounty land on 7 January 1835 [Brumbaugh, *Revolutionary War Records*, 223]. He was a "Free Mulatto" head of a Culpeper County household of 5 "other free" in 1810 (called William Bunda) [VA:8].

Joe Butler was a "mulatto" listed among seven deserters drafted out of Prince George County, Virginia, for whom a reward was offered in the 28 November 1777 issue of the *Virginia Gazette* [Purdie edition, p.3, col. 3].

Reuben Byrd applied for a pension in Powhatan County on 15 June 1820 at the age of 56 years. He testified that he enlisted in Hillsborough, North Carolina, and served in Captain

James Gunn's Regiment of Dragoons. Benjamin Sublett testified that he met Reuben, a 16 or 17-year-old "Mulatto boy," while serving in the Revolution in May 1780. Gabriel Gray testified that Reuben served as "Boman" for his brother Lieutenant William Gray [NARA, S.37776, M804, Roll 243, frame 0362; http://fold3.com/image/11036948]. He was head of a Petersburg household of 5 "other free" in 1810 [VA:121b]. He registered in Petersburg on 9 June 1810: *a brown Mulatto man, five feet seven inches high, forty seven years old, born free in Essex County, a stone mason* [Register of Free Negroes 1794-1819, no. 576].

John Caine enlisted for 18 months on 23 September 1780: *age 23, 5'3-1/2" high, born in Fairfax County, Yellow complexion* [Register & description of Noncommissioned officers & Privates, LVA accession no. 24296, by http://revwarapps.org/b69.pdf (p.62)].

William Cannady was presented for not listing his wife as a tithable in York County on 21 November 1765. He was a soldier in the Revolution on 17 August 1778 and 21 June 1779 when the York County court allowed his wife Frances Kennedy a subsistence payment [Judgments & Orders 1763-5, 90, 126; 1768-70, 299; Orders 1774-84, 170, 219].

James Carter was a six-year-old "negro" bound as an apprentice to Thomas Pettit on 14 August 1765 and bound to Anne Pettit, widow, on 13 January 1778 in Northampton County, Virginia [Minutes 1765-71, 8, 33]. He was a "Mulatto" or "free Negro" taxable in Northampton County from 1787 to 1805 [PPTL, 1782-1823, frames 64, 125, 207, 345, 408, 447, 467, 530]. He was a resident of Northampton County when he appeared in court to apply for a pension for his services in the Revolution, stating that he enlisted from Northampton County for 18 months early in the war to garrison a fort on Kings Creek in Northampton County and served the time. Six months after his discharge he crossed the Chesapeake Bay and enlisted in Portsmouth in the 2nd Virginia Regiment of Artillery commanded by Colonel Thomas Marshall. He received bounty land of 200 acres for the five years of service [NARA, S.9162, M804, frame 614 of 668; http://fold3.com/image/12845878].

William Carter enlisted in the Revolution for 18 months from Charles City County on 12 September 1780: *age 22, 5'9" high, yellow complexion, a sawer, born in Charles City* [Register & description of Noncommissioned officers & Privates, LVA accession no. 24296, by http://revwarapps.org/b69.pdf (p.41)].

John Case, a "Mulatto" and brother of William Case, died while serving in the Revolution according to the 11 June 1807 deposition of John Cropper, Jr., of Accomack County, former Lieutenant Colonel of the 9th Virginia Regiment. He stated that William and John had no wives or children, and Betty Case "of this county" who was an infant during the war, was their only legal representative [LVA, Digital Collections, Case, John, Revolutionary War Bounty Warrants].

William Case, a "Mulatto," died while serving in the Revolution [NARA Bounty Land Warrant 1826-100, http://fold3.com/image/12751811].

William Cassidy was taxable in Norfolk County in 1801 and 1803, counted in a list of "free Negroes and Mulattoes" on Tanner's Creek in Norfolk County in 1801 [PPTL, 1791-1812, frames 383, 462]. He appeared in Princess Anne County court on 6 October 1811 when he testified for the Legislative petition of Aaron Weaver. He stated that he was born in Northumberland County and served with Aaron for three years aboard the galley *Protector* under captains Conway and Thomas [Legislative Petitions of the General Assembly, 1776-1865, Accession no. 36121, Box 309, folder 62, Weaver, Aaron, Digital Collections, LVA]. He registered in York County on 16 December 1822: *a dark mulatto about 65 years of age 5 feet four Inches high...born free* [Register of Free Negroes 1798-1831, no.163]. He received bounty land based on his discharge from Captain John Thomas of the Galley *Protector* which stated that he served in the Navy from 6 January 1777 to 26 January 1780 [Revolutionary War Bounty Warrants, Casity, William, Digital Collections, LVA].

James Causey served as a seaman in the Revolution for three years, received a discharge from James Markham, captain of the ship *Dragon*, on 16 February 1780 and assigned (signing) his bounty land on 23 August 1783 to Mr. Joseph Sanders [Revolutionary War Bounty Warrants, Causey, James, Digital Collection, LVA]. He was taxable in Northumberland County from 1785 to 1813 [PPTL 1782-1812, frames 283, 603, 621, 653, 668, 682] and a "free mulatto" head of a Northumberland County household of 3 "other free" in 1810 [VA:975].

Charles Charity enlisted in the Revolution on 2 September 1780 for 1-1/2 years: *age 24, 5'6-1/2" high, a planter, born in Surrey, black complexion* [Register & description of Noncommissioned officers & Privates, LVA accession no. 24296, by http://revwarapps.org/b69.pdf (p.26)]. He enlisted in the Revolution at Hampton, Virginia, under Captain Hugh Woodson in Colonel Green's 10th Regiment, and was discharged in Winchester. He applied for a pension in July 1827 in Newby District, South Carolina, at the age of 70 years [NARA S.39317, M804, http://fold3.com/image/12804208; http://fold3.com/image/12804208].

Randolph Charity was recruited for 3 years in Captain Nathan Fox's 6th Virginia Regiment on 24 March 1777 and died 10 July 1777 [NARA, M246, Roll 103, frames 154, 157, 160, 178, 180 of 756; http://fold3.com/image/9563516].

Sharod/ Sherwood Charity was in the muster of Colonel John Green's detachment of the 6th Virginia Regiment taken at Petersburg on 12 December 1780: *no. 28, Sherod Charaty, age 36, 5"7-1/2", a Shomaker, engaged 9 Oct 80, Lunenburg* [New-York Historical Society, Muster and pay rolls of the War of the Revolution, 1775-1783, II:598-9; http://babel.hathitrust.org].

Allen Chavis was listed in the payroll and muster of Captain James Lucas in the 4th Virginia Regiment commanded by Colonel Thomas Elliot from 1 April 1777 to 1 June 1777: listed as dead or deserted in July 1777 [NARA, M246, roll 99, frame 619, 653, 656, of 760; http://fold3.com/image/9163533].

Anthony Chavis was a taxable "Blackman" in Island Creek District, Granville County, in 1803 [Tax List 1803-09, 42] and head of a Granville County household of 7 "other free" in 1810 [NC:858]. He died in Granville County in May 1831 according to the survivor's pension application of his son Peter [NARA, R.1889-1/2, M805, reel 180, frame 145; http://fold3.com/image/12037220; Revolutionary War Bounty Warrants, Chavers, Anthony, 1840, Digital Collection, LVA]. Anthony received a certificate for his pay [Eckenrode, *List of the Revolutionary Soldiers of Virginia*, 64, citing Auditors' Account XXXI:55 at LVA].

Edward Chavis was "a free Negro Boy" bound out as an apprentice by the Amelia County court on 22 December 1757 [Orders 1746-51, 192; 1757-60, 36, 45; 1760-3, 44]. He and Samuel Chavous enlisted in the Revolution on 28 August 1777. He was in the payroll of the 14th Virginia Regiment in March 1778 and in June 1778: sick at Valley Forge, and he and Samuel were in the payroll of the 18th Regiment in April 1779: mustered at Middlebrook on 7 May 1779 [NARA, M246, roll 109, frames 163, 175, 209; roll 112, frame 714; http://fold3.com/image/10104087].

George Chavis was the son of Margaret Chaves, a "Mulatto Girl" bound out in Charles City County in 1750. He was bound out as an apprentice in 1761 [Orders 1737-51, 574; 1758-62, 302, 313]. He was listed in the 3rd Virginia Company commanded by Major Samuel Finley from 1 September 1782 to 1 May 1783: called George Chavour, listed with John Chavour [NARA, M246, roll 113, frames 672, 674; http://fold3.com/image/9648474].

Isaac Chavis enlisted in the Revolution on 3 February 1777, a pioneer listed in the muster of the 14th Virginia Regiment commanded by Colonel Charles Lewis from 29 April 1777 to December 1777, wounded at Monmouth and at Valley Forge in July 1778, and paid a bounty of $20 to enlist in Charlotte County for 3 years between July and November 1778 [NARA, M246, roll 112, frames 111, 613, 619, 631, 637, 642, 649; http://fold3.com/image/10102100].

He was head of a Granville County household of 3 "other free" in 1800, 3 "other free" and a white woman in 1810 [NC:858], and 1 "free colored" in Mecklenburg County, Virginia, in 1820. His heirs Jacob Chavos, William Chavos, Sally **Brandom** and Patsy **Scott** applied for a land grant for his services in the Revolution, stating that he was a "free man of color of Charlotte County" who enlisted in the 14th Virginia Regiment in March 1777 and was included in the muster roll of Captain Michaux. Their petition was rejected [Chavos, Isaac: Petition, 1837, Revolutionary War Rejected Claims Records, Digital Collections, LVA]. However, there is a record that he served [Eckenrode, *List of the Revolutionary Soldiers of Virginia*, 65].

James Chavis, son of "Rebecca Chavis a Free Negro," was bound out in Amelia County on 28 August 1760 [Orders 1751-5, 149; 1760-3, 44]. He was listed in the payroll of Captain Dudley's 2nd Virginia State Regiment commanded by Colonel Gregory Smith from 1 July 1778 to November 1779, in the same list as John and Rhode **Brandom** and Elias **Pettiford** [NARA, M246, roll 96, frames 532, 535, 541, 545, 547; http://fold3.com/image/10081826, 10081833, 10081873]. He received bounty land for his service [Revolutionary War Bounty Warrants, Chavis, James, Digital Collection, LVA]. He was head of a Mecklenburg County household of 10 "free colored" in 1820.

John Chavis enlisted in the Revolution while resident of Mecklenburg County, Virginia, in 1780: *age 26, 5'9-1/2" high, a planter, born in Brunswick County, black hair, swarthey complexion* [Register & description of Noncommissioned officers & Privates, LVA accession no. 24296, by http://revwarapps.org/b69.pdf (p.26)]. He was called John Shivers on 16 November 1818 when he made a declaration in Southampton County court that he was a soldier in the Revolutionary War by voluntary enlistment [Minutes 1816-9, unpaged]. He was called Jack Chavis in 1810 when he was head of a Southampton County household of 3 "other free" [VA:77].

John Chavis enlisted in the 5th Virginia Regiment in December 1778 and served for three years. Captain Mayo Carrington, in a bounty warrant written in March 1783, certified that Chavis had "faithfully fulfilled [his duties] and is thereby entitled to all immunities granted to three year soldiers" [Mecklenburg County Legislative Petition of 14 December 1820]. He was listed in the payroll of Captain Mayo Carrington's Company in Morristown in November 1779 [NARA, M246, Roll 102, frames 545, 548, 552 of 774; http://fold3.com/image/9946464]. He was taxable in Mecklenburg County in 1785 and 1786 [PPTL 1782-1805, frames 99, 127, 211]. On 20 April 1818 his sons John, Charles, and Randolph Chavis of Mecklenburg County gave their power of attorney to Melchizedek Roffe to collect money due to them from the state treasurer for their father's service in the Revolution [Mecklenburg County DB 17:218-9]. William O. Goode, former member of the General Assembly from Mecklenburg County, wrote a letter in support of the petition to the Legislature made by his son Randall. Goode stated that John and his brother Anthony Chavis were wagoners in the Revolution who were issued certificates of public debt at the end of the war, about £21 for Anthony (signed by Captain Young) and £89 for John (signed by Captain Carrington) [Mecklenburg County Legislative Petitions of 14 December 1820 and 19 January 1836, LVA].

Joshua Chavos, Jr., served in the Revolution [Eckenrode, *Virginia Soldiers of the American Revolution*, I:93, citing Auditors' Account XVIII:516 at LVA].

Robert W. Chavis. See Robert Walden.

Samuel Chavis, a "Melatto boy," was bound as an apprentice in Lunenburg County in April 1751 [Orders 1748-52, 396]. He enlisted in the Revolution on 28 August 1777. He was in the payroll of the 14th Virginia Regiment in March 1778, sick at Valley Forge in the same list as Edward and Isaac Chavous in June 1778, in the payroll of the 18th Regiment in April 1779, and mustered at Middlebrook on 7 May 1779 [NARA, M246, roll 109, frames 163, 175, 209; roll 112, frames 714, 723; http://fold3.com/image/10104087]. On 14 August 1789 he assigned his rights to his land warrant for services in the Revolution [Revolutionary Bounty Warrants,

Chavis, Samuel, Digital Collections, LVA]. He was a "free Negro" taxable in Dinwiddie County in 1801 and a "free" taxable in 1802 [PPTL, 1790 A, p.3; 1790 A, p.3; 1801 B, p.25; 1802 A, p.4]. He was counted the "list of free Negroes and Mulattoes" in Mecklenburg County from 1813 to 1815 [PPTL, 1806-28, frames 307, 417, 435].

Shadrack Chavis enlisted in the Revolution on 1 August 1778 for three years and was listed in the roll of Captain William Taylor's Company of the 2nd Virginia Regiment commanded by Christian Febiger, Esquire, for July 1778 to August 1779: sick at Valley Forge in July 1778 [NARA, M246, roll 96, frames 136, 176, 180, 182 of 736; http://fold3.com/image/10069450, 10079300]. He was called Shadrach Shavers when he appeared in Stafford County court on 14 December 1818 and on 12 February 1821 to apply for a pension for his service in the Revolution. He stated that he enlisted for three years in the spring of 1778 at Valley Forge in the 2nd Virginia Regiment commanded by Colonel Febiger and injured one of his ankles which rendered him incapable of service, so he came to Virginia with Captain Cunningham. Captain George Burroughs deposed that he knew Shadrack in the service and that he was acting as bowman to Captain John P. Harrison of the 2nd Virginia Regiment [NARA, S.38368, M804, Roll 2159, frame 1393 of 1408; http://fold3.com/image/16443948]. Shadrack Shavers was a "B.M." taxable in Stafford County from 1810 to 1813 [PPTL, 1782-1813, frames 737, 800, 858] and head of a Stafford County household of 3 "free colored" in 1820.

John Chubb enlisted in the Revolution in Loudoun County, Virginia, on 19 March 1781 and was sized on 28 May: *age 23, 5'5-1/2" high, black complexion, planter, born in and residing in Montgomery County, Maryland* [The Chesterfield Supplement or Size Roll of Troops at Chesterfield Court House, LVA accession no. 23816, by http://revwarapps.org/b81.pdf (p.67)]. He may have been identical to Jonathan Chubb who enlisted in the 3rd Maryland Regiment on 1 January 1782 [NARA, M246, Roll 34, frame 398 of 587; http://fold3.com/image/12006667]. He served in the 6th Virginia Regiment under Lieutenant Colonel Thomas Posey from 1 April to 1 September 1782, served in Captain Clough Shelton's Company of the 1st Virginia Battalion from 1 December 1782 to 1 May 1783 and received 100 acres bounty land [NARA, M246, roll 113, frame 712; M881, Roll 1089, frames 323-6 of 1808; http://fold3.com/image/23299172].

William Clark was in the list of men in the Amherst County Militia in 1781 [William & Mary Digital Archives, Swem Library's Special Collections, Cabell Papers Box 2, Folder11.pdf]. He was taxable in Amherst County from 1782 to 1820: a "man of color" in 1811, 1812, and 1815, a "Mulatto" in 1813, a planter over the age of 45 in a list of "Free Negroes & Mulattoes" in 1816 and 1818 [PPTL 1782-1803, frames 9, 23, 44, 54, 70, 97, 136, 195, 225, 257, 326, 347, 370, 393, 419, 450, 479; 1804-23, frames 21, 62, 103, 144, 165, 188, 209, 230, 253, 326, 403, 537, 551, 584].

William Clark was a "Mulatto" taxable in Culpeper County from 1790 to 1801 [PPTL 1782-1802, frames 640, 684, 818] and a "Free Mulatto" head of a Culpeper County household of 7 "other free" in 1810 [VA:18]. On 7 December 1816 he obtained "free papers" in Culpeper County which were recorded later in Ross County, Ohio: *William Clerke, a Mulatto man, 50 or 60, 5'7", served in the Revolutionary War in 1780 and 1781...is a free man, who has a wife and several children, and wishes to visit his mother in law in Frederick Co., at Charles Carter's place.* William was 64 years old on 22 August 1820 when he appeared in Culpeper County court to apply for a pension for his services in the Revolution. He served in the 15th Virginia Regiment under Captain Thomas Edmunds [Madden, *We Were Always Free*, 191-199; NARA, W.6687, M804, Roll 570, frame 795 of 940; http://fold3.com/image/13747831].

Henry Cockran was sick at White Plains on 8 September 1778 and on the payroll of Captain Augustine Tabb's Company of the 2nd Virginia State Regiment in August 1779. Joseph Selden drew his final pay of £57 on 15 March 1785 [NARA, M246, roll 97, frame 79 of 720; M881, Roll 946, frames 2509-2528 of 2864; http://fold3.com/image/23017945]. He was taxable in Goochland County from 1787 to 1816: a "Mulatto" living near Duval Carroll's in 1804 [PPTL, 1782-1809, frames 163, 175, 279, 357, 479, 616, 686, 738, 821]. He was head of a Goochland County household of 8 "other free" in 1810 [VA:689]. He registered as a "free Negro" in Goochland County on 12 August 1815: *a free man of color of Yellow complexion about five feet eight inches high, about fifty three years old, short black curled hair...free born* [Register of Free Negroes, p.89, no.171].

John Cockran was a "FN" taxable in the northern district of Campbell County in 1807 [PPTL, 1785-1814, frame 693], and head of a Campbell County household of 1 "other free" in 1810 [VA:853]. He appeared in the Hustings Court of Lynchburg on 4 March 1828 to apply for a pension. He stated that he enlisted for 18 months in March 1781 in Captain Bohannon's Company of Colonel Davis's Virginia Regiment and served until August 1782 [NARA, S.39353, M804, roll 592, frame 16 of 559; http://fold3.com/image/12856487].

Francis Cole enlisted in the Revolution on 1 August 1780: *age 23, 5'10" high, a waggoner, born in Fairfax County, residing in Prince William County, black complexion* [Register & description of Noncommissioned officers & Privates, LVA accession no. 24296, by http://revwarapps.org/b69.pdf (p.62)].

Thomas Cole was listed among seven deserters from Thomas W. Ewell's Company of State Troops in a 20 June 1777 advertisement in the *Virginia Gazette*, described as: *a dark mulatto, about 5 feet 7 inches high living in Prince William County* [Purdie edition, p.1, col. 3]. He was a fifer in Captain Thomas W. Ewell's Muster Roll of July 1780 [NARA, M246, roll 94, frame 729 of 742; http://fold3.com/image/10073280]. He enlisted for three years in the 1st Virginia Regiment on 15 March 1780 and received a discharge from Lieutenant J. Harper on 2 May 1783 [Revolutionary War Bounty Warrants, Cole, Thomas, Digital Collections, LVA]. He was taxable in the lower district of Prince William County in 1786, 1787, 1792, and from 1794 to 1798, called a "free Black" in 1798 [PPTL, 1782-1810, frames 71, 95, 203, 254, 309, 362].

Francis Coley/ Cooley, born in Charles City County, Virginia, enlisted there in the militia in 1777 and moved to Halifax County, North Carolina, in 1779. He volunteered for six months in Halifax County and then settled in Brunswick County, Virginia, as an overseer for one Othen (Owen?) Myrick. He moved to Smith County, Tennessee, from where he petitioned for a pension on 28 November 1833 [NARA, S.3197, M804, Roll 609 , frame 465 of 618; http://fold3.com/image/12745128]. He was listed in the state census for North Carolina in the 6th District in 1786.

James Coley, born in Charles City County, Virginia, served in the Revolution in Virginia and then enlisted in Halifax County, North Carolina. He lived in Montgomery County, Tennessee, about 12 years and then moved to Humphreys County, Tennessee, where he appeared in court to apply for a pension on 18 September 1833 [NARA, S.3188, M804, Roll 643, frame 218 of 651; http://fold3.com/image/13181021]. He was head of a Halifax County, North Carolina household of 7 whites in 1790 [NC:62].

Robin Cooley, born before 1776, was head of a Halifax County, North Carolina household of 6 "free colored" in 1830. The 25 February 1842 session of the Halifax County court allowed him to use his gun in the county. He was called Robin Coley when he appeared in Halifax County court on 17 February 1844 and testified that his sister Sally Coley, widow of Jeffrey Coley, a Revolutionary War pensioner, died in Halifax County on 26 December 1843 and he was her heir [NARA, W.4160, M804, Roll 609, frame 494 of 618; http://fold3.com/image/12743960]. Jeffrey Coley was head of a Halifax County, North Carolina household of 5 whites in 1790 [NC:62].

John Collins was taxable in King William County as a "Mulatto" in 1813 and 1814 [Land Tax List 1782-1832]. In June 1837 his widow Jane Collins applied for a pension for his services in the Revolution, stating that he enlisted in King William County in September 1777 and served for three years: under Captain David Pannel and later Colonel Elias Edmunds when the regiment went southwards. They were married in Williamsburg in April 1780, her maiden name was **Richeson (Richardson)**, and he died in August 1821 leaving no children [NARA,

W.6736, M804, Roll 613, frame 645 of 761; http://fold3.com/image/12861980].

Mason Collins enlisted in the Revolution for 1-1/2 years while residing in King William County on 8 September 1780: *age 21, 5'11" high, a sailor, born in King William County, yellow complexion* [Register & description of Noncommissioned officers & Privates, LVA accession no. 24296, by http://revwarapps.org/b69.pdf (p.26)]. He was taxable in King and Queen County from 1804 to 1820: taxable on 2 tithables from 1807 to 1812, called a "Mulatto" in 1807, a "free Negro" from 1809 to 1812, over the age of 45 in 1815 [PPTL, 1804-23]. He made a declaration in King and Queen County court to obtain a pension for his services in the 11th Virginia Regiment. He declared that he had traveled north as bowman to an officer named Holt Richeson in 1777 and enlisted while in the State of Pennsylvania [NARA, S.39355, M804, Roll 614, frame 373; http://fold3.com/image/15202544]. He was head of a King William County household of 5 "free colored" in 1830.

William Collins was probably the third son of Mary Collins of King William County who received £25 public assistance on 13 May 1779 because she had three sons serving in the Continental Army [Creel, *Selected Virginia Revolutionary War Records*, III:106 (abstract of Auditors' Account, Volume II:119, LVA].. He was taxable in King William County from 1787 to 1813: listed as a "Mulatto" in 1813 [PPTL 1782-1832; Land Tax 1782-1811].

James Cooper was a "Black" or "person of color" taxable in Augusta County from 1800 to 1819 [PPTL 1796-1810, frames 192, 238, 337, 383, 434, 485, 530, 579, 622; 1811-20, frames 31, 76, 97, 118, 163, 250, 311, 427, 588]. He was a 70-year-old "free man of color" who applied for a pension while residing in Augusta County, Virginia, on 26 June 1820. He stated that he had enlisted in Goochland County and that his family consisted of himself and Sukey **Orchard**, a free woman of color upwards of 50 years old, who lived with him. His application included a certificate dated October 1787 from a justice of the peace in Goochland County, describing him as a "molatto Free man," which was to be used as a pass to travel to North Carolina and Georgia. He had been a waiter under Colonel Bluford and continued until his time was out [NARA, S.39362, M804, Roll 647, frame 566 of 621; http://fold3.com/image/12703900; Revolutionary War Pensions, Cooper, James, Digital Collections, LVA]. He was head of an Augusta County household of 2 "other free" and a white woman over 45 in 1810 [VA:371]. His son Pleasant received a warrant for bounty land for his service [Revolutionary War Bounty Warrants, Cooper, James, Digital Collections, LVA].

John Cooper was a black complexioned soldier, 5'5-1/4" high, a waggoner, born in Albemarle County and residing there when he entered the Revolution as a substitute in Goochland County on 24 March 1781 for 1-1/2 years [The Chesterfield Supplement or Size Roll of Troops at Chesterfield Court House, LVA accession no. 23816, by http://revwarapps.org/b81.pdf (p. 43)].

Francis Cousins married Mary **Martin** in Goochland County on 15 December 1759, "Mulattoes both" [Jones, *The Douglas Register*, 4]. He received £34 for serving as a soldier in the Revolution [NARA, M881, Roll 1091, frame 1079; http://fold3.com/image/23761275]. He was taxable in Powhatan County on 2 horses from 1787 to 1788, a "M" taxable in 1789, a "Mo" taxable in 1793 [PPTL, 1787-1825, frames 4, 17, 31, 90] and head of a Goochland County household of 8 "other free" in 1810 [VA:687].

James Cousins enlisted in the Revolution from Goochland County on 1 April 1782 and was sized the following day: *age 23, 5'6" high, black complexion, Negro, planter, born in Goochland County* [The Chesterfield Supplement or Size Roll of Troops at Chesterfield Court House, LVA accession no. 23816, by http://revwarapps.org/b81.pdf (p.97)]. He was taxable in the upper district of Goochland County in 1790 [PPTL, 1782-1809, frame 235].

Gustavus/ Travis D. Croston appeared in Hampshire County court to make a declaration to obtain a pension for his service in the Revolution. He stated that he enlisted in Alexandria and served for three years. He made a second declaration in court on 18 July 1820, stating that he enlisted in Newport (Charles County), Maryland, served as a private from 1778 to 1783 and was discharged in Alexandria, Virginia [NARA, S.39379, M804, Roll 701, frame 728 of 810; http://fold3.com/image/13009229]. He was head of a Hampshire County household of 9 "other free" in 1810 [VA:833], 11 "free colored" in 1820 [VA:281] and 2 "free colored" in 1840 [VA:8].

Thomas Creco enlisted for 18 months on 2 January 1782: *age 24, 5'7-1/2" high, black complexion, residing in Northampton County, Virginia, born in Hispaniola* [The Chesterfield Supplement or Size Roll of Troops at Chesterfield Court House, LVA accession no. 23816, by http://revwarapps.org/b81.pdf (p.101)].

John Cuff was listed in the payroll of Captain Joseph Scott's Company of the 1st Virginia Regiment commanded by Colonel James Hendricks from November 1777 to March 1778 [NARA, M246, Roll 92, frames 643, 673 of 715; http://fold3.com/image/9093909]. He was head of a Gates County, North Carolina household 9 "other free" in 1790 [NC:23], 8 in 1800 [NC:264], and 2 in 1810 [NC:835].

William Cuff, a "free man of Colour," appeared in Botetourt County court on 11 December 1826 to apply for a pension for his services in the 1st Virginia Regiment commanded by Colonel Campbell in Captain Stribling's Company in the Revolution. He enlisted in 1780, was in the Battles of Guilford Courthouse and Eutaw Springs and served until 1782. He had a wife of about 40-50 years of age and two sons ages 11 and 14 [NARA, S.39347, M804, Roll 594, frame 59 of 685; http://fold3.com/image/12853986 (Coff, William)]. He was a "free Negro" taxable in Botetourt County in 1794 and from 1810 to 1813: taxable on 2 tithes in 1813 and 1814 [PPTL, 1783-1822, frames 223, 665; 1811-22, frames 59, 103, 147] and head of a Fluvanna County household of 8 "other free" in 1810 [VA:474].

Charles Cuffee was called the son of "free Negro" Sarah Coffe when he was bound apprentice to Nathaniel Sikes in Norfolk County on 19 May 1763 [Orders 1763-65, 15]. He registered in Norfolk County on 16 April 1799: *Born free as is of age & his hight five feet six inches 3/4* [Cuffee, Charles (M, 37): Free Negro Certificate, 1799, African American Narrative Digital Collection, LVA]. He enlisted in the Revolution in 1780 for 18 months in the 11th Virginia Regiment under Captain Adam Wallace and Colonel Abraham Bluford, and he applied for and was granted a pension while a resident of Princess Anne County on 7 June 1830 when he was 75 years old [NARA, W.9402, M804, Roll 707, frame 381 of 744; http://fold3.com/image/14750811.

William Cuffee was head of a Norfolk County household 3 "other free" in 1810 [VA:794] and a "free Negro" taxable in St. Bride's Parish in 1812 and 1813 [PPTL, 1791-1812, frame 802; 1813-24, frame 11]. He was apparently identical to William McCuffy who was residing in Norfolk County when he enlisted in the Revolution in August 1780. He was sized on 3 March 1781: *age 18, 5'8-1/2" high, farmer, born in Norfolk County, Black complexion* [Register & description of Noncommissioned officers & Privates, LVA accession no. 24296, by http://revwarapps.org/b69.pdf (p.85)].

Daniel Cumbo was living in Charles City County on 29 September 1768 when there was an ad in the *Virginia Gazette* offering a reward for the capture of a "mulatto" slave named Daniel who was passing as a freeman named Daniel Cumbo [Purdie and Dixon edition, p. 3, col. 1]. He was in the 1st Virginia Regiment from March 1777 to December 1778 and received his final pay of £54 on 20 June 1783 [NARA, M246, Roll 92, frames 283, 325 of 715; http://fold3.com/image/22419700]. He was taxable in James City County in 1813: counted with 1 male and 1 female in a list of "Free Persons of Colour above 16 years" in 1813 [PPTL, 1800-15].

John Cumbo died before 26 July 1791 when the overseers of the poor of Charles City County bound his orphan daughter Mourning Cumbo to George Hubbard until the age of 18 [DB 4:61]. He may have been the John Cumbo who served in the Revolution from Charles City County [Gwathmey, *Historical Register of Virginians in the Revolution*, 198]. A John Cumbo

22

was the servant of Colonel Lamb of the 2d New York Regiment of Artillery from January to April 1783 at West Point [NARA, M246, Roll 117, frames 737, 741, 743 of 919; http://fold3.com/image/9230775].

Michael Cumbo enlisted in the 6th Virginia Regiment on 12 September 1777, was sick at the Yellow Spring Hospital in the June 1778 muster commanded by John Gibson (with Richard Cumbo), and was listed as deceased in the September 1778 muster. Parker Bailey received his final pay of £66 on 7 December 1784 [NARA, M246, Roll 103, frames 485, 488, 491, 494, 497 of 756; M853, Roll 22, http://fold3.com/image/286702942]. His widow Mildred Cumbo received £60 for support of herself and her two children by order of the Charles City County court on 14 July 1779 [Creel, *Selected Virginia Revolutionary War Records*, III:138, citing Auditors' Account, Volume II:261, LVA].

Peter Cumbo was a soldier from Charles City County who served in the Revolution [Gwathmey, *Historical Register of Virginians in the Revolution*, 198]. He was in the muster of the 3rd Virginia Regiment from February to April 1778, in Captain John Payton's muster in August 1778 at White Plains and discharged in February 1779 at Middlebrook [NARA, M246, Roll 98, frames 432, 675 of 789; http://fold3.com/image/21958424]. He may have been the Peter Cumbo who was listed as "runaway" in the 1783 tax list for Brunswick county, Virginia, in 1783 [PPTL 1782-99, frame 61] and sued by the churchwardens of Meherrin Parish, Brunswick County, on 24 January 1785 [Orders 1784-8, 59, 85].

Richard Cumbo enlisted in the 6th Virginia Regiment for three years on 5 September 1777, was sick at Yellow Spring Hospital in the May 1778 muster commanded by John Gibson, and present for the September 1778 muster. Mi Cumbo received his final pay of £36 between 30 April 1783 and 23 March 1784 [NARA, M246, Roll 103, frames 485, 488, 491, 494, 497 of 756; M853, Roll 22, http://fold3.com/image/286702951].

Stephen Cumbo was a soldier from James City County who served in the Revolution [Gwathmey, *Historical Register of Virginians in the Revolution*, 198]. Mr. Norvells received his final pay of £20 on 18 June 1784 [NARA, M881, Roll 1091, frame 1276 of 2235; http://fold3.com/image/23762198]. He was taxable in James City County from 1782 to 1814: taxable on 3 horses and 4 cattle in 1782, a "Mulatto" taxable in 1785, taxable on 2 horses and 6 cattle in 1787 and 2 tithes and a horse in 1800. He was counted with a male and a female in a list of "Free Persons of Colour above 16 years" in James City County in 1813 [PPTL, 1782-99; 1800-15]. He was entitled to but had not received bounty land by 1835 [Brumbaugh, *Revolutionary War Records*, I:202].

William Cumbo was paid for services to the Revolution [Creel, *Selected Virginia Revolutionary War Records*, I:62].

____ Cumbo was the son of Fortune Cumbo, the mother of a poor soldier in the Continental Service on 17 December 1778, 20 May 1779 and 19 August 1779 when the Halifax County, Virginia court issued a certificate to the Treasurer that she had been provided with public assistance [Pleas 1774-9, 236, 384, 414; 1779-83, 65].

Abraham Cuttillo served three years in Colonel Marshall's Virginia Regiment of Artillery according to an affidavit from Captain James W. Bradley on 31 March 1784 [Revolutionary Bounty Warrants, Kertiller, Abra., Digital Collections, LVA]. He was head of a York County household of 6 "other free" in 1810 [VA:873]. On 21 May 1838 Henry Buchanan, aged 77 of York County, deposed that Abraham Cottiler, a "free man of color" from York County, enlisted in the Revolution in 1779, served at the Battle of Yorktown, and died about 30 years previous [Revolutionary War Rejected Claims, Cottiller, Abraham, Digital Collections, LVA].

Frank Cypress was bound apprentice in Surry County in 1754, bound apprentice in Lunenburg County in November 1760 [Orders 1759-61, 191] and listed in the Surry County account of the estate of Dr. Patrick Adams in 1771 [WB 12:248]. He enlisted in the Revolution on 13 October 1780: *age 30, 5'6-1/4" high, a taylor, born and residing in Surry County, yellow complexion* [Register & description of Noncommissioned officers & Privates, LVA accession no. 24296, by http://revwarapps.org/b69.pdf (p.75)].

John Davise, appeared in Westmoreland County court on 30 June 1818 and testified that he enlisted with Captain Elisha Callender, commander of the ship *Dragon*, for three years. Captain Eleazer Callender, commander of the ship Dragon, certified that John Davise entered on board the ship on 3 September 1777 as a landsman and was paid until 20 January 1779. Ambrose **Lewis**, "a Blackman" and pensioner, testified that he found Davise on board when he first boarded the ship. John died on 9 March 1838, and his widow Amy Davis, nee **Griffis**, applied for a survivor's pension [NARA, W.19138, M804, roll 770, frame 15 of 717; http://fold3.com/image/16220496]. John was listed as a private aboard the *Dragon* on 2 September 1779 [Brumbaugh, *Revolutionary War Records, Virginia*, 8]. He and his wife Amea were "Molattoes" farming in Westmoreland County in 1801 with two children of the **Locus** family in their household [*Virginia Genealogist* 31:40]. Amea **Griffin** was a "Molato" girl valued at 100 shillings in the 21 November 1766 Northumberland County estate of Stephen Chilton [Record Book, 1766-70, 56-7].

Daniel Davis, "a mulatto" born in Lancaster County, enlisted for the war and deserted from the ship *Gloucester* near Warwick with William **Smith**, a Creole born in Barbados, according to an advertisement in the 2 August 1780 issue of the *Virginia Gazette* [Dixon and Nicholson edition, p. 2, col. 3]. Daniel Davis was listed as a private aboard the ship *Dragon* on 2 September 1779 and a seaman who served for three years and was entitled to bounty land [Brumbaugh, *Revolutionary War Records, Virginia*, 8, 68].

George Day was among a group of Revolutionary War seamen who deserted from the ship *Tartar* and for each of whom a $100 reward was offered by Thomas Grant of the Chickahominy Shipyard in the 11 September 1779 issue of the *Virginia Gazette*: ...*George Day, and Augustine Boyd, all of Wicomico parish, Northumberland county* [Dixon and Nicholson edition, p. 3, col. 2]. George apparently returned to his ship and served out his term because Captain John Thomas certified in February 1780 that George Day enlisted on 10 February 1777, served three years, and discharged his duty truly and faithfully [Revolutionary War Bounty Warrants; Day, George; Sailor, 1780, Digital Collection, LVA]. He was a "free negro" head of a Northumberland County household of 5 "other free" in 1810 [VA:976].

Thomas Day enlisted as a mariner in the Virginia Navy on 7 July 1777 and served as a seaman for three years according to a certificate signed by Captain John Thomas on 5 April 1785. Thomas assigned his rights to the pay and bounty land to Matthew Pate [Revolutionary War Bounty Warrants; Day, Thomas, Seaman, Voucher 1785, Digital Collection, LVA]. He may have been related to George Day since he enlisted 3 days before him and received a certificate from Captain John Thomas, the same person who certified George Day's service.

Frederick Demmery, born say 1738, served as a soldier in the infantry in Virginia. Mr. Ridley received his final pay of £23 on 23 November 1785 [NARA, M881, Roll 1091, frame 1641 of 2235; http://fold3.com/image/286702949]. He was living in Southampton County, Virginia, on 28 August 1780, when he made his will, proved 8 November 1781, David Demmery executor [WB 3:348]. He named Richard Demmery, head of a Northampton County, North Carolina household of 6 "other free" in 1800 [NC:435] and Micajah Demmery, a "Black" person 12-50 years old living alone in Captain Dupree's District of Northampton County in 1786 for the North Carolina state census [WB 3:348].

Charles Dobbins was living in Dinwiddie county when he enlisted in the Revolution as a substitute on 6 June 1782 and was sized the same month: *age 20, 5'6-2/4" high, yellow complexion, a planter* [The Chesterfield Supplement or Size Roll of Troops at Chesterfield Court House, LVA accession no. 23816, by http://revwarapps.org/b81.pdf (p.101)]. He was listed in the roll and muster of the 3rd Company commanded by Major Samuel Finley from 1 December 1782 to 1 May 1783. And a Charles Dobbins was listed as sick and absent in the 9 July 1778 muster of the 9th Virginia Regiment in Brunswick and in the muster of Captain Peter Minor's Company of the 5th Virginia Regiment at Pompton Plains, New Jersey, on 1

December 1778 as having died on 15 October 1778 [NARA, M246, roll 113, frames 674, 752; roll 102, frames 347, 419 of 774; http://fold3.com/image/9946253]. He was taxable in Powhatan County in 1794, 1795 and a "Mo" taxable there from 1802 to 1806 [PPTL, 1787-1825, frames 105, 117, 239, 255, 277, 293, 316]. Henry Skipwith of Cumberland County, Virginia, placed an ad in the 19 April 1783 issue of the *Virginia Gazette* claiming that "a tall slim mulatto man named Tom, about twenty years of age, five feet six and three quarters high...and resembles an Indian from whom he is descended," had run away and been received as a substitute in Dinwiddie County, brought to Cumberland Old Court-house with the recruits of that county, re-enlisted for the war the previous fall, went by the name of Charles Dobbins, then cut off his forefinger in order to marry a free woman, near Fine Creek Mill in Powhatan County, who had determined never to have a husband in the Continental Army, and supposed this mutilation would procure him a discharge [Hayes edition, http://www2.vcdh.virginia.edu/gos/explore.html].

William Dobbins and Charles Dobbins were the sons of Sarah Dobbins who was released from her service by the Cumberland County court on 26 August 1752 [Orders 1749-51, 316; 1752-8, 40; 1758-62, 371]. Sarah was old and infirm in 1811 when she in a list of "Free Negroes and Mulattoes" in Powhatan County [A List of Free Negroes and Mulattoes within the County of Powhatan, 1811, African American Narrative Digital Collection, LVA]. William was discharged from his service by the Cumberland County court on 27 July 1772 [Orders 1770-2, 315]. On 27 October 1784 William Gatewood received his final pay of £15 for serving in the Revolution [NARA, M881, Roll 1024, frame 871 of 1650 http://fold3.com/image/286702733].

Elijah Donathan was most likely the son of William Donathan, a "Mullatto," who petitioned the Spotsylvania County court for his freedom in 1734 [Orders 1734-5, 285]. William Donathan was living in present-day Henry County, Virginia, when he sold his land to Jacob **Chavis**, and Elijah Donathan owned land in Henry County. His widow Rachel Donathan applied for a survivor's pension, stating that her husband was drafted in the militia in Wilkes County, Georgia, and marched to St. Augustine, Florida [NARA, R.3004, M804, Roll 830, frame 782; http://fold3.com/image/17545326]. His descendants were listed as white in the census.

Emanuel Driver was listed in the payroll of Peter Bernard's 2nd Virginia Regiment from 1778 to 1779 (in the same list as William Driver) [NARA, M246, Roll 96, frames 331, 336, 344, 347, 380 of 736; http://fold3.com/image/10081035]. He received a discharge from Captain Machen Boswell on 8 April 1784 for serving three years and received bounty land [Revolutionary War Bounty Warrants, Digital Collection, LVA]. He was head of a Kingston Parish, Gloucester County household of 5 free persons in 1783 [VA:53], taxable in Kingston Parish on his own tithe and 2 horses in 1784, 4 cattle in 1787, taxable on his own tithe from 1788 to 1790 [PPTL, 1782-99]. In July 1835 his heirs William Driver and John Driver, son of John Driver, testified that Emanuel enlisted in the 2nd Virginia Regiment in 1776 and was discharged in 1780 or 1781. The claim was rejected [Revolutionary War Rejected Claims, LVA, Virginia Memory Collections].

John Driver deposed that his father John Driver enlisted in the 2nd Virginia Regiment and resided in Mathews County. He was taxable in Kingston Parish, Gloucester County, from 1783 to 1790: taxable on 4 cattle in 1783, 3 in 1785, 5 in 1787 [PPTL 1782-99]. And he was a "Mulatto" taxable in Gloucester County from 1801 to 1803 [PPTL 1800-20]. A John Driver was due bounty land for service in the Revolution as a seaman but had not received it by 25 November 1834 [Brumbaugh, *Revolutionary War Records*, 215].

William Driver received a discharge from Captain Machen Boswell on 8 April 1784 for serving three years in the 2nd Virginia Regiment and received bounty land [Revolutionary War Bounty Warrants, Digital Collection, LVA]. He was head of a Kingston Parish, Gloucester County household of 3 free persons in 1783 [VA:53], taxable in Kingston Parish from 1784 to 1790: on his own tithe and a horse in Kingston Parish from 1784 to 1789 [PPTL, 1782-99] and head of a Chatham County, North Carolina household of 2 "other free" in 1800.

25

He (or perhaps a younger William Driver) was a "Mulatto" taxable in Gloucester County in 1809 and from 1812 to 1820 [PPTL 1800-20].

Luke Duncan enlisted in the Revolution for 18 months while resident in Norfolk County on 23 September 1780: *age 40, 5'8" high, a farmer, born in Norfolk County, Black complexion* [Register & description of Noncommissioned officers & Privates, LVA accession no. 24296, by http://revwarapps.org/b69.pdf (p.69)].

Solomon Duncan enlisted in the Revolution on 22 September 1780: *age 39, 5'8" high, a blacksmith, born in Pasquotank County, North Carolina, residing in Princess Anne County, yellow complexion, deserted* [Register & description of Noncommissioned officers & Privates, LVA accession no. 24296, by http://revwarapps.org/b69.pdf (p.44)]. He was a "Free Black" head of a Princess Anne County household of 5 "other free" in 1810 [VA:450].

Bartholomew Dungee served in the Revolution according to a statement made by his older brother William [LVA chancery file 1803-002, http://virginiamemory.com/collections/chancery]. He was listed in Captain William Cherry's Company of the 4th Virginia Regiment commanded by Major Isaac Beall from March to May 1778: *sick at Valley Forge and died on 16 July 1778* [NARA, M246, Roll 100, frame 826 of 865; Roll 99, frames 694, 743, 749 of 760; http://fold3.com/image/22629177].

James Dungee completed three years service in the Virginia State Artillery, was discharged on 12 September 1780, and received bounty land [Revolutionary War Bounty Warrants, Dungy, James, Digital Collections, LVA; Brumbaugh, *Revolutionary War Records, Virginia*, 336]. He was head of a Prince Edward County household of 7 "other free" in 1810 [VA:562].

Matthew Dungee received £6 pay as bounty for serving in the 4th Virginia Regiment commanded by Colonel Robert Lawson on 16 February 1778 [NARA, M246, Roll 99, frame 749 of 760; http://fold3.com/image/9161780].

William Dungee served in the Revolution as a matross in the artillery and was eligible for bounty land [NARA, M246, Roll 114, frame 43 of 492; http://fold3.com/image/9946731; Brumbaugh, *Revolutionary War Records, Virginia*, 202]. In April 1799 he stated in Cumberland County, Virginia court that he was the "oldest brother and heir at law of Bartholomew Dungee who departed this life in the year [blank] being a soldier in the American Army in the late Revolutionary War" [LVA chancery files 1799-003; 1803-002, http://virginiamemory.com/collections/chancery/]. He was head of a Cumberland County household of 5 "other free" in 1810 [VA:114].

Charles Dunston, son of Patience Dunston, was bound apprentice to John Howell in Cumberland Parish, Lunenburg County, in April 1751. He was called "a poor soldier in the service of the United States" on 8 May 1780 when the Mecklenburg County, Virginia court allowed his wife Elizabeth Dunston a barrel and a half of corn and 50 pounds of bacon for the support of herself and two children [Orders 1779-84, 34, 53]. He was a substitute in the Revolution from Wake County [Revolutionary War Pay Vouchers, http://familysearch.org/ark:/61903/3:1:3QSQ-G9W8-NYD] and received his final settlement for his service in the Revolutionary War in Orange County [*The North Carolinian* VI:755].

Joseph Dunstan was a soldier who was born in James City County and enlisted there in the Revolution on 1 September 1780: *age 15, 5'3/4" high, a farmer, yellow complexion* [Register & description of Noncommissioned officers & Privates, LVA accession no. 24296, by http://revwarapps.org/b69.pdf (p.44)]. He was taxable in James City County from 1783 to 1812 [PPTL 1782-99; 1800-15].

Wallace Dunstan was a soldier from Halifax County, Virginia, who deserted Captain Shem Cook's Second Georgia State Battalion. On 27 October 1777 Cook placed an advertisement in the *Virginia Gazette* offering "mulattoes" Wallace Dunstan and James **Smith** of Halifax County (and 10 other soldiers, including a sergeant) a pardon if they returned [Purdie edition,

John Epps was counted in the "List of Free Negroes & Mulattoes in the Lower District of Lunenburg County" in March 1802 [Lunenburg County, Free Negro, Slave Records, 1802-1803, p.1, LVA] and head of a Wilkes County, North Carolina household of 9 "free colored" in 1820 [NC:519]. He testified in his pension application that he was born in Lunenburg County, enlisted there for 12 months, and was then drafted there in the militia in 1781. He was granted a pension while residing in Person County, North Carolina, on 8 February 1836 [NARA, S.8423, M804, Roll 932, frame 208 of 603; http://fold3.com/image/17565757].

William Epps enlisted in the Revolution and was in the list of men from Mecklenburg County under the command of Captain Reuben Vaughan who were on a detachment to the southward under immediate command of Colonel Mason in 1779 [Elliott, Katherine, *Revolutionary War Records, Mecklenburg County, Virginia* (1964), 162-3, citing Edmund W. Hubbard Papers, Southern Historical Collection, UNC Chapel Hill, NC]. He was counted in the "List of free Negroes & Mulattoes" in the lower District of Lunenburg near Flatrock Creek in 1802 and 1803 with his wife Caty and children: George, Priscilla, William, Thomas & James Cutillow [Lunenburg County, Free Negro, Slave Records, 1802-1803, p.1, LVA]. His widow Catherine was counted as a (26-44)-year-old white woman with 8 "other free" persons in her household in the 1810 census for Lunenburg County.

Benjamin Evans was in the list of men in the service of the Amherst County Militia in 1781 [William & Mary Digital Archives, Swem Library's Special Collections, Cabell Papers Box 2, Folder11.pdf]. He was head of an Amherst County household of 6 "Mulattoes" in 1785 [VA:84].

Charles Evans enlisted for 18 months in the Revolution in Mecklenburg County as a substitute on 2 October 1780 and was sized on 18 March 1781: *age 19, 5'4-1/4" high, yellow complexion, a farmer, born in Petersburg* [The Chesterfield Supplement or Size Roll of Troops at Chesterfield Court House, LVA accession no. 23816, by http://revwarapps.org/b81.pdf (p.7)].

Godfrey Evans enlisted as a substitute for Dick Evans and was in the list of men from Mecklenburg County under the command of Captain Reuben Vaughan who were on a detachment to the southward under immediate command of Colonel David Mason in 1779 [Elliott, Katherine, *Revolutionary War Records, Mecklenburg County, Virginia* (1964), 162-3, citing Edmund W. Hubbard Papers, Southern Historical Collection, UNC Chapel Hill, NC]. Richard Evans was called a "Mallotto" when Dinwiddie, Crawford & Company sued him in Mecklenburg County court on 14 June 1773 for a debt of £19 [Orders 1773-9, 24].

John Evans enlisted in the Revolution from Cumberland County, Virginia, on 12 March 1781 and was sized a year later: *age 18, 5'4" high, yellow complexion, a shoemaker, born in Cumberland County* [The Chesterfield Supplement or Size Roll of Troops at Chesterfield Court House, LVA accession no. 23816, by http://revwarapps.org/b81.pdf (p.7)].

Philip Evans, the "Mulotto" son of Ann Evans, was bound apprentice to the Rev. Robert Fergeson in Bristol Parish on 10 November 1748 [Chamberlayne, Register of Bristol Parish, 134]. He was a "mulatto" who was listed among 7 deserters drafted out of Prince George County, Virginia, for whom a reward was offered in the 28 November 1777 issue of the *Virginia Gazette* [Purdie edition, p.3, col. 3]. His widow Aggy was a "Mulatto" taxable on 2 free male tithes in Prince George County in 1804, 1806, 1810 and 1811 [PPTL, 1782-1811, frames 602, 652, 721, 742] and was head of a Prince George County household of 11 "other free" in 1810 [VA:537].

Thomas Evans was a wagoner living in the lower district of Lunenburg County in 1802 and 1803 when he was counted in the "List of free Negroes & Mulattoes" [LVA, Lunenburg County, Free Negro & Slave Records, 1802-1803]. He was a "free man of Colour" about 63 years of age on 23 December 1819 when he applied for a pension in Lunenburg County for his services in the Revolution. He stated that he enlisted in September 1777 while resident in Mecklenburg County and served until 1780 [23 December 1819 Lunenburg County Legislative Petition, LVA]. He was listed in the payroll of Captain Dudley's 2nd Virginia State Regiment commanded by Colonel Gregory Smith from March to December 1778, listed with James **Chavers**, Elias and Drury **Pettiford**, and John and Rhode **Brandom** [NARA, M246, Roll 96, frames 528, 538, 548 of 736; http://fold3.com/image/10081826, 10081833, 10081847, 10081851, 10081867, 10081873].

David Fargus enlisted for the war in Chesterfield County in 1781: *age 15, 4'9-3/4" high, yellow complexion, a weaver* [The Chesterfield Supplement or Size Roll of Troops at Chesterfield Court House, LVA accession no. 23816, by http://revwarapps.org/b81.pdf (p.9)].

Benjamin Farrow enlisted in the Revolution as a substitute in Goochland County on 20 March 1781 for 18 months and was sized in April the same year: *age 21, 5'3-3/4" high, yellow complexion, a waiter, born in Goochland County* [The Chesterfield Supplement or Size Roll of Troops at Chesterfield Court House, LVA accession no. 23816, by http://revwarapps.org/b81.pdf (p. 9)]. He received his final pay of £17 on 25 February 1783 [NARA, M881, Roll 1092, frame 89 of 2281; http://fold3.com/image/23344368]. He was a "Free Negro" taxable in the northern district of Campbell County from 1800 to 1805 [PPTL, 1785-1814, frames 484, 544, 622].

John Farrow enlisted in the Revolution from Goochland County on 9 March 1781 for 18 months and was sized about the same time: *age 21, 5'2-1/2" high, yellow complexion, a waggoner, born in Richmond City* [The Chesterfield Supplement or Size Roll of Troops at Chesterfield Court House, LVA accession no. 23816, by http://revwarapps.org/b81.pdf (p.9)]. Benjamin Farrow received his final pay of £17 [NARA, M881, Roll 1092, frame 91 of 2281; http://fold3.com/image/23344373]. John Farrar was a "Mulatto" taxable in Powhatan County from 1788 to 1792 [PPTL, 1787-1825, frames 18, 32, 46, 60, 77]. He and Benjamin Farrow were on a list of soldiers who had served in the Revolution but had not received bounty land by 7 January 1835 [Brumbaugh, *Revolutionary War Records*, 237].

___ F_gin enlisted in the Revolution: *age 28, 5'8-3/4" high, sandy hair, blk eyes, blk Complection, planter* [The Chesterfield Supplement or Size Roll of Troops at Chesterfield Court House, LVA accession no. 23816, by http://revwarapps.org/b81.pdf (p.9)].

Andrew Ferguson and his father served in the Revolution. He appeared in Monroe County, Indiana, on 16 August 1838 to apply for a pension for his services, stating that he was born in Dinwiddie County, Virginia, and was drafted there in January 1780 at the age of 15 by General Green. Two weeks previous to being drafted in company with his father (Andrew Peeleg as he was called), he was taken prisoner by the British. They ran away from them because they whipped them with cat o' nine tails, and they fell in with the American soldiers under Green. He was wounded in the head at Guilford and stayed about a month in the iron works in North Carolina. He was tended by Doctor Harris and Doctor Sidney. Daniel **Strother**, another pensioner, visited him in the hospital in Charlotte County, Virginia. Mr. Ferguson sent one of his sons for him, and he got home in November 1781. He appeared in court again on 8 January 1851 to apply for a full pension in place of the half pension he was then receiving. He stated that he was pressed into service in Dinwiddie County with his father Andrew Ferguson. He stated that he was born free, his father being a free man and his mother a free woman [NARA, S.32243, M804, Roll 966, frame 44 of 1168; http://fold3.com/image/17570759]. He was head of a Monroe County, Indiana household of 2 "free colored" in 1830.

John Fields was a "Mulatto" taxable in Buckingham County in 1774 [LVA, List of Tithables, 1774, p.6]. He was living in Amherst County on 18 May 1781 when he enlisted in the Revolution for 18 months. He was sized on 22 June the same year: *age 48, 5'7-1/2" high, black complexion, a farmer, born in Charles City County* [The Chesterfield Supplement or Size Roll of Troops at Chesterfield Court House, LVA accession no. 23816, by http://revwarapps.org/b81.pdf (p.65)]. He was head of a Buckingham County household of 4 "other free" in 1810 [VA:806] and was a taxable "man of color" in Amherst County in 1811 and 1812 [PPTL 1804-23, frames 211, 233].

Burwell Flood enlisted in Isle of Wight County on 20 August 1777 and was listed in the 11th and 15th Virginia Regiment (with Daniel **Goff**) on 20 August 1777 [NARA, M246, Roll 110, frame 493 of 768; http://fold3.com/image/9952883; http://fold3.com/image/9952883]. He enlisted in the Revolution in Williamsburg, while residing in Mecklenburg County, in January 1780 after serving three years with the 15th Virginia Regiment and was sized in 1781: *age 24, 5'6-1/2" high, yellow complexion, a cooper, born in Sussex County* [The Chesterfield Supplement or Size Roll of Troops at Chesterfield Court House, LVA accession no. 23816, by http://revwarapps.org/b81.pdf (p.9)]. He registered in Petersburg on 19 August 1794: *a brown Mulatto man, five feet seven and a half inches high, thirty eight years old, born free & raised in Mecklenburg County* [Register of Free Negroes 1794-1819, no. 49].

Michael Flood enlisted in the Revolution for two years in July 1779 in Petersburg while residing in Sussex County and was sized in 1781: *age 15, 5' high, yellow complexion, a planter, born in Sussex County, served Colonel Buford for 1 year* [The Chesterfield Supplement or Size Roll of Troops at Chesterfield Court House, LVA accession no. 23816, by http://revwarapps.org/b81.pdf (p.9)].

William Flora was counted in a list of "free Negroes" as a pedlar living in Portsmouth, Norfolk County, in 1801 [PPTL, 1782-91, frames 392, 485, 567, 613, 643, 682; 1791-1812, frames 22, 82, 172, 354, 463, 646, 742; 1813-24, frames 101, 251]. He was listed in the payroll of Captain William Grimes in the 15th Virginia Regiment under Lieutenant Colonel James Innes from 1776 to 1779 [NARA, M246, Roll 113, frame 439 of 752; http://fold3.com/image/22938237]. He received bounty land based on his application from Norfolk County on 16 July 1806 which stated that William Floray, a man of colour, served in the 16th Virginia Regiment until the close of the war and was held in high esteem as a soldier [Revolutionary War Bounty Warrants, Floray, William, Digital Collections, LVA]. He was said to have fought in the battle at Great Bridge, Norfolk County, in the Revolution, prying loose the last board in the bridge to prevent the British from attacking his retreating comrades [Jackson, *Virginia Negro Soldiers*, 34; WPA, *The Negro in Virginia*, 23].

Lewis Fortune enlisted in the Revolution on 20 September 1780 for 1-1/2 years: *age 16, 5'7" high, a planter, born in Caroline County, residing in Essex County, black complexion* [Register & description of Noncommissioned officers & Privates, LVA accession no. 24296, by http://revwarapps.org/b69.pdf (p.67)]. He received £30 final pay as a soldier in the infantry on 18 November 1785 [NARA, M881, Roll 1092, frame 356 of 2281; http://fold3.com/image/286702962]. He was a "Mo" or "free Black" taxable in Powhatan County from 1792 to 1813 [PPTL, 1787-1825, frames 76, 92, 105, 118, 132, 162, 362, 438].

Samuel Fortune enlisted in the Revolution from Powhatan County for 18 months on 29 August 1781 and was sized the same day: *age 32, 5'4-1/4" high, black complexion, a planter, born in Caroline County* [The Chesterfield Supplement or Size Roll of Troops at Chesterfield Court House, LVA accession no. 23816, by http://revwarapps.org/b81.pdf (p.65)]. He was listed in the muster of the 5th Virginia Regiment in September 1782: "died 4 August 1782 Great S. Hospital" [NARA, M246, Roll 113, frame 664 of 752; http://fold3.com/image/23301380].

Shadrack Fortune enlisted in the Revolution in Accomack County in April 1782 for 18 months as a substitute and was sized: *age 24, 5'2-1/2" high, black complexion, a gardner, born in Accomack County* [The Chesterfield Supplement or Size Roll of Troops at Chesterfield Court House, LVA accession no. 23816, by http://revwarapps.org/b81.pdf (p.65)].

George Francis was a resident of South Carolina who enlisted in the Revolution for the duration of the war in Virginia about 1781: *age 28, 5'4" high, black complexion, born in*

South Carolina [The Chesterfield Supplement or Size Roll of Troops at Chesterfield Court House, LVA accession no. 23816, by http://revwarapps.org/b81.pdf (p.65)].

Anthony Freeman enlisted in the Revolution from Amelia County on 11 September 1780: *age 19, 5"3-1/4" high, a planter, born in Amelia County, black complexion* [Register & description of Noncommissioned officers & Privates, LVA accession no. 24296, by http://revwarapps.org/b69.pdf (p.42)].

Charles Freeman was a "Mulatto Boy" living in Nottoway Parish, Amelia County, on 28 June 1759 when the court ordered the churchwardens to bind him as an apprentice to John Howsing [Orders 1757-60, 224]. He enlisted in the Revolution for 18 months from Amelia County on 11 September 1780: *age 21, 5'6" high, planter, black complexion, born in Amelia County* [Register & description of Noncommissioned officers & Privates, LVA accession no. 24296, by http://revwarapps.org/b69.pdf (p.42)].

John Freeman enlisted in the 15th Virginia Regiment in December 1776 for three years, served as a waiter to Captain Samuel Hogg, and died as a prisoner of war on Haddril's Point according to a certificate from Captain Hogg on 8 June 1787. His heirs Squire **Osborne**, a free person of Colour, and others applied for his bounty land [Revolutionary War Bounty Warrants, Freeman, John, Digital Collections, LVA].

Stephen Freeman and his brother John Freeman were soldiers in the Revolution whose heirs received bounty land. Jane **Collins**, a free woman of Colour, testified on 14 May 1840 that their heirs were Molly **Holt**, Rhody **Arnold**, Billy **Sampson** and Squire **Osborn**, free persons of Colour. Stephen received £103 for his services prior to January 1782 according to an auditor's certificate [NARA, B.LWt. 2393-100, M804, roll 1024, frame 312 of 952; http://fold3.com/image/20171576]. He may have been the Stephen Freeman who was a wagoner in the muster of Major Stephenson's Company of the 5th and 11th Virginia Regiment commanded by Colonel Russell from June 1779 to November 1779 [NARA, M246, frames 668, 677, 683 of 774; http://fold3.com/image/9946602]. Squire **Osborn** was a "F.N." tithable in New Kent County from 1799 to 1815: taxable on 2 slaves over 16 and a horse in 1799, a slave 12-16 in 1801, listed with his unnamed wife in 1813 [PPTL, 1791-1828, frames 332, 345, 359, 433, 444, 455, 466, 477, 488, 494, 500, 503, 516]. Molly **Holt**, Rhody **Arnold** and Billy **Sampson** lived in King William County on or near the Pamunkey Indian Reservation. The **Holt** family descended from George **Holt**, born 20 October 1737, the "Bastard Son of Ann **Holt** a free mulatto woman," who was baptized on 23 July 1738 in St. Peter's Parish, New Kent County [Chamberlayne, Vestry Book and Parish Register of St. Peter's, 545].

Nathan Fry was probably a descendant of Jane Fry who was living in Washington Parish, Westmoreland County, on 9 February 1713/4 when she bound her one-year-old "mulatto" son William Fry to Jonas Williams [DW 1716-20, 66]. Nathan was a "coloured man," aged about 68 or 69 on 2 June 1823, and living in Richmond when he stated that he enlisted in the Minute Service with Daniel Duval of Henrico County in 1775, went to Savannah, Georgia, and served under Captain Mosby in Colonel Elbert's Regiment against the Creek Indians as a drummer until he was taken as a waiter to Major Duval, batman to Baron Steuben, and was discharged in Richmond in 1781 or 1782. He also stated that he was born free in Westmoreland County [NARA, S.39545, M804, Roll , Roll 1031; frame 596 of 1051; http://fold3.com/image/22758110]. He was a "F.N." taxable in the upper district of Henrico County from 1790 to 1813 [PPTL 1782-1814, frames 376, 402, 486, 593, 661, 823; Land Tax Lists 1799-1816].

Dennis Garner enlisted in the Revolution for 18 months from Isle of Wight County on 28 September 1780: *age 26, 5'6-1/4" high, a farmer, born in Isle of Wight County, yellow complexion* [Register & description of Noncommissioned officers & Privates, LVA accession no. 24296, by http://revwarapps.org/b69.pdf (p.72)]. He was listed on the payroll of Captain Edmund's Company of the 15 Virginia Regiment in June 1777 but deserted in July 1777 [NARA, M246, roll 113, frame 189; http://fold3.com/image/9639784].

Abraham Goff was a "Mulatto" taxable in Buckingham County in 1790 [PPTL 1782-97] and head of a Botetourt County household of 5 "other free" in 1810 [VA:625]. He was a "free man of Colour" who testified in Bedford County, Virginia court to obtain a pension for his service in the Revolution, stating that he enlisted in January 1777 in Cumberland County, Virginia, in the 10th Virginia Regiment under Captain Mayo Carrington and served in the company of Captain Alexander Parker. He was taken prisoner in Charleston, re-enlisted and discharged at Yorktown after serving four years [NARA, S.39596, M805, Roll 362, frames 56-65; http://fold3.com/image/22805793]. He registered in Bedford County on 26 October 1820: *aged 77, Mulatto, 5 feet 11 inches, Born free* [Register of Free Negroes 1820-60, p.3].

Daniel Goff made a declaration in Boone County, Kentucky, on 4 February 1833 in order to obtain a pension for his services in the Revolution. He was living in Chesterfield County when he enlisted in the 15th Virginia Regiment for three years. He served under Captain Dandridge, then Major Wallace and General Woodford and was at the Battle of Monmouth. James Taylor testified that Daniel, a "poor colored man," came to live with him in Campbell County, Virginia, in 1793 as a gardener and laborer [NARA, S.15586, M805, Roll 362, frame 97; http://fold3.com/image/22806017].

John Goff was listed in the muster of Lieutenant Gibbs of the 15th Virginia Regiment on 3 February 1778 next to Abram Goff in the same list as Daniel Goff, all enlisted for 3 years on 5 September 1777. John died on 16 May 1778 according to the May muster at Valley Forge [NARA, M246, Roll 113, frames 291, 300, 303 of 752; http://fold3.com/image/9641918].

Moses Goff, born say 1760, was a soldier in the Revolution from Cumberland County. On 24 March 1783 Abram Goff received his final pay of £56 [NARA, M881, Roll 1092, frame 793 of 2281; http://fold3.com/image/286702747]. He was a "f. Mo" taxable in the upper district of Cumberland County [PPTL, 1782-1816, frames 33, 89, 122, 155, 257, 294, 353, 428, 486, 523, 559]. He was a "M"(ulatto) taxable in Buckingham County from 1810 to 1821 [PPTL 1810-26].

Samuel Goff enlisted in the Virginia Continental Line on 15 September 1777 and was killed at Paulus Hook on 16 August 1779 according to a certificate signed by Captain Mayo Carrington and presented by Samuel's brother Abraham Goff in Cumberland County court [Orders 1779-84, 496; Revolutionary War Bounty Warrants, Goff, Samuel, Digital Collections, LVA]. Moses Goff received his final pay of £38 on 6 March 1784 [NARA, M881, Roll 1092, frame 794 of 2281; http://fold3.com/image/23001032, 286702752].

Zachariah Goff served in the Revolution. On 24 March 1783 Abram Goff received Zachariah's final pay of £35 for serving in the infantry [NARA, M881, Roll 1092, frame 797 of 2218; http://fold3.com/image/286702747]. He was taxable in Prince Edward County in 1784 and 1785 [PPTL 1782-1809, frames 130, 145] and a "Melatto" taxable in Campbell County from 1788 to 1792 [PPTL, 1785-1814, frames 84, 150, 212]. He was called a "free mulatto" on 19 August 1793 when the Campbell County court found him not guilty of poisoning Micajah Moorman [Orders 1791-7, 219]. On 28 February 1796 the Cumberland County court ordered the clerk to issue him a certificate of freedom "it appearing to the court that the said Zachariah by birth and parentage is intitled to the same" [Orders 1792-7, 613]. He enlisted in Cumberland County in 1777 under Captain Mayo Carrington in the 10th Virginia Regiment, served under General Charles Scott, served for three years and was discharged in Richmond. On 25 September 1851 his widow Betsy Goff, a "free Negroe," testified that they were married in June 1796, that her maiden name was Betsy **Moss**, and that her husband died in 1823 [NARA, W.2730, M805, Roll 362, frames 288-295; http://fold3.com/image/22806134].

Charles Going/ Gowens was taxable in Henry County from 1783 to 1790 [PPTL, 1782-1830, frames 302, 352] and taxable in Patrick County from 1791 to 1795 [PPTL, 1791-1823, frames 151, 177, 207]. He was about 70 years old on 22 October 1833 when he applied for a Revolutionary War pension, stating that he enlisted in September 1779 for 6 months under Captain Jonathan Hamley, marched to South Carolina where he was under Colonel Munroe and guarded provisions and public stores. He enlisted again in May 1781 for three months under Captain Sheldon and went to the Dan River where they suppressed the Tories. He was born in Henry County, lived there until 1797, then moved to Kentucky and moved to Gallatin in 1815 [NARA, S.31072, M805, Roll 368, frame 0144; http://fold3.com/image/21819909].

David Going was a "Mulo" taxable in Halifax County, Virginia, from 1792 to 1806 and a ' planter in the list of "free Negroes & Mulattoes" in 1801 [PPTL, 1782-1799, frames 7, 71, 302, 417, 442, 732, 819; 1800-12, frames 59, 187, 517, 676]. He registered in Halifax County on 11 October 1802: *aged about forty eight years, six feet and a half inch high, light yellow Colour, inclining to white, straight hair ..born free* [Register of Free Negroes, no.20]. He was head of a Wythe County household of 8 "other free" in 1810. He appeared in Hamilton County, Tennessee court and testified that he volunteered in the militia under Colonel William Terry at Halifax courthouse for about three months, was drafted for three months and served in the militia under Captain Bates at Bibbs Ferry, and was drafted and marched by Captain Prigmore to Portsmouth where he served under General Washington until the surrender of Cornwallis. He moved to Grayson County, Virginia, for three years, then to Wythe County for ten years, then to Grainger County, Tennessee [NARA, S.3406, M805, Roll 362, frames 27-30; http://fold3.com/image/22046872].

Frederick Goen was head of a Sumner County, Tennessee household of 10 "free colored" in 1820 and a "free man of Color" who appeared in Lawrence County, Alabama court to apply for a pension for services in the militia during the Revolution. He stated that he was born on the Meherrin River in the part of Brunswick County, Virginia, from which Greensville was formed after the war, and he was about 16 years old when drafted. He served as a cook and looked after horses [NARA, R.4167, M805, Roll 362, frames 14-24; http://fold3.com/image/22046834].

Jacob Gowen, brother of Charles and William Going of Henry County, was taxable in Henry County from 1784 to 1787 [PPTL, 1782-1830, frames 88, 253], taxable in Patrick County in 1791, 1792, 1798 and 1800 [PPTL, 1791-1823, frames 151, 251, 288], and head of a Stokes County, North Carolina household of 6 "other free" in 1800 [NC:495]. He was about 70 years of age and living in Vermillion County, Illinois, on 7 June 1832 when he applied for a Revolutionary War pension, stating that he enlisted in July 1780 in the militia under Colonel Elifus Shelton in Henry County and marched to the Big Dan River to protect the area from the Tories. He enlisted a second time in 1781 as a substitute for John Berry and served in the regiment commanded by Colonel John Waller. He made entrenchments and conveyed timber and other materials for the breastwork at Yorktown and was discharged after the surrender of Cornwallis. He was born in Henry County, Virginia, lived in Kentucky for about 30 years, then lived for 7 years in Vincennes, Indiana [NARA, S.32273, M805, Roll 1368, frame 0115; http://fold3.com/image/21817288]. He was counted as white in the 1830 census for Vermilion, Illinois, a male between 70 and 80 years of age.

James Gowing was in Captain James Franklin's Company of the 10th Virginia Regiment on 31 May 1777, in the same list as Shadrack **Battles**, listed as deceased on 1 January 1778 [NARA, M246, Roll 108, frames 308, 332 of 1044; http://fold3.com/image/9096387].

John Goin enlisted in the Revolution on 14 February 1778 for one year and was listed in the May 1778 payroll of Captain Mosely's Company of the 7th Virginia Regiment at Valley Forge and the December 1778 payroll of the 5th Regiment mustered on 13 January 1779 at Middlebrook, New Jersey. He was discharged in February 1779 [NARA, M246, Roll 105, frame 74 of 806; Roll 102, frames 38, 44 of 774; http://fold3.com/image/9680943]. He may have been the John Going who was taxable in Henry County from 1782 to 1790: taxable on a horse and 3 cattle in 1782, taxable on Ward Barrett's tithe in 1786, living on the Dan River from 1787 to 1790 [PPTL, 1782-1830, frames 8, 88, 158, 218, 253], and taxable on the Dan River in Patrick County from 1791 to 1805: taxable on 2 tithes in 1802, 1804, 1805 [PPTL, 1791-1823, frames 150, 343, 396]. He was called John Going, Sr., "Molatto," in Patrick County in 1812 and was in a list of "free Negroes & Mulattoes" in 1813 and 1814 [PPTL, 1791-1823, frames 537, 598, 614]. Another John Goan was head of a Grainger County household of 9 "other free" in 1810 and a third John Going was head of a Smithland,

Livingston County, Kentucky household of 7 "other free" and a slave in 1810.

Joshua Going was drafted into the Revolution from Louisa County for 18 months on 17 April 1781 and was sized on 14 May: *age 28, 5'7-1/4" high, yellow complexion, born in Louisa County* [The Chesterfield Supplement or Size Roll of Troops at Chesterfield Court House, LVA accession no. 23816, by http://revwarapps.org/b81.pdf (p.55)]. He was a "Mula" taxable in Albemarle County in 1813 [PPTL, 1800-1813, frames 29, 117, 208, 297, 435, 522, 567].

Raverly Going enlisted in the 6th Virginia Regiment and died in the army according to an affidavit by Lieutenant Bell of the regiment who was living in Charles City County on 21 March 1818. Freeman and James **Brown** of Charles City County (heads of "other free" Charles City County households in 1810) deposed that Nancy **Smith**, wife of Michael Smith was the only heir of Raverly Going, deceased. She received land warrant no. 5484 for 100 acres and was living in Charles City County in 1808 [Revolutionary War Bounty Warrants, Going, Raverly, Digital Collections, LVA]. Raverly was apparently identical to David Going who was listed as deceased on 11 May 1778 in the 6th Virginia Regiment commanded by Colonel John Gibson 1778. John Bell was one of the lieutenants in that muster [M246, Roll 103, frame 485 of 756; http://fold3.com/image/9565261].

Sherrod Going enlisted in the Revolution for three years in the 14th Virginia Regiment and enlisted again for 18 months in Albemarle County on 20 March 1781. He was sized on 19 April 1781: *age 21, 5'8-1/2", yellow complexion, born in Louisa County, former service: 14th Va. Regt, 3 yrs* [The Chesterfield Supplement or Size Roll of Troops at Chesterfield Court House, LVA accession no. 23816, by http://revwarapps.org/b81.pdf (p.11)]. He was head of an Albemarle County household of 12 "other free" in 1810 [VA:196] and 9 "free colored" in 1820. He was a "man of colour" who appeared in Albemarle County court to apply for a pension for 3 years service in the 14th Regiment under Colonel Charles Lewis and another service of 18 months. He was at the Battles of Germantown and Monmouth and the Siege of Yorktown. He owned 200 acres on one of the spurs of the Blue Ridge when he applied [NARA, W.7545, M804, roll 1087, frame 234; http://fold3.com/image/22778244].

William Going was in a list of "free Negroes & Mulattoes" in Henry County in 1813 and 1814 [PPTL, 1782-1830, frames 150, 177, 207, 234, 288, 343, 369, 396, 455, 515, 553, 598, 616]. He appeared in Hawkins County, Tennessee court on 20 May 1819 and applied for a pension for his service in the Revolution. He stated that he enlisted in the Spring of 1780 at Halifax County, Virginia courthouse under Captain Tilman Dixon in the 18th Regiment commanded by Henry Dixon. They marched to join General Greene in Guilford, North Carolina, in March 1781 and then to the Battle of Camden. He was later drafted in the company of Captain Jonathan Hamley and joined General Greene at the Siege of Ninety Six [NARA, W.7546, M804, Roll 1087, frame 280 of 1089; http://fold3.com/image/22778397].

Zephaniah Going was head of a Roane County, Tennessee household of 6 "free colored" in 1830. He was about 76 years old and living in Hawkins County, Tennessee on 18 December 1834 when he applied for a Revolutionary War pension, stating that he volunteered in Henry County under Captain Consiganer and Colonel John Haston, was marched to Guilford courthouse and discharged in August 1779. He was drafted in July 1779 under Captain Rubel, marched to Yorktown and discharged after the surrender of Cornwallis [NARA, R.4165, M805, Roll 368, frame 0134; http://fold3.com/image/21817728].

Oliver Griffin enlisted in the Revolution as a substitute from Northampton County, Virginia, for 18 months on 8 September 1780 and was sized on 14 May 1781: *age 34, 5'7-3/4" high, yellow complexion, Indian features, a sailor, born in Northampton County, old 18 mo man* [The Chesterfield Supplement or Size Roll of Troops at Chesterfield Court House, LVA accession no. 23816, by http://revwarapps.org/b81.pdf (p.55)].

Moses Grimes was a "mulatto" who served in the Virginia Regiment commanded by Colonel Gibson and waited on Colonel Brent during the Revolution. He was married to a 45-year-old "mulatto" woman named Jane **Wilson** on 2 October 1779 when Cuthbert Bullitt of Dumfries,

Virginia, placed an ad in the *Maryland Journal and Baltimore Advertiser* which stated that she had run away, perhaps to her husband or to the plantation of her former master Colonel George Mason or to Mrs. Page, among whose slaves she had a number of relations [Windley, *Runaway Slave Advertisements*, II:232-3]. He was listed as a wagoner in the July 1779 muster of Captain Thomas Ewell's Company in the 1st Virginia Regiment commanded by Colonel George Gibson [NARA, M246, roll 93, frame 565]. He was a soldier who received clothing on 29 November 1779 [NARA, M853, Roll 22, http://fold3.com/image/286702242].

Christopher Guy, born say 1762, enlisted as a substitute for John Guy and was in the list of men from Mecklenburg County under the command of Captain Reuben Vaughan who were on a detachment to the southward under immediate command of Colonel David Mason in 1779 [Elliott, Katherine, *Revolutionary War Records, Mecklenburg County, Virginia* (1964), 162-3, citing Edmund W. Hubbard Papers, Southern Historical Collection, UNC Chapel Hill, NC]. He was a "Mulatto" taxable in Mecklenburg County from 1806 to 1817 [PPTL, 1806-28, frames 35, 135, 163, 235, 341, 390, 596] and head of a household of 2 "free colored" in 1820 [VA:159b].

William Guy was head of a Granville County, North Carolina household of 7 "other free," a white woman over 45 years of age, and a white woman 16-26 years old in 1810 [NC:890]. He called himself "a free man of Color" on 5 February 1833 when he made a declaration in Granville County court in order to obtain a pension for his services in the Revolution. He testified that he was about 70 years old, was born in Brunswick County, Virginia, and lived in Mecklenburg County, Virginia, when he enlisted as a substitute for Jack Goode for six months in 1779 at Mecklenburg courthouse. He served under Captain Vaughan and was at the Battle of Stono Ferry. He was drafted in 1781, served under Captain Stephen Mabry and Colonel Lewis Burwell, marched to the Siege of York and was discharged after the surrender of Cornwallis [NARA, W.17969, M804-1149; M805, Roll 384, frame 0381; http://fold3.com/image/21447376].

Peter Hackett was a soldier in the Revolution whose final pay of £8 was received by Colonel Cropper on 20 December 1783 [NARA, M853, Roll 22; http://fold3.com/image/286702940]. He was in a list of soldiers of the Virginia Line whose names were on the register but had not received bounty land by 7 January 1835 [Brumbaugh, *Revolutionary War Records*, 246]. He was a "Free Negro" taxable in the northern district of Campbell County from 1787 to 1807, listed the same day as Peter Hacket, Jr., in 1807 [PPTL, 1785-1814, frames 85, 119, 331, 459, 697]. He was head of a Campbell County household of 11 "other free" in 1810 [VA:869].

Peter Haley received a land warrant for Revolutionary War service as a seaman on 9 December 1783 based on his discharge from Captain William Saunders in 1780 [Revolutionary War Bounty Warrants, Sallard, Eliphalet, Digital Collections, LVA; Brumbaugh, *Revolutionary War Records*, 345, 604]. On 16 September 1783 he received his final pay of £66 for serving as a sailor in the Navy [M853, Roll 22, http://fold3.com/image/286702489]. He registered as a "free Negro" in York County on 28 April 1802: *a bright mulatto with woolly hair high forehead...5 feet 6-1/2 Inches high...about 45 years of age...addicted to the intemperate use of ardent Spirits* [Register of Free Negroes 1798-1831, no.19]. He was head of a York County household of 4 "other free" and a slave in 1810 [VA:875].

George Harmon was head of an Accomack County household of 9 "other free" in 1800 [*Virginia Genealogist* 2:153] and 5 "other free" in 1810 [VA:29]. On 3 June 1807 late Lieutenant Colonel John Cropper, Jr., certified that George Harman "Mulatto" served until the end of the Revolution [Revolutionary War Bounty Warrants; Oldham, George, Digital Collections, LVA]. His only heirs Betsy, Comfort, Leah and Sarah Harmon applied for a pension for his service in Accomack County court on 25 September 1832 [Orders 1832-36, 16].

Stephen Harmon was head of an Accomack County household of 9 "other free" in 1810 [VA:100]. Scarborough Bloxam, a midshipman aboard the *Accomac*, testified that Stephen

Harmon, Tire Harmon and Joshua **Perkins** enlisted in the war, served on board the vessel during the Revolution and were discharged [Revolutionary War Bounty Warrants; Bayly, Robert, Digital Collections, LVA; http://fold3.com/image/11129094]. Fanny Harmon received bounty land warrant no. 7251 for his service and no. 7252 for the service of Tire Harmon [Brumbaugh, *Revolutionary War Records*, 292].

Tire Harmon served on board the *Accomac* according to testimony by midshipman Scarborough Bloxam [Revolutionary War Bounty Warrants; Bayly, Robert, Digital Collections, LVA]. Fanny Harmon received bounty land warrant no. 7252 for his service [Brumbaugh, *Revolutionary War Records*, 292]. Fanny Harmon was head of an Accomack County household of 8 "free colored" in 1830.

Edward Harris registered in Chesterfield County on 9 January 1809: *color yellow, age 40 years, stature 5 feet 7 inches born free* [Jesper, Archer (M, 30): Free Negro Register, 1809, African American Narrative Digital Collection, LVA]. He was head of a Charles City household of 5 "other free" in 1810 [VA:959] and a "Mulattoe" taxable in Chesterfield County from 1810 to 1827, living on James Scott's land with his 6 children in 1811 [PPTL, 1786-1811, frames 782, 824; 1812-27, 67, 338, 434, 471, 507, 552, 584, 619, 651, 685]. He appeared in Chesterfield County court to apply for a pension for his service in the Revolution, stating that he enlisted in Amelia County in Colonel Richard Campbell's Regiment in 1780, was at the Battles o f Guilford Courthouse and Ninety Six, and was discharged in January 1782. He owed Mr. James B. Scott, on whose land he lived, two years rent of £40 [NARA, S.37992, M804, Roll 1198, frame 1017 of 1169; http://fold3.com/image/23204526].

Isham Harris was called "Isham Harris, Son of Patty Stewart" on 13 October 1763 when he was ordered bound to Amos Tims, Jr., by the Lunenburg County court. On 13 April 1769 the court ordered Isham bound instead to John **Evans** (alias **Eppes**) [Orders 1763-64, 257; 1766-69, folio 202]. He was a "FN" taxable in Pittsylvania County in 1797 [PPTL 1782-97, frame 768]. He applied for a pension for services in the Revolution at the age of 84 years on 8 August 1843 in Rutherford County, North Carolina, stating that he was born in Charlotte County, Virginia, in 1759, entered the service in Lunenburg County as a substitute for __ Jones, served under Brigadier General Stevens who joined General Gates at the Battle of Camden. He was then drafted by Captain Walker and joined General Washington at Gloucester in the Siege of Yorktown. His claim was rejected [NARA, R.4654, M804, roll 1199, frame 197 of 947; http://fold3.com/image/22990280].

James Harris was head of a Charles City County household of 5 "other free" in 1810 [VA:958]. He was a resident of Charles City County on 17 August 1820 when he appeared in court to apply for a pension for his services in the Revolution. He stated that he enlisted in February 1778 in Charles City County, was marched to Valley Forge under Captain Callohill Minnis, entered the company under the command of Colonel Richard Parker of the 1st Virginia Regiment, and was discharged in Middlebrook, New Jersey [NARA, S.38006, M804, Roll 1199, frame 521 of 947; http://fold3.com/image/22990334].

James Harris, born on 14 January 1748 in Dinwiddie County, was a "free man of Color" residing in Patrick County on 12 February 1835 when he appeared there in court to make a declaration to obtain a pension for service in the Revolution. He stated that he moved from Dinwiddie County to Orange County, North Carolina, in 1775, resided in Orange County until 1781 and then moved to the part of Henry County that later became Patrick County. He was drafted while resident in Hillsborough, Orange County, in 1776 under Colonel Archibald Lytle and marched to Charleston where he was under the command of Colonel Thompson. He was employed at storing up the breastwork on the east side of the island and fought under Colonel Thompson at Sullivan Island. They marched to Savannah, Georgia, and then to St. Augustine, Florida. He was drafted again on 13 July 1780 under General Gregory, marched to Camden and was employed in doing various duties about the camp. His widow Keziah was about 80 years old on 10 April 1855 when she appeared in Patrick County court to obtain a widow's pension. She stated that her maiden name was Keziah **Minor** and that she and James had married in Rockingham County, North Carolina, in April 1801, that her husband died about 1842 or 1843, and that he was a horse-keeper. On 12 February 1860 she appeared before a notary public in Highland County, Ohio, where she had moved with her son, to ask that her pension be moved from Patrick County to Cincinnati [NARA, W.11223, M804, Roll 1199, frame 350 of 947; http://fold3.com/image/22990952]. James was a "Mulatto" taxable in Patrick County in 1799, listed with 2 tithes in 1799, 1804 and 1805 [PPTL, 1791-1823, frames 269, 428, 598] and head of a Patrick County household of 6 "free colored" in 1830. His widow Keziah was head of a Patrick County household of 4 "free colored" in 1840 and an 80-year-old "Mulatto" woman, born in Virginia, counted in the 1850 census [VA:389]

John Harris was a "Mulatto" taxable in Dinwiddie County in 1790 and 1792 and a "free" taxable from 1794 to 1801 when he was listed as a cooper in the same district (Braddock Goodwyn's) as another "free" John Harris [PPTL 1801 B, p.7]. He was called a "free man of Colour" on 27 April 1818 when he made a declaration in Prince George County to obtain a pension for his services, stating that he enlisted in 1777 in the 15th Virginia Regiment. He was taken from the regiment and made a servant to President Monroe who was then the major of horse and aide-de-camp to Lord Sterling. He was discharged in the Spring of 1779, and re-enlisted in 1780 under Colonel William Davies for abut six months, employed principally in building the barracks at Chesterfield courthouse. He made a second declaration on 18 May 1821 in the Hustings Court of Petersburg, stating that he was about 69 years old and residing in Dinwiddie County in the immediate vicinity of Petersburg. He was a cooper by trade [NARA, S.37997, M805, Roll 401, frame 0640; http://fold3.com/image/22610207].

John Harris was born in Prince George County and residing in Dinwiddie County when he enlisted on 6 June 1782 for 3 years in the Revolution: *age 21, 5'4-1/2" high, yellow complexion, hasel eyes* [The Chesterfield Supplement or Size Roll of Troops at Chesterfield Court House, LVA accession no. 23816, by http://revwarapps.org/b81.pdf (p.103)]. He was called a soldier who enlisted in the Revolution in Petersburg and served as a drummer according to the 3 July 1852 application made by his children, who were living in Wilkes County, North Carolina [CR 104.923.2 by *NCGSJ* V:251-2].

William Harris was listed in the payroll of Captain Thomas Massie's 6th Virginia Regiment for the months of November 1777 and January 1778 [NARA, M246, roll 103, frames 346, 348 of 756; http://fold3.com/image/9564581]. He was a deserter from Captain Thomas Massie's new recruits for the 6th Virginia Regiment according to the 21 November 1777 issue of the *Virginia Gazette* which offered a reward for his return, describing him as *a mulatto fellow about five feet eleven inches high, the veins in his leg much broke, appear in knots, he was enlisted in New Kent, but expect he is lurking about Charles City* [Purdie's edition, p.3, col. 3].

James Hartless was in a list of men in Amherst County called into militia service in 1781 [William & Mary Digital Archives, Swem Library's Special Collections, Cabell Papers Box 2, Folder11.pdf]. The Hartless family of Amherst County descended from Henry Hartless, a "mulatto," who was indicted by the Spotsylvania County court on 4 May 1761 for cohabiting with a white woman [Orders 1755-65, 208].

Peter Hartless made a declaration in Amherst County court to obtain a pension for his service in the Revolution, stating that he was born in Caroline County, was drafted in the militia in 1779 or 1780 under Captain Philip Buckner, was drafted for two short tours in 1781, but was never in any engagements. He returned to Caroline County until 1787 when he moved to Amherst County. Bounty land was issued to Lawrence **Mason** for Peter's service in the North Carolina Militia during the War of 1812 [NARA, S.5740, M804. Roll 1210, frame 0249; http://fold3.com/image/22991169]. He was head of an Amherst County household of 3 "other free" in 1810 [VA:288].

William Hartless made a declaration in Amherst County court on 17 September 1832 to obtain a pension for his service in the Revolution. He stated that he was born in Caroline County, moved to Amherst County when he was 23 years old, and entered the militia in Albemarle County in 1779 for one month, was drafted from Amherst County in 1781 for three months which he spent in Guilford County under General Greene, and did another tour of three months which culminated at Yorktown [NARA, S.5498, M804-1210, frame 260 (frame 274 of 1007; http://fold3.com/image/22991192]. He was head of an Amherst County household 13 "other free" in 1810, and 6 "free colored" and a 26-44 year old white woman in 1820.

John Hathcock was living in Southampton County on 5 October 1771 when he and his mother Sarah agreed to his indenture to Arthur **Byrd** for 12 years [Judgment Papers, 1773, frames 44-5]. On 11 March 1773 the court ordered the churchwardens of St. Luke's Parish to bind him and Aaron Heathcock, "poor children," and on 11 June 1773 the court ordered the churchwardens to bind him to Arthur **Byrd** (head of a Northampton County, North Carolina household of 5 "other free" in 1790) [Orders 1772-7, 134, 213]. He petitioned the Virginia Legislature on 9 October 1792 that he enlisted as a solider in the State in September 1779, served until January 1782 and received a discharge at Portsmouth from his commanding officer Captain Browne [Hathcock, John: Petition, Southampton County, 1792-10-09, Legislative Petitions Digital Collection, LVA]. He was head of a Halifax County, North Carolina household of 4 "other free" in 1810 [NC:27] and 7 "free colored" in 1820 [NC:151].

James Hawkins was about 57 years old with no family living with him on 14 October 1820 when he made a declaration in Fluvanna County to obtain a pension for his service in the Revolution. He stated that he enlisted for two years in 1779 or 1780 in the regiment commanded by Colonel Harris. "Being a Coloured man," he was taken as a waiter to Major Chrogham. He received a land warrant for three years service and died on 21 January 1824 [NARA, S.37991, M804, Roll 1227, frame 0576 (frame 590 of 915; http://fold3.com/image/22759297].

John Hawkins enlisted in the Revolution from Frederick County on 7 June 1781 and was sized on 7 December 1781: *age 22, 5'4" high, yellow complexion, born in Frederick County* [The Chesterfield Supplement or Size Roll of Troops at Chesterfield Court House, LVA accession no. 23816, by http://revwarapps.org/b81.pdf (p.57)].

Peter Haw(s)/How and William Hawes were serving aboard the galley *Gloucester* on 4 November 1777 when the Keeper of the Public Store was ordered to deliver them articles of clothing, "on their paying for the same" [U.S. Government Printing Office, Naval Documents of the American Revolution, 11:160; http://ibiblio.org/anrs//docs/E/E3/ndar_v11p05.pdf]. He was head of a Lancaster County, Virginia household of 9 "Blacks" in 1783 [VA:56] and 6 "other free" in 1810 [VA:349]. On 1 November 1834 Peter's heirs applied for bounty land for his and his brother William's services in the Revolution. They stated that William Haw entered the State Navy in 1776, was on board the *Dragon* in 1777 under the command of Captain James Markham, and died in the service. William was from Lancaster County and had only one brother Peter Haw. Their petition included an affidavit that Peter Haws's name was on the army register as receiving £60.10 as the balance of his pay as a seaman on 9 March 1787 [Revolutionary War Rejected Claims, Haw, William, Digital Collection, LVA]. Peter was listed on 25 November 1834 as a seaman who served three years and was due bounty land [Brumbaugh, *Revolutionary War Records, Virginia,* 216].

William Haws, brother of Peter Haws, was a seaman aboard the *Dragon* according to an affidavit by a fellow seaman aboard the ship, John **Davis**, who testified for the bounty land claim of James Jennings on 7 February 1834 and named five of the officers and 52 members of the crew who served faithfully for three years and were discharged at the Chickahominy Ship Yard [Revolutionary War Bounty Warrants, Jennings, James (p.9), Digital Collection, LVA]. He was listed aboard the ship *Gloucester* on 5 July 1779 and aboard the *Dragon* on 2 September 1779. He served three years, died in service aboard the *Dragon* and was entitled to bounty land [Brumbaugh, *Revolutionary War Records*, 8, 14, 68].

Baker Hazard, a "mulatto man," ran away from John Scott's plantation in Fauquier County on 17 June 1777 according to the 25 July 1777 issue of the *Virginia Gazette* [Purdie edition, p.3, col. 1]. He was described in the 19 July 1780 issue of the *Virginia Gazette* as *a mulatto man,*

37

almost white, about 5 feet 8 inches high, pitted with the smallpox, born in Virginia (where he is now supposed to be) and waited on Mr. Gill of the Maryland regiment of light dragoons until he was taken prisoner last summer [Dixon & Nicholson edition]. He was in Calmes's Company of the 2nd Virginia regiment commanded by Christian Febiger in March 1777, October 1779 and August 1780 [NARA, M246, roll 95, frames 504 and 552 of 744; http://fold3.com/image/10069735]. This appears to be a different Baker Hazard than the one who was advertised as a runaway "mulatto" in the 25 July 1777 issue of the *Virginia Gazette* as having run away "the 17 June last" since the soldier was on the payroll for March 1777 [Purdie edition].

Ephraim Hearn enlisted in the 1st Virginia Regiment in January or February 1778 and served until the regiment was taken prisoner in Charleston in May 1780. They were placed on board prison ships until the general exchange in 1781 according to an affidavit by Colonel Mennis on 22 March 1796 when Ephraim received bounty land [Revolutionary War Bounty Warrants, Hern, Ephraim, Digital Collections, LVA]. He was a "man of colour" about 84 years old on 8 August 1829 when he made a declaration in Gloucester County court to obtain a pension for his services in the Revolution [NARA, 38020, M804, Roll 1242, frame 0662; http://fold3.com/image/27159669]. He was head of a Gloucester County household of 6 "other free" in 1810 [VA:657].

Elisha Heathcock was among a group of soldiers from Brunswick County, Virginia, who deserted from the 2d Georgia Battalion on 16 February 1777 according to the 7 March 1777 issue of the *Virginia Gazette* [Purdie edition, p. 4, col. 3]. (See the Haithcock/ Hathcock family of North Carolina).

Caleb Hill enlisted for 18 months in the Revolution from King William County on 8 September 1780 and was sized about the same time: *age 31, 5'7" high, born in King & Queen County, yellow complexion* [Register & description of Noncommissioned officers & Privates, LVA accession no. 24296, by http://revwarapps.org/b69.pdf (p.27)].

Zachariah Hill, son of "free mulatto" Hannah Hill, was bound out as an apprentice in Culpeper County on 18 May 1758. He was 24 years old in 1777 when he complained to the Halifax County, Virginia court that he had been treated as a slave. The court ordered him released [Pleas 9:194]. He was paid for serving in the militia in Halifax County in 1781 [Eckenrode, *Virginia Soldiers of the American Revolution*, I:218, Executive Communications, 178, loose manuscripts at the LVA]. He was a "Mulatto" taxable in the southern district of Halifax County, Virginia, from 1806 to 1812 [PPTL, 1800-12, frames 521, 629, 682, 804, 949, 1032]. He and Thomas Hill were heads of a Sullivan County, Tennessee household of 7 "free colored" in 1830.

John Hobson was a soldier who served three years in the 2nd State Regiment and received a discharge on 27 February 1780 which was certified by Captain Augustine Tabb and Lieutenant J. Hardyman on 2 July 1783 [Revolutionary War Bounty Warrants, Hopson, John, Digital Collection, LVA]. His son James registered as a "free Negro" in York County on 21 October 1805: *a bright Mulatto about 22 years of age 5 feet 7-3/4 Inches high, long curly black Hair, Hazle eyes, thick Eye brows* [Register of Free Negroes, 1798-1831, no. 32; Bell, Charles Parish Registers, 106]. He was head of a York County household of 6 "other free" in 1810 [VA:876].

Bartholomew Holmes enlisted in the Revolution from King William County in 1778 and was sized in 1781: *age 23, 5'7-1/4" high, yellow complexion, a farmer, born in James City, served in the 15th V.R.* [The Chesterfield Supplement or Size Roll of Troops at Chesterfield Court House, LVA accession no. 23816, by http://revwarapps.org/b81.pdf (p.79)]. He received an affidavit from Lieutenant Giles Raines of the 15th Regiment that he enlisted on 21 December 1776 and served for three years and a certificate from Captain Samuel Jones of the 11th Regiment that he enlisted on 23 December 1778 and served for the war [Revolutionary War Bounty Warrants, Holmes, Bartlett, Digital Collection, LVA]. He was about 64 years old on 1 August 1820 when he applied for a pension in Washington County, Maryland. He enlisted in Virginia under Colonel Russell for three years in December 1775, re-enlisted at Middlebrook for the duration of the war and was discharged after the Siege of Yorktown. He was in the Battles of Germantown, Monmouth, Stony Point, Charleston, Yorktown and Paulus Hook [NARA, S.34926, M804, roll 1313, frame 102 of 947; http://fold3.com/image/23390996].

Thomas Howell and his wife Lucy Howell were the parents of several children whose births were recorded in St. Peter's Parish, New Kent County [NSCDA, *Parish Register of St. Peter's*, 163]. He was taxable in New Kent County from 1790 to 1807: taxable on 2 tithes from 1803 to 1805, listed as a "M"(ulatto) in 1806 and 1807 [PPTL 1782-1800, frame 146; 1791-1828, frames 229, 307, 370, 420, 431]. He was a "free Negro" taxable in the upper district of Henrico County from 1811 to 1814: listed with his unnamed wife in 1813 [PPTL 1782-1814, frames 664, 758, 823] and head of a Richmond City household of 6 "other free" in 1810 [VA:345]. On 29 August 1836 he appeared in the Hustings Court of Richmond and testified that he was 76 years old, he entered the militia under Captain Waldy Clopton in August 1780 and was later drafted in New Kent County. And he stated that he was born in St. Peter's Parish, New Kent County, and served with Thomas Clopton who confirmed that he served with him under his brother Waldy Clopton. His application was rejected, but there is a record of a Thomas Howell who received £48 as the balance of his full pay on 2 September 1783 [NARA, M804, roll 1347, R.5300; http://fold3.com/image/24162797, 23349791].

William Holmes enlisted in the Revolution for 1-1/2 years while residing in King William County on 2 September 1780: *age 40, 5'10-1/2" high, a planter, born in King William County, yellow complexion.* He was probably identical to the William Holms who was sized about a year later: *age 43, 5'10" high, Negro complexion, farmer, residing in King William County* [The Chesterfield Supplement or Size Roll of Troops at Chesterfield Court House, LVA accession no. 23816, by http://revwarapps.org/b81.pdf (pp. 13, 34)].

David Howell enlisted in the Revolution on 3 January 1777 for three years, but he was discharged after serving two years and eight months "on account of his inability's" according to his 6 October 177_ discharge from Captain Robert Woodson of the 9th Virginia Regiment [Revolutionary War Bounty Warrants, Howel, David, Digital Collection, LVA]. Mr. Ford received his final pay of £48 on 21 April 1784 [NARA, M881, Roll 1092, frame 2049 of 2281]. He registered in Powhatan County on 19 December 1822: *Age: 59; Color: Dark Brown; Stature: 5'6-1/2"; Born Free* [Register of Free Negroes, nos. 65].

Isaac Howell was a black complexioned soldier, 5'5-1/4" high, born in Powhatan County, who entered the service on 24 March 1781 for 1-1/2 years, and had previously served as a waiter for a year in the 7th Virginia Regiment when he was sized at the Powhatan County court house on 27 April 1781 [The Chesterfield Supplement or Size Roll of Troops at Chesterfield Court House, LVA accession no. 23816, by http://revwarapps.org/b81.pdf (p. 41)]. Captain Pryor received his final pay of £19 on 11 February 1783 [NARA, M881, Roll 1092, frame 2053 of 2281]. He was head of a Buckingham County household 6 "other free" in 1810 [VA:810].

Robert Howell and his wife Mary were the parents of several "Free Mulatto" children baptized in St. Peter's Parish, New Kent County [NSCDA, *Parish Register of St. Peter's*, 162]. He was a "Freeman of Colour" who enlisted in New Kent County under Captain Peter Wright in the artillery and died in the service a year or two afterwards according to testimony by Henry Maderias on 8 February 1809. Benjamin Crump testified that Thomas Howell was Robert's heir at law and that his parents were lawfully married [Revolutionary War Bounty Warrants, Howel, Robert, Digital Collections, LVA]. His son Thomas was taxable in New Kent County from 1790 to 1807: listed as a "M"(ulatto) in 1806 and 1807 [PPTL 1782-1800, frame 146; 1791-1828, frames 229, 268, 307, 344, 370, 395, 420, 431].

Joseph Hughes enlisted in the Revolution in Culpeper County, Virginia, before December 1781 when he was sized: *age 31, 5'9-1/4" high, black complexion, a planter, born in Newcastle, Pennsylvania* [The Chesterfield Supplement or Size Roll of Troops at Chesterfield

Court House, LVA accession no. 23816, by http://revwarapps.org/b81.pdf (p.79)].

Luke Hughes was listed among the slaves in Cadwelder Dade's estate inventory which was proved in Stafford County on 14 July 1761: "Luke...to serve till 31" [Wills, Liber O, 1748-63, 400]. He was listed in the payroll of Captain Robert Powell and Captain Reubin Briscoe in the 3rd Virginia Regiment in August 1778 [NARA, M246, Roll 98, frames 556, 565 of 789; http://fold3.com/image/9680894]. He registered in King George County on 27 October 1800: *a dark molatto man with long grey hair, about sixty years, was born in this County, served Cadwellder Dade untill he was thirty one years of age* [Register of Free Persons, no.16]. He was a "Mulatto" taxable in Culpeper County from 1798 to 1802 [PPTL 1782-1802, frames 687, 781, 820, 865] and a "free Mulatto" head of a Culpeper County household of 3 "other free" in 1810 [VA:40].

William Hughes enlisted in the Revolution from Caroline County on 26 March 1781 and was sized about a month later: *age 33, 5'7" high, yellow complexion, a shoemaker, born in Caroline County* [The Chesterfield Supplement or Size Roll of Troops at Chesterfield Court House, LVA accession no. 23816, by http://revwarapps.org/b81.pdf (p. 57)]. He was head of a Spotsylvania County household of 2 "other free" and a slave in 1810 [VA·113b].

Hardy Hunt enlisted from Southampton County for the duration of the war on 3 September 1780 and was sized about the same time: *age 16, 5'3-1/4" high, planter, born in Southampton, Negro complexion* [Register & description of Noncommissioned officers & Privates, LVA accession no. 24296, by http://revwarapps.org/b69.pdf (p.27)]. He appeared in Southampton County court on 18 September 1792 and petitioned for pay for his services in the Revolution. John **Haithcock** testified that he served together with him, and Samuel Tinsley testified that he remembered a "Mulatto man by the name of Hardy Hunt" who served with him [Hunt, Hardy, 1795-11-19, Legislative Petitions Digital Collection, LVA]. He was a "F.N." or "M" taxable in Southampton County in 1803 and 1806 [PPTL 1782-92, frames 639, 658, 710, 758, 873; 1792-1806, frames 63, 91, 171, 382, 415, 518, 694, 844].

William Jackson enlisted in the Revolution in King William County for 18 months on 3 September 1780: *age 26, 5'5-1/2" high, a groom, born in Hanover County, yellow complexion* [Register & description of Noncommissioned officers & Privates, LVA accession no. 24296, by http://revwarapps.org/b69.pdf (p.9)].

William Jackson was a "free man of Colour" or "blackman" who was about 65 years old in October 1825 when he appeared in Bedford County to apply for a pension for his service in the Revolution. He stated that he entered the war in 1780 or 1781 at Amherst Court House and served for three years under colonels Posey, Febiger and Augustine Muhlenburg and was at Charleston and Cumberland courthouse. He served for a few weeks as a waiter [NARA, W.7877, M804, roll 1401, frame 1064; http://fold3.com/image/24144820].

Thomas James was a soldier in the Revolution who resided in Albemarle County in 1780 when he entered the service. He deserted in Goochland County on the way to Chesterfield County court house: *age 25, 5'4" high, born in Chesterfield County, yellow complexion* [Register & description of Noncommissioned officers & Privates, LVA accession no. 24296, by http://revwarapps.org/b69.pdf (p.63)].

Anthony Jasper, son of Elizabeth Jasper of Charles City County [Orders 1737-51, 287], was probably a brother of Hannah Jasper who was indicted by the York County court on 20 November 1749 for failing to list herself as a tithable [Orders 1746-52, 256, 277, 284]. He was the father of Johnny **Peters** who was baptized in Bruton Parish, James City and York counties, on 4 June 1748 [Bruton Parish Register, 8]. He may have been the Anthony Jasper who served as a soldier in the infantry in the Revolution. William Gordon received his final pay of £28 on 15 December 1784 [NARA, M881, Roll 1093, frame 146 of 2068; http://fold3.com/image/23285601].

John Jeffries was taxable in Meherrin Parish, Brunswick County, Virginia, from 1782 to 1787. His son Thomas appeared in Orange County, North Carolina court on 26 May 1837 to obtain a pension for his father's services in the Revolution. He stated that his father was born in Halifax County, Virginia, in 1733 (perhaps date in error and place meant to be Halifax County, North Carolina), was drafted in the fall of the years 1780 and 1781, that his father was very infirm and blind in December 1832 when he moved him to Orange County, and that his father died 4 December 1834 leaving no widow [NARA, S.8754, M804, Roll 1409, frames 350-1; http://fold3.com/image/24019756]. His son Thomas was head of an Orange County household of 9 "other free" in 1810 [NC:817] and 7 "free colored" in 1820 [NC:406].

John Jeffries was head of an Orange County, North Carolina household of 5 "free colored" in 1820 [NC:342]. He enlisted in Brunswick County, Virginia, in 1780, was marched to Hillsborough and then to South Carolina where he guarded the prisoners taken by General Morgan at the Battle of Cowpens. He resided in Brunswick County until 1808 when he moved to Orange County. He served in the place of his father Andrew Jeffreys [NARA, W.26158, M804, Roll 1409, frame 0363; http://fold3.com/image/24019847].

John, a "French negro man," was jailed in York County, Virginia, on 8 July 1777 and informed the jailer that he was a freeman and had run away from the brig *Northampton* which was under the command of Captain Bright according to the 1 August 1777 issue of the *Virginia Gazette* [Purdie edition, p. 4, col. 1].

James Johns was serving in the Revolution in 1778 when the Goochland County court allowed his wife Mary £12 [Gwathmey, *Historical Register of Virginians in the Revolution*, 419; Creel, *Selected Revolutionary War Records*, III:100, citing Auditors' Account Volume II:94, LVA]. J. Hopkins and William H. Miller certified that John Johns was the legal representative of James Johns who departed his life in the Continental Army. John Johns was called the brother of James Johns in March 1789 when he assigned his right to bounty land due for the service of James Johns [Revolutionary War Bounty Warrants, Johns, James, Digital Collection, LVA]. J. Hopkins and William H. Miller were "Gentlemen" from Goochland County [PPTL, 1782-1809, frame 220]. William Combs Johns left a 1788 Goochland County will, proved on 21 June 1789, naming his daughter Susannah **Banks** and son John Johns [DB 15:5]. Susannah Johns married Jacob **Banks**, "Mulattoes both," in Goochland County in 1775 [Jones, *The Douglas Register*, 347].

Charles Johnston enlisted as a substitute from Essex County for 18 months in October 1780 and was sized on 5 April 1781: *Age 18, 5'6" high, yellow complexion, a farmer, born in Essex County* [The Chesterfield Supplement or Size Roll of Troops at Chesterfield Court House, LVA accession no. 23816, by http://revwarapps.org/b81.pdf (p.15)].

Britton Jones was head of a Greensville County household of 4 "free colored" in 1820 [VA:262]. He petitioned the legislature on 26 October 1793, stating that he was drafted in the militia in Greensville County in 1782, performed a tour of duty for six months, and received a discharge in Portsmouth from his commanding officer Captain Armstead which he was able to produce [Jones, Britton: Petition, 1793-10-26, Southampton County, Legislative Petitions Digital Collections, LVA]. He registered as a "Free Negro" in Greensville County on 1 April 1825: *free born of a Yellowish Complexion about Sixty-two years old, 5 feet 10-1/4 inches high...a planter* [Register of Free Negroes, 1805-32, no. 140].

Burwell Jones was a "man of colour" hired by Daniel McKie of Lunenburg County to take his place in the Revolution. Burwell went together with McKie to Brunswick County court house where Colonel Davie accepted him as a substitute. McKie was later informed that Burwell died in the service [NARA, R.6750, M804, roll 1690, frame 420 of 891 and http://fold3.com/image/24220878].

James Keemer was in Captain Benjamin C. Spillar's Company of the 2nd Virginia State Regiment at White Plains on 8 September 1778 [NARA, M246, roll 96, frame 323 of 736; http://fold3.com/image/9679714]. He received clothing in 1780 [Gwathmey, *Historical*

He was head of a Northampton County, North Carolina household of 11 "other free" in 1800 [NC:466] and 6 in 1810 [NC:731].

Jesse Kelly was bound to serve Lewis lee as an apprentice for 31 years when John Crittendon and Luke Cannon, officers of the 15th Virginia Regiment, recruited Jesse to serve in the Revolution. Lee brought a suit against them in King William County court that lasted almost 9 years and awarded him £35 for the loss of his servant. Crittendon and Cannon's King William County petition to the General Assembly of Virginia for reimbursement was rejected [Crittendon, John & Cannon, Luke: Petition, 1791-10-26, Legislative Petitions, Digital Collections, LVA]. Jesse registered in Surry County as a free Negro on 11 April 1799: *a free born - mulatto man of a bright complexion...has a bushy head of hair* [Hudgins, Register of Free Negroes, 6].

George Kendall was taxable in Prince William County from 1796 to 1810: called a "Free Molatto" in 1799, a "yellow" man in 1806 and 1809, taxable on 3 tithes in 1809 and 1810 [PPTL, 1782-1810, frames 313, 402, 462, 643, 707, 736]. He appeared in Prince William County court on 3 November 1834 at the age of 93 and stated that he entered the service in Captain Drew's Company of Colonel Charles Porterfield's Light Infantry Regiment and was at the Battles of Guilford and Yorktown where he was under Colonel Dabney. He was born in King George County, had his indentures showing his age, and enlisted in the town of Falmouth about three years before the termination of the war [NARA, R.5859, M804, roll 1470, frame 469 of 1069; http://fold3.com/image/24947929]. He received a discharge stating that he enlisted for the war on 5 January 1780 and served his time [Revolutionary War Bounty Warrants, Kendall, George, Digital Collections, LVA].

William Kersey was head of a Warren County, North Carolina household of 10 "other free" in 1800 [NC:814], 11 in 1810 [NC:765], and 7 "free colored" in 1820 [NC:798]. He was called William Carsey in his pension application in which he stated that he was born in Southampton County in 1761, enlisted at Sussex County courthouse in 1777, and was marched to Georgetown where they were inoculated for smallpox. He spent the winter at Valley Forge and was then in the Battle of Monmouth. He was taken prisoner at Charleston and spent over a year on a prison ship and then marched to Williamsburg where he was discharged after serving four years. He moved to the part of Bute County, North Carolina, which became Warren County and re-enlisted there in 1782 [NARA, W.29906-1/2, M804, Roll 493, frame 768 of 790; http://fold3.com/image/12179994].

John Key appeared in Lunenburg County, Virginia court to petition for a pension for his service in the Revolution. He stated that he entered the 1st Virginia Regiment as a substitute for Christopher Carlton. His widow was Faithy Lester [NARA W.10163, M804, Roll 1478, frame 78 of 1326; http://fold3.com/image/24200551]. Faith Lester was the daughter of Isam Lester who was counted in a list of "free Negroes and Mulattoes" in the lower district of Lunenburg County near Hawkins' Ford in 1802 and 1803 with his children: Ermin, Faith, Bolling, Jones, Anna, and Ellick [Lunenburg County, Free Negro & Slave Records, 1802-1803, LVA].

Francis King was head of an Abingdon Parish, Gloucester County household of 7 free persons in 1784 [VA:68] and a "mulatto" taxable in Gloucester County in 1801 [PPTL, 1782-1799; 1800-20]. He received a discharge from Captain Machem Boswell on 27 May 1783 that he had enlisted in the 2nd Virginia Regiment in June 1777, re-enlisted in 1779 and served for the war [Revolutionary War Bounty Warrants, King, Francis, 1783, Digital Collections, LVA]. He was listed as a waiter to Lieutenant Colonel Thomas Posey, enlisted for the war, on the muster from January 1782 to March 1783 when he was transferred to Virginia. He received his final pay of £67 on 27 October 1783 [NARA, M881, Roll 1089, frames 920-7 of 1808].

Henry Lattimore enlisted in the Revolution in Fairfax County and was sized on 15 March 1781: *age 22, 5'8" high, yellow complexion, planter, resident of Fairfax County, born in Charles County, Maryland* [The Chesterfield Supplement or Size Roll of Troops at Chesterfield Court House, LVA accession no. 23816, by http://revwarapps.org/b81.pdf

(p.91)]. He was listed in the roll and muster of Captain Claugh. Shelton's 1st Virginia Battalion from 1 September to 1 May 1783 (with William **Wedgebare** and Sawney **Whistler**) [NARA, M246, roll 113, frames 709, 712; http://fold3.com/image/9649552]. He received his discharge from the 1st Virginia Regiment on 6 July 1783 [Revolutionary War Bounty Warrants, Latimer, Henry, Digital Collections, LVA].

Drury Lawrence petitioned the Amelia County court on 26 June 1755 (when he was about 30 years of age) to be discharged from his indenture to Charles Irby [Orders 1754-8, n.p.]. On 9 November 1769 the Lunenburg County court presented Richard Claiborne, Gentleman, for not listing him as a tithable [Orders 1769-77, 5]. He was apparently identical to Jury Larrance, an "Indian" taxable in Cumberland Parish, Lunenburg County, in Henry Blagrave's list for 1772 [Bell, *Sunlight on the Southside*, 291, 293, 339, 361]. (The original tax lists have not survived). Drury enlisted in the Revolution in Brunswick County, Virginia, on 20 August 1780 and was sized in 1781: *born in Prince George County, residing in Dinwiddie County, Age 55, 5'3-1/2" high, grey hair, yellow complexion, a farmer* [The Chesterfield Supplement or Size Roll of Troops at Chesterfield Court House, LVA accession no. 23816, by http://revwarapps.org/b81.pdf (p.19)].

John Laws, brother of Timothy and William Laws, was a boatswain's mate on the *Dragon* according to the testimony of John S. Kesterson of Northumberland County [Laws, Timothy: Revolutionary Bounty Warrants, Digital Collections, LVA]. His nephew Daniel Laws was head of a Lancaster County household of 10 "free colored" in 1840.

Timothy Laws was a gunner who served on the *Tempest* and died in the service in 1782. He was listed as a gunner the account of necessaries delivered to the officers on board the *Tempest* on 30 December 1779. His heirs received $730 as bounty for his service. His nephew Daniel Laws received $730 as bounty for his service [Laws, Timothy: Revolutionary Bounty Warrants, Digital Collections, LVA]. Timothy was issued a warrant of £219 on 7 September 1779 for re-enlisting [Creel, *Selected Virginia Revolutionary War Records*, III:159, citing Auditors' Account, Volume III:53, LVA]. Daniel was head of a Lancaster County household of 10 "free colored" in 1840, a "Black" farmer with Margaret Laws, age 37, and $400 worth of real estate in the 1850 Northumberland County census.

William Laws, the older brother of Timothy, was a seamen aboard the *Defiance* for three years, and died "soon after peace was declared according to an affidavit by John S. Kesterson of Northumberland County on 6 March 1838. Kesterson also stated that a family of Laws lived in the county at the time of the Revolution "and their descendants ever since." His widow may have been Chris Laws, born about 1760, who registered in Lancaster County on 16 June 1806: *Age 46, Color dark...emancipated by Doodridge P. Chichester* [Burkett, *Lancaster County Register of Free Negroes*, 2], head of a Lancaster County household of 4 "other free" in 1810 [VA:352].

Ambrose Lewis was a "Mulatto" child bound out in Spotsylvania County with Charles Lewis on 5 April 1771. He was paid for serving as a seaman aboard the *Dragon* in the Revolution from 30 March 1778 to 20 January 1779, was on a list of seamen on the *Dragon* on 2 September 1779, and was on a list of seamen who had served in the navy for 3 years. Fanny and Hannah Lewis received his bounty land warrant no. 8082 for his service as a seaman, but he also received bounty land warrant no.2503 as a soldier [Brumbaugh, *Revolutionary War Records*, 8, 12, 69, 352, 462]. On 4 May 1787 the Spotsylvania County court called him "a soldier who got wounded in General Gates' defeat" when it ordered that he receive a pension. The order was renewed each year through 1795 [Minutes 1786-7, 102, 158; Orders 1787-92, 48, 236; 1792-5, 78, 240]. He stated that he enlisted on 15 April 1776 as a seaman aboard the galley *Page* until 30 March 1778, then aboard the *Dragon* until 15 April 1779 and then as a soldier in the 2nd Virginia Regiment commanded by Colonel George Stubblefield until August 1780 when he was wounded at the battle of Camden [NARA, S.36041, M804, Roll 1554, frame 249 of 909; http://fold3.com/image/25072024; Revolutionary War Bounty Warrants, Lewis, Ambrose, Digital Collections, LVA].

43

Charles Lewis was a "Mulatto" child living in King George County on 5 April 1771 when the court ordered the churchwardens of Brunswick Parish to bind him and his brother Ambrose Lewis to William Buckham [Orders 1766-90, 158]. He was paid for serving as a seaman aboard the *Dragon* in the Revolution from 15 April 1778 to 20 January 1779, was on a list of seamen on the *Dragon* on 2 September 1779, and was on a list of seamen who had served in the navy for 3 years. Fanny Lewis and others received his bounty land warrant no. 8083 [Brumbaugh, *Revolutionary War Records*, 8, 12, 69, 352]. The pension application of Ambrose Lewis includes an affidavit from a soldier that Charles and Ambrose were brothers who both served in the Revolution. Also, John **Davis**, a seaman aboard the *Dragon*, made a deposition for the bounty land claim of James Jennings on 7 February 1834 and named Charles and Ambrose Lewis as 2 of 52 members of the crew [Revolutionary War Bounty Warrants, Jennings, James (p.9), Lewis, Charles, Digital Collections, LVA].

Beverly Liggin was paid $22 for serving as a fifer in the Revolution [NARA, M881, Roll 1093, frames 1135, 1136 of 2068]. He was a "Mo" taxable in Powhatan County in 1791 [PPTL, 1787-1825, frame 62], taxable in Rockbridge County in 1796 and 1798, called a "Free Negroe" in 1801 and 1802 [PPTL 1787-1810, frames 243, 309, 394, 426].

Jeremiah Liggon served three years as a soldier in the Revolution served three years. His final pay of £34 was received by William Wood on 10 November 1784 [NARA, M881, Roll 1093, frames 1138, 1139 of 2068; http://fold3.com/image/23297458; Brumbaugh, *Revolutionary War Records*, 252]. He registered in Chesterfield County on 10 October 1800: *son of William Liggan and Hanah Liggan were free persons at his birth. Guleelmus Wood. A Blak man aged between thirty five and forty years, about five feet nine inches high, stout made, the son of Hanah Ligon a Black woman now living in this county. The said Hanah Ligon lived with a certain Thomas Smith as an apprentice or servant about forty five or forty eight years past. From the expiration of her service with said Smith has lived in this county as a free woman, that she intermarried with William Ligon a melatow who served his time as an apprentice with John Branch of this county. They raised several children* [Ligon, Jeremiah (M, 35): Free Negro Affidavit, 1800, and Liggan, Jeremiah (M): Free Negro Certificate, 1800, African American Narrative Digital Collection, LVA].

James Lines enlisted for 18 months in Amherst County while residing in Cumberland County in 1781: *age 50, 5'10" high, yellow complexion* [The Chesterfield Supplement or Size Roll of Troops at Chesterfield Court House, LVA accession no. 23816, by http://revwarapps.org/b81.pdf (p.19].

Thomas Lively was a "Mulatto" living with his two children on James Scott's land in Chesterfield County in 1809 and 1811 [PPTL, 1786-1811, frames 162, 198, 268, 301, 374, 563, 689, 738]. His daughter Sally obtained a certificate of freedom in Chesterfield County on 14 January 1833: *a free mulatter woman, lived on my plantation some years ago Whilst there gave birth to a boy called Dick. I knew Sally Lively's father and mother forty years ago and they have always been reputed to be free. Her father is at this time receiving annually a pension for his services in the revolutionary war. Robt. Clarke* [Lively, Sally (F): Free Negro Affidavit, 1833, African American Narrative Digital Collection, LVA]. He was a "man of Colour," who enlisted in Chesterfield County in the 5th Virginia Regiment in 1777, was discharged at Annapolis and re-enlisted at Chesterfield courthouse a few months later. He was at the Battles of Wilmington, Monmouth (where he lost his right eye) and Augusta and was taken prisoner at Charleston [NARA, S.38144, M804, Roll 1573, frame 42; http://fold3.com/image/27253533].

"Indian" Robin Loyd, a "person of color," was residing in Jennings County, Indiana, and was about the age of 80 on 12 February 1838 when he made a declaration to obtain a pension for his services in the Revolution. He stated that he enlisted at Dinwiddie County courthouse and had resided in Dinwiddie for many years after the war, went to North Carolina for a few years, and had been living in Indiana for more than 20 years. John Grimes of Ripley County, Indiana,

44

testified for him that Indian Robin, "a negro man," had served as a footman and also as a soldier in the light horse service. Bartholomew Turner of Jennings County testified that he had seen a "Negro man" named Indian Robin as a soldier on horseback and armed for battle [NARA, R.6501, M804, Roll 1596, frame 0594; http://fold3.com/image/27257831].

Claude Lomanaintrom enlisted for the war as a substitute in Fairfax County on 19 February 1781 and was sized the same day: *age 19, 5'8" high, yellow complexion, a taylor* [The Chesterfield Supplement or Size Roll of Troops at Chesterfield Court House, LVA accession no. 23816, by http://revwarapps.org/b81.pdf (p.19].

Charles Lucas received a certificate of freedom in Loudoun County on 13 May 1816: *This day Robert Sears appeared and made Oath before me that Charles Lucas a Man of Colour Aged Upward of Seventy Years is a free man (& was born free) & Served Capt. Howsen Hoe of Prince William County--Untill he was thirty one years of Age, Agreeable to a former Law of the State of Virginia.* He and his wife Nancy were identified in the 29 October 1811 Loudoun County certificate of freedom of their son William Lucas: *I do certify that Charles Lucas and Nancy Lucas his wife has live near me for twenty odd years two mulattos I always believed them free born consequently the Bearer William Lucas being the son of the above must be born free...Henry Washington* [Lucas, Townsend M., Loudoun County, Virginia, Records of Free Negroes, 1778-1838 (bound book at Thomas Balch Library in Loudoun County)]. He was a seaman aboard the galley *Henry* in an undated muster taken before 8 April 1778. He was entitled to bounty land since he served as a seaman for three years [Brumbaugh, *Revolutionary War Records*, 15, 69, 252]. He was head of a Prince William County household of 15 "other free" in 1810 [VA:523].

James Lucas was listed as a seaman who had served three years in the Revolution and was due bounty land [Brumbaugh, *Revolutionary War Records*, 69, 216]. He was taxable in King George County from 1786 to 1793, called "free Jim Lucas" [PPTL, 1782-1830, frames 28, 48, 100, 111, 118]. He registered in King George County on 1 May 1800: *a dark Mulatto man aged about ___ years, and about five feet ___ Inches, was bound to Thomas Massey, Senr. of this County to serve till the age of thirty one years* [Register of Free Persons 1785-1799, no.12].

John Lucas received pay from 10 September 1777 to 20 January 1779 for service as a seaman aboard the *Dragon* [Brumbaugh, *Revolutionary War Records*, 12]. He was also named as a seaman aboard the *Dragon* in an affidavit by a fellow seaman, John **Davis**, aboard the ship, who testified for the bounty land claim of James Jennings on 7 February 1834 and named five of the officers and 52 members of the crew who served faithfully for three years and were discharged at the Chickahominy Ship Yard [Revolutionary War Bounty Warrants, Jennings, James (p.9), Digital Collection, LVA]. He was a "free Neg" or "Black" taxable in Stafford County from 1783 to 1792: listed by John **DeBaptist** in 1787 [PPTL 1782-1813, frames 106, 151, 218, 226, 263].

Joseph Lucas enlisted in the Revolution from Powhatan County for 18 months as a substitute on 11 March 1782 and was sized the same day: *age 21, 5'9-1/4" high, yellow complexion, born in Powhatan County* [The Chesterfield Supplement or Size Roll of Troops at Chesterfield Court House, LVA accession no. 23816, by http://revwarapps.org/b81.pdf (p.83)]. He was a "free Bk" taxable in Powhatan County in 1790 [PPTL, 1787-1825, frame 48]. He registered as a free Negro in Goochland County on 18 July 1809: *five feet nine and an half inches high, about forty five years of age, short curled hair intermingled with Grey...free born* [Register of Free Negroes, p. 32]. He was head of a Henrico County household of 6 "other free" in 1810 [VA:998].

Joseph Longdon enlisted for the war on 12 September 1780: *age 27, 5'7" high, a blacksmith, born in Fairfax County, residing in Alexandria, black complexion* [Register & description of Noncommissioned officers & Privates, LVA accession no. 24296, by http://revwarapps.org/b69.pdf (p.35)].

John Macklin was described as a "free mulatto" who lived near the lower Mecklenburg County store of Dinwiddie, Crawford, & Company and owed them £3 on 1 September 1775 [*Virginia Genealogist* 15:291]. He was "poor soldier in the service of the United States," whose wife Frances was living in Mecklenburg County on 13 March 1780 when the court ordered Reuben Morgan to supply her with 2 barrels of corn for her support [Orders 1779-84, 19].

Richard McGee enlisted in the Revolution as a substitute in King George County in August 1780 for 18 months and was sized on 15 April 1781: *age 22, 5'9-1/2" high, sandy colored hair, hazel eyes, yallow complexion, a weaver, born in King George County* [The Chesterfield Supplement or Size Roll of Troops at Chesterfield Court House, LVA accession no. 23816, by http://revwarapps.org/b81.pdf (p.21)].

Bennett McCoy/ McKey was head of a Westmoreland County, Virginia household of 4 "other free" in 1810 [VA:780]. He was about 61 years old on 23 May 1818 when he appeared in Westmoreland County and made an affidavit (signing) to apply for a pension for his services in the Revolution. He was drafted in Westmoreland County in September 1777 for three years, was in Middlebrook and at the Battle of Monmouth. He enlisted under Captain Lawrence Butler for the duration of the war. He served in the 15th Regiment and was taken prisoner at Charleston. He was living on 7 acres of land in a small house with two children, aged 12 and 10. General Alexander Parker testified for him that he served for at least 9 months, was taken prisoner with him in Charleston and acted as a bowman or cook for Captain Beeles [NARA, S38197, M804, Roll 1690, frame 353 of 891; http://fold3.com/image/24220794; McGuye, Bennet: Revolutionary War Bounty Warrants, Digital Collection, LVA]. He made an affidavit for the rejected Revolutionary War claim of Jesse McKey (writing too faint to read) [McKey, Jessey: Revolutionary War Rejected Claims, Digital Collection, LVA].

George McCoy married Elizabeth **Nickens**, 24-year-old daughter of Nathaniel **Nickings**, 10 March 1788 Orange County, Virginia bond. He was a "B.M." (blackman) taxable in Augusta County in 1796 and 1797 [PPTL 1796-1810, frames 32, 69], a "free Negro" or "Melatto" taxable in Rockingham County in 1798, 1800, 1804, 1809 and a laborer taxable on 2 horses at Sam McWilliam's in 1810 [PPTL 1795-1813, frames 143, 199, 294, 460, 634]. He was head of a Rockingham County household of 3 "other free" in 1810 [VA:130b] and 2 "free colored" persons over the age of 45 in 1820. He appeared in Rockingham County court on 26 February 1821 and signed an affidavit to give his attorney in Richmond power to petition the Virginia Legislature in his name for compensation on 24 February 1821 for wounds he received at Buford's defeat in the Revolutionary War. He received a warrant for $30 [Virginia Revolutionary War State Pensions, McCoy, George, 1822, Digital Collection, LVA].

James McKoy was listed as a "free Molatto" farmer living on his own land in Westmoreland County in 1801 ["A List of Free Mulattoes & Negroes in Westmoreland County" *Virginia Genealogist*, 31:40] and head of a Westmoreland County household of 4 "other free" in 1810 [VA:778]. He appeared in Westmoreland County, Virginia court to apply for a pension for his services in the Revolution, stating that he was born in Saint Mary's County, Maryland, and moved with his father to Westmoreland County when he was about 8 years of age. He entered the war in the year 1778 and was placed on guard at a place called Sandy Point on the Potomac River under the command of Lord Dunmore and then to a place called Hamilton Hall under command of Captain Rochester, then to several other locations for a month or two at a time. In 1781 he was drafted to go down to Yorktown for a total enlistment time of about 15 months [NARA, S.5750, M804, Roll 1692, frame 809 of 914; http://fold3.com/image/24327054]. He was listed in the 1840 census for Westmoreland County as an 80-year-old pensioner, a "free colored" man living by himself, called James C. McKoy, Sr.

Thomas Mahorney, a "free man of colour," enlisted in the Revolution in January 1777 in Westmoreland County. He appeared in Westmoreland County court to apply for a pension, declaring that he served in the 2nd Virginia Regiment under Captain Robert Lovell, was in the

Battle of Monmouth, that he was discharged in New Jersey, and that his family consisted of his wife Mima and son Jack, both slaves [NARA, S.38166, M804, Roll 1615, frame 0568 (frame 580 of 764 on ancestry.com); http://fold3.com/image/23394967].

Daniel Malbone, a "young Molloto lad...lawfully begotten," was set free by the 27 January 1766 Princess Anne County will of Reodolphus Malbone, Sr., "if in case the Law allow it" [Deed Book 9, part 2, 580-1]. He was apparently identical to Daniel Malbone, a "free mulatto," who owed John Gardner of Princess Anne County £2.15 on 25 November 1773 [Princess Anne County Loose Papers, Box A 17, LVA, cited by Creecy, *Virginia Antiquary*, 76]. He was taxable in the Lower Precinct of the Eastern Shore of Princess Anne County in 1782 and 1783 with (his wife?) a slave over the age of 16 named Phebe and infants under the age of 16 named Daniel and Love and a "Free Negro" taxable in the Lower Western Shore Precinct (the same precinct as the **Anderson** family) in 1784, also taxable that year on slave John Francis who was under the age of 16. On 5 November 1787 William Reynolds received his final pay of £30 for serving in the infantry during the Revolution [NARA, M881, Roll 1093, frame 1848-9 of 2068 (Daniel Malburne)]. In 1787 and 1790 he was taxable on only horses and cattle; in 1792 on a slave over the age of 16 and 3 horses; in 1793 on only 2 horses; in 1807 he was a "F.B." taxable on a horse; in 1809 he was taxable on a slave over 16 and a slave aged 12 to 16. He paid $15 for a retailer's license in 1809 [PPTL, 1782-9, frames 551, 576, 605, 691, 693; 1790-1822, frames 19, 44, 67, 375, 399].

Wilmore Male enlisted in the Continental Line for three years in January 1777 and was in the Battles of Monmouth and Stony Point [Revolutionary War Bounty Warrants, Mail, Welmore, Digital Collections, LVA]. He enlisted from the part of Berkeley County, Virginia, that became Jefferson County, moved to Hampshire County in 1790 and applied for a pension from Hampshire County on 27 May 1818 at the age of 60 [NARA, S.38171, M804, Roll 1615, frame 744 of 764; http://fold3.com/image/23395021]. He was head of a Hampshire County household of 8 "other free" in 1810 [VA:826].

William Martin enlisted in the Revolution for the length of the war while resident in Pittsylvania County in March 1778 and was sized on 15 April 1781: *age 19, 5'5-1/2" high, yellow complexion, born in Cumberland County, former service: 11th Va Regt 1 year* [The Chesterfield Supplement or Size Roll of Troops at Chesterfield Court House, LVA accession no. 23816, by http://revwarapps.org/b81.pdf (p.21)].

Littlebury McKinny enlisted in the Revolution for the length of the war in Sussex County, Virginia, about 27 July 1782 when he was sized: *age 16, 5'1-1/2" high, yellow complexion, born in Sussex County* [The Chesterfield Supplement or Size Roll of Troops at Chesterfield Court House, LVA accession no. 23816, by http://revwarapps.org/b81.pdf (p.107)].

James Mealy registered as a free Negro in Goochland County on 18 December 1822: *about fifty eight years old, about five feet ten inches high...yellowish complexion and was free born* [Register of Free Negroes, p.136]. He was drafted from Goochland County in May 1781, was attached to the company of Captain Tolls and was at the Siege of Yorktown [NARA, S.9408, M804, Roll 1704, frame 641 of 740; http://fold3.com/image/27177003].

Isaac Meekins, born 19 April 1754,"Son of Mary Mekins, a free negroe woman" [NSCDA, Parish Register of St. Peter's, 97], received pay for military service in the Revolution [Eckenrode, *Virginia Soldiers in the American Revolution*, I:206, citing Auditors Account XVIII:612 at LVA]. He was taxable in New Kent County from 1783 to 1803 and from 1807 to 1814: taxable in 1785 on a slave named Sally who was called his wife Sarah in 1786; taxable on 2 free male tithables in 1807 and 1809, 3 in 1810 and 1811, 2 in 1812, a "fN" listed with his unnamed wife in 1813 [PPTL 1782-1800, frames 21, 67, 89, 117, 131, 149; 1791-1828, frames 384, 396, 409, 420, 452, 444, 455, 466, 477, 491, 503].

Elisha Milton left a Southampton County will, proved 21 August 1797, naming his daughter Ann **Bowser** and Randolph Milton [WB 5:2]. Randolph was head of a Southampton County household of 8 "other free" in 1810 [VA:71]. He may have been the Elisha Milton (written Millon) who served in the Revolution. On 23 March 1785 John White received his final pay of £25 for serving in the cavalry during the Revolution [NARA, M881, Roll 1094, frame 223 of 1764; http://fold3.com/image/286702815].

James Milton enlisted in the Revolution and died of smallpox at Bunker Hill [Brown, *Genealogical Abstracts, Revolutionary War Veterans Script Act, 1852*, 139; Gwathmey, *Historical Register of Virginians in the Revolution*]. He received a discharge for three years service on 18 August 1780 from Captain Wm Spiller by order of Lieutenant Colonel Edmunds. He was the brother of Ann Melton who married Thomas **Bowser** [Revolutionary War Bounty Warrants, Melton, James, Digital Collections, LVA]. He received £79.17.10 for service in the infantry, drawn by Colonel Mason on 14 October 1783 [Creel, *Selected Virginia Revolutionary War Records*, I:91].

John Milton received a discharge for three years service as a soldier in Colonel Marshall's Regiment of State Artillery on 23 August 1780 from Captain Wm Spiller by order of Lieutenant Colonel Edmunds [Revolutionary War Bounty Warrants, Melton, John, Digital Collections, LVA]. He received £79.17.10 for service in the infantry, drawn by Colonel Mason on 14 October 1783 [Creel, *Selected Virginia Revolutionary War Records*, I:91]. He was head of a Hertford County, North Carolina household of 3 "other free" in 1800.

Ambrose Month received a pension for his services in the Revolution based on his application from Knox County, Tennessee, on 7 January 1834, at the age of 69. He stated that he was born at the Hawfields in Spotsylvania County. He was drafted from spotsylvania county, was wounded at the Battle o f Guilford Courthouse and was at Yorktown for the surrender of Cornwallis. He stated that he was of mixed blood, part Shawnee and part Negro and was born free. His widow and his former slave Daphney, "a free Negro of full blood," received a widow's pension [NARA, W.7477, M804, Roll 1750, frame 15 of 857; http://fold3.com/image/24864672].

Adderson Moore enlisted in the Revolution from Chesterfield County in August 1780: *age 16, 4'9" high, a planter, born in Chesterfield County, Yellow Mulatto complexion* [Register & description of Noncommissioned officers & Privates, LVA accession no. 24296, by http://revwarapps.org/b69.pdf (p.28)].

Charles Morris enlisted in the Revolution on 12 September 1780 for the duration of the war from Charles City County: *age 17, 5'2" high, planter, born Charles City County*. He was sized again in April 1781 when his height was listed as 5'4" and his complexion black [Register & description of Noncommissioned officers & Privates, LVA accession no. 24296, by http://revwarapps.org/b69.pdf (pp.21, 36)]. He was a "Mulatto" taxable in Chesterfield County from 1798 to 1810 [PPTL, 1786-1811, frames 358, 543, 620, 662, 717, 753, 799] and head of a Chesterfield County household of 2 "other free" in 1810 [VA:70/1062]. He obtained a certificate of freedom in Chesterfield County on 8 August 1814: *about forty eight years old, brown complexioned, born free* [Register of Free Negroes 1804-53, no. 224].

Francis Morris enlisted in the Revolution from Petersburg on 11 September 1780: *age 28, 5'5-1/4" high, S. carpenter, born in Henrico County, yellow complexion* [Register & description of Noncommissioned officers & Privates, LVA accession no. 24296, by http://revwarapps.org/b69.pdf (p.12)].

Jack Morris, an orphan, no race indicated, was bound apprentice in Chesterfield County on 7 September 1750 [Orders 1749-54, 77]. He was a soldier in the Continental Line on 7 February 1778 when the Chesterfield County court ordered that his wife Mary receive £6 public money [Orders 1774-8, 158]. His wife may have been the Mary Morris who registered in Petersburg on 19 August 1794: *a brown Mulatto woman, five feet one inches high, forty eight years old, born free & raised in Chesterfield County* [Register of Free Negroes 1794-1819, no. 57].

Nathaniel Morris served in the 5th Virginia Regiment (raised in Richmond) from 1777 until the end of the war according to an affidavit from former Captain John Henry Fitzgerald on 18 August 1796 that Nathaniel Morris, a "black man," served with him [Revolutionary War Bounty Warrants, Morris, Nathaniel, Digital Collections, LVA]. Perhaps his wife was Jane Morris who received £6 by order of the Henrico County court for the support of herself and children while her husband was serving in the Revolution [Creel, *Selected Virginia Revolutionary War Records*, III:130 (abstract of Auditors' Account, Volume II:228, LVA].

Anthony Morrison was listed as a seaman aboard the ship *Gloucester* on 4 November 1777 [U.S. Government Printing Office, Naval Documents of the American Revolution, 11:160, http://ibiblio.org/anrs//docs/E/E3/ndar_v11p05.pdf], and on 5 July 1779. He was listed among the seamen entitled to bounty land for three years service. Sarah Morrison received bounty land warrant no. 8048 for his service [Brumbaugh, *Revolutionary War Records*, 14, 70, 358]. He was head of a Lancaster County household of 3 "free colored" in 1820. Sarah appeared in Lancaster County court on 7 April 1834 to state that she was the only heir of Anthony Morrison, deceased, who was a seaman in the State Navy [Revolutionary War Bounty Warrants; Morrison, Anthony, Digital Collections, LVA].

Ezekiel Moses enlisted in the Revolution from Northampton County, Virginia, on 12 March 1781 for 18 months: *age 18, 5'2" high, yellow complexion, T smith, born in Northampton County.* On 23 July 1782 he was listed as a silversmith in the size roll as having been sentenced to serve 3 years and 3 months by a court martial [The Chesterfield Supplement or Size Roll of Troops at Chesterfield Court House, LVA accession no. 23816, http://revwarapps.org/b81.pdf (pp.21, 107)]. He was listed as a fifer when he was paid $22 in 1783 and as soldier in the infantry on 5 April 1783 when General Morgan received his pay of £32 [NARA, M881, Roll 1094, frames 568, 571 of 1764; http://fold3.com/image/287703068; http://fold3.com/image/23279242]. He was a "Mulatto" delinquent taxable in Northampton County in 1786 [*Virginia Genealogist* 20:269] and taxable in Northampton County from 1792 to 1796, called a "free Nego" from 1797 to 1800 [PPTL, 1782-1823, frames 140, 182,1 231, 251, 289]. He was taxable in York County from 1803 to 1814 [PPTL, 1782-1841, frames 288, 297, 307, 341, 392, 409].

Henry Moss was ordered bound out as an apprentice by the churchwardens of Raleigh Parish in Amelia County on 24 March 1757 [Orders 1754-8, n.p.]. He enlisted in the Revolution on 28 August 1777 and was in the muster of the 4th Virginia Regiment from March 1778 to December 1779 [NARA, M246, roll 99, frames 250, 430, 544, 546, 548; roll 100, frames 665, 830; http://fold3.com/image/10081049]. He received a certificate from Major Charles Pelham that he served from 18 August 1777 to July 1781 [Revolutionary War Bounty Warrants, Moss, Henry, Digital Collections, LVA]. He was taxable in Powhatan County from 1789 to 1791 and from 1803 to 1817: called a "Mullo" in 1790, called a "F.B." from 1813 to 1815 [PPTL, 1787-1825, frames 36, 48, 63, 262, 280, 321, 366, 443, 463, 488, 538]. He was about 42 years old on 1 July 1796 when he was described by the 1 July 1796 issue of a Virginia newspaper as: *born a free Negro in one of the lower Counties of this state...his father was a black and his mother a mulatto, but he has turned white; he was in the Virginia Line in the last war* [Headley, *18th Century Newspapers*].

Isaac Needham, enlisted in the Revolution on 15 September 1780: *age 17, 4'9-1/2 " high, a farmer, born in Annapolis, Maryland, residence: Westmoreland County, yellow complexion* [Register & description of Noncommissioned officers & Privates, LVA accession no. 24296, by http://revwarapps.org/b69.pdf (p.13)]. Captain Selden received his final pay of £5 on 21 October 1782 and £11 on 25 February 1783 [NARA, M881, Roll 1094, frames 769, 770 of 1764].

Benjamin Newell enlisted as a substitute while resident in Culpeper County on 20 September 1780 and was sized on 18 March 1781: *age 28, 5'7-1/4 " high, yellow complexion, born in Gloucester County* [The Chesterfield Supplement or Size Roll of Troops at Chesterfield Court House, LVA accession no. 23816, by http://revwarapps.org/b81.pdf (p.23)].

Edward Jones Nicken enlisted as a seaman in the Virginia State Navy on 1 August 1777 for three years, served aboard the *Tartar*, and received bounty land [Revolutionary War Bounty Warrants, Nicking, Edward, Digital Collections, LVA]. He was an able seaman who assigned his final pay of £84 to James Allen on 5 August 1786 [NARA, M880, Roll 4; http://fold3.com/image/286914548]. He was serving aboard the *Gloucester* on 5 July 1779 and drew bounty land warrant no. 2427 [Brumbaugh, *Revolutionary War Records*, 14, 217]. He was taxable in the lower end of New Kent County on the south side of Warrenny Road from 1782 to 1815: taxable on a slave named Roger in 1785; taxable on a slave in 1792; removed to Richmond in 1794; taxable in New Kent County on a slave in 1796 and 1804; called a "FN" in 1806; taxable on 2 free males in 1809; listed as a "Person of Colour" with his unnamed wife in 1813 [PPTL 1782-1800, frames 36, 100, 190, 213; 1791-1828, frames 372, 409, 432, 455, 476, 491, 503, 516, 574].

Hezekiah Nickens was serving as a seaman aboard the *Gloucester* in the Revolution on 5 July 1779 and served for three years. James Nickins and others drew his warrant no. 8396 [Brumbaugh, *Revolutionary War Records*, 14, 70, 361]. He, Nathaniel and Richard Nickins were issued spirits aboard the *Tempest* on 9 December 1779 [NARA, W.7284, M804, Roll 988, frame 976 of 983; http://fold3.com/image/17885364]. His final pay of £57 was drawn by Captain Sanders on 31 January 1787 [NARA, M853, http://fold3.com/image/286702512].

James Nickens enlisted in the Revolution for the length of the war while resident in Lancaster County and was sized in April 1781: *age 18, 5'1-1/2" high, yellow complexion, a planter, born in Princess Anne County, engaged Mar 80 in Essex County, former service: served for 18 months in Buford's detacht* [The Chesterfield Supplement or Size Roll of Troops at Chesterfield Court House, LVA accession no. 23816, by http://revwarapps.org/b81.pdf (p.23)]. He was serving in the Revolution in July 1781 when forage was delivered to him at Prince Edward County courthouse on several days in July 1781 for the wagon and riding-horses used in the Revolution [NARA, M853, Roll 30, http://fold3.com/image/286751367]. He was taxable in Prince William County from 1796 to 1798 and from 1806 to 1813: called a "Dark" man in 1805 and 1806, a "yellow" man in 1809 and 1813 [PPTL, 1782-1810, frames 315, 341, 368, 598, 645, 709], taxable in Essex County in 1795 [PPTL, 1782-1819, frame 266] and head of an Essex County household of 3 "other free" in 1810. He was about 59 years old and living in Falmouth on 27 April 1818 when he made a declaration in court to apply for a pension. He stated that he served as a seaman for three years on board the ships *Tempest, Revenge & Hero* which were then commanded by Captains Muter and Westcott, but he had forgotten the name of the captain of the *Tempest*. He then enlisted in the land service at Lancaster courthouse, was marched by Nicholas Currell to he headquarters of Baron Steuben at Cumberland courthouse, remained there some time and was then placed under Captain Drury Ragsdale and Fleming Gains of Colonel Harrison's Regiment of Artillery which was marched to join the Southern Army under General Green in South Carolina where he was in the Battle of Eutaw Springs. After the war he returned to Virginia and had resided there ever since. He was a 62-year-old "Free Man of Color," said to be living alone in Stafford County on 16 August 1820 when he repeated much of what he had stated in his 27 April 1818 declaration, did not mention any sea service, but added that he was stationed in the rear at the Battle of Eutaw Springs, in charge of baggage belonging to Fleming Gains and John T. Brooke, officers in Harrison's Regiment. His pension for service in the artillery commenced on 27 April 1818. On 27 April 1818 Charles West testified before Judge William Dade of Stafford County that James Nickens enlisted on board the sally *Norfolk Revenge* and served aboard that vessel with him for two years and three months, and on 13 October 1818 John T. Brooke certified that James Nickens was a soldier in the First Regiment of Artillery under Colonel Charles Harrison [NARA, S.38262, M804, Roll 1820, frame 630 of 1213; http://fold3.com/image/25389006]. James Nickers private, was issued bounty land warrant no. 7391 for 200 acres which he assigned to John Metcalf. And James Nickins received warrant no. 1716 for service in the State Navy [Brumbaugh, *Revolutionary War Records*, 8, 312, 360]. He was head of a Stafford County household of 6 "free colored" in 1820, 1 "free colored" over the age of 55 with a white woman aged 30-40 in 1830, and a pensioner living in Stafford County, age 85, head of a household of 1 "free colored" man and woman 55-100 years of age in the 1840 census. He was about 72 on 7 November 1831 when he appointed an agent in Washington to apply for bounty land for his service under Corporal Lieutenant Gains at the Battle of Eutaw Springs. His deposition said nothing about service as a seaman, but it included the discharge by (Captain) James Markham of James Nickens, a seaman belonging to the ship *Dragon*, on 24(?)th June 1780 for three years in the service and his assignment of his right to the bounty land to Mr. Joseph Landers on 4 July 1783 [Revolutionary War Bounty Warrants, Nicking, James, Digital Collections, LVA].

James Nicken sued Edward Ingram for freedom from his indenture on 11 September 1764 in Northumberland County court. He was called James Nicken alias Bateman when the court ordered him to serve Ingram for four more years [Orders 1762-66, 411, 435]. James Bateman and James, Edward and Hezekiah Nicken were serving aboard the Gloucester on 4 November 1777 when the Keeper of the Public Store was ordered to deliver them articles of clothing, "on their paying for the same" [U.S. Government Printing Office, Naval Documents of the American Revolution, 11:160, http://ibiblio.org/anrs//docs/E/E3/ndar_v11p05.pdf]. They were listed on board the *Gloucester* shortly before it was dismantled on 5 July 1779 [Brumbaugh, *Revolutionary War Records*, 14]. And James Wicking or Nicking was listed as one of the seamen aboard the galley *Dragon* who were wanting provisions for 30 days on 2 September 1779. He was called a seaman belonging to the ship *Dragon* when he received his discharge for three years service as a seaman in the Revolution on 24 June 1780. He assigned (signing) his right to his land warrant to Joseph Landers on 4 July 1783 [Revolutionary War Bounty Warrants, Nickens, James, Digital Collections, LVA]. On 10 April 1835, about the same time as the Fauquier County branch of the family applied for bounty land for the service of James Nickens, Jemima **Bass** of Norfolk County applied in Norfolk County court which certified that she was the widow of Willis **Bass** and only heir of her father James Nickens and his brother Nathaniel Nickens [Court Minutes 24:139]. She was 66 years old when she deposed that she was a resident of the county of Norfolk, that during the Revolution James Nickens and his brother Nathaniel Nickens served on board a vessel named the *Caswell* and were regularly discharged after the war. Nathaniel Nickens died leaving no wife or child; the nearest relative he left was James Nickens who was also a seaman, and that James Nickens died leaving her as his only child and heir [Revolutionary War Rejected Claims, Nickens, James, Digital Collections, LVA; NARA, M804, Roll 1820, frame 630 of 1213].

James Nicken was taxable in Lancaster County in John Nicken's household in 1775 and 1776 [Tithables 1745-95, 14, 18]. He may have been the James Nickens who was a seaman belonging to the ship *Dragon* and received a discharge for three years service in the Revolution on 24 June 1780. He assigned (signing) his right to his land warrant to Joseph Landers on 4 July 1783 [Revolutionary War Rejected Claims, Nickens, James, Digital Collections, LVA; NARA, S.38262, M804. Roll 630 of 1213; http://fold3.com/image/25389006] He was head of a Lancaster County household of 9 "Blacks" in 1783 [VA:55]. He obtained a certificate of freedom for himself, his wife and children in Lancaster County on 4 December 1786 which he recorded in Fauquier County on 29 April 1806. He was a "F. Negroe" head of a Fauquier County household of 8 "other free" in 1810, called James Nickens, Sr. [VA:368] and 11 "free colored" in 1820. On 3 September 1834 James Nickens, Elizabeth Nickens, and Judy **Watkins** appeared in Frederick County court to apply for the survivors' pension of their father James Nickens and their brother Hezekiah Nickens, a seaman in the Virginia State Navy who died during the war. The application of his heirs for bounty land was denied based on the fact that a James Nickens of Stafford County had already received bounty land and was receiving a pension [Revolutionary War Rejected Claims, Nickens, James, Digital Collections, LVA; NARA, S.38262, M804, Roll 1820, frame 630 of 1213].

John Nickens was a "free mulatto" head of a Northumberland County household of 10 "other free" in 1810 [VA:990]. He served in the Virginia Navy during the Revolution [Stewart, *The history of Virginia's navy of the revolution*, 231, citing Auditors' Account book XXIX:78].

Nathaniel Nickens was listed aboard the *Tempest* on a 7 December 1779 return of spirits provided to the ship [Brumbaugh, *Revolutionary War Records*, 32, 70, 371]. He served as an ordinary seaman aboard the ship *Tempest* under Captain Celey Saunders for three years ending in July 1780 according to an affidavit he received from Captain William Saunders on 25 July 1786. He assigned his right to all his claims and his bounty land to William Bigger in Lancaster County court on 30 July 1786 [Revolutionary War Bounty Warrants, Nicken, Nathl, Digital Collections, LVA]. He was also listed as a seaman aboard the *Dragon* (listed with James and William Neakins) according to an affidavit by a fellow seaman aboard the ship, John **Davis**, who testified for James Jennings on 7 February 1834 and named five of the officers and 52 members of the crew [Revolutionary War Bounty Warrants, Jennings, James (p.8), Digital Collection, LVA]. He was head of a Lancaster County household of 3 "Blacks" in 1783 [VA:55].

Richard Nickens was listed as a seaman aboard the ship *Tempest* during the Revolution on 7 December 1779 [Brumbaugh, *Revolutionary War Records*, 32]. He registered in Lancaster County on 17 October 1803: *Age 52, Color mulatto...born free* [Burkett, *Lancaster County Register of Free Negroes*, 1]. He made a deposition (signing) in Lancaster County court on 14 December 1819 for a pension for his services, stating that he enlisted in the Revolution for three years, went to Hampton with Captain Pollard and was placed on board the galley *Hero* commanded by Captain Barrett where he served 18 months, then on board the ship *Tempest* under command of Captain Celey Saunders where he also served 18 months and was honorably discharged at Chickahominy Ship Yard by Lieutenant Steel when the ship was laid up. His final pay as a seaman of £69 was drawn by Colonel Heath on 2 August 1783 [NARA, M880, Roll 4; http://fold3.com/image/286914564]. He received Virginia State pension no. 307 [Legislative Petitions, Nicken, Richard, Digital Collection, LVA]. He appeared in Lancaster County court to apply for a pension on 17 December 1832 [NARA, S.5830, M805, reel 0615, frame 0187; http://fold3.com/image/25388922]. He received bounty land warrant no. 1477 [Brumbaugh, *Revolutionary War Records*, 360].

Robert Nickens enlisted in the Revolution while resident in Lancaster County as a substitute for 18 months in 1780 and was sized in April 1781: *age 18, 5'8" high, black complexion, a farmer, born in Frederick County* [The Chesterfield Supplement or Size Roll of Troops at Chesterfield Court House, LVA accession no. 23816, by http://revwarapps.org/b81.pdf (p.23)]. On 5 April 1785 Doctor Ball received his final pay of £14 for serving in the infantry [NARA, M881, Roll 1094, frames 845, 846 of 1764; http://fold3.com/image/23282733]. He was granted a certificate of his free birth by the Lancaster County court on 16 February 1796 [Orders 1792-9, 256]. He was in a list of soldiers whose name appeared on the army register but had not received bounty land by 7 January 1835 [Brumbaugh, *Revolutionary War Records*, 259].

William Nickens was bound to Richard Hutchings in Lancaster County on 18 February 1773 [Orders 1770-78, 300]. He was called William Neakins, when he, Nathaniel and James Neakins were seamen aboard the *Dragon* according to an affidavit by a fellow seaman, John **Davis**, who testified for the bounty land claim of James Jennings on 7 February 1834 and named five of the officers and 52 members of the crew who served faithfully for three years and were discharged at the Chickahominy Ship Yard [Revolutionary War Bounty Warrants, Jennings, James (p.9), Digital Collection, LVA]. He received bounty land warrant no. 337 for service in the Virginia State Line [Brumbaugh, *Revolutionary War Records*, 360]. He served in the artillery as a drummer. T. Graves received his final pay of £83 on 24 May 1783 [Revolutionary War Bounty Warrants, Nickins, William, Digital Collections, LVA; NARA, M881, Roll 1094, frames 843, 8444 of 1764; http://fold3.com/image/23282720].

William Oats was a drummer listed in the payroll of Captain Nathaniel Morris's Company of the 9th Virginia Regiment commanded by Colonel George Matthews in May and October 1777 [NARA, M246, Roll 107, frame 768 of 808; http://fold3.com/image/9682293 and 23225254]. He was a "free mulatto" head of a Northumberland County household of 4 "other free" in 1810 [VA:991].

Robert Owls (Howell?), a "free man of colour," was about 80 years old (according to information he obtained from his parents) on 27 May 1818 when he appeared in Opelousas, St. Landry Parish, Louisiana, on 27 May 1818 to apply for a pension for his service in the Revolution. He stated that he was drafted to serve in the militia of Princess Anne County, Virginia, and then enlisted in Essex County in Captain Andrew Wallace's Regiment commanded by Colonel Abram Buford. He was at Buford's Defeat and the Battle of Eutaw Springs. He presented an affidavit from A. Buford in Frankfurt, Kentucky, on 7 November 1802 that Robert Owls, a yellow man, then a resident of Jefferson County, Kentucky, had served in his regiment in 1779 and 1780 and was said to be free born [NARA, S.36713, M804, roll 1856, frame 1011 of 1331; http://fold3.com/image/25873976]. He may have been identical to Robert Old, a fifteen-year-old "free Malatto" bound by the churchwardens of Princess Anne county to Edward Cannon to serve until the age of twenty one in 1770 [Orders 1770-3, 15].

Benjamin Payne enlisted in the Revolution as a substitute from Buckingham County in 1782 and was sized about the same time: *age 20, 5'6" high, yellow complexion, born in Buckingham County* [The Chesterfield Supplement or Size Roll of Troops at Chesterfield Court House, LVA accession no. 23816, by http://revwarapps.org/b81.pdf (p.61)].

Charles Payne, black complexion, was a planter born in Westmoreland County, who entered the Revolution in King George County as a substitute for three years on 4 April 1781 [The Chesterfield Supplement or Size Roll of Troops at Chesterfield Court House, LVA accession no. 23816, by http://revwarapps.org/b81.pdf (p. 25)]. He registered in King George County on 10 November 1801: *a dark mulatto man aged about thirty five years, about five feet six inches high, rather spare...born in this County of free parents* [Register of Free Persons, no.36].

Evan Payne was taxable in Fauquier County from 1802 to 1806: a "free Negro" in 1804, a "Mulatto" in 1805; a "free negro" in 1806 [PPTL, 1797-1807, frames 413, 632, 659, 768, 791]. He was a "mulatto" listed among 14 deserters from Lieutenant John Tankersley's troops. Tankersley offered a reward for their delivery to King George courthouse in the 3 October 1777 issue of the *Virginia Gazette* [Purdie edition, p. 3, col. 1].

Joshua Payne was a black complexioned soldier, 5'4" high, a farmer born in Westmoreland County who entered the war as a substitute in King George County on 4 April 1781 to serve for two years in the Navy [The Chesterfield Supplement or Size Roll of Troops at Chesterfield Court House, LVA accession no. 23816, by http://revwarapps.org/b81.pdf (p. 25)]. He was listed in the muster of the 5th Virginia Regiment in September 1782 [NARA, M246, Roll 113, frame 664 of 752; http://fold3.com/image/9648376]. John White received his final pay of £17 on 31 July 1783 [NARA, M881, Roll 1089, frame 1201 of 1808; http://fold3.com/image/286702828]. He was head of a Rockingham County, North Carolina household of 5 "other free" in 1800 [NC:491].

Charles Pierpoint, born about 1763, was a five-year-old "Mullatto" boy living in Loudoun County on 11 August 1768 when the court ordered the churchwardens of Cameron Parish to bind him to William Suthard until the age of twenty-one [Orders 1767-70, 110]. He (called Charles Pearpoint) enlisted as a substitute for the War in Loudoun County on 19 March 1781 and was sized on 28 May 1781: *age 18, 5 feet 8 inches, blk Hair, Hazl Eyes, yellow Complexion, Indian Features, a planter, residence Loudoun County, born Frederick County, Maryland* [The Chesterfield Supplement or Size Roll of Troops at Chesterfield Court House, LVA accession no. 23816, by http://revwarapps.org/b81.pdf (p.61)].

Andrew Pebbles appeared in King and Queen County to apply for a pension, stating that he was a Mulatto who served under Captain George Lee Turberville of Westmoreland County who was a recruiting officer. He joined the camp at Valley Forge under Captain Lewis Booker of the 15th Virginia Regiment for two years. He was a miller with a wife who was a slave [NARA, S.38297, M804, Roll 1899, frame 395 of 1727; http://fold3.com/image/25981200].

Joshua Perkins was a member of Captain Windsor Brown's Virginia Company of Troops in Williamsburg when Brown advertised in the 6 June 1777 issue of the *Virginia Gazette* that he had deserted. Brown described him as: *a mulatto, about 5 feet 6 or 7 inches high, 24 or 25 years old, and is a straight made fellow; had on a short striped jacket, a felt hat bound round with French lace* [Purdie edition, p. 3, col. 3]. He was in Captain Thomas Edmunds's muster of the 15th Virginia Regiment in Morristown on 1 July 1777, listed as being sick in Virginia, but he was in the muster at White Plains on 1 September 1778 [NARA, M246, roll 113, frame 189 of 752; roll 110, frame 484 of 768; http://fold3.com/image/9639818; http://fold3.com/image/9953749].

Joshua Perkins was a seaman in the Revolution. Scarborough Bloxam, a midshipman aboard the *Accomac*, testified that Joshua enlisted in the war, served on board the vessel during the Revolution and was discharged. [Revolutionary War Bounty Warrants; Bayly, Robert, Digital Collections, LVA]. He received 100 acres bounty land warrant no. 93 and Sally Perkins received no. 8241 for his services [Brumbaugh, *Revolutionary War Records*, 193, 363]. His only heir Sally Perkins applied for his pension in Accomack County on 29 March 1834 [Orders 1832-36, 21, 313].

Nimrod Perkins was bound as an apprentice shoemaker to William Sacker James in Accomack County on 28 August 1765 [Orders 1764-65, 489]. He was taxable in Accomack County in 1785 and 1790 [PPTL, 1782-1814, frames 154, 347], a "Mulatto" taxable in Northampton County in 1787 and 1788 [PPTL, 1782-1823, frames 74, 81], and head of an Accomack County household of 2 "other free" and a white woman in 1800 [*Virginia Genealogist* 2:13]. Zadock Bayley testified in Accomack County court on 1 July 1830 that he frequently went on board the Navy vessel *Accomac* and saw Nimrod Perkins ("b.m") serving as a drummer [Revolutionary War Bounty Warrants; Perkins, Nimrod, Digital Collections, LVA]. He enlisted as a drummer on board the galley *Diligence* from 1777 until 1781, and he had received a Virginia military land warrant for 100 acres [Orders 1828-32, 537; NARA, S.5904, M804, roll 1912, frame 356 of 988; http://fold3.com/image/27174273].

Anthony Peters served three years as a soldier in the Revolution and received a bounty land warrant based on the affidavit of Lieutenant Wyatt Coleman of Dabney's Legion on 2 March 1786. He assigned his rights to the warrant to Jones Allen in the presence of William Eaton, a magistrate of York County [Revolutionary War Bounty Warrants, Peters, Anthony, Digital Collections, LVA]. Jones Allen collected his pay of £101.3.7 on 6 May 1786 [Creel, *Selected Virginia Revolutionary War Records*, I:102]. He was taxable in Simon **Gillett**'s York County household in 1784 and 1786 and head of a household of 2 "free Negroes & mulattoes over 16" in 1813 [PPTL, 1782-1841, frames 91, 107, 130, 394, 410]. He was head of a York County household of an "other free" man, 7 slaves and a white woman aged 26-45 in 1810 [VA:304].

James Peters was a seaman on the payroll of the galley *Henry* in the Revolution in an undated list before 8 April 1778. He received warrant no. 4368 [Brumbaugh, *Revolutionary War Records*, 15, 371]. Lieutenant Joshua Singleton certified on 16 August 1787 that he had served aboard the galley *Henry* from January 1777 until January 1780. He assigned his rights to the land to William Reynolds on 21 June 1787 with Philip Brownley as witness [Revolutionary War Bounty Warrants, Peters, James, Digital Collections, LVA]. He was presented by the grand jury of Middlesex County on 24 November 1783 for failing to list himself as a tithable [Orders 1783-4, 16; 1784-6, 7]. He did not list himself there, and was probably the James Peters who was a "Mulatto" taxable in Culpeper County in 1789 (2 tithes), 1790 and 1796 (a tithe and 2 slaves) [PPTL 1782-1802, frames 305-6, 335, 608].

Jesse Peters registered as a "free Negro" in Surry County on 9 January 1796: *son of Lucy Peters a free mulattoe, a resident of the county, a dark mulattoe man aged about 32 years, pretty well made short hair, 5'11" high* [Back of Guardian Accounts Book 1783-1804, no. 17]. Jesse was called a "Free man of Color" in his application for a pension in which he stated that he enlisted with Captain John Lucas in Surry County and fought in the Battles of Guilford Courthouse, Camden and Eutaw Springs [NARA, R.8146, M804;

http://fold3.com/image/25933183].

Drury Pettiford was head of a Stokes County, North Carolina household of 11 "other free" in 1810 [NC:607]. He was listed in the payroll of Captain Dudley's 2nd Virginia State Regiment commanded by Colonel Gregory Smith from July to December 1778 (with Elias Pettiford) [NARA, M246, Roll 96, frame 545 of 736; http://fold3.com/image/10081826, 10081833, 10081847, 10081873] and served for 3 years. He was in the Battles of Monmouth and Stony Point [NARA, S.41954, M804, roll 1920, frame 59 of 1326; http://fold3.com/image/27177513].

Edward Pettiford, son of Lewis Pettiford, was ordered bound apprentice in Mecklenburg County, Virginia, on 9 March 1778 [Orders 1773-9, 395]. He enlisted in the 5th Virginia Regiment in 1778 and served for the length of the war according to the affidavit of Captain Mayo Carrington [Revolutionary War Bounty Warrants, Pediford, Edward, Digital Collections, LVA]. Lewis Pettiford was a "Black" taxable in the 1758 Granville County, North Carolina tax list of Nathaniel Harris, taxable in 1764 with his wife Catherine and daughter in Samuel Benton's list [CR 044.701.19] and a "Mulo" taxable in the southern district of Halifax County, Virginia, in 1794 [PPTL, 1782-1799, frame 544].

Elias Pettiford was listed in the payroll of Captain Dudley's 2nd Virginia State Regiment commanded by Colonel Gregory Smith from August to December 1778 [NARA, M246, Roll 96, frame 545 of 736; http://fold3.com/image/10081826, 10081833, 10081847, 10081873]. He enlisted in Donoho's Company of the 10th North Carolina Regiment on 14 June 1781 and left the service in 1782 [Clark, *The State Records of North Carolina*, XVI:1138]. On 4 October 1832 William Whicker appeared in Fayette County, Ohio court and testified that "he got one Elias Pettiford, a Colored, to take his place in the Revolution [NARA, S.17194, M804, Roll 2547, frame 555 of 822; http://fold3.com/image/28017843].

Richard Pettigrew served on board the galley *Accomac* commanded by Captain Underhill from the time the galley was ready until she was laid up. A certificate was issued in the name of the seaman on 26 April 1785 for £47 which was given to Colonel Cropper for services prior to 1 January 1782. He remained in Accomack County for a few years after the war ended, then moved to Delaware and died a few months before 1 December 1835. He had no widow living, so Leah **Collins**, his child, was his only heir at law according to testimony by several witnesses in Kent County, Delaware. Leah, about 40 years of age, appeared in Accomack County court on 29 November 1836 to apply for his pension, stating that she had received a warrant for his three years of service [NARA, S.46639, roll 1920, frame 323 of 1326]. Richard was a "free Negro" taxable in Kent County, Delaware, in 1797 [Delaware Archives film RG 3535, roll 4, 1785-1798, frame 184], head of a Mispillion, Kent County household of 6 "other free" in 1800 and 9 "other free" in 1810 [DE:93].

_____ Phillips was a black complexioned soldier, born in Fauquier County, who entered the service in Culpeper County, was 5'6-1/2' high, a planter, enlisted on 29 April 1781 for 1-1/2 years [The Chesterfield Supplement or Size Roll of Troops at Chesterfield Court House, LVA accession no. 23816, by http://revwarapps.org/b81.pdf (p. 25)], apparently identical to Philip Phillips who was taxable in Culpeper County from 1787 to 1802: taxable on a horse from 1787 to 1795, taxable on (his brother) William Phillips and Thomas **Timbers** in 1791 [PPTL, 1782-1802, frames 164, 225, 267, 319, 377, 628, 847]. Eckenrode has his name as Philip Phillips [Eckenrode, *List of the Revolutionary Soldiers of Virginia (Supplement)*, 240, citing (Culpeper) Rev. War vol. 1, Reg. 25]. On 20 August 1781 William Roberts sold him 130 acres in Culpeper County for only £5.6 which may have been his way of paying Philip for substituting [DB K:338]. He may have been the "FN" Philip Philips who was taxable in Loudoun County from 1807 to 1820: taxable on his unnamed son in 1812, his wife and son on J. Nichols's land in 1813 [PPTL, 1798-1812; 1813-] and head of a Loudoun County household of 12 "free colored" in 1820.

Joseph Pierce enlisted in the Revolution from New Kent County about 1780: *age 45, 5'6-1/4" high, a planter, born in Nansemond County, Molatto complexion, for 5 years by order of a court martial Decr 9th 1780* [Register & description of Noncommissioned officers & Privates, LVA accession no. 24296, by http://revwarapps.org/b69.pdf (p.80)].

Francis Pierce, a "free man of Colour," appeared in Boone County, Missouri, on 1 May 1837 to apply for a pension of his service in the Revolution. He was born free near Port Royal in Caroline County and enlisted there at the age of 17 with Captain Philip Buckner for five years. He served under Colonel Samuel Haws and acted as his servant [NARA, R.8235, M804, Roll 1933, frame 591 of 1115; http://fold3.com/image/27214473]. He was head of a Spotsylvania County household of 1 "other free" and 6 slaves in 1810 [VA:100].

John Pinn enlisted aboard the galley *Protector* as a mariner on 8 February 1777 and served until 8 February 1780 according to his discharge from the ship's Commander John Thomas [Revolutionary War Bounty Warrants, Pinn, John, Digital Collections, LVA]. He was a "Free" head of a Northumberland County household of 3 "Blacks" in 1782 [VA:37].

John Pinn was living in Boston, Massachusetts on 28 October 1842 when he applied for a pension for his services in the Revolution. He stated that his father Robert Pin was a Mustee and his mother a Cherokee who were inhabitants of Lancaster County, Virginia, at a place called Indian Town near Carter's Creek. He and his father served in Captain William Yerby's Company of Artillery: he as a powder boy. He had moved to Boston about 1792 and married Nancy Coffin about ten years later. She died about 1820. He testified that his brothers Jim and William also served and that Jim died in the service. He was described as "a coloured man - apparently of Indian Origin and is a person of good report amongst our mercantile community both here and at Salem" [NARA, R.8264, M804, Roll 1938, frames 0637-51; http://fold3.com/image/27251398].

Rawley Pinn was a "Mulatto" taxable in Buckingham County in 1774 [LVA, List of tithables, 1773-1774, p. 6; http://familysearch.org/search/catalog/274745, film 30684, image 6], head of an Amherst County household of 7 persons in 1783 [VA:47], and 8 "Mulattos" in 1785 [VA:84]. He was in the list of men in the Amherst County Militia in 1781 [William & Mary Digital Archives, Swem Library's Special Collections, Cabell Papers Box 2, Folder11.pdf].

Thomas Pinn was a "free Negro boy" living in Richmond County, Virginia, on 7 May 1764 when the court ordered the churchwardens of North Farnham Parish to bind him out to William Downman, the same man Robert Pinn was bound to in Lancaster County on 11 May 1751 [Orders 1762-5, 227]. He may have been the Thomas Pinn who died on 11 January 1778 according to the January 1778 payroll of Captain Abner Crumb's 1st Virginia Regiment [NARA, M246, Roll 94, frame 507 of 742; http://fold3.com/image/10071434].

William Pinn was named in the Revolutionary War pension application of his brother John Pin, perhaps the William Penn who was head of a Maryland household of 1 "other free" in 1790 [MD:52].

John Pipsico appeared in the District of Columbia court on 16 June 1818 to apply for a pension for this service in the Revolution. He stated that he enlisted in Fairfax County, served in Captain Snead's Company of Colonel Campbell's Virginia Regiment in 1780 or 1781 and was in the Battles of Guilford Courthouse, Eutaw Springs, Camden and Ninety Six [NARA, S.36230, M804, roll 1939, frame 1028 of 1351; http://fold3.com/image/27236218]. He was head of an Alexandria household of 3 "free colored" in 1820.

Obediah Plumly was listed in the payroll of the 3rd Georgia Battalion commanded by Lieutenant John McIntosh from 1 November 1779 to 1 February 1780 [NARA, M246, roll 32, frame 65 of 117; http://fold3.com/image/7661921]. He enlisted in the Revolution as a substitute for 18 months while resident in New Kent County on 6 June 1782 and was sized on 26 June: *age 20, 5'6-3/4" high, yellow complexion, born in New Kent County* [The Chesterfield Supplement or Size Roll of Troops at Chesterfield Court House, LVA accession no. 23816, by http://revwarapps.org/b81.pdf (p. 61)]. He was head of a Northampton County, North Carolina, household of 7 "other free" in 1790 [NC:76], 11 in 1800 [NC:469] and 3 in 1810 [NC:739].

Thomas Poe was presented by the York County court on 17 December 1764 for failing to list his wife as a tithable, and on 18 June 1787 the court discharged him from paying taxes, probably due to old age [Judgments & Orders 1746-52, 473; 1759-63, 298, 312; 1763-5, 320; 1772-4, 437; 1784-7, 468]. He and his wife Sarah Pow, "free Mulattas," registered the ___ 1766 birth of their son Thomas in Bruton Parish [Bruton Parish Register, 30]. He was taxable in York County on 2 tithables, 3 horses and 9 cattle in 1782, 2 horses and 6 cattle in 1785, 2 tithables in 1786, and exempt from personal tax from 1788 to 1792 when he was taxable on 2 horses [PPTL, 1782-1841, frames 69, 92, 109, 131, 143, 164, 184]. He received bounty land for serving three years as a soldier in the 1st Virginia State Regiment based on the testimony of Colonel J. Allison of James City County and the certificate of Benjamin C. Waller, C.C, a justice of York County that Thomas had made oath before him that he had never before proved or claimed his right for the service [Revolutionary Bounty Warrants, Poe, Thomas, 1780, Digital Collections, LVA].

Robert Randall, "a free black man," applied for a pension in Hanover, Grafton County, New Hampshire, on 2 May 1818 for service in the Revolutionary War. He stated that he enlisted in Fairfax County, Virginia, under Lieutenant Rogers who brought him to Rhode Island where he joined the regiment under Colonel Patterson. His widow Hannah Randall applied for benefits on 13 May 1820, stating that she had sons James (age 15) and Edward (12) at home and two children who lived at a distance from her [NARA, S.45165, M804, roll 1999, frame 808 of 957; http://fold3.com/image/26201642].

Joseph Ranger was a 72-year-old "man of Colour" and resident of St. John's Parish, Elizabeth City County, when he appeared in court on 25 October 1832 to make a declaration to obtain a pension for his service in the Revolution. He stated that he enlisted as a seaman in Northumberland County on board the galley Hero and then the ship Dragon for a total of four years. He was issued 100 acres of bounty land [NARA S.7352, M804, Roll 2000, frame 1220 of 1277; http://fold3.com/image/27992134]. He was a seaman aboard the Dragon according to an affidavit by a fellow seaman aboard the ship, John Davise, who testified for the bounty land claim of James Jennings on 7 February 1834 and named five of the officers and 52 members of the crew [Revolutionary War Bounty Warrants, Jennings, James (p.8), Digital Collection, LVA]. He was taxable in Elizabeth City County from 1809 to 1815: taxable on slave in 1809 and 1810, in a list of "free negroes & mulattoes" in 1813 [PPTL 1782-1820, frames 258, 271, 283, 295, 315, 334, 342].

John Rolls/ Rawls was residing in Caroline County when he was drafted into the Revolution from Culpeper County on 17 March 1781 for 18 months. He was sized on 4 May 1782: age 48, 5'3-1/4" high, black complexion [The Chesterfield Supplement or Size Roll of Troops at Chesterfield Court House, LVA accession no. 23816, by http://revwarapps.org/b81.pdf (p.75)]. He was a "Mulatto" taxable in Culpeper County from 1786 to 1802 [PPTL 1782-1802, frames 157, 194, 336, 418, 435, 529, 567, 609, 693, 743, 867]. He was called John Rawls when he appeared in Shenandoah County court to apply for a pension, stating stated that he enlisted at Culpeper courthouse, served in the regiment of Captain Reuben Fields, and was at the Battle of Guilford Courthouse and the Siege of Yorktown [NARA, S.39056, M804, Roll 2079, frame 534 of 1300; http://fold3.com/image/15532577].

Daniel Redcross was in the muster roll of Captain John Winston's 14th Virginia Regiment in the Revolution from 1777 to 1778. He died on 15 November 1778 according to the 24 December 1778 muster at Middlebrook [NARA, M246, http://fold3.com/image/9639177; M246, Roll 113, frame 91 of 752]. See Charles Evans and John Epps in this list.

John Redcross was in the list of men in the service of the Amherst County Militia in 1781 [William & Mary Digital Archives, Swem Library's Special Collections, Cabell Papers Box

2, Folder11.pdf]. His daughter Nancy married James **Pinn**, 27 August 1799 Amherst County bond. James was head of an Amherst County household of 6 "other free" and a slave in 1810 [VA:302]. John Redcross was probably related to Henry Redcross who was taxable in Amherst County in 1803 and a "Mulatto" taxable there in 1813 [PPTL 1782-1803, frame 594; 1804-23, frame 260].

John Redcross was listed as a deserter from Captain Lang's 2nd Virginia Regiment in the Revolutionary War [NARA, M246, Roll 96, frames 721, 726, 732 of 736; http://fold3.com/image/10082925]. He apparently returned, completed his service, was discharged, and received bounty land warrant no. 4748 for three years service in the State Line which he assigned to Jones Allen on 15 July 1783 [Revolutionary War Bounty Warrants, Digital Collections, LVA]. He was head of a York County household of 10 "other free" in 1810 [VA:882].

John Redman was taxable in the western district of Hardy County: counted in the "list of Free Negroes & Molattoes" from 1801 to 1813 [PPTL 1786-1806, frames 348, 357, 396-7, 459-60; 1807-1850, frame 183, 256]. He made a declaration in Hardy County court to obtain a pension for his services in the Revolution, stating that he enlisted in Winchester, Virginia [NARA, W.5691, M805, Roll 679, frame 0611; http://fold3.com/image/15171417].

Richard Redman enlisted in the Revolution from Fauquier County for 18 months on 20 September 1780 and was sized about the same time: *age 21, 5'4-1/2" high, a planter, born in Fauquier County, yellow complexion* [Register & description of Noncommissioned officers & Privates, LVA accession no. 24296, by http://revwarapps.org/b69.pdf (p.54)]. He was taxable in the western district of Hardy County in a "list of Free Negroes & Mulattoes" from 1809 to 1816 [PPTL 1786-1806, frames 471; 1807-1850, frames 57, 104, 166, 183, 266, 328, 343]. He was head of a Hardy County household of 2 "free colored" in 1830.

Abram Reed was a "free man of Colour by birth" who had always lived in Nansemond County and was about 79 years old on 13 May 1833 when he applied for a pension for his service in the militia digging embankments at Portsmouth during the Revolution [NARA, S.7364, M805, Roll 678, frame 0148; http://fold3.com/image/14120863].

Ameriah Reed applied for a pension for his service in the Revolution, stating the he enlisted in 1778 and had always lived in Nansemond County [NARA, R.8627, M805, Roll 678, frame 0154; http://fold3.com/image/14120943]. He was a "FN" taxable in Nansemond County in 1815 [PPTL, 1815-37, frame 26].

Amos Reed was a 75-year-old "free man of Colour by birth" who applied for a pension in Nansemond County on 13 May 1833 for his service in the Revolution. Joseph Ross and James Wright testified that they had seen him in the service but could not say how long he served [NARA, R.8628, M805, Roll 678, frame 0166; http://fold3.com/image/14121021].

Clement Reed was the "mullatoe" son of Jane Reed who was bound as an apprentice by the Southampton County court on 13 December 1759 [Orders 1759-63, 11]. He enlisted in the Revolution for 3 years on 9 January 1777 and was in the muster of Captain Peter Jones's Company of the 14th Virginia Regiment, sick at Lancaster in February 1778, and in the muster of the 5th and 11th Regiment in July 1779 [NARA, M246, roll 102, frame 683 of 774; roll 112, frames 350, 403 of 826; http://fold3.com/image/9946602].

Raymond Reed was a "mullatto" child bound as an apprentice by the Southampton County court on 11 May 1758 [Orders 1754-9, 434]. He enlisted in the Revolution for 3 years and was on the payroll of Captain Thomas Edmunds's Company of the 15th Virginia Battalion from June 1777 to March 1778 [NARA, M246, roll 113, frames 212, 224, 226, 237, 243 of 752; http://fold3.com/image/9640342].

Wilmoth Rich was ordered bound as an apprentice by the churchwardens of North Farnham Parish, Richmond County, in May 1749 [King, *Register of North Farnham Parish*, 157; Orders 1746-52, 161]. He was probably identical to Willm Rich who received bounty land based on his discharge on 1 March 1780 from Major Charles Magill for serving three years [Revolutionary War Bounty Warrants, Rich, William, Digital Collections, LVA]. He received his final pay on 6 August 1783 [NARA, M881, Roll 1095, frame 327 of 2014; http://fold3.com/image/286702521]. William was head of a Lancaster County household of 5 "Blacks" in 1783 [VA:55].

Godfrey Richardson enlisted in the Revolution from Stafford County for 18 months on 1 August 1780: *age 39, 5'6" high, a blacksmith, born in Essex County* [Register & description of Noncommissioned officers & Privates, LVA accession no. 24296, by http://revwarapps.org/b69.pdf (p.30)]. He received his final pay of £36 on 23 July 1783 [NARA, M881, Roll 1095, frame 353 of 2014]. He was entitled to bounty land [Brumbaugh, *Revolutionary War Records*, 263].

Charles Riley was a "free Negro" taxable in Middlesex County, Virginia, from 1801 to 1819 [PPTL 1782-1819, frames 197, 217, 225, 272, 282, 313, 322, 343]. He was a "coloured man," aged about 85, who applied for a pension for his services in the Revolution. He stated that he was a resident of Middlesex County when he enlisted, served from January 1780 to 1 November 1781, was sometimes sent on express between the troops in Middlesex, Gloucester, and Caroline counties, sometimes sent out upon foraging service and once helped guard a captured British vessel [NARA, M804, R.8824, Roll 2048, frame 812 of 1496; http://fold3.com/image/1/16183885].

Anthony Roberts was called "Anthony Roberds Mulatto" when his payment of 5 shillings was entered in the account of the York County estate of John **Peters** which was recorded in court on 15 September 1760 [W&I 21:20]. He was listed in the muster of Captain John Camp's Company of the 1st State Regiment commanded by Colonel George Gibson on 12 November 1777: enlisted for 3 years, and in the payroll of Captain Charles Ewell's Company on May 1779: listed next to Anthony **Peters** [NARA, M-246, roll 94, frames 67, 418, 671, 677, of 1421]. On 22 April 1783 he received a certificate from Captain Ab. Crump that he had served since January 1777 until his discharge [Revolutionary War Bounty Warrants, Roberts, Anthony, Digital Collection, LVA].

Godfrey Roberts was taxable in York County from 1788 to 1814: a "FN" in 1813 and 1814 [PPTL, 1782-1841, frames 144, 164, 195, 212, 247, 267, 288, 318, 342, 367, 394, 411] and head of a York County household of 9 "other free" in 1810 [VA:881]. He was deceased on 21 September 1833 when Anselm Bailey of Henrico County testified that Godfrey enlisted in the Revolution under Colonel Diggs for three years and served under Thomas Meriwether [Revolutionary War Rejected Claims, Roberts, Godfrey, Digital Collections, LVA]. Godfrey was listed as a landsman on Captain Elliott's payroll for the galley *Safeguard* from 1 March 1777 to 16 June 1777 and as a seaman entitled to bounty land for three years service [Brumbaugh, *Revolutionary War Records, Virginia*, 28, 71].

Hezekiah Roberts was head of a St. George Parish, Accomack County household of 3 "other free" in 1800 (called Kiah) [*Virginia Genealogist* 2:160]. He received bounty land in 1784 based on his service of three years and discharge from Colonel W. Brent in May 1780 [Revolutionary War Bounty Warrants, Roberts, Hezekiah, Digital Collections, LVA].

John Roberts was drafted from Accomack county on 25 January 1782 to serve in the Revolution for 18 months and sized on 4 May 1782: *age 30, 5'3" high, black complexion, born in Accomack County* [The Chesterfield Supplement or Size Roll of Troops at Chesterfield Court House, LVA accession no. 23816, by http://revwarapps.org/b81.pdf (p.75)].

David Robertson enlisted for 18 months on 22 September 1780: *age 19, 5'7-1/2" high, a planter, born in Dosset (Dorchester County), Maryland, residence: Middlesex County, yellow complexion* [Register & description of Noncommissioned officers & Privates, LVA accession no. 24296, by http://revwarapps.org/b69.pdf (p.54)]. He was on the muster until May 1783 and received 100 acres [NARA, M881, Roll 1088, frames 1321-6 of 1808].

Jonathan Ross served as a fifer in the Revolution. Samuel Ferguson received his final pay of £61 on 11 October 1784 [NARA, M881, Roll 1095, frame 680 of 2014; http://fold3.com/image/23624799]. He was a "Mulatto" taxable on a horse in Culpeper County from 1782 to 1802 [PPTL 1782-1802, frames 23, 83, 195, 336, 417, 496, 693, 867].

Reuben Ross was on the payroll of Captain Richard Stephen's Company of the 10th Virginia Regiment commanded by Colonel Edward Stephens from 28 March to 1 June 1777 [NARA, M246, roll 108, frame 785 of 1044; http://fold3.com/image/9098429]. He married Sally Terrel, 25 October 1791 Culpeper County bond. On 3 June 1799 Catherine Tearel (Terrell), George Tearel, Reuben Ross and his wife Sally, and Jonathan Ross and his wife Eleanor sold two lots in the town of Stevensburg which was probably land inherited from his father-in-law [DB 468]. He was a "Mulatto" taxable in Culpeper County from 1782 to 1802 [PPTL 1782-1802, frames 23, 83, 195, 336, 417, 496, 609, 693, 823, 867] and a "F. Mo." head of a Culpeper County household of 9 "other free" and a white woman in 1810 [VA:68]. He may have been the husband of Siby Ross of Culpeper County who was the wife of a soldier who received payment for her support on 7 June 1779 [Creel, *Selected Virginia Revolutionary War Records,* III:119, citing Auditors' Account II:334].

Peter Rouse, a "free man of colour," was about 57 years old on 4 November 1818 when he applied (signing) for a pension in Bedford County, Pennsylvania. He stated that he enlisted in the 2nd Virginia Regiment under Captain William Campbell in Dinwiddie County, Virginia, in 1778 and served until the surrender of Cornwallis. His application for a pension included two passes dated 27 April 1807: *Peter Rouse is a free man, that his parents & relations resided in this County. That I knew him in the capacity of a soldier in the regiment commanded by Colo George Gibson. J Nicholas* and one from William Campbell of Orange County, Virginia on 15 September 1807: *he and his parents also were born free.* He was described as a "yellow man" [NARA, S.23880, M805, Roll 706, frame 0545; http://fold3.com/image/15535547]. He was head of a Northampton County, North Carolina household of 9 "other free" in 1800 [NC:473].

John Rowe, a "free man of Colour," made a declaration in Botetourt County court to obtain a pension for his services in the Revolution. He stated that he enlisted in 1778 with Colonel Febiger in the 2nd Regiment in New Jersey and served until the end of the war. He also stated that he was in the Battles of Monmouth and Stony Point and the Siege of Yorktown [NARA, S.39045, M804, Roll 2072, frame 0209; http://fold3.com/image/14131371]. He was head of a Fluvanna County, Virginia household of 1 "other free" in 1810 [VA:478]. He registered in Nottoway County on 5 November 1818 and again in Botetourt County on 13 March 1820: *58 years, Black Colour, 5 feet 8 inches* [Free Negroes Registered in the Clerks Office of Botetourt County, no.29].

George Russell appeared in Smith County, Tennessee, on 15 August 1820 to apply for a pension for his services in the Revolution. He served in the 15th Virginia Regiment for a year and 9 months and was in the Battles of Rugeley's Mill and Camden. He was a "colored man" who was born in Brunswick County, Virginia, and returned there after his service in the spring of 1779 [NARA, S.39059, M804, Roll frame 54 of 829; http://fold3.com/image/14067393]. He was head of a Wake County, North Carolina household of 11 "other free" in 1790 [NC:103] and 4 in 1800 [NC:791].

Samuel Russell enlisted in the Revolution for 18 months from Loudoun County on 23 September 1780: *age 19, 5'2-1/2" high, a planter, born in Berkeley County, hair dark brown, eyes gray, complexion black, Deserted. Reg. 8* [Register & description of Noncommissioned officers & Privates, LVA accession no. 24296, by http://revwarapps.org/b69.pdf (p.54)]. He

60

produced an affidavit in Rockbridge County on 6 July 1818 that he enlisted in the Revolution on 1 September 1780 and served 18 months, and he appeared in Rockbridge County court to make a second deposition, stating that he served under Captains Peyton, Scott & Anderson, Colonel Davis and General Baron Steuben for 18 months in the 3rd Virginia Regiment in 1780 and 1781 [NARA, W.26423, M804, roll 2101, frame 271 of 829; http://fold3.com/image/14068041].

John Saunders enlisted in the Revolution for 18 months as a substitute while resident in Henrico county on 16 April 1781 and was sized 11 days later on 27 April: *age 16, 5'1-1/2" high, black complexion, a farmer, born in Hanover County* [The Chesterfield Supplement or Size Roll of Troops at Chesterfield Court House, LVA accession no. 23816, by http://revwarapps.org/b81.pdf]. He was head of a Henrico County household of 3 "other free" in 1810 [VA:980].

William Santy/ Santee took the oath of allegiance in Sussex County, Virginia, on 24 November 1777 [Tithables, 1753-1782, frame 824, LVA microfilm no. 90]. He enlisted as an "artifiler" (artificer?) with Captain Lawrence Rowse for three years on 31 October 1777 and served until his discharge [Revolutionary War Bounty Warrants; Santee, William, Digital Collection, LVA]. He married Mazy **Blizzard**, 7 February 1786 Sussex County, Virginia bond. He was taxable in St. Andrew's Parish, Greensville County, from 1792 to 1794 [PPTL, 1782-1830, frames 149, 156, 172] and was in the "List of Free Negroes & Mulattoes" for Sussex County from 1804 to 1806: with (wife) Mason Santy and children Betsy and Lucy [List of Free Negroes & Mulattoes, 1801-1812, frames 17, 23, 32, LVA microfilm no. 221].

Alexander Scott was a "free man of colour" who was in Amherst County in 1832 when he received bounty land for his service in the Revolution [Revolutionary War Bounty Warrants, Digital Collections, LVA].

Drury Scott, "mulattoe" son of Nanny Scott, was bound as an apprentice blacksmith on 27 April 1767 in Southam Parish, Cumberland County (which became Powhatan County in 1777) [Orders 1764-7, 459]. He was taxable in the southern district of Bedford County from 1800 to 1809: called a "free N" in 1807 [PPTL 1782-1805, frames 463, 479, 496, 531, 658; 1806-16, frames 30, 153, 288, 469]. He was a "free man of colour" who appeared in Clarke County, Kentucky court to make a declaration to obtain a pension for service in the Revolution. He stated that he enlisted in Powhatan County for three years in the 10th Regiment. He was in the Battles of Brandywine and Germantown, was taken prisoner in Charleston, and was under Colonel Febiger at the Siege of Yorktown. He was a rough carpenter with no one in his family but his wife who was a slave [NARA, S.35644, M804, Roll 2135, frame 994 of 1004; http://fold3.com/image/14186355].

Jesse Scott registered in Petersburg on 16 August 1794: *a light Mulatto man five feet six & 1/2 inches high who served as a Soldier & a free man during the American Revolution about thirty four years old* [Register of Free Negroes 1794-1819, no. 9].

John Scott, a "person of color," or "a free black man," received bounty land for his service in the Revolution in the 10th Virginia Regiment commanded by Captain Thomas Posey which he sold to Charles Jones of Prince Edward County, Virginia. He was in Clement County, Ohio, on 2 November 1809 when he appointed an attorney to receive his warrant. He was in Hamilton Township, Warwick County, Ohio, when he made a declaration to obtain a pension [NARA, S.46522, M804, roll 2137, frame 805 of 1207; http://fold3.com/image/16237261].

John Scott, the "mulattoe" son of Nanny Scott, was bound as an apprentice blacksmith to Robert Moore in Cumberland County, Virginia court on 27 April 1767 [Orders 1764-7, 459]. He may have been the John Scott who was a soldier that died in the service of the State according to testimony of (his mother?) Nanny Scott and (brother?) Andrew Scott in Henrico County court on 4 February 1788 [Orders 1787-9, 169]. Drury Scott and Nanny Scott testified in Henrico County court on 4 February 1788 that Axom Scott was the legal representative of

John Scott, a soldier who died in the service of the State [Orders 1787-9, 169; 1789-91, 184, 417, 430].

Littleberry Scott enlisted as a substitute in the Revolution for the length of the war while resident in Henrico County on 28 March 1781 and was sized on 27 April the same year: *age 18, 5-2-1/2" high, yellow complexion, a farmer, born in Charles City County* [The Chesterfield Supplement or Size Roll of Troops at Chesterfield Court House, LVA accession no. 23816, by http://revwarapps.org/b81.pdf (p.45)]. Captain Stoakley received his final pay of £17 on 9 August 1783 [NARA, M881, Roll 1095, frame 993 of 2014; http://fold3.com/image/286702864. He registered in Petersburg on 2 June 1801: *a light brown Mulatto man, five feet four inches high, forty years old, born free & raised in Charles City County* [Register of Free Negroes 1794-1819, no. 256].

Nicholas Scott was a "free Mulatto man" living in Halifax County, Virginia, on 6 May 1758 when he was tried for having shot and killed John Herring with Jacob Cogar as his accomplice. He was sent to Williamsburg for further trial where he was reprieved by the Governor but ordered to leave Virginia [Pleas 2:330, 336, 452, 471]. He may have been the Nicholas Scott who enlisted in the Revolution while resident in Charles City County for 18 months on 22 September 1780: *age 52, 5'4-1/2" high, a sailor, born in Henrico County, yellow complexion* [Register & description of Noncommissioned officers & Privates, LVA accession no. 24296, by http://revwarapps.org/b69.pdf (p.38)].

William Scott enlisted in the Revolution for the length of the war while resident in Dinwiddie County, Virginia, probably in September 1780 (no date but dates on either side of him are in September 1780) and was sized on 1 March 1781: *age 28, 5'6-1/2" high, a carpenter, born in Charlestown, Bk Hair, Blk Eyes, Yellow Complexion* [Register & description of Noncommissioned officers & Privates, LVA accession no. 24296, by http://revwarapps.org/b69.pdf (p.60)]. He registered in Petersburg on 16 August 1794: *a light Mulatto man five feet six inches high, about forty one years old, who served in the American Army during the Revolution* [Register of Free Negroes 1794-1819, no. 10].

Thomas Shaw enlisted for 18 months as a substitute in Culpeper County in September 1780: *age 40, 5'4-3/4" high, complexion all Blk, a planter, residence Culpeper County, born in Stafford County* [The Chesterfield Supplement or Size Roll of Troops at Chesterfield Court House, LVA accession no. 23816, by http://revwarapps.org/b81.pdf (p.29].

John Simmons enlisted in the Revolution for 18 months while resident in Caroline County on 20 September 1780: *age 45, 6'2-1/2" high, a carpenter, born in Essex County, yellow complexion* [Register & description of Noncommissioned officers & Privates, LVA accession no. 24296, by http://revwarapps.org/b69.pdf (p.77)].

Randolph Sly enlisted for 18 months on 23 September 1780: *age 25, 5'6-3/4" high, a planter, born in Caroline County, Black complexion. Enlisted for the war, but received no bounty Deserted* [Register & description of Noncommissioned officers & Privates, LVA accession no. 24296, by http://revwarapps.org/b69.pdf (p.60)]. He was apparently identical to Randall Shly who enlisted in the 2nd Maryland Regiment on 22 April 1782 (though his height is quite different): *residence: Virginia, age 24, 5'10" height, complexion: Negro, paid £8 bounty* [NARA, M246, roll 34, frame 434 of 587; http://fold3.com/image/12007228].

Charles Smith, of Henrico County, deserted from Captain Pope's command in Williamsburg about 10 days previous, according to an ad offering $20 reward on 1 August 1777, and describing him as: a stout well formed Mulatto, about 5 feet 10 inches high *[Virginia Gazette,* Dixon & Hunter edition, p. 8, col. 1].

Elijah Smith enlisted as a substitute in the Revolution for 18 months from Norfolk County on 15 August 1780 and was sized on 5 April 1781: *age 55, 5'4-1/4" high, black complexion, Indian features, a farmer, born in Norfolk County* [The Chesterfield Supplement or Size Roll of Troops at Chesterfield Court House, LVA accession no. 23816, by http://revwarapps.org/b81.pdf (p.29)]. He was a "Free Black" head of a household of 8 "other free" Princess Anne County in 1810 [VA:475].

James Smith enlisted as a substitute in the Revolution from Bedford County in February 1778 and was sized on 5 April 1781: *age 35, 5'9" high, black complexion, right eye out, blacksmith, born in Prince George County* [The Chesterfield Supplement or Size Roll of Troops at Chesterfield Court House, LVA accession no. 23816, by http://revwarapps.org/b81.pdf (p.29)].

James Smith was a "mulatto" from Halifax County, Virginia, who was one of the deserters from Captain Shem's 2d Georgia Battalion who were offered a free pardon on their return to duty, according to the 28 November 1777 issue of the *Virginia Gazette* [Purdie edition, p.3, col. 1].

Joseph Smith enlisted in the Revolution from Dinwiddie County on 6 June 1782 and was sized on 26 June: *age 25, 5'7-3/4" high, yellow complexion, born in Prince George County* [The Chesterfield Supplement or Size Roll of Troops at Chesterfield Court House, LVA accession no. 23816, by http://revwarapps.org/b81.pdf (p.113)].

Lewis Smith enlisted as a substitute from Dinwiddie County for 18 months on 6 June 1782 and was sized on 26 June: *age 22, 5'6-3/4" high, black complexion, a planter, born in Prince George County* [The Chesterfield Supplement or Size Roll of Troops at Chesterfield Court House, LVA accession no. 23816, by http://revwarapps.org/b81.pdf (p.113)]. He was a "free man of Colour" who was living in Dinwiddie County when he made a declaration in court to obtain a pension for service in the Revolution. He stated that he was born in Prince George County and removed to Dinwiddie County just before the war and resided there ever since. He enlisted in 1779 as a bowman for Captain Covington [NARA, S.6112, M804, roll 2226, frame 169 http://fold3.com/image/16878961]. He was a "free Black" taxable in Petersburg in 1813 [PPTL 1800-1833, frame 413].

William Smith, a Creole born in Barbados, and Daniel **Davis**, "a mulatto" born in Lancaster County, enlisted for the war and deserted from the ship *Gloucester* near Warwick according to an advertisement in the 2 August 1780 issue of the *Virginia Gazette* [Dixon and Nicholson edition, p. 2, col. 3]. Daniel **Davis** was listed as a private aboard the ship *Dragon* on 2 September 1779 and a seaman who served for three years and was entitled to bounty land [Brumbaugh, *Revolutionary War Records, Virginia*, 8, 68].

William Smothers enlisted in the Revolution while residing in Powhatan County for the length of the war and was sized on 8 March 1782: *age 19, 5'3-1/2" high, black hair, yellow eyes, black complexion, born in Albemarle County* [The Chesterfield Supplement or Size Roll of Troops at Chesterfield Court House, LVA accession no. 23816, by http://revwarapps.org/b81.pdf (p.73)]. He was taxable in Powhatan County from 1793 to 1804, called a "Mo" in 1793 and 1803 [PPTL, 1787-1825, frames 98, 123, 111, 138, 170, 193, 230, 266, 282]. He appeared in Cumberland County, Virginia court to apply for a pension for his services in the Revolution, stating that he enlisted in 1781 in Captain Stephen Southall's Virginia Regiment commanded by Colonel Charles Harrison and served until the close of the war [NARA, S.38375, M804, roll 2238, frame 588; http://fold3.com/image/17371111].

Edward Sorrell was 79 years old when he applied for a Revolutionary War pension in Northumberland County court on 14 August 1832. He enlisted in Northumberland and served two years from 1779 until the surrender of Cornwallis. He stated that he was in the 2nd Virginia Regiment under Colonel Porterfield and was in the Battles of Point of Fork and Camden where both he and Colonel Porterfield were wounded, he went to the western part of Virginia to get wagons and teams for the army and was sent to retrieve Colonel Porterfield who was paroled from prison near Camden [NARA, W.26493, M804, Roll 2246, frame 0911 (frame 925 of 1319 on ancestry.com); http://fold3.com/image/17117544]. He was a "free mulatto" head of a Northumberland County household of 10 "other free" in 1810 [VA:996].

James Sorrell was head of a Northumberland County household of 6 "Black" persons in 1782 [VA:37]. On 15 October 1783 Captain Thomas received his pay of £91.10.10 for his service as a gunner's mate in the Virginia Navy [Creel, *Selected Virginia Revolutionary War Records*, I:108]. In 1833 his heirs applied for bounty land for his services in the Navy and included his discharge papers from Captain John Thomas who certified that James enlisted in the Navy on 10 January 1777 as a gunner's mate for three years, discharged his duty faithfully, and was discharged on 10 January 1780 [Revolutionary War Bounty Warrants, Sorrell, James, 1783, Digital Collections, LVA]. (His brother?) Edward Sorrell was 80 years old on 17 May 1833 when he testified that James had enlisted in the galley *Hero* under Captain John Thomas in 1776 and later transferred to the ship *Tartar*. The claim was rejected [Revolutionary War Rejected Claims, Sorrell, James, 1834, Digital Collections, LVA].

Thomas Sorrell was listed among the "Free Molattoes" living on Thomas Rowand's land in Westmoreland County in 1801 [*Virginia Genealogist* 31:41]. He enlisted in the Revolution in 1780 under Captain Thomas Downing of Northumberland County, was marched to Hillsborough, then to South Carolina where he was in the Battle of Camden, marched to Richmond 18 months later to complete his service, and then returned to Northumberland County [NARA, S.6137, M804, Roll 2246, frame 0992 (frame 1003 of 1319 on ancestry.com); http://fold3.com/image/17117917].

Richard Spinner was bound by the Amelia County court as an apprentice to Joel Bevill on 22 January 1756 [Orders 1755-7, 26], was listed as "Dick" in the Amelia County household of James Bevill in 1762 [List of Tithables, 1736-77, LVA; http://familysearch.org/search/catalog/670006, film 1902616, images 450, 452], and was head of an Albemarle County household of 8 "free colored" in 1820. He was a "Coloured man," who appeared in Albemarle County court on 2 October 1832 at the age of 90 and stated that he was born a slave in Amelia County. He moved to Mecklenburg County with his master Joel Bevel who set him free in that county. After his emancipation he enlisted in Mecklenburg County for 3 years under Captain William Green and Captain Lewis Burwell. He was a substitute for Billy Stanley and was engaged in fatigue duty such as cutting wood and later in driving wagons [NARA, S.6140, M804, roll 2259, frame 605 of 1119].

Abel Spriggs and Thomas **Wood** were "mulattoes" listed among the deserters from the ship *Dragon* who were allowed until 20 July 1779 to return without punishment according to the 3 July 1779 issue of the *Virginia Gazette* [Dixon's edition, p. 3, col. 2]. They apparently returned since Abm Sprigg and Thomas **Wood** were seamen aboard the *Dragon* according to an affidavit by a fellow seaman aboard the ship, John **Davis**, who testified for the bounty land claim of James Jennings on 7 February 1834 and named five of the officers and 52 members of the crew who served faithfully for three years and were discharged at the Chickahominy Ship Yard [Revolutionary War Bounty Warrants, Jennings, James (p.8), Digital Collection, LVA].

Simon Stephens was a resident of Accomack County who was a cook and seaman aboard the Accomac during the Revolution according to the application of his and Stephen Stephens' heirs for bounty land. Their application included the certificates for their final pay on 27 April 1785. Simon's name also appears as a cook on board the *Accomac* in the State Navy records. Simon's heir Simon Stephens received bounty land warrant no. 7376 in 1833 [Brumbaugh, *Revolutionary War Records*, 376; Revolutionary War Bounty Land Warrants; Stevens, Simon; Powell, Solomon; Digital Collections, LVA].

Stephen Stephens was a seaman in the State Navy during the Revolution. His heir Stephen Stephens received bounty land warrant no. 7376-7 [Brumbaugh, *Revolutionary War Record*, 313, 376; Revolutionary War Bounty Land Warrants, Stevens, Simon, Digital Collections, LVA].

Barnett Stewart was head of a Chatham County, North Carolina household of 5 "other free" in 1810 [NC:200] and head of a Sumner County, Tennessee household of 10 "free colored" in 1820. He was "a free man of Colour" who was drafted in 1776 from Brunswick County, Virginia, where he was born and raised. He served as a cook [NARA, S.1727, M804, Roll 2289, frame 820 of 1236; http://fold3.com/image/18359714].

Edward Stewart enlisted as a substitute in the Revolution in Dinwiddie County for 18 months on 6 June 1782 and was sized on 26 June: *age 23, 5'11-1/4" high, yellow complexion, a planter, born in Chesterfield County* [Register & description of Noncommissioned officers & Privates, LVA accession no. 24296, by http://revwarapps.org/b69.pdf (p.68)]. He obtained a certificate of freedom in Chesterfield County on 11 June 1810: *forty eight years old, yellow complexion, born free* [Register of Free Negroes 1804-53, no. 131].

Edward Stewart enlisted in the Revolution in Amelia County for 18 months on 11 September 1780: *age 15, 5'3-1/2" high, a planter, born in Chesterfield County, yellow complexion* [Register & description of Noncommissioned officers & Privates, LVA accession no. 24296, by http://revwarapps.org/b69.pdf (p.68)]. He received his final pay of £36 on 21 June 1783 [NARA, M881, Roll 1095, frame 1807 of 2014].

Jack Stewart, a "mulatto," was listed among 7 deserters drafted out of Prince George County, for whom a reward was offered by Ensign Benjamin Grey in the 28 November 1777 issue of the *Virginia Gazette* [Purdie edition, p. 3, col. 3]. He was a "Mulatto" taxable in Chesterfield County on a tithe and 3 horses from 1788 to 1807 [PPTL, 1786-1811, frames 73, 148, 206, 286, 508, 585, 717].

John Stewart enlisted as a substitute in the Revolution from Dinwiddie County for 18 months on 6 June 1782 and was sized on 26 June: *age 24, 5'11-1/4" high, yellow complexion, a planter, born in Prince George County* [Register & description of Noncommissioned officers & Privates, LVA accession no. 24296, by http://revwarapps.org/b69.pdf (p.68)]. He was a "Mulo" taxable in Powhatan County from 1787 to 1810 [PPTL, 1787-1825, frames 10, 68, 124, 193, 351, 370, 386] and a "Free Black" head of a Powhatan County household of 26 "other free" and 3 slaves in 1810 [VA:2].

Jordan Stewart was taxable in his father William Stewart's Mecklenburg County household in 1790 [PPTL, 1782-1805, frame 329] and head of a Chatham County household of 8 "other free" in 1810 [NC:193]. He appeared in Wake County, North Carolina court and applied for a pension for his service in the Revolution, stating that he was born in Dinwiddie County, moved to Mecklenburg County, Virginia, where he joined the militia at the age of 26 years on 4 February 1780 and served for seven months. He was marched to within 20 or 30 miles of Guilford Court House where he met his father William Stewart, a soldier who was returning with a great many others after the Battle of Guilford Court House. He had lived in Wake County since the war [NARA, R.10160, M804, roll 2291, frame 715 of 945; http://fold3.com/image/18358007].

Nathan Stewart enlisted in the Revolution in Caroline County on 20 March 1781 and was sized on 18 May: *age 34, 5'8-1/2" high, black complexion, Black, born in Jamaica* [The Chesterfield Supplement or Size Roll of Troops at Chesterfield Court House, LVA accession no. 23816, by http://revwarapps.org/b81.pdf (p.45)].

Samuel Stewart was taxable in Surry County from 1783 to 1816: called a "FN" in 1809, listed with 2 "free Negroes & Mulattoes above the age of 16" in 1813 [PPTL, 1782-90, frames 368, 398; 1791-1816, 17, 169, 271, 384, 462, 574, 616, 657, 757, 866] and head of a Surry County household of 6 "free colored" in 1830. He was a "Free Negroe" who appeared in Surry County court to apply for a pension for his services in the Revolution, stating that he enlisted in Brunswick County, Virginia, in the 4th Virginia Regiment in February 1777, was at Valley Forge, the Battle of Monmouth, re-enlisted at West Point and was discharged at Middlebrook in February 1779 [NARA, W.7220, M804, Roll 2292, frame 280 of 875; http://fold3.com/image/18485949].

Thomas Stewart, born about 1742 in Mecklenburg County, Virginia, enlisted in Captain Dawson's Company in Lunenburg County under General Gibson and was at Valley Forge and Guilford Courthouse [NARA, W.4594, M805, Roll 772, frame 69 and M804, Roll 2289, frame 374 of 1236; http://fold3.com/image/18359225]. He was called "Thomas Stewart a Dark Man" by the 17 September 1792 Person County, North Carolina court when the court exempted him from payment of poll tax [Minutes 1792-6]. He was head of a Person County household of 7 "other free" in 1800 [NC:598] and 11 in 1810.

Thomas Tann and his wife Sarah Tan were "free mulattos" who recorded the birth of their son Thomas in Bruton Parish, James City and York counties, in 1766 [Bruton Parish Register, 28]. He enlisted for three years in Isle of Wight County on 26 December 1776 and was listed as deceased in the 1 July 1777 muster of Captain Thomas Edmunds's Company in the 15th Virginia Battalion [NARA, M246, roll 110, frame 285 of 768; roll 113, frame 189; http://fold3.com/image/9639784; http://fold3.com/image/9952883].

James Tate/ Teet was a "Molatto" farmer living with (his wife?) Sarah Teet and children in Westmoreland County in 1801 [Virginia Genealogist 31:42] and head of a Westmoreland County household of 7 "free colored" in 1820. He was about 91 years old the next September when he appeared in Westmoreland County court on 28 January 1833 for a pension for his service in the Revolution. He was called into service in the militia in Westmoreland County under Captain James Muse to defend against the British invasion by small vessels at Pope's Creek [NARA, M804, S.7696, Roll 2355, frame 283 of 607, Teete, James; http://fold3.com/image/18352288].

Jesse Tate entered the service on the galley Dragon on 10 September 1777 and was paid on 20 January 1779. He was listed as one of the crew of the Dragon which was waiting for provisions on 2 September 1779, listed as entitled to bounty land, but had not received it by 23 November 1834 [Brumbaugh, Revolutionary War Records, 8, 13, 71, 217]. He was head of a Richmond County household of 8 "other free" in 1810 [VA:395].

Jacob Teague was head of an Accomack County household of 7 "other free" in St. George's Parish in 1800 [Virginia Genealogist 2:164] and 6 "other free" in 1810 [VA:65]. He was a "man of color" who appeared in Accomack County court to apply for a pension for his service in the Revolution on 2 August 1820. He enlisted in the 11th Virginia Regiment under Captain Thomas Parker and Colonel Arthur Campbell and served 18 months [NARA, S.41235, M804, Roll, 2354, frame 204; http://fold3.com/image/18334056].

Buckner Thomas was a "man of Colour" who resided in Nottoway County when he appeared there in court to make a declaration to obtain a pension for his service in the Revolution. He stated that he enlisted in Dinwiddie County in September 1777 for three years, served in the 14th Virginia Regiment, was at the Battle of Paulus Hook, was in a scouting party at Scotch Plains, guarded the wagons and baggage at Stony Point, and marched to defend Charleston under Captain Peter Jones when the 10th Regiment was formed from the 14th [NARA, S.41248, M804, Roll 2367, frame 416 of 858; http://fold3.com/image/18729500]. He was in the muster of Captain Peter Jones's Company of the 10th Virginia Regiment from February to August 1779 with Isham Valentine [NARA, M246, Roll 109, frame 87, 102 of 795; http://fold3.com/image/10067205; S.41248, M804, Roll 2367, frame 416 of 853; http://fold3.com/image/18729500]. He was a "Black" tithable in Nottoway County from 1791 to 1812 (called Buck Thomas) [PPTL 1789-1822].

James Thomas, a "Colored man," enlisted in Norfolk County and served for 3 years as a boatswain aboard the brig Northampton in the Revolution. James Barron described him as: a fellow of daring and though a man of color was respected by all the officers who served with him. In 1840 Nancy Bell, his sole heir, received two land warrants of 1,333 acres each for his service [Thomas, James, 1840, Revolutionary War Bounty Warrants, Digital Collection, LVA].

John Thomas was drafted into the Revolution for the length of the war from Caroline County on 26 March 1781 and was sized on 14 May 1781: *age 30, 5'11-1/2" high, yellow complexion, a shoemaker, born in Prince George County* [The Chesterfield Supplement or Size Roll of Troops at Chesterfield Court House, LVA accession no. 23816, by http://revwarapps.org/b81.pdf (p.51)].

William Thomas enlisted in the Revolution for 18 months while resident in Charles City County on 22 September 1780: *age 21, 5'7" high, a planter, yellow complexion, born in Charles City County* [Register & description of Noncommissioned officers & Privates, LVA accession no. 24296, by http://revwarapps.org/b69.pdf (p.39)]. He was taxable in Upper Westover Precinct of Charles City County in 1784, taxable on 2 horses from 1788 to 1793, a "Mulattoe" taxable in 1813 and 1814 [PPTL, 1788-1814] and head of a household of 3 "free colored" in 1820. He appeared in Charles City County court to apply for a pension for his service in the Revolution, stating that he enlisted at Charles City courthouse in 1777 and was at Valley Forge under the company commanded by Lieutenant Carrol Minnis of the 1st Virginia Regiment. He was discharged in 1779 and reenlisted for 18 months in Charles City County just prior to the siege of York and marched to Chesterfield courthouse where he entered the company commanded by Captain Joseph Scott for about 3 weeks when he was taken into the family of General Peter Muhlenburg and discharged in Shenandoah County [NARA, S.38435, M804, roll 2372, frame 540 of 934; http://fold3.com/image/18338890].

Perkins Thomson, Jr., was in a list of drafts from Charles City County who deserted according to an ad placed in the 28 November 1777 issue of the *Virginia Gazette* by Lieutenant John Dudley: *Perkins Thomson, jun., who is twenty five years of age, of a yellow complexion, a shoemaker by trade, and is lurking about a place called Fo(u)ntain's Creek in Brunswick County* [Purdie edition, p. 3, col. 2]. He may have been related to Perkin Thompson who was taxable on 5 slaves in Charles City County in 1783 [PPTL, 1783].

Peter Toyer enlisted in the Revolution as a substitute for 18 months while resident in Gloucester County in August 1780 and was sized in 1781: *age 19, 5'2" high, black complexion, a farmer, born in Gloucester County* [The Chesterfield Supplement or Size Roll of Troops at Chesterfield Court House, LVA accession no. 23816, by http://revwarapps.org/b81.pdf (p.31)]. Major Poulson received his final pay of £34 for his service in the Revolution on 26 June 1783 [NARA, M881, Roll 1096, frame 501 of 2087; http://fold3.com/image/286702883].

George Tyler enlisted in the in the Revolution as a substitute in Goochland County for 18 months on 13 September 1780: *age 23, 5'6-1/2" high, black complexion, some of his fingers off, a planter or waiter*; in another list: *born in Louisa County* [The Chesterfield Supplement or Size Roll of Troops at Chesterfield Court House, LVA accession no. 23816, by http://revwarapps.org/b81.pdf (p.31) and http://revwarapps.org/b69.pdf (p.39)]. Thomas Aslin received his final pay of £35 on 27 September 1783 [NARA, M881, Roll 1096, frame 687 of 2087; http://fold3.com/image/286702885]. He was taxable in the upper district of Goochland County from 1787 to 1815: a "Mulatto" planter near Charles Watkins's shop in 1804, living on Joseph Woodson's land in 1811, exempt in 1815 [PPTL, 1782-1809, frames 157, 184, 227, 349, 367, 626, 698; 1810-32, frames 87, 270]. He was head of a Goochland County household of 3 "other free" in 1810 [VA:717]. He registered as a free Negro in Goochland County on 16 December 1814: *a free man of color about Sixty years old, about five feet six inches high, yellow complexion, short curled hair intermixed with grey...free born* [Register of Free Negroes, p.84, no.159]. He applied for a pension in Goochland County in 1781 for 18 months service [NARA, S.41,276, M804, Roll 2432, frame 0669; http://fold3.com/image/19973375].

Joseph Tyler was a slave called "Indian Joe" when he sued for his freedom from Charles Hutcherson, executor of John Thomson, in Louisa County court on 13 July 1767. He was described as a "Mulatto, or Indian Man" in Gabriel Jones's company of marines in Culpeper County on 2 September 1776 when Jones advertised in the *Virginia Gazette* that he had recovered a silver spoon which Joseph "had (stolen) from a Negro Boy belonging to Major

Carr of Louisa County" [Dixon's edition, p. 3, col. 2].

William Underwood, alias Wedgebare, enlisted in the Revolution in Culpeper County for the length of the war on 19 March 1781 and was sized about a month later: *William Wegbare, age 19, 5'2-3/4" high, yellow complexion, born in Loudoun County* [The Chesterfield Supplement or Size Roll of Troops at Chesterfield Court House, LVA accession no. 23816, by http://revwarapps.org/b81.pdf (p.35)]. William Underwood was head of a Wilkes County, North Carolina household of and 9 "other free" in 1800 [NC:66]. He was head of a Haywood County household of 3 "free colored" and 1 white male aged 30-40, including an 80-year-old Revolutionary War pensioner in 1840 [NC:111]. He was called William Wedgebare alias William Underwood when he testified that he enlisted for the duration of the war on 19 March 1780 in Culpeper County. He served under Baron Steuben, was at the Siege of Yorktown, was marched south and was at the evacuation of Charleston and was in Savannah [NARA, W.2292, M804, Roll 2520, frame 35 of 1387; http://fold3.com/image/29311044].

Anthony Valentine enlisted in the Revolution from Charles City County for 18 months on 22 September 1780: *age 33, 5'8" high, planter, born in Charles City County, black complexion* [Register & description of Noncommissioned officers & Privates, LVA accession no. 24296, by http://revwarapps.org/b69.pdf (p.22)].

Charles Valentine was listed in a 13 March 1779 offer of a reward in the *Virginia Gazette* for deserters from the infantry of the Virginia State Garrison Regiment stationed near Williamsburg. The advertisement described him as: *a mulatto, born in Surry County, Virginia, 28 years old, 5 feet 9 inches high, well made* [Dixon's edition, p. 2, col. 2]. He was sized at the Chesterfield County court house sometime after 1 September 1780: *residence: Sussex County, deserted (no age, size or complexion shown)* [Register & description of Noncommissioned officers & Privates, LVA accession no. 24296, by http://revwarapps.org/b69.pdf (p.22)]. He was head of a Brunswick County, Virginia household of a "free colored" man over 45 years of age in 1820 [VA:672].

Edward Valentine enlisted in the Revolution from Dinwiddie County as a substitute on 6 June 1782 and was sized on 26 June: *age 21, 5'6-1/4" high, black complexion, a planter, born in Dinwiddie County* [The Chesterfield Supplement or Size Roll of Troops at Chesterfield Court House, LVA accession no. 23816, by http://revwarapps.org/b81.pdf (p.33); Eckenrode, *Virginia Soldiers of the American Revolution, II (Supplement)*:308, citing Revolutionary Army Vol. I:33 at LVA]. He received $20 pay between 1782 and 1783 [NARA, M881, Roll 1096, frame 721 of 2087].

Isham Valentine, born about 1766, enlisted in the Revolution from Dinwiddie County as a substitute on 6 June 1782 and was sized on 26 June: *age 16, 5'9" high, black complexion* [The Chesterfield Supplement or Size Roll of Troops at Chesterfield Court House, LVA accession no. 23816, by http://revwarapps.org/b81.pdf (p.33)].

Isham Valentine, born say 1755, enlisted in the Revolution for 3 years on 6 September 1777 and was listed in the payroll of Captain Peter Jones's Company in the 14th Virginia Regiment commanded by Colonel William Davis at White Plains in 1778. Hy Williams received his final pay of £55 on 20 December 1784 [NARA, M881, Roll 931, frames 1442-1489 of 1871; http://fold3.com/image/22609320]. He applied for bounty land and received a certificate from Colonel William Davis on 15 December 1784 that he had been a soldier in his regiment to the northward, was at Middlebrook in 1779, and was captured at Charleston. And Colonel William Epes, an officer in Davis's regiment, certified that Isham was inducted on 12 September 1777 for three years and was discharged. Isham assigned his bounty land to Henry Watkins on 11 December 1784 [Revolutionary War Bounty Warrants, Digital Collection, LVA]. He and his wife Caty were the parents of Nancy Valentine who registered in Surry County on 25 May 1818: *daughter of Isham Valentine & Caty his wife of Surry County free people of Colour the said Nancy Valentine is about 37 years old of a bright Complexion tolerable straight made...is 5'3-1/2" high* [Hudgins, Surry County Register of Free Negroes, 68].

Luke Valentine was in a list of militia marched by Captain Adam Clements from Bedford County to the assistance of General Green in South Carolina on 1 May 1781 [NARA, M246, Roll 114, frame 128 of 492; http://fold3.com/image/9946836], called a "free man of Colour" on 13 November 1832 when he made a declaration in Campbell County in order to obtain a pension for his service in the Revolution [NARA, S.6299, M804, Roll 2438, frame 590 of 1811; http://fold3.com/image/19914802]. He was head of a Campbell County household of 10 "other free" in 1810 [VA:848].

Benjamin Viers was a "F. Negro" taxable in Augusta County in 1797, 1798 and 1805 [PPTL 1796-1810, frames 56, 92, 421] and a "F.N." taxable in Botetourt County from 1809 to 1820 [PPTL 1787-1810, frames 620, 653; 1811-1822, frames 13, 48, 90, 92, 269, 310, 356, 391, 443]. His pension application states that he was born on 3 September 1752 in Charlotte County, Virginia. He was a "free coloured man" who enlisted in Revolutionary War service in Henry County, Virginia, in October 1775. He served in the 14th and 10th Virginia Regiments. He marched to Valley Forge, Trenton, and Stony Point, and was at the Battles of White Plains, Brandywine, Monmouth and the Siege of Yorktown [NARA, S.6313, M804, Roll 2459, frame 1260 of 1360; http://fold3.com/image/20125436]. On 26 February 1787 John Henderson received his final pay for serving as a wagoner [NARA, M881, Roll 1096, frame 818 of 2087].

Robert Walden enlisted for four years as a substitute in the Revolution from Dinwiddie County on 29 June 1782 and was sized the same day: *age 28, 4'11" high, yellow complexion, a farmer, born in Dinwiddie County* [The Chesterfield Supplement or Size Roll of Troops at Chesterfield Court House, LVA accession no. 23816, by http://revwarapps.org/b81.pdf (p.91)]. He was called Robert **Chavis** when he was listed as a tithable in Dinwiddie County with Batt and Isham **Chavis** in 1788, called Robert Walden in 1789 [PPTL, 1782-90 (1788 B, p.5), (1789 A, p.21)], apparently identical to Robert W. **Chavers** who received bounty land for his service in the Revolution, enlisted for 3 years on 3 June 1782 according to his discharge on 2 November 1784 [Revolutionary War Bounty Warrants, Chavers, Robert W., Digital Collection, LVA].

James Wallace was living in Williamsburg on 11 July 1780 when he enlisted in the Revolution for the duration of the war: *age 28, 5'3-1/4" high, a planter, born in New Kent County, black complexion* [Register & description of Noncommissioned officers & Privates, LVA accession no. 24296, by http://revwarapps.org/b69.pdf (p.43)]. He was about 75 years old on 13 August 1832 when he made a declaration in James City County to obtain a pension for his services in the Revolution. "Being a Coloured man," he acted as a cook for Colonel Porterfield and guarded prisoners. He enlisted in James City County and returned there after the war [NARA, S.7834, M804, Roll 2479, frame 0558; frame 572 of 1232; http://fold3.com/image/19822757]. He was taxable in James City County from 1786 to 1813: listed as a "Mulatto" in 1805 and 1806, taxable on 2 tithables in 1806, 3 in 1809, 2 in 1810, taxable on 2 tithables and a "free person of colour" (probably his wife) in 1813 [PPTL 1782-99; 1800-15].

Joseph Wallace, a "free man of color," appeared in Charles City County on 25 April 1835 at the age of 80 and stated that he was engaged by the army under Lord Dunmore in James City County to subdue the Indians before the Revolution, early in the Revolution enlisted in Bedford County for three years under Captain John Bard, then under Captain Alexander Cummings and served until the end of the war [NARA, R.11068, M804, Roll 2480, frame 53 of 1173; http://fold3.com/image/20354572; Revolutionary War Bounty Warrants, Digital Collections, LVA].

Abraham Warren/ Warrick was living in Frederick County when he enlisted in the Revolution and was sized about July 1782: *age 39 5'4-1/2" high, blk complexion, residing Frederick County, born Loudoun county, enlisted for the war* [The Chesterfield

69

Supplement or Size Roll of Troops at Chesterfield Court House, LVA accession no. 23816, by http://revwarapps.org/b81.pdf (p.91-2)]. General Morgan received his final pay of £87 on 7 April 1783 [NARA, M881, Roll 1096, frames 1044-7 of 2087].

Moses Watkins (son-in-law of James **Nickens**) served as a soldier in the infantry. On 27 February 1784 Colonel Gaskins received his final pay of £35 [NARA, M881, Roll 1096, frame 1092 of 2087; http://fold3.com/image/23329340]. He was a "Mulatto" taxable in Culpeper County from 1789 to 1794 [PPTL 1782-1802, frames 307, 338, 416, 437, 498] and a "free negro" taxable in Fauquier County in 1798 [PPTL 1797-1807, frame 100].

Edward Watson enlisted in the Revolution from Caroline County on 23 September 1780: *age 18, 5'3" high, a farmer, born in Caroline County, yellow complexion* [Register & description of Noncommissioned officers & Privates, LVA accession no. 24296, by http://revwarapps.org/b69.pdf (p.66)].

Aaron Weaver was head of a Lancaster County household of 3 free persons and a slave in 1783 and a "F.B." taxable on a horse in the Eastern Branch Precinct of Princess Anne County from 1784 to 1815 [PPTL, 1782-89, frames 600, 719; 1790-1822, frames 21, 47, 104, 112, 179, 206, 252, 299, 347, 419, 479, 534]. He registered in Princess Anne County on 27 September 1800: *Aaron Weaver & Martha Nicken were married in the county of Northumberland the 7th February 1766. The above Aaron Weaver & Martha Nicken were born free* [Weaver, Aaron (M): Free Negro Affidavit, 1800, African American Narrative Digital Collection, LVA]. He was a "F.B." head of a Princess Anne County household of 4 "other free" in 1810 [VA:479]. He petitioned the legislature for a pension for his services in the Revolution, stating that he served as a seaman for 3 years aboard the galley *Protector* and ship *Tartar* and was wounded. William **Cassady** of Northumberland County, aged 56, deposed that he served with him and witnessed Aaron being wounded. He received State pension no. 442 and bounty land warrant VA 1477 [Legislative Petitions of the General Assembly, 1776-1865, Accession no. 36121, Box 309, folder 62; Virginia Revolutionary War Pension Applications, LVA, digitized].

Elijah Weaver was a "Mulatto" bound out by his "Mulatto" mother Ann **Kelly** on 24 May 1755 to serve Benjamin Waddy of Lancaster County for three years [LVA, chancery suit 1765-001, digitized]. John Keys received his final pay of £81 on 11 July 1783 for his service in the Revolution [NARA, M881, Roll 1096, frame 1170 of 2087; http://fold3.com/image/23329624]. He registered as a "free Negro" in Lancaster County on 18 July 1803: *Age 66, Color dark...born free* [Burkett, *Lancaster County Register of Free Negroes*, 1]. He was a Revolutionary War veteran who died intestate in Lancaster County before 15 September 1834 when his heirs Spencer Weaver, Elijah Weaver, Mary **Pinn**, Agatha **Bell**, Betsy Weaver, and Polly the wife of Armstead **Nicken** were named in court [Orders 1834-41, 37]. The application for his bounty warrant for Revolutionary War service included a Lancaster County affidavit by Richard **Nicken**, a near-neighbor of Elijah, that Elijah served on board the *Dragon* or *Tartar* for 3 years as a seaman. And it included a note that he had received £58 as the balance of his full pay as a seaman on 27 October 1783 [Revolutionary War Bounty Warrants, Weaver, Elijah, Digital Collection, LVA].

John Weaver petitioned the Lancaster County court on 19 October 1786 for his freedom from Susannah Leland who was holding him in servitude until the age of 31 [Orders 1786-9, 32]. He registered as a "free Negro" in Lancaster County on 19 September 1808: *Age 48, Color yellow, Height 5'3-1/4* [Burkett, *Lancaster County Register of Free Negroes*, 1]. He was a Revolutionary war veteran who died before 19 May 1834 when his only heir Betty Weaver was named in Lancaster County court [Orders 1834-41, 7]. Dorcas left a 23 July 1820 Lancaster County will, proved 21 August the same year, naming her son Spencer **Bell** and grandchildren John Weaver **Bell**, James **Bell**, and Nancy **Bell** [WB 28:208].

John Weaver was residing in Richmond City when he enlisted in the Revolution in Northumberland County for two years on 16 June 1782 and was sized the same day: *age 25, 5'4" high, black complexion, Negro, a planter, born in Lancaster County* [The Chesterfield Supplement or Size Roll of Troops at Chesterfield Court House, LVA accession no. 23816, by http://revwarapps.org/b81.pdf (p.91)]. He was taxable in Portsmouth and Elizabeth River Parish in Norfolk County, Virginia, in 1788 and 1789 and from 1796 to 1806: called a "Mulatto" in 1798, 1800 and 1804; a labourer in Western Branch Precinct in a "List of Free Negroes and Mulattoes" in 1801 [PPTL, 1782-1791, frames 633, 652; 1791-1812, frames 180, 235, 261, 306, 364, 384, 569, 584]. He was head of a Northampton County, North Carolina household of 3 "other free" in 1810 [NC:750], 5 "free colored" in Hertford County in 1820 [NC:206] and 3 "free colored" in Hertford County in 1830. On 13 October 1828 he made a declaration in Hertford County court that he served in the Virginia Line in a regiment that was commanded by colonels Davis, then Cambell, then Quebeck but lost his discharge in a sea wreck soon after the war. He received bounty land. James **Smith** testified for him [NARA, B.LWt.1391-100, M805, Roll 845, frame 272; http://fold3.com/image/28295899]. He may have been identical to the John Weaver who received bounty land by virtue of a voucher by Lieutenant Colonel Ed. Carrington in 1783 that John Weaver the bearer belonged to the Fifth Troop in the 1st Regiment of Light Dragoons commanded by Colonel George Baylor and had leave of absence. He served for 3 years [Revolutionary War Bounty Warrants, Weaver, John, Digital Collection, LVA].

Richard Weaver was an indentured servant who ran away from Robert Dudley of King and Queen County who offered a reward for his return in the 21 March 1771 *Virginia Gazette*, describing him as *a young Negro fellow...about 19 years of age, of a yellow complexion, and very spare, had on when he went off a grey serge coat and waistcoat, lined with red, and a pair of leather breeches* [Rine edition, p. 4, col. 3]. He may have been the Richard Weaver who was on the muster of Captain Samuel Hawes's Company in the 2nd Virginia Regiment in July 1777 and in Captain Richard Stevens's Company of the 10th Virginia Regiment in November 1777, enlisted until February 1778 [NARA, M246, Roll 96, frame 205 of 736; Roll 108, frames 755, 797, 801 of 1044; http://fold3.com/image/9098496]. Joseph Saunders received his final pay of £64 on 29 August 1786 [NARA, M881, Roll 1096, frame 1179 of 2087].

Henry Welch enlisted in the Revolution from Culpeper County for 18 months on 19 March 1781 and was sized about a month later: *age 19, 5'3-3/4" high, yellow complexion, born in King George County* [The Chesterfield Supplement or Size Roll of Troops at Chesterfield Court House, LVA accession no. 23816, by http://revwarapps.org/b81.pdf (p.35)].

James West was head of a Fredericksburg household of 9 "other free" and a slave in 1810 [VA:111a]. He may have been the James West who was listed as one of the seamen aboard the galley *Dragon* during the Revolution, received pay on 20 January 1779, was entitled to bounty land for three years service, but had not received the land by 7 January 1835 [Brumbaugh, *Revolutionary War Records*, 7, 13, 72, 277, 608].

Alexander/ Sawney Whistler enlisted as a substitute for a year in the Revolution from Middlesex County on 11 February 1782 and was sized the same day: *age 20, 5'4-1/2" high, black complexion, a farmer, born in Middlesex County* [The Chesterfield Supplement or Size Roll of Troops at Chesterfield Court House, LVA accession no. 23816, by http://revwarapps.org/b81.pdf (p.91)]. He received a warrant for 200 acres in 1784 which he assigned to Richard Smith on 30 July 179_ [NARA, BlWt. 12683, M804, Roll 2549, frame 0028; frame 42 of 1058 on http://ancestry.com; http://fold3.com/image/28019381; Revolutionary War Bounty Warrants, Whistler, Sawny, Digital Collection, LVA]. He was a "Black" taxable in the lower district of King and Queen County in 1801 [PPTL, 1782-1803]. He registered in Middlesex County on

26 June 1805: *born free; 40 years of age; Black complexion* [Register of Free Negroes 1800-60, p.15].

Benjamin Whitmore enlisted in the Revolution in Fairfax County on 22 December 1782 and was sized on 8 April 1783: *aged 19, 5'5-1/2" high, dark complexion, Mulatto, baker in Alexandria, born in Fairfax County* [The Chesterfield Supplement or Size Roll of Troops at Chesterfield Court House, LVA accession no. 23816, by http://revwarapps.org/b81.pdf (p.117)].

Charles Whitson enlisted for the war on 22 December 1782 and was sized on 8 April 1783: *age 14, 5'9-1/2" high, black complexion Mulatto, born in Fairfax County* [The Chesterfield Supplement or Size Roll of Troops at Chesterfield Court House, LVA accession no. 23816, by http://revwarapps.org/b81.pdf (p.117)].

Charles Wiggins enlisted in the Revolution from Isle of Wight County, Virginia, for 18 months on 1 October 1780: *age 40, 5'7-1/2" high, a farmer, born in Isle of Wight* [Register & description of Noncommissioned officers & Privates, LVA accession no. 24296, by http://revwarapps.org/b69.pdf (p.66)].

Daniel Williams, a "Colourd" man, appeared in Philadelphia County court to apply for a pension, stating that he was born in Accomack County, Virginia, where he was drafted into the army as a wagoner and had charge of a wagon and two horses until the end of the war. He returned home to Accomack County after the war and remained there for several years, then moved to Maryland for 13 years and came to Philadelphia where he had resided for 27 years. On 28 April 1835 John **Blake**, a "Colourd man" who was about 76, testified that he was born in Accomack County and lived near and was well acquainted with Daniel Williams, a "Colourd" man, who was drafted into the army to drive teams, that he was a free-born man and was gone for four or five years. He had resided in Philadelphia about 15 years past, where he again met Williams and "has frequently seen him engaged in driveing the team" [NARA, R.11569, M804, Roll 2586, frame 736 of 751; http://fold3.com/image/28467470]. He may have been the Daniel Williams for whom Mr. Broadhead received final pay of £11 on 30 July 1784 [NARA, M881, Roll 1096, frame 1560 of 2087].

Matthew Williams was a "Mulatto" bound to Servant Jones by the Warwick County court on 3 July 1760 [Minutes 1748-62, 322, 325, 334, 337]. He was a "Free Man of colour" who appeared in Southampton County court to make a declaration to obtain a pension. He stated that he was living in Southampton County when he enlisted at Cabin Point for 18 months. He stated that he was at the Battle of Guilford Courthouse where he was wounded in the knee by a musket ball and was at the Siege of Yorktown [NARA, S.6414, M804, roll 2592, frame 857 of 967; http://fold3.com/image/28351789]. He registered in Southampton County on 12 July 1810: *age 55, Blk, 5 feet 7-1/2 inches, free born* [Register of Free Negroes 1794-1832, no. 589].

William Williams was a "Mulatto" bound to Servant Jones by the Warwick County court on 3 July 1760 [Minutes 1748-62, 322, 325, 334, 337]. He served three years as a soldier in the 2nd Virginia State Regiment for the term of his enlistment according to a certificate from Colonel William Brent on 12 June 1780 in James City County. James McClung, a justice of York County, certified that William Williams made oath before him that he had never before proved his right to land for his military service [Revolutionary War Bounty Warrants, Williams, William, 1780, Digital Collections, LVA]. He and his wife Rachel, "Free Mulattoes," registered the birth of their daughter Lydia in Bruton Parish, James City and York counties, on 5 January 1783 [Bruton Parish Register, 35]. He was taxable in Warwick County from 1783 to 1798: taxable on 2 horses and 10 cattle in 1783 and 1786, called a "free Negro" in 1785, a "Mulatto" starting in 1789, taxable on 4 horses in 1793, 2 tithes in 1795, 1797 and 1798 [PPTL

1782-1820, frames 219, 229, 238, 246, 253, 257, 271, 279]. He was taxable in York County from 1792 to 1806: called "free Negro" in 1805.

Peter Wilson was a "Mo" taxable in Halifax County, Virginia, from 1792 to 1799 [PPTL, 1782-1799, frames 7, 58, 79, 202, 427, 614, 686, 711, 931] and a "F.B." head of a Giles County household of 10 "other free" and a white woman in 1810 [VA:643, 1021]. He may have been the Peter Wilson whose final pay of £36 for service in the Revolution was received by Sam Matthews on 16 April 1784 [NARA, M881, Roll 1096, frame 1727 of 2087]. His widow Dicey **Cumbo** applied for a pension for his service in the Revolution. She stated that he served under Captain George Walton in the Virginia and Georgia Line [NARA, R.11662, M804, Roll 2609, frame 231 of 1437; http://fold3.com/image/28761628].

Charles Wood was taxable in Lancaster County from 1795 to 1814: taxable on 2 tithes from 1800 to 1802, 3 in 1803, 2 in 1806, in the list of "free negros & Mulattoes above the age of sixteen" in 1813 [PPTL, 1782-1839, frames 134, 192, 244, 292, 385, 399], head of a Lancaster County household of 5 "other free" and a white male under 10 years old, probably identical to the Charles Wood who was a "free Mulatto" head of a Northumberland County household of 5 "other free" in 1810. He may have been the Charles Wood who was a soldier in the infantry during the Revolution and assigned his right to payment of £25.12.0 to Mr. Brodhead on 3 August 1784 [Creel, *Selected Virginia Revolutionary War Records*, I:118; NARA, M881, Roll 1096, frame 1804 of 2087; http://fold3.com/image/23331620].

Jesse Wood enlisted in the Revolution from King William County on 8 September 1780: *age 16, 4'10" high, a planter, born in Hanover County, yellow complexion* [Register & description of Noncommissioned officers & Privates, LVA accession no. 24296, by http://revwarapps.org/b69.pdf (p.23)]. He was a "free man of color" living in Fluvanna County when he applied for a pension, stating that he enlisted in King William County in 1778 and was discharged in Fluvanna County in 1782 [NARA, S.7962, M804, Roll 2627, frame 1005 of 1213; http://fold3.com/image/28480466]. He was a "Mulatto" taxable in the upper district of Goochland County from 1804 to 1813 [PPTL, 1782-1809, frame 698; 1810-32, frames 20, 88, 112, 177] and head of a Goochland County household of 6 "other free" in 1810 [VA:722].

John Wood was paid £6 as a seaman on 16 June 1783, the payment received by Captain Richard Taylor on the same day he received Philip Wood's pay [Creel, *Selected Virginia Revolutionary War Records*, I:120]. He was a seaman aboard the *Tempest* according to testimony by James Jennings, listed before Philip and Thomas Wood and after Joseph **Ranger** [Wood, John; Jennings, James (pp.8-10): Revolutionary Bounty Warrants, Digital Collections, LVA]. John was taxable in Northumberland County from 1795 to 1812: called a "Black" man from 1805 [PPTL 1782-1812, frames 439, 448, 461, 480, 495, 508, 518, 568, 578, 605, 627, 661, 676].

Jonathan Wood, "a Free negroe," applied for a pension in Isle of Wight County on 6 January 1835. He stated that he was drafted into the militia from Surry County, Virginia, in 1776 and served several tours of 6 weeks each. James Johnson, a captain in the militia during the war, certified that Jonathan had served at least two tours of 6 weeks each [NARA, R.11793, M804, roll 2628, frame 1018 of 1371; http://fold3.com/image/28756126]. He was head of an Isle of Wight County household of 7 "free colored" in 1830.

Philip Wood was a soldier in June or July 1778 in Colonel Marshall's Regiment, re-enlisted and served until the end of the war according to an affidavit from Captain Christopher Roane on 25 April 1783. Philip was a seaman aboard the *Tempest* according to an affidavit by James Jennings who listed the members of the crew. Jennings listed Joseph **Ranger**, John Wood, Philip Wood and Thomas Wood consecutively [Wood,

Phillip; Jennings, James (pp.8-10): Revolutionary Bounty Warrants, Digital Collections, LVA]. Captain R^d Taylor received his final pay of £6 as a seaman on 16 June 1786. Captain Taylor also received the final payment of seaman John Wood of £20 on the same date [M853, Roll 22; http://fold3.com/image/286702539]. Philip is not found in the early census or tax records.

Robert Wood, "a man of Colour", enlisted in the 3rd Virginia Regiment in the early part of the war, then enlisted in the State Artillery Regiment commanded by Colonel Marshall and served during the war according to an affidavit by J. Marshall, former captain of the 11th Regiment. He enlisted in Fauquier County and applied for a pension in Washington, D.C., on 6 August 1818 [NARA, S.39909, M804, roll 2629, frame 1281 of 1290; http://fold3.com/image/28761011].

Thomas Wood and Abel **Spriggs** were "mulattoes" listed among the deserters from the ship Dragon who were allowed until 20 July 1779 to return without punishment according to the 3 July 1779 issue of the *Virginia Gazette* [Dixon's edition, p. 3, col. 2]. They apparently returned since Ab^m **Sprigg** and Thomas Wood were seaman aboard the Dragon according to an affidavit by a fellow seaman aboard the ship, John **Davis**, who testified for the bounty land claim of James Jennings on 7 February 1834 and named five of the officers and 52 members of the crew who served faithfully for three years and were discharged at the Chickahominy Ship Yard [Revolutionary War Bounty Warrants, Jennings, James (p.8), Digital Collection, LVA]. He was paid for serving on the Dragon between 21 April 1778 and 20 January 1779, was listed as a seaman aboard the Dragon on 2 September 1779, and qualified for bounty land by serving three years [Brumbaugh, *Revolutionary War Records*, 8, 13, 72, 218]. He was a "free Negro" taxable in Lancaster County in 1813 [PPTL, 1782-1815, frame 385].

William Wynn was a taxable "Mulatto" in King William County in 1813 and was included in the list of "Free Negro and Mulattoes" for 1833 [A List of free Negroes and Mulattoes in the County of King William for the year 1833, African American Digital Narrative Collection, LVA]. He was about 75 years old on 23 December 1833 when he appeared in King William County court and applied for a pension for his services in the Revolution. He stated (signing) that he was born in King William County and drafted under Captain John Catlett and joined the regiment under Colonel Holt Richeson [NARA, S.11699, M804, Roll 2616, frame 485 of 1296 http://fold3.com/image/28362798].

Lewis Hinton was one of only a relatively few slaves that received his freedom by serving in the Revolution. He enlisted for his master William Hinton who served on board the Dragon. Hinton's health became so bad that he was permitted to leave the service, and Lewis took his place. He served under captains Callender, Hamilton and Chamberlayne [NARA, S.10831, M804, roll 1287, frame 944 of 958; http://fold3.com/image/23384208].

Tim Jones was about 86 years old on 15 July 1833 when he appeared in York County court to apply for a pension for his services in the Revolution. He stated that he enlisted under Captain Edward Digges in the 3rd Virginia Regiment for four years as a substitute for his master Rolling Jones [NARA, S.18063, M804, http://fold3.com/image/24627808].

Jack Knight and William Boush were two "negro slaves" belonging to the Commonwealth who had faithfully served on board armed vessels which were no longer in service. On 30 October 1789 the Legislature passed a law manumitting them, but "saving all legal or equitable rights of all claimants" [Hening, *The Statutes at Large*, XIII:103].

Caesar, the slave of Mary Tarrant of Elizabeth City, entered very early into the service of his country as a pilot of the armed vessels. The assembly enacted a law on 14 November 1789 that the executive should contact Mary Tarrant for the purchase of Caesar, and if she should agree, pay for his freedom [Hening, *The Statutes at Large*, XIII:102]. His heirs received bounty land in 1831 [Revolutionary War Bounty Warrants, Terrant, Caesar, Digital Collections, LVA].

William Beck was the "Mulatto" slave of Thomas Walker, Jr., who served in the Revolution with Walker and was emancipated by the Virginia Legislature in October 1779 after Walker petitioned for his freedom [Walker, Thomas, Jr.: Petition, Albemarle County, 1779-10-23, Legislative Petitions Digital Collection, LVA; Hening, *Statutes at Large*, X:211].

Emanuel, a Negro, was serving aboard the *Tempest* on 7 October 1779 [Stewart, *The History of Virginia's Navy of the Revolution*, 185].

Pluto, a "negroe belonging to Mr. William Brough of Elizabeth City County," served on board the boat *Patrick* for three years according to an affidavit by Richard Barron on 19 January 1781 [Revolutionary War Bounty Warrants, Pluto, Digital Collections, LVA].

"Negro" Seamen Abram, Bachus, Boston, Charles, Daniel, Emanuel, George, Jack, James, Kingston, Peter, Tom, and Will were entitled to bounty land for service in the Virginia Navy [Brumbaugh, *Revolutionary War Records, Virginia*, 70, 214-8].

"Mulatto" Frank served as a seaman in the Virginia Navy and received bounty land [Revolutionary War Bounty Warrants, Frank, Mulatto, Digital Collections, LVA].

James Wimbish freed his slave Toby alias William Ferguson in 1786 for his service as a soldier in the late American War [Charlotte County DB 4:fol. 170 cited by Nicolls, *Passing Through this Troubled World*, 62].

Saul, the property of George Kelly of Norfolk County performed many essential services to the Commonwealth during the war, was set free by the Legislature by law passed on 13 November 1792 which directed that a person be appointed to jointly ascertain with his master what value should be paid for him from public funds [Hening, *The Statutes at Large*, XIII:619].

James, a slave the property of Wm Armistead, Gentleman, of New Kent County in 1781 entered the service of Marquis Lafayette, and at the peril of his life frequented the British Camp and executed important commissions entrusted to him by the marquis. He applied to the Legislature which passed an act in October 1786 granting him full freedom and appointed someone to value him so that his master could be compensated by the state [Hening, *The Statutes at Large*, VII:380-1]. James Lafayette was a free Negro taxable in New Kent County on a slave and 3 horses in 1805 [PPTL, 1791-1828, frames 442, 487].

Aaron Brister enlisted in the town of Dumfries in Prince William County, Virginia, in the company commanded by Thomas Helms in the 3rd Virginia Regiment commanded by Colonel Weadon for two years in 1776. He was discharged in Philadelphia. He was head of a Palmyra, Ontario County, New York household of 5 "free colored" in 1820. He appeared in the town of Palmyra on 27 April 1818 to apply for a pension. His widow Betsy Tolliver applied in 1836. They married about 1777 or 1778 when they were both slaves [NARA, W.17341, M804, roll 342, frame 527 of 764; http://fold3.com/image/12838865].

Thomas Camel/ Campbell, "a black man," was the slave of Colonel Martin Picket of Virginia. He was free and in Madison County, New York on 7 June 1832 when he

75

applied for a pension. He stated that he entered the service in September 1776 under Captain Wilson in Culpeper County, Virginia, where he was then resident and was marched to join the main army under George Washington [NARA, R.1609, M804, roll 453, frame 80 of 866; http://fold3.com/image/12314424]. He was head of a household of 9 "free colored" in Oneida, Augusta County, New York, in 1820.

William Canonbrig was drafted for 18 months while resident in Bedford County on 6 April 1781 and was sized in 1782: *age 20, 5'11-1/4" high, black complexion, born in Fluvanna County* [The Chesterfield Supplement or Size Roll of Troops at Chesterfield Court House, LVA accession no. 23816, by http://revwarapps.org/b81.pdf (p.97)].

Peter McAnelly applied for a pension in Knox County, Indiana, on 7 September 1832. He was born in Louisa County, Virginia, and resided there until 1790. He served in the militia as a substitute for Anthony Thompson and served for a total of 9 months. Daniel **Strother** testified that he was acquainted with Peter at Little York during the Revolution [NARA, S.16467, M804, roll 1662, frame 734 of 1107; http://fold3.com/image/23667354]. Peter was head of a Knox County, Indiana household of 2 "free colored" in 1840.

Ned Streater, "a free man of color, appeared in Nansemond County court on 2 November 1833 to apply for a pension for his service in the Revolution. He entered the service in 1780 under Captain Ellington Knott in the Nansemond County Militia as a substitute for his master Willis Streater and served for 12 months. His master died in 1814, and he finally recovered his freedom by suit in Nansemond County court in April 1824 [NARA, S.7645, M804, roll 2313, frame 470 of 1266; http://fold3.com/image/18465965].

Daniel Strother was born in South Carolina and raised in Anson County, North Carolina. He entered the service in Charlotte County, Virginia, and served as a wagoner under General Greene. Andrew **Ferguson** and Peter **McNelly/ McNally** testified for him. His application was rejected because he did not serve in a military capacity [NARA, R.10275, M804, roll 2316, frame 164 of 1050; http://fold3.com/image/19454198]. He was head of a Polk County, Missouri household of 4 "free colored" in 1840.

OTHER POSSIBLE VIRGINIA SOLDIERS

Thornton Allman/ Almond enlisted in the Revolution for 3 years as a private and was in the muster and payroll of Captain John Gregory's company of the 15th Virginia Regiment from 26 December 1776 to April 1779 when the regiment was at Middlebrook. From June 1779 to November 1779 he was in John Hobb's Company of the 5th and 11th Regiment with Robert Mush (an Indian) and Bartholomew Holmes, a "yellow" complexioned soldier, who were both from King William County [NARA, M246, roll 110, frames 202, 204, 283, 365, 377, of 768; roll 102, frames 707, 719 of 774, http://ancestry.com; http://fold3.com/image/9643187, 9643230, 9643268, 9463302]. He is not listed in any record after the war and did not apply for bounty land, but a Thornton Almond who was born about 1812 was a "Mulatto" counted in the 1850 census for King William County.

Benjamin Ash enlisted in Isle of Wight County on 1 February 1777 for three years, was in the muster of Captain Wills' Company of the 15 Virginia Regiment in 1778 and in Colonel William Russell's 5th and 11th Regiments at the camp near Morristown on 9 December 1779, in the same list as Giles **Bowry/ Bowers** of Southampton County [NARA, M246, Roll 110, frame 293 of 768; Roll 102, frame 651 of 774; http://fold3.com/image/9952883]. He may have been a member of the mixed-race Ash(e) family of Southampton County.

76

Elvin Ash was in the Muster of Captain James Harris's Company of the 15th Virginia Regiment for the month of March 1778, listed as deceased on 15 March 1778 [NARA, M246, Roll 113, frame 297 of 752; http://fold3.com/image/9641598]. He may have been a member of the mixed-race Ash(e) family of Southampton County.

Larkin Beazley died on 1 August 1778 while serving at White Plains according to the testimony of Captain Thomas Upshaw. His brother Leroy Beazley, who applied in Fredericksburg court, received bounty land for his service [Beazley, Larkin: Revolutionary Bounty Warrants, Library of Virginia Digital Collection, LVA]. No one by the name Leroy Beazley is found in the records, but a Larkin Beazley was head of a Spotsylvania County household of 1 "other free" in 1810.

Stephen Bowles was listed as dead in the November 1777 muster of the 4th Virginia Regiment [NARA, M881, Roll 972, frame 1581 of 2184; http://fold3.com/image/22717393]. He may have been the brother of Bartlett Bowles who was taxable in Louisa County in 1782 and 1785 [PPTL, 1782-1814] and taxable in Fredericksville Parish, Albemarle County, from 1793 to 1813: taxable on 2 horses in 1793, listed as a "Mulatto" in 1812 and 1813 [PPTL, 1782-1799, frames 382, 446, 477, 512, 550, 585; 1800-1813, frames 24, 68, 113, 156, 202, 245, 291, 339, 382, 429, 473, 517, 562]. Bartlett registered as a "free Negro" in Albemarle County on 6 September 1803 [Orders 1801-3, 225] and was head of an Albemarle County household of 2 "free colored" in 1820.

Levin Bundick served in the Virginia Navy from Accomack County [Bundick, Levin: Revolutionary Bounty Warrants, Library of Virginia Digital Collection, LVA], perhaps the Levi Bundick who was head of an Accomack County household of 7 "other free" in 1800.

Rebecca Chaves was the "free Negro" mother of Adam Chavis who was bound out by the Amelia County court on 19 September 1740 [Orders 1735-46, 125; 1754-8, n.p.; 1757-60, 195; 1760-3, 44]. Adam Chevis was on the payroll of Captain Callohill Mennis's Company in the 1st Virginia Regiment for the month of April 1778 [NARA, M246, roll 92, frame 553 of 715; http://fold3.com/image/9093719].

Robert Corn died before 8 May 1783 when his unnamed mother received his final pay of £36 for serving in the Revolution in Virginia [NARA, M881, Roll 1091, frame 995 of 2235; http://fold3.com/image/286702708]. He may have been related to the Robert Corn who was head of a Wake County, North Carolina household of 3 "other free" in 1790 [NC:106] and 1 in 1800 [NC:756].

John Cowage, born say 1746, was a "Mollatto Boy" valued at £24 in the 24 June 1752 Goochland County estate of Henry Miller [DB 6:352-4]. He was called John Cowigg when he served in the Revolution from Goochland County as a wagoner in the service of supply [Jackson, *Virginia Negro Soldiers*, 32]. He was taxable in Goochland County from 1787 to 1807: called a "Mulatto" in 1793, a "freed Negroe" in 1794, a "Mulatto" in 1803 and 1807. His wife was probably "Clarissa Cowig free negroe" who was taxable on her son John Cowig in 1813 [PPTL, 1782-1809, frames 163, 190, 311, 376, 405, 568, 650, 803; 1810-32, 139].

Henry Curtis, a "Mulatto," was ordered bound to George Henry as an apprentice carpenter by the Fauquier County court on 28 August 1769 [Minutes 1768-73, 132, 141]. He may have been the Henry Curtis who was serving aboard the boat *Liberty* in November 1779 when the seamen were supplied their rations of rum. He received a discharge from Captain John Thomas of the galley *Protector*, stating that he enlisted on 12 October 1778, served faithfully, and was discharged on 12 October 1781. He received bounty land warrant no. 3271 [Brumbaugh, *Revolutionary War Records*, 21, 67, 333; Revolutionary War Bounty Warrants, Curtice, Henry, 1784, Digital Collections, LVA]. He was taxed in Caswell County, North Carolina, in 1790 [NC:79], and was head of a Person County household of 4 "other free" in 1800 [NC:596] and 2 in Caswell County in 1810 [NC:468].

Stephen Davenport was said to have been a soldier in the Revolution from York County [Jackson, *Virginia Negro Soldiers*, 34], but Jackson did not cite the source for this. He is listed by Eckenrode [Eckenrode, *Virginia Soldiers in the American Revolution*, I:129, citing Auditors Account XVIII:534].

John DeBaptist was said to have served in the Revolution as a seaman aboard the *Dragon* [http://waymarking.com]. He was born in St. Kitts in the West Indies and moved to Fredericksburg, Virginia. His widow Franky Baptist was head of a Fredericksburg, Spotsylvania County household of 6 "other free" and 2 slaves in 1810 [VA:113b]. A Jean Babtiste served in the infantry [Babtiste, Jean: Revolutionary Bounty Warrants, Library of Virginia Digital Collection, LVA].

Solomon Evans was issued a pay warrant for service in the Charles City County Militia on 17 April 1781 [*Charles City County Historical Society Newsletter* 6:10-14, citing Auditors' Account XVIII:558-9, LVA].

John Goin received a warrant for £80 in lieu of clothing on 14 December 1779 for his service in the Revolution [Creel, *Selected Virginia Revolutionary War Records*, III:223, citing Auditors' Accounts III:220, LVA].

Isaac Jackson complained to the Prince Edward County court against his master Samuel Wallace in April 1769. He was a "free Negro" head of a Charlotte County household of 7 "other free" in 1810 [VA:68]. He registered in Charlotte County on 18 August 1815: *a Black looking man, five feet six & half inches high 67 years of age Sep. 1815. Son of Dorcas Jackson a free Mulato born free & Lived in Prince Edward & Charlotte and has lately Removed to Halifax, a Carpenter & Weever by trade.* He may have been the Isaac Jackson who received a discharge from Lieutenant Samuel Baskerville and General P. Muhlenberg at Winchester Barracks on 11 June 1783, stating that he had served since August 1777 [Revolutionary War Bounty Warrants, Jackson, Isaac, 1783, Digital Collections, LVA].

James Jameson was taxable in James City County from 1782 to 1814: called a "mulatto" in 1805, taxable on 2 free tithes in 1809 and 1810, called a "mulatto" from 1811 to 1813 and "cold." in 1814 [PPTL, 1782-99; 1800-15]. He and his wife Jane, "Free mulattoes," baptized their daughter Nancy in Bruton Parish, James City County, on 26 February 1785 [Bruton Parish Register, 36]. He may have been the James Jameson who received payment for services in the Revolution [Eckenrode, *Virginia Soldiers of the American Revolution*, I:238, citing Auditors' Account XXII:70 (Accounts from 24 May 1784 to 14 December 1784)].

James Maclin, alias **Roberts**, was added to the list of tithables in Elizabeth City County on 7 November 1764 [Court Records 1760-9, 262]. He may have been the James Macklin who received bounty land based on his discharge by Lieutenant Colonel W. Washington for three years service in the 3rd Virginia Regiment of Light Dragoons on 23 December 1780 [Revolutionary War Bounty Warrants, Macklin, James, 1780, Digital Collections, LVA].

Jeremiah Meekins enlisted in the Revolution in March 1777 for three years, was sick at Valley Forge in Captain John Anderson's 5th Virginia Regiment in August 1778; on command, in charge of General Woodford's baggage in November 1779 [NARA, M246, Roll 99, frame 106 of 760; Roll 98, frame 244 of 789; http://fold3.com/image/22038275]. He may have been related to David, Joseph and Christmas Meekins who were heads of "black" New Kent County households in 1782 [VA:36].

Hardy Milton was not found by the sheriff in Southampton County on 10 October 1782 when his property was attached for a £3.12 debt he owed John Wright [Orders 1778-84, 247]. He received bounty land for three years service in Colonel Marshall's Regiment of the State Artillery, based on the certification of Captain William Spiller by order of Lieutenant Colonel Edmonds on 18 August 1780 [Revolutionary War Bounty Warrants, Melton, Hardy, 1783, Digital Collections, LVA]. He was probably the Hardy Melton who was counted as white in Cheraws District, South Carolina, in 1790.

Isham Milton/ Melton received a discharge for 3 years' service in Colonel Marshall's Regiment of Artillery on 23 August 1780 from Captain William Spiller [Revolutionary War Bounty Warrants, Melton, Isham, 1780, Digital Collections, LVA]. He received pay of £79.17.10 for 3 years service in the infantry, drawn by Colonel Mason on 14 October 1783 [Creel, *Selected Virginia Revolutionary War Records*, I:91]. He received a pension while resident in Edgecombe District, South Carolina, based on his testimony on 5 June 1818 [NARA, M804, S.38,944, Roll 1709, frame 543 of 743; http://fold3.com/image/27259535]. He was counted as white in the 1810 census for Edgefield District.

Samuel Monoggon was said to have been a soldier in the Revolution from Gloucester County [Jackson, *Virginia Negro Soldiers*, 29]. He was head of a Gloucester County household of 3 "other free" in 1810 [VA:409a] and 3 "free colored" in 1820 [VA:192].

George Morris, born 19 December 1740, was called the son of Winefred Morris, a "free Mullatto," when his birth was registered in Christ Church Parish, Middlesex County. He was taxable on 2 tithes in Gloucester County in 1770 and 1771 [Tax List 1770-1, 99], taxable in Petsworth Parish, Gloucester County, on 2 free tithes and 8 cattle in 1782 and 1784, taxable in Ware Parish in 1785 and 1786, taxable on 3 tithes in 1787, and taxable in 1788 [PPTL, 1782-99]. Another George Morris, born say 1762, was taxable in York County from 1784 to 1814: taxable on 3 horses and 9 cattle in 1784, taxable on a slave in 1788 and 1789, called George Morris, Sr., when he was taxable on 2 tithes in 1794 and 1799, listed as a "free Negro" in 1814 [PPTL, 1782-1841, frames 87, 142, 163, 203, 212, 288, 318, 341, 355, 409]. A George Morris was listed in the Revolutionary War accounts from 24 May to 14 December 1784 [Eckenrode, *Virginia Soldiers of the American Revolution*, I:319, citing Auditors' Account XXII:329 (Accounts from 24 May to 14 December 1784].

Isham Reed enlisted in the Revolution on 14 July 1777, was sick but present for the March 1778 Muster of Captain James Harris's Company of the 15 Virginia Regiment and died on May 6, 1778 at Valley Forge [NARA, M246, Roll 113, frames 297, 303; http://fold3.com/image/9461918]. He may have been a member of the mixed-race Reed family of Southampton County.

Ephraim Stephens, son of Amey Stephens, was bound apprentice to John Tankard in Northampton County, Virginia, on 10 January 1775 [Minutes 1771-7, 277]. He registered as a "free Negro" in Northampton County on 11 June 1794 [Orders 1787-9, 64; 1789-95, 193, 354]. He may have been the Ephraim Stephens who served in the Revolution. William Satchell received his final pay of £36 on 28 February 1782 [NARA, M881, Roll 1095, frame 1766 of 2014].

Spencer Thomas served in the Virginia Battalion of Northumberland County [Gwathmey, *Historical Register of Virginians in the Revolution*, 767; Eckenrode, *Virginia Soldiers of the American Revolution*, 434, citing War 4:372 at LVA]. Charles Jones received his final pay of £18 on 26 February 1784 [NARA, M246, 679 of 752; M881, Roll 1088, frame 1851 of 1808; http://fold3.com/image/23306931]. He was taxable in Northumberland County from 1787 to 1812: taxable on a slave from 1788 to 1798; listed as a "Blk" taxable from 1806 to 1812; taxable on 2 free males from 1809 to 1811 [PPTL 1782-1812, frames 323, 331, 352, 368, 382, 396, 412, 426, 447, 479, 508, 517, 540, 554, 568, 577, 605, 626, 643, 675]. He was a "free mulatto" head of a

Northumberland County household of 7 "other free" in 1810 [VA:996]. Note, however, that there was also a white man named Spencer Thomas in Northumberland County about the same age.

Edward Wilkerson was said to have been a soldier from Chesterfield County in the Revolution [Jackson, *Virginia Negro Soldiers*, 64].

VIRGINIA INDIANS

George Langston served three years in the Revolution from King William County in the 7th Virginia Regiment under Captain Holt Richeson and received bounty land for his services [Revolutionary War Bounty Warrants, Langston, George, 1817, Digital Collection, LVA].

Gideon Langston was an Indian boy attending William & Mary College in 1754 [*William & Mary College Quarterly* VI:188]. He was one of the headmen of the Pamunkey Indians who petitioned the Virginia Legislature on 4 December 1812 [Pamunkey Indians: Petition, King William County, 1812-12-04, Legislative Petitions Digital Collection, LVA]. He was an Indian taxable on a slave in King William County in 1809 [PPTL, 1782-1832]. He and William Samson were living in King William County in 1818 when they received bounty land for three years service in the Revolution under Captain Holt Richeson in the 7th Virginia Regiment [Revolutionary War Bounty Warrants, Froman, Temple, 1818, Digital Collection, LVA].

William Langston was one of the only seven surviving men of the Pamunkey Indians who petitioned the Virginia Assembly to sell a small tract of their land in 1748 [Winfree, *The Laws of Virginia*, 416-7]. He or a younger William Langston was a private in Captain James Gray's Company of the 15th Virginia Regiment in the Revolution, from August 1777 to December 1777, reported as sick on most rosters and deceased in the muster for February 1778. The musters included Robert Mush, Elias Peay, Edmund Absolam, and several other soldiers whose widows or dependents received support from the King William County court in 1779. William Bigger received his final pay of £15 [NARA M246, Roll 113, frames 322, 325, 328, 331, 337, 340 of 752; http://fold3.com/image/9642083, 9642136, 9642178, 9642229, 9642251, 9642291; NARA, M881, Roll 1084, frame 897]. Therefore, William's widow must have been the Sukey Langston, widow, who received support from the King William County court on 23 June 1779, called Lucy Langton when she was allotted £12 support on 6 November that year [Quarles, John: Petition, 1779-11-06 and 1779-06-23, Legislative Petitions Digital Collection, LVA]. Lieutenant Henry Quarles certified that William Langston served for three years and was dead by February 1778. His bounty land was assigned to George Langston [Revolutionary War Bounty Warrants, Langston, William, 1786, Digital Collections, LVA].

Nanney Major, a widow, was allowed payment to widows and orphans of soldiers in the Revolution from King William County on 23 June 1779 and 6 November 1779 [Quarles, John: Petition, 1779-11-06 and 1779-11-23, Legislative Petitions of the General Assembly, 1776-1865, Accession Number 36121, Box 134, Folders 4 & 6, Digital Collections, LVA]. A relative, Nancy Major, was in the "list of Blacks above the age of sixteen" for the Upper District of Henrico County in 1813 [PPTL, 1782-1814, frame 759]. She died on Sunday, 12 September 1819 at her home in Henrico County from domestic violence. Her husband John, the slave of Thomas Cowls was in the habit of beating his wife "severely and frequently" according to a statement made by witness Agness Langston to a Henrico County coroner's inquisition on Monday, 13 September 1819. Agness stated that she lived with Nancy for some time, that Nancy was in good health before Saturday night, that John came there and beat her very much, and she died the following morning. John, a slave hired that year by Mr. Hailey, was also present and confirmed Agness Langston's statement [Major, Nancy: Coroner's Inquisition, 1819, African American Narrative Digital Collection, LVA].

Sarah Major was allowed payment to widows and orphans of soldiers in the Revolution from King William County on 23 June 1779 and 6 November 1779 [Quarles, John: Petition, 1779-11-06 and 1779-11-23, Legislative Petitions of the General Assembly, 1776-1865, Accession Number 36121, Box 134, Folders 4 & 6, Digital Collections, LVA].

James Morton enlisted in Loudoun County for 18 months on 19 March 1781 and was sized on 28 May 1781: *age 20, 5 Feet 3 Inches, blk Hair, dark Eyes, yellow Complexion, Indian features, a sailor, born Boston, Massachusets* [The Chesterfield Supplement or Size Roll of Troops at Chesterfield Court House, LVA accession no. 23816, by http://revwarapps.org/b81.pdf (p.53)].

Robert Mursh/ Mush, born about 1758, was apparently the descendant of James Mush, a Chickahominy Indian who confessed to burning down the cabin of another Chickahominy Indian named Tom Perry in May 1704 [McIlwaine, *Executive Journals of the Council*, II:364, 376]. Robert was a Pamunkey Indian who served in the Revolution from King William County. His mother was probably Sarah Mush, a widow of a soldier in the Revolution, who was allowed £24 by the King William County court in June 1779 [Quarles: John: Court Record, King William County, 1779-06-23, Legislative Petitions Digital Collection, LVA]. Robert was a member of the Pamunkey Tribe who became a Baptist minister and was living on 50 acres of land in York District, South Carolina, on 25 October 1820 with wife Elizabeth when he applied for a pension. He enlisted in 1776 and served for three years [NARA, W.8416, M804, roll 1797, frame 15 of 1084; http://fold3.com/image/25346090].

George Sampson enlisted in the 15th Virginia Regiment for three years about December 1775 and died in the service after June 1777 according to an affidavit from Lieutenant Giles Raines. On 29 June 1789 his widow Nanny Sampson of King William County certified that Reuben Sampson was his legal representative. Reuben assigned his right to the bounty land to William Bigger with Robert Mush as witness [Revolutionary War Bounty Warrants; Sampson, George, Digital Collections, LVA]. Nanney Sampson was his widow who was allowed payment to widows and orphans of soldiers in the Revolution from King William County on 23 June 1779 and 6 November 1779 [Quarles, John: Petition, 1779-11-06 and 1779-11-23, Legislative Petitions of the General Assembly, 1776-1865, Accession Number 36121, Box 134, Folders 4 & 6, Digital Collections, LVA]. Reuben was taxable on 2 horses in the Pamunkey Indian Town in King William County in 1799 [PPTL, 1782-1832].

William Sampson was living in King William County when he and Gideon Langston enlisted and served three years in the Revolution under Captain Holt Richeson in the 7th Virginia Regiment. They received bounty land in 1818 [Revolutionary War Bounty Warrants, Froman, Temple, 1818, Digital Collection, LVA].

Simon Turner, an "Iindian," died in the fall of the year 1776 in Revolutionary service before he and Holladay Revell reached the regiment to which they were assigned according to testimony by Revell on 7 April 1831 [Revolutionary War Bounty Warrants, Turner, Simon; Revell, Holladay, 1831, Digital Collections, LVA]. Simon was probably from the Nottoway Indian Tribe of Southampton County.

NORTH CAROLINA

Joseph Allen was a "Mullatto" taxable in William Allen's Granville County household in 1767 [Tax List 1767-1809] and a 22-year-old "mullatto" planter listed in the 25 May 1778 Granville County Militia Returns [T.R., Box 4, folder 4].

Caleb Archer was in a list of militia men drafted from Hertford County in the Third Division commanded by Major George Little [T.R. Box 5, Folder 20]. He was allowed £26 pay for service in the Revolution from 10 November 1777 to 10 August 1778 [Haun, *Revolutionary Army Accounts*, vol.II, Book 2, 280]. On 7 June 1792 he appointed James Carraway of Cumberland County his attorney to receive his payment for services in the Continental line in 1778 and 1779 [*NCGSJ* VIII:98]. He was head of a Hertford County household of 5 "other free" in 1790 [NC:26] and 9 in 1800.

Ezekiel Archer was taxable in Hertford County in District 5 on 3 cattle and 2 horses in 1779 [GA 30.1]. He received voucher no. 2005 for £12 in Edenton District on 16 August 1783 for military service in the Revolution [North Carolina Revolutionary Pay Vouchers, 1779-1782, http://familysearch.org/ark:/61903/1:1:Q2WT-L51X, Archers, Ezekiel]. He was head of a Hertford County household of 7 "other free" and 3 slaves in 1800.

Demcey Archer was a private who enlisted in Ely's Company of the 7th North Carolina Regiment in the Revolution for three years in November 1777 and died on 14 February 1778 [Clark, *The State Records of North Carolina*, XVI:1005]. His heir Baker Archer (son of "Free Mulatto" Thomas Archer) received 640 acres of bounty land for his service [N.C. Archives, S.S. file no. 984a, call no. S.108.385 http://archives.ncdcr.gov/doc/search-doc; also abstracted by Haun, *North Carolina Revolutionary Army Accounts*, pt. 15].

Jacob Archer received voucher nos. 1960 and 2309 for a total of £21 specie on 1 August 1783 and 26 August 1783 in Edenton District for military service in the Revolution [North Carolina Revolutionary Pay Vouchers, 1779-1782, http://familysearch.org/ark:/61903/1:1:Q2WT-5Q3K, Archers, Jacob]. He was head of a Hertford County household of 8 "other free" in 1790 [NC:26].

Jesse Archer was a private who served and died in the Revolution [DAR, *Roster of Soldiers from North Carolina in the American Revolution*, 184]. His heir Baker Archer received 640 acres of bounty land for his service [N.C. Archives, S.S. file no. 225, call no. S.108.351, http://archives.ncdcr.gov/doc/search-doc; also abstracted by Haun, *North Carolina Revolutionary Army accounts*, pt. 15].

John Archer was a "free Mulatto" taxable in the household of John Sholer, Jr., in an untitled Bertie tax list for 1765. In 1766 he was taxable in William Whealer's household, and in 1767 he was in Henry Bunch's household in Jonathan Standley's list [CR 10.702.1]. By 1779 he was in Martin County where he was taxable as a married man [GA 30.1]. He received £9 in Halifax District for military service in the Revolution [North Carolina Revolutionary Pay Vouchers, 1779-1782, http://familysearch.org/ark:/61903/1:1:Q2WT-LLZ9, John Archer].

Thomas Archer was head of an Orange County, North Carolina household of 5 "free colored" in 1820 [NC:352]. He was identified as a Revolutionary War soldier and father of Nancy, wife of Elias **Roberts**, in Elias' Chatham County free papers. The papers stated that Thomas Archie had resided in Chatham County for 23 years but was living in Orange County, North Carolina, when the papers were issued on 10 February 1823 [Orange County, Indiana DB D:432].

Zachariah Archer was taxed in Jonathan Stanley's 1766 Bertie Tax List. In 1772 he was head of a household with Sarah Archer, possibly his wife, in the list of Thomas Ward, adjacent to John Archer [CR 10.702.1. He received £9 in Halifax District in June 1783 for service in the Revolution [North Carolina Revolutionary Pay Vouchers, 1779-1782, http://familysearch.org/ark:/61903/1:1:Q2WT-LT39, Zachariah Archer]. In the 1787 State Census for Martin County he had 8 persons in his District 7 household. He was head of a Martin County household of 6 "other free" and a white woman in 1790 [NC:68], 1 "other free" and a white woman in 1800 [NC:383], and 2 "other free" in Edgecombe County in 1810 [NC:771].

Archibald Artis, born say 1753, was paid for serving in the militia in Wilmington District, North Carolina, during the Revolution [DAR, *Roster of Soldiers from North Carolina in the American Revolution*, 415]. He received voucher no. 511 in New Bern District for £9 specie on 19 August 1782 for militia duty in Anson County as per Captain Griffen's payroll http://familysearch.org/ark:/61903/1:1:Q2WT-RSCG]. He died before November 1782 when Stephen **Powell** was granted administration of his estate in Johnston County on a bond of £200. The account of sales of the estate totaled a little over £43 [Haun, *Johnston County Court Minutes*, III:232]. He was mentioned in the Revolutionary War pension application of Holiday **Haithcock** which had a testimonial by William Bryan, a justice of the peace: *..This affiant remembers that one mulatto was in his company as a common soldier whose name Archibald Artis* [NARA, R.4812, M804, roll 1263, frame 437; http://fold3.com/image/22996357].

John Artis enlisted in 1781 in Colonel Hall's Company of Abraham Shepard's 10th North Carolina Regiment. He and John Godwin were imprisoned for robbery in Halifax on 15 August 1781. He left the service on 1 November 1782. Benjamin McCulloch drew his final pay [Clark, *The State Records of North Carolina*, 17:190, 16:1007, 15:609; *N.C. Historical & Genealogical Register*, II:128]. He appeared in Cumberland County, North Carolina court to apply for a pension and claim 12 months pay as a private in the Revolution. He stated that he enlisted in May 1781 and joined Captain Clem Hall's Company of the 2nd Regiment. William **Lomack** testified on his behalf [NARA, S.41416, M804, http://fold3.com/image/10951920]. He was head of an Orange County, North Carolina household of 5 "free colored" in 1820 [NC:354].

Joseph Artis was paid for service in the militia in Wilmington District during the Revolution [DAR, *Roster of Soldiers from North Carolina in the American Revolution*, 415; North Carolina Revolutionary War Pay Vouchers, http://familysearch.org/ark:/61903/1:1:Q2WT-L5Z3], perhaps the Josiah Artis who was in a list of men raised for the Continental Line [T.R, Box 4, Folder 43, http://digital.ncdcr.gov/cdm/compoundobject/collection/p16062coll26/id/701/rec/2].

Thomas Artis served in the Revolution from North Carolina [N.C. Archives, State Treasurer Record Group, Military Papers, Revolutionary War Army Accounts, IV:35, folio 3].

William Baley was head of a Hertford County, North Carolina household of 6 "other free" and a white woman in 1790. He may have been the William Bailey who received voucher no. 3444 for £6 specie for military service in Edenton District on 29 September 1784 [North Carolina Revolutionary Pay Vouchers, 1779-1782, http://familysearch.org/ark:/61903/1:1:Q2WT-LR4T].

Council Bass enlisted as a musician for 9 months on 20 July 1778 [Clark, *The State Records of North Carolina*, XVI:1018] and was listed as a fifer in the roll of Lieutenant Colonel William L. Davidson's Company on 23 April 1779 [NARA, M246, roll 79, frame 142 of 323; http://fold3.com/image/10200387]. He was head of a Northampton County household of 7 "other free" and 2 slaves in 1790 [NC:74].

Elijah Bass enlisted in the 10th Regiment of the North Carolina Line as a substitute for Ebenezar Riggan on 10 February 1781 and was killed in the battle of Eutaw Springs on 8 September 1781. His widow married Benjamin **Richardson** with Philip **Pettiford** as bondsman [NARA, W.4061, M804, Roll 2038, frames 533, 528; http://fold3.com/image/14161295].

Hardy Bass enlisted for 12 months in Donoho's Company of the 10th North Carolina Regiment on 14 June 1781 and left the service on 14 June 1782 [Clark, *The State Records of North Carolina*, XVI:1020]. He received pay voucher no. 178 for £13 specie in Halifax in 1782 as well as no. 120 for £4 on 1 June 1781, endorsed on the back, "Hardy Bass, Volunteer, Granville County" [North Carolina Revolutionary Pay Vouchers, 1779-1782, http://familysearch.org/ark:/61903/1:1:Q2WT-L2QX, Bass, Hardy]. He was head of a Granville County household of 4 "other free" in 1800.

Reuben Bass may have been one of 7 males in Benjamin Bass, Sr.'s Granville County household in the 1786 state census. He received voucher no. 175 in Hillsboro for £9 specie on 11 June 1783 for military service in the Revolution [North Carolina Revolutionary Pay Vouchers, 1779-1782, http://familysearch.org/ark:/61903/1:1:Q2WT-5RNS, Bass, Ruben]. He was head of a Wake County household of 7 "other free" in 1800 [NC:753].

Samuel Bell was born in Surry County, Virginia, in May 1749. He was living in Sampson County, North Carolina, in February 1782 when he volunteered in Captain Coleman's Company under Major Griffith McRae and Colonel Lytle. He marched to Wilmington, to Georgetown, and to Charleston, but was never in any engagement. After the war, he lived in Sampson County until about 1807 when he moved to Robeson County where he applied for and was granted a pension on 31 August 1832 [NARA, S.6598, M804, Roll 207, frame 0489; http://fold3.com/image/11030605]. He was head of a Sampson County household of 10 "other free" in 1790, 15 in 1800 [NC:509], 5 in Robeson County in 1810 [NC:234], and 2 "free colored" in Robeson County in 1820 [NC:309].

John Benson was drafted in the Dobbs County Militia for 12 months service in the Revolution: *age 23, 5'8", Black complexion, a planter* [T.R., Box 6, folder 22, http://digital.ncdcr.gov/cdm/compoundobject/collection/p16062coll26/id/985/rec/3]. His heirs received 640 acres for his service [DAR, *Roster of Soldiers from North Carolina in the American Revolution*, 277].

Absolem Bibby was 7 years old in November 1771 when the Bute County court ordered him bound an apprentice planter to John Pinnion [WB A:227]. He enlisted in the Tenth Regiment, Dixon's Company, of the N.C. Continental Line on 18 May 1781 for one year and was discharged on 21 May 1782 [Clark *The State Records of North Carolina* XVI:1021]. He was head of a Franklin County household of 4 "other free" in 1790 [NC:58] and 1 "other free" in 1810 [NC:825].

Edmund Bibby was ordered bound to John Pinnion in Bute County in November 1771 [Minutes 1767-76, 194; WB A:218]. He was listed among the Continental soldiers from Bute County who enlisted for 9 months on 3 September 1778: *Edmon Bibby, Place of Abode Bute County, born N.C., 5'4", 20 years old, Dark Hair, Dark Eyes* [T.R., Box 4, folder 35]. His heirs received military land warrant no. 3928 for 640 acres, entered on 22 July 1795 and issued 7 March 1796 [N.C. Archives S.S. 1096, call no. S.108.385, http://archives.ncdcr.gov/doc/search-doc].

Edward Bibby was a "Malatoe Child" bound apprentice to Colonel Thomas Armstrong in Cumberland County, North Carolina, on 21 January 1758 [Minutes 1755-9, 33]. He may have been identical to Edward Bubby who enlisted in Raiford's Company in the

10th North Carolina Regiment on 2 June 1781 and completed his service on 3 June 1782 [Clark, *The State Records of North Carolina*, XVI:1020]. He was head of a Cumberland County household of 1 "other free" in 1810, called Ned Beebe [NC:565].

Solomon Bibby was 7 years old in November 1771 when the Bute County court ordered him bound an apprentice planter to Peter Goodwin [WB A:233]. He received a pension for his Revolutionary War service as a private in the Tenth Regiment, Yarborough's Company, of the North Carolina Continental Line in 1781. He was living near Sandy Creek in the part of Franklin County which was formed from Bute County when he volunteered. He was called a "free person of Color" on 18 June 1841 when he applied for a pension while living in Franklin County. He stated that he served in the 10th North Carolina Regiment and also as a waiter for General Jethro Sumner. He cared for the horses and guarded the baggage wagons during the Battles of Camden, Guilford Courthouse and Eutaw Springs [NARA, S.6644, M804, Roll 233, frame 182 of 763; http://fold3.com/image/10967901].

David Bizzell received pay voucher nos. 2028, 2342, and 2705 for £12 on 16 August 1783, £10 on 26 August 17__ and £7 on 29 December 1783 in Edenton District for military service in the Revolution [North Carolina Revolutionary Pay Vouchers, 1779-1782, http://familysearch.org/ark:/61903/1:1:Q2WT-PBK6, Byzel, David]. He was head of a Hertford County household of 3 "other free" in 1800.

Enos Bizle/ Bizzel enlisted on 10 September 1777 for three years and was in the muster of Colonel John Patton's Company of 2nd North Carolina Battalion at White Plains on 9 September 1778 [Clark, *The State Records of North Carolina*, XIII:516]. He apparently died in service since his heir David Bizzell received a military warrant of 640 acres for his service [North Carolina and Tennessee, Revolutionary War Land Warrants, 1783-1843, Roll 1, Revolutionary Warrants, 1783-1799 (Nos. 22-387), 120 (http://ancestry.com)]. David was head of a Hertford County household of 3 "other free" in 1800.

Solomon Bizzell was head of a Hertford County household of 11 "other free" in 1790 [NC:26] and 11 in 1800. He received £11 for service in the Revolution on 1 August 178__ [North Carolina Revolutionary Pay Vouchers, 1779-1782, http://familysearch.org/ark:/61903/1:1:Q2WT-531R, Bizells, Solomon].

William Bussell was head of a Robeson County household of 5 "other free" in 1790 [NC:48]. William Bizzel received voucher no. 321 for £10 specie in Wilmington District on 12 December 1781 for military service in the Revolution [North Carolina Revolutionary Pay Vouchers, 1779-1782, http://familysearch.org/ark:/61903/1:1:Q2WT-P5Q1, Bizzel, William].

Jacob Black received voucher no. 3655 for £9 specie in Hillsboro on 20 August 1783 for military service in the Revolution [North Carolina Revolutionary Pay Vouchers, 1779-1782, http://familysearch.org/ark:/61903/1:1:Q2WT-L5HQ, Black, Jacob]. He was head of an Orange County household of 3 "other free" in 1800 [NC:513].

Martin Black enlisted in New Bern for three years in Stevenson's Company of the North Carolina Continental Line on 16 May 1777. He stated that he was marched to Georgetown on the Potomac where the troops were inoculated against smallpox; he was in the Battles of Monmouth and Stony Point and was later taken prisoner at Charleston. Isaac **Perkins** testified that he enlisted on the same day as Martin and served with him [NARA, S.41441, M805, Roll 92, frame 0147; http://fold3.com/image/11042872]. He was head of a Carteret County household of 2 "other free" in 1790 [NC:128] and an Onslow County household of 4 "other free" in 1800 [NC:143].

Benjamin Blango enlisted in Hogg's Company for 9 months on 20 July 1778 and received a total of £25 specie for service in the Continental Line [Clark, *The State Records of North Carolina*, XVI:1018; North Carolina Revolutionary Pay Vouchers, 1779-1782, Benjamin Blango, http://familysearch.org/search/collection/1498361]. He was a deceased soldier of Beaufort County whose estate was administered before June 1792 by Sarah Blango [*NCGSJ* XVIII:72].

Moses Blango enlisted in Hogg's Company on 20 July 1778 and received a total of £25 specie for service in the Continental Line [Clark, *The State Records of North Carolina*, XVI:1018; North Carolina Revolutionary Pay Vouchers, 1779-1782, Moses Blango, http://familysearch.org/search/collection/1498361]. He was a deceased soldier of Beaufort County whose estate was administered before June 1792 by Sarah Blango [*NCGSJ* XVIII:72].

Solomon Blango and Tom Blango were in the list of men in the Beaufort County Regiment of Militia on 20 April 1781 [T.R., Box 7, folder 15, http://digital.ncdcr.gov/cdm/compoundobject/collection/p16062coll26/id/1107/rec/10]. He was head of a Beaufort County household of 1 "other free" in 1790 [NC:126].

Thomas Blango was paid for military service in the New Bern District Militia during the Revolution [DAR, *Roster of Soldiers from North Carolina in the American Revolution*, 404], was paid £9 for service in the Continental Army on 15 January 1782 [Clark, *Colonial Soldiers of the South*, 781; DAR, *Roster of Soldiers from North Carolina in the American Revolution*, 404; North Carolina Revolutionary Pay Vouchers, 1779-1782, http://familysearch.org/ark:/61903/1:1:Q2WT-LGR2] and was head of a Beaufort County household of 10 "other free" in 1790 [NC:125].

John Blanks was a "Mixt Blood" taxable in his own Bladen County household in 1774, a "Black" taxable in 1775, and head of a household of 2 Blacks 12-50 years old and 4 over 50 or under 12 in 1786 [Byrd, *Bladen County Tax Lists*, I:29, 124; II:36, 142, 169, 202]. He served in the Revolution from North Carolina [N.C. Archives, State Treasurer Group, Military Papers, Revolutionary War Army Accounts, Blanks, John, VIII:37, Folio 4; W-1:12; IX:93, Folio 1; V:18, Folio 3; VI:29, Folio 3; http://archives.ncdcr.gov/doc/search-doc]. He received voucher no. 823 for £9 specie in Wilmington District on 15 February 1782 for his service in the militia [North Carolina Revolutionary Pay Vouchers, 1779-1782, http://familysearch.org/ark:/61903/1:1:Q2WT-RS7Q]. He was head of Bladen County household of 8 "other free" in 1790 [NC:188].

David Boon enlisted in Ballard's Company of the 10th North Carolina Regiment for 9 months on 20 July 1778. H. Murfree received his final pay [Clark, *The State Records of North Carolina*, XVI:1019; XVII:193]. He was head of a Northampton County household of 1 "other free" in 1810 [NC:714] and 10 "free colored" in Hertford County in 1820 [NC:182].

Elisha Boon enlisted in Baker's Company in the 10th North Carolina Regiment for 9 months on 20 July 1778 [Clark, *The State Records of North Carolina*, XVI:1018]. He may have been the Elisha Boon who was head of a Northampton County household of 4 "free colored" in 1820 [NC:218]. He was about 61 when he appeared in Wake County court on 13 June 1818 to apply for a pension for his service in the Revolution, stating that he enlisted early in the war as a volunteer in Nash County under the command of Captain Isaac Horn who marched his company to Halifax where he was put under the command of Captain John Baker of the 10th Regiment for 9 months about July 1778. He moved to Lexington, Kentucky, by 7 June 1824 [NARA, S.35196, M804, roll 288, frame 14 of 842; http://fold3.com/image/14438017].

James Boon was a "Mixt. Blood" taxable in Hertford County in 1770 [Fouts, *Tax Receipt Book*, 31] and head of a Gates County household of 1 "other free" in 1790 [NC:23]. He may have been the James Boon who enlisted for 9 months in Bradley's

10th North Carolina Regiment on 20 July 1778. John Sheppard received his final pay of £23 in Halifax [Clark, *The State Records of North Carolina*, XVI:1019; XVII:193]. And he may have been the James Boon whose heirs received warrant no. 1493 of 640 acres for service in the Revolution [N.C. Archives, S.S. no. 1498, call no. S.108.357, http://archives.ncdcr.gov/doc/search-doc]. In February 1790 the Gates County court ordered his twelve-year-old orphan son Thomas Boon bound an apprentice shoemaker to Thomas Marshall. The inventory of his estate was recorded in Gates County court on 20 February 1794 [Fouts, *Minutes of County Court of Pleas and Quarter Sessions 1787-93*, 8, 14].

Lewis Boon, "bastard Mulatto of Patt Boon," was bound apprentice in Bertie County, North Carolina, in 1774. He enlisted in the Revolution for 9 months in Baker's Company on 20 July 1778 [Clark, *The State Records of North Carolina*, XVI:1018]. He was head of a Northampton County, North Carolina household of 9 "other free" in 1800 [NC:429], 5 in Halifax County in 1810 [NC:5], and 5 "free colored" in Halifax in 1820 [NC:142]. He appeared in Halifax County court to apply for a pension for his service in the Revolution, stating that he enlisted in Bertie County for 9 months in July 1778 in Captain Blount's Company. He was born in 1757 in Bertie County, moved to Northampton County and had been living in Halifax County for the previous 40 years [NARA, S.6683, M804, Roll 288, frame 247 of 842; http://fold3.com/image/14438482].

Willis Boon enlisted in William's Company of the 5th North Carolina Regiment for 2-1/2 years in 1777 and was omitted in February 1778 [Clark, *The State Records of North Carolina*, XVI:1013]. He was about 70 when he appeared in Chowan County court on 11 October 1820 to apply for a pension for his services in the Revolution, stating that he enlisted for 2-1/2 years in Captain John Pugh William's Company and served until the Battle of Germantown when he was transferred to Polk's Regiment and served until the end of the war. He had no one in his family but his elderly wife. His application included a certificate from Colonel Nicholas Long [NARA, S.41455, M804, roll 288, frame 409 of 842; http://fold3.com/image/14438694]. He was head of a Chowan County household of 2 "free colored" in 1820 (man and a woman over 45) [NC:118].

Saul Bowers, "of Craven County," received pay voucher no. 11 on 1 August 1782 for £35 specie for military service in the Revolution from Craven County [North Carolina Revolutionary Pay Vouchers, 1779-1782, http://familysearch.org/ark:/61903/1:1:Q2WT-PY4B]. He was head of a Craven County household of 3 "other free" in 1790 [NC:131].

James Bowser was drafted from the Third Division of the Hertford County Militia between 1779 and 1780. Others in this list included Caleb **Archer**, Mark **Manley**, Moses **Manley**, Junr., Carter **Nickens**, Gabriel **Manley**, and Henry **Chavers** [T.R., Box 5, folder 20].

Randal Bowser/ Bowers was listed in the payroll of Captain William Caldwell's Company of the 3rd South Carolina Regiment commanded by Colonel William Thompson in July and August 1779 [NARA, M246, roll 89, frame 171; http://fold3.com/image/9679437]. He was head of a Hertford County household of 6 "other free" in Moore's District in 1800 [NC:133].

Moses Branch, born before 1776, was head of a Robeson County household of 1 "other free" in 1800 [NC:363] and 1 "free colored" in 1820 [NC:297]. He received £2 specie in Wilmington District on 14 November 1781 for his service in the militia [North Carolina Revolutionary Pay Vouchers, 1779-1782, http://familysearch.org/ark:/61903/1:1:Q2WT-GM2Z, Branch, Moses].

David Braveboy was a taxable "Mulato" in Bladen County in 1769, taxable with his wife in 1772, a "Mixt Blood" taxable on himself, his wife and daughter in 1774, a "Molato" taxable in 1776, and taxable on 1 poll and 250 acres in 1784 [Byrd, *Bladen County Tax Lists*, I:16, 43, 71, 80, 93, 123, 134; II:67, 74; Bladen County Tax List (1763, 1784)]. He received voucher no. 1183 for £9 in Wilmington District on 27 September 1782 for military service in the Revolution [North Carolina Revolutionary Pay Vouchers, 1779-1782, http://familysearch.org/ark:/61903/1:1:Q2WT-5FDB, Braveboy, David]. In his 20 October 1787 Robeson County will be named his wife Lydia and children [WB 1:10]. Lydia was head of a Robeson County household of 7 "other free" in 1790 [NC:48].

Jacob Braveboy, a "bastard Mulattoe, was about 15 when the May 1774 Bertie County court bound him out as an apprentice bricklayer [Haun, Bertie County Court Minutes, IV:74]. He enlisted for 2-1/2 years as a private in Williams' Company of the 2nd North Carolina Battalion on 9 May 1776 and was discharged on 10 November 1778 [Clark, *The State Records of North Carolina*, XVI:1013]. He was listed in Benjamin Williams's Company of the 2nd North Carolina Battalion commanded by Colonel John Patten for January 1778, and was listed in Hardy Murfree's Company of the 2nd North Carolina Battalion on 9 September 1778 at White Plains, in the same list as William **Sweat** [NARA, M246, roll 79, frames 115, 122 of 323; http://fold3.com/image/10200094]. He was head of a Martin County household of 10 "other free" in 1800 [NC:387].

John Braveboy was a "Black" tithable in Tyrrell County in 1755 [T.O. 105, box 1], head of a Beaufort County household of 1 "other free" and 6 slaves in 1790 [NC:127], 1 "other free" in 1800 [NC:4], and 1 in 1810 [NC:116]. He was called John Brayboy when he volunteered for three years as a soldier in Carteret County in September 1778 [T.R., Box 4, folder 36, http://digital.ncdcr.gov/cdm/compoundobject/collection/p16062coll26/id/651/rec/162]. He enlisted on 27 August 1778 for 3 years in Captain Ballard's Company in the North Carolina Continental Line but was listed as a deserter a little over a year later on 29 October 1779 [Clark, *The State Records of North Carolina*, XVI:1020].

John Braveboy was a "free Mulatto" tithable in Abraham Sullivent's household in the 1770 Bertie tax list of David Standley, and he was taxable with his mother in Standley's 1771 list [CR 10.702.1, box 2]. In 1774 he was a "Negro" head of his own household in David Standley's list. In 1779 he was taxable on an assessment of £243 in District 6, Martin County [GA 30.1]. In 1790 he was head of a Martin County household of 7 "other free" and a white woman: John Braveboy & mother [NC:68]. He sold his pay for military service in the Revolution to Thomas Hunter, commissioner for Martin County on 1 September 1782 [North Carolina Revolutionary Pay Vouchers, 1779-1782, http://familysearch.org/ark:/61903/1:1:Q2WT-56S4, Braveboy, John].

Samuel Braveboy received voucher no. 1734 for £9 specie on 3 March 1784 in Salisbury, Rowan County, North Carolina, for military service in the Revolution [North Carolina Revolutionary Pay Vouchers, 1779-1782, http://familysearch.org/ark:/61903/1:1:Q2WT-5997, Brayboy, Samuel]. He was head of a Cheraw District household of 1 "other free" male over the age of 16, 1 male "other free" under 16, and 1 female "other free" in 1790 [SC:380].

Benjamin Brewington enlisted in Quinn's Company of the 10th North Carolina Regiment for nine months on 20 July 1778. He received £23 pay for service in the Revolution [Clark, *The State Records of North Carolina*, XVII:193, 1018]. His rights to military land warrant no. 1515 of 640 acres were assigned to Alexander Ewing on 17 January 1789 [N.C. Archives S.S. file 893, call no. S.108.354, http://archives.ncdcr.gov/doc/search-doc].

Joshua Brewington was head of a New Hanover County household of 5 "other free" in 1800 [NC:311] and 5 "free colored" in 1820 [NC:225]. He was 77 years old on 19 September 1836 when he appeared in New Hanover County court to make a declaration to obtain a pension for his services in the Revolution. He stated that he was born in 1759 or 1760 in the part of Duplin County that became Sampson County, served in a company of 9 months raised in Duplin County in February or March 1779, was in the Battle of Stono Ferry, lived 10 to 12 years in Sampson County after the war and then moved to New Hanover County. There was a record of his enlistment but no record of service. He was a "person of Colour" who died on 22 November 1836 [NARA, S.8091, M804, Roll 332, frame 14 of 905; http://fold3.com/image/10990898].

Lewis Brewington received voucher no. 1839 on 16 March 1782 for £20 specie and no. 5559 for £20 on 5 February 1784 in Wilmington District for military service in the Revolution [North Carolina Revolutionary Pay Vouchers, 1779-1782, http://familysearch.org/ark:/61903/1:1:Q2WT-G3S9, Bruenton, Lewis; Brewinton, Lusis]. He was head of a New Hanover County household of 4 "other free" in 1800 [NC:311].

John Brooks was a Revolutionary War pensioner in North Carolina [Clark, *The State Records of North Carolina*, XXII:571] and head of a Robeson County household of 5 "other free" in 1800 [NC:367] and 7 in 1810 [NC:147]. He claimed to be 95 or 96 years old on 30 May 1853 when he applied for a pension for service in the Revolution and was still living in Robeson County on 22 March 1858 when he applied for (and received) bounty land. He stated that he served four years and was in the Battle of Camden. In May 1853 Nancy **Locklier** (nearly 100 years of age) had known him for about 85 years. Mrs. Rachel **Locklier** (about 90 years old) stated that she had known him for the previous 85 years. Mrs. Rhody **Locklier** (nearly 100 years of age) had known him for the last 90 years [NARA, S.6732, M804, Roll 353, frame 421 of 889; http://fold3.com/image/13939742].

William Brown appeared in Hertford County court in May 1833 to apply for a pension for his service in the Revolution. He stated that he was drafted for 9 months in January 1779 in the Hertford County Militia under Captain Harris, marched to Kinston, then marched to South Carolina under Captain Roundtree. He was later employed in destroying batteaus and boats to prevent Cornwallis and his men from crossing the Chowan River on his way northward. Major Isaac Carter testified that he had seen William serving in the militia [NARA, R.1349, M804, Roll 381, frame 156 of 830]; http://fold3.com/image/11035184]. William was listed as a draft from Hertford County on 5 November 1778 [T. R., Box 4, Folder 41, http://digital.ncdcr.gov/cdm/compoundobject/collection/p16062coll26/id/696/rec/42]. He was head of a Hertford County household of 8 "free colored" in 1830 [NC:188].

Kedar Bryan(t) enlisted for 12 months in Captain Hall's 10th North Carolina Regiment on 1 February 1782 and received voucher no. 332 for military service in the Revolution [Clark, *The State Records of North Carolina*, XVI:1022; North Carolina Revolutionary Pay Vouchers, 1779-1782, http://familysearch.org/ark:/61903/1:1:Q2WT-G7QL, Bryan, Kedar]. He was head of a Fayetteville household of 4 "other free" in 1790 (Kedar Bryant) [NC:42], 4 in New Hanover County in 1800 (Cato Bryan) [NC:311], and 7 "free colored" in Fayetteville in 1820 (Cader Briant) [NC:189].

Clement Bunch enlisted in Lytle's Company of the 10th North Carolina Regiment in 1782 for 18 months [Clark, *The State Records of North Carolina*, XVI:1023]. The Bunch family of North Carolina descended from an African slave and a white woman in colonial Virginia [http://familytreedna.com/groups/coremelungeon/dna-results].

David Burnett enlisted in Blount's Company of the 5th North Carolina Regiment on 2 April 1776 for the war and was omitted in February 1778 (likely deceased) [Clark, *The State Records of North Carolina*, 1013; Crow, *Black Experience in Revolutionary North Carolina*, 98; *A History of African Americans in North Carolina*, 36-7]. He died without heirs, and his 640 acre military land warrant was assigned to the University of North Carolina [North Carolina and Tennessee, Revolutionary War Land Warrants, 1783-1843, Roll 14: William Hill Warrants, 1811-1837 (Nos. 676-1131), frames 142-3 of 540, http://ancestry.com].

Sawney/ Sanders Burnett was head of a Johnston County household of 12 "other free" in 1790 [NC:140], 11 "other free" in Orange County, North Carolina, in 1800 [NC:544] and 10 in 1810 [NC:956]. On 8 August 1783 he was called Saunders Burnet of Johnston County when he received voucher no. 1189 for £9 specie for military service in the militia during the Revolution [North Carolina Revolutionary Pay Vouchers, 1779-1782, http://familysearch.org/ark:/61903/1:1:Q2WT-PN7S, Burnet, Saunders].

William Burnett was head of a Dobbs County household of 5 "other free" in 1790 [NC:137]. He was drafted in the Dobbs County Militia for 12 months service in the Revolution in February 1781: *age 23, 5'4", Black complexion, a planter* [T.R., Box 6, folder 22, http://digital.ncdcr.gov/cdm/compoundobject/collection/p16062coll26/id/985/rec/3]. He may have been the William Barnett of Wayne County who received voucher no. 2046 for £4 specie on 12 December 1783 for militia duty during the Revolution [North Carolina Revolutionary Pay Vouchers, 1779-1782, http://familysearch.org/ark:/61903/1:1:Q2WT-5YDH, Barnett, William]. He was a "Mulatto" who enlisted with the 10th Regiment in 1780 and was said to have died without heirs [Crow, *Black Experience in Revolutionary North Carolina*, 98].

John Butler was a taxable "Mollato" in William Butler's household in the 1774 Bertie County list of Humphrey Nichols [CR 10.702.1, box 1]. He was living in Bertie County on 17 November 1820 when he applied for a pension for his services in the Revolution, stating that he enlisted in May 1776 at Windsor, Bertie County, in the North Carolina Line [NARA, S.41463, M804, Roll 437, frame 391; http://fold3.com/image/12035260]. He was head of a white Bertie County household in 1820.

Moses Byrd enlisted as a musician in Lewis's Company of the North Carolina Continental Line in Halifax County, North Carolina, in 1776 and was omitted in January 1778. He mustered again in Taylor's Company for 2-1/2 years in January 1779. H. Montfort received his final pay [Clark, *The State Records of North Carolina*, XVI:1012, 1024, XVII: 192]. He was a "Mulatto" taxable in Southampton County in 1802 [PPTL 1792-1806, frames 156, 183, 261, 373, 509, 615].

Nathan Byrd received voucher no. 6817 in Halifax District on 4 June 1782 for £3 specie for service in the Revolution [North Carolina Revolutionary Pay Vouchers, 1779-1782, http://familysearch.org/ark:/61903/1:1:Q2WT-53RJ, Byrd, Nathan]. He was head of a Northampton County household of 8 "other free" in 1790 [NC:76].

Philip Byrd was listed among the "Black" members of the undated colonial muster roll of Captain James Fason's Company [T.R., box 1, folder 3]. He was in the 15 March 1780 return of troops for Northampton County [T.R., box 6, folder 11] and received voucher no. 5908 for £9 on 13 February 1782 in Halifax District for his military service in the Revolution. He assigned his right to the payment to Micajah **Walden** [North Carolina Revolutionary Pay Vouchers, 1779-1782, http://familysearch.org/ark:/61903/1:1:Q2WT-LLGH]. He was head of a Northampton County household of 5 "other free" in 1790 [NC:76].

Solomon Byrd was called Solomon Burd of Northampton County in August 1783 when he received voucher no. 9033 for his service in the Revolution [North Carolina Revolutionary Pay Vouchers, 1779-1782, http://familysearch.org/ark:/61903/1:1:Q2WT-P5HL]. He was head of a Northampton County household of 5 Black males, 4 white females and a white male in Captain Winborne's District for the 1786 state census.

William Carroll received voucher no. 306 for £19 specie in New Bern, Craven County, on 1 August 1783 for military service in the Revolution [North Carolina Revolutionary Pay Vouchers, 1779-1782, http://familysearch.org/ark:/61903/1:1:Q2WT-RSDX, Carroll, William]. He was head of a Beaufort County household of 4 "other free" in 1790.

Emanuel Carter received voucher no. 126 for £12 specie by the auditors for the counties of Washington and Sullivan on 20 June 1782 for service in the Revolution [North Carolina Revolutionary Pay Vouchers, 1779-1782, http://familysearch.org/ark:/61903/1:1:Q2WT-L2YW]. He was listed in the North Carolina Revolutionary War Army Accounts [N.C. Archives, State Treasurer Group, Military Papers, Revolutionary Army Accounts, I:81, folio 2]. He was head of a Robeson County household of 5 "other free" in 1790 [NC:50].

George Carters received voucher no. 1178 for £21 specie in Edenton on 4 November 1782 for military service in the Revolution [North Carolina Revolutionary Pay Vouchers, 1779-1782, http://familysearch.org/ark:/61903/1:1:Q2WT-LGQF]. He was head of a Carteret County household of 10 "other free" in 1790 [NC:129].

Isaac Carter enlisted for 3 years and was in the muster of Captain Clement Hall's Company in the 2nd North Carolina Battalion commanded by Colonel John Patten at White Plains on 9 September 1778 with Isaac **Perkins**, Martin **Black**, Cader/ Cato **Copeland** and Sesar **Santee** [NARA, M246, roll 79, frame 106 of 323; http://fold3.com/image/10199799]. He was head of a Craven County household of 5 "other free" in 1790 [NC:131].

John Carter enlisted in Captain Quinn's 10th Regiment commanded by Colonel Davidson for 9 months on 20 July 1778. He was engaged in skirmishes near West Point and Kings Ferry. He made a declaration in September term 1820 Craven County court to obtain a pension. He died before 30 July 1821 [NARA, R.1749, M805, Roll 166, frame 497; http://fold3.com/image/15571476]. He was identical to John Caster who enlisted in Quinn's Company on 20 July 1778 [Clark, *The State Records of North Carolina*, XVI:1034]. He may have been one of two John Carters who were heads of "other free" Carteret County households in 1790 [NC:128, 129].

John Edward Carter was a "man of color" living in Duplin County during the Revolution when a company of troops hired him to serve for a year. He went to Charleston, was taken prisoner by the British and never heard from again [NARA, R.10316, M804, Roll 2247, frame 1009 of 1172; http://fold3.com/image/17127338].

Joshua Carter was head of a Craven County household of 4 "other free" in 1790 [NC:130]. He received £4 pay for 40 days service in the Craven County Militia under Major John Tillman in an expedition to Wilmington [Haun, *Revolutionary Army Accounts, Journal A, 141*].

Mark Carter was a "Molato" taxable in the Bladen County household of (his father?) James Carter in 1776, head of a Bladen County household of 1 white male from 21 to 60 and 2 white females in 1786 [Byrd, *Bladen County Tax Lists*, I:5, 34, 81, 94, 103, 134; II:68, 76, 182-4]. He received voucher nos. 657 and 4408 for a total of £30 specie in Wilmington District on 6 February 1782 and 27 August 1783 based on the payroll for the militia [North Carolina Revolutionary Pay Vouchers, 1779-1782, http://familysearch.org, Carter, Mark]. He was taxable on 200 acres in Bladen County in Captain Regan's District in 1784 and head of a Robeson County household of 4 "other free" in 1800.

Moses Carter was about three years old on 18 April 1758 when the Cumberland County court ordered him bound to James Wright [Minutes 1755-59, 32]. He was a "man of color" who enlisted as a private in Captain Joseph Rhodes's 1st North Carolina Regiment on 19 July 1782 until 1 July 1783. He made a declaration to obtain a pension in Sampson County on 25 October 1820 [NARA, S.41470, M805, Roll 167, frame 0077; http://fold3.com/image/12701515]. He was head of a Sampson County household of 9 "other free" in 1790 [NC:52] and 6 "free colored" in 1820 [NC:278].

Solomon Carter received voucher nos. 245 and 2274 on 18 December 1781 and 22 March 1782 for £1.10 in Wilmington District for service in the militia [North Carolina Revolutionary Pay Vouchers, 1779-1782, http://familysearch.org/ark:/61903/1:1:Q2WT-L27R, Carter, Solomon]. He was counted as white in the 1790 Duplin County census: head of a household of 2 males, 1 female, and 3 slaves [NC:190] and counted as "other free" in Duplin County in 1800: head of a household of 4 "other free" and 3 slaves.

Jonathan Case was on the payroll of Captain Alexander Whitehall's Company of North Carolina Militia commanded by Colonel Samuel Jarvis on 2 June 1780 [Clark, *The State Records of North Carolina* XVII:1054]. He enlisted in Bailey's Company of the 10th North Carolina Regiment on 17 May 1781 and left the service on 17 May 1782. Isles Simmons received his final pay of £32 [Clark, *The State Records of North Carolina* XVI:1036; XVII:202]. He was living in Currituck County on 2 June 1791 when he applied for a pension for 18 months service as a Continental soldier [*NCGSJ* VIII:213]. He was head of a Currituck County household of 4 "other free" in 1790 [NC:21] and 10 in 1800 [NC:138].

Joseph Case was head of a Currituck County household of 6 "other free" in 1800 [NC:138]. He made a declaration in Currituck County court on 10 May 1820 to obtain a pension for his services in the Revolutionary War. He stated that he was at the Battle of Stono and Siege of Charleston and was made a waiter to Colonel Bradley [NARA, S.41472, M805, Roll 168; M804, Roll 492, frame 159 of 783; http://fold3.com/image/12751875].

Bartholomew Chavers received pay of $70 as a private in the Continental Line in the Revolution from 1 August 1782 to 15 November 1783 which was approved by Captain Bradley and Lieutenant Colonel Thomas Hogg [NARA, U.S. Revolutionary War Miscellaneous Records (Manuscript File), 1775-1790s, Records Pertaining to Troops of particular States, 14395-6, frames 7-11 of 397; http://ancestry.com]. He was head of a Northampton County, North Carolina household of 6 "other free" and 2 slaves in 1800.

Caesar Chavis was in Captain William Ashburn's Militia in Bertie County on 8 April 1780 [T.R., Box 7, folder 8, http://digital.ncdcr.gov/cdm/compoundobject/collection/p16062coll26/id/1086/rec/1]. He enlisted in Carter's Company of the 10th Regiment of the North Carolina Line on 19 May 1782. H. Murfree received his final pay of £23 [Clark, *The State Records of North Carolina*, XVI:1037; XVII:99]. He was head of a Bertie County household of 7 "other free" in 1790 (Cezar Chevat) [NC:12]. He was the grandchild of "Free Caesar" **Cook** of Bertie County.

Drury Chavers enlisted as a soldier in Bailey's Company of the 10th Regiment of the North Carolina Line in Edenton on 25 May 1781 and left the service on 25 May 1782. Thomas Person received his final pay of £20 [Clark, *The State Records of North Carolina*, XVI:1035; XVII:199]. Drewry Chavis was a substitute from Granville County [North Carolina Revolutionary Pay Vouchers, 1779-1782, http://familysearch.org/pal:/MM9.3.1/TH-1951-32743-9856-78?cc=1948361].

Henry Chavis was in a list of militia men drafted from Hertford County in the Third Division commanded by Major George Little between 1778 and 1780 [T.R. Box 5, folder 20]. He was taxable on 170 acres and 1 poll in Hertford County in Nathan Harrel's list for 1784 [GA 64.1]. He was a soldier who served in the Revolution from November 1778 to August 1779. His widow Peggy made a deposition in Hertford County on 14 July 1792 to obtain his pay. William **Manly** attested to her statement [*NCGSJ* VIII:214]. Voucher no. 404 was issued for "Henry Chavers, late a soldier in the Continental Line," for £20 on 1 May 1792 [North Carolina Revolutionary Pay Vouchers, 1779-1782, http://familysearch.org/ark:/61903/1:1:Q2WT-R7J4, Chavers, Henry].

Ishmael Chavis was paid for service in the Wilmington District Militia during the Revolution [DAR, *Roster of Soldiers from North Carolina in the American Revolution*, 325].

Richard Chavers was head of a Richmond County household of 5 "other free" in 1790 [NC:46] and as "Bud" Chavers, a taxable "Molato" in Archibald McKissak's Bladen County household in 1776 [Byrd, *Bladen County Tax Lists*, II:68], head of an Anson County household of 8 "other free" in 1800 [NC:224]. He was listed in the North Carolina Revolutionary War Army Accounts [N.C. Archives, State Treasurer Group, Military Papers, Revolutionary Army Accounts, IX:122, folio 3; http://archives.ncdcr.gov/doc/search-doc].

Shadrack Chavis received voucher no. 866 on 15 February 1782 in the District of Wilmington for £7 for his service in the militia [North Carolina Revolutionary Pay Vouchers, 1779-1782, http://familysearch.org/ark:/61903/1:1:Q2WT-L2PR, Schavons, Shadrick]. He was head of a Bladen County household of 6 "other free" in 1810 (called Shadrack Shavers) and called Shadrack Chavus when he was head of a Columbus County, North Carolina household of 2 "free colored" (55-100) in 1830.

Sherwood Chavis, son of Beck Chavis, was bound as an apprentice by the churchwardens in Amelia County on 24 March 1763 [Orders 1763, 30]. He, Isaac **Malone**, alias **Rouse**, and Joseph and Elijah **Locklear** were in the Salisbury, Rowan County, North Carolina jail on suspicion of robbery on 2 April 1779. They were released when no evidence appeared against them, and they were willing to enlist in the Revolution [Clark, *The State Records of North Carolina*, XIV:287].

Solomon Chavis was head of a Halifax County household of 2 "other free" in 1810 [NC:13]. Jer. Nelms received his final pay of £28 for service in the North Carolina Continental Line [Clark, *The State Records of North Carolina*, XVII:198].

William Chavis died while serving from North Carolina in the Revolutionary War. His unnamed heirs received a warrant for 640 acres which they assigned to William Phillips before 6 December 1797 [North Carolina and Tennessee, Revolutionary War Land Warrants, 1783-1843, Survey Orders (Nos. 1-3992), no. 5058. (http://ancestry.com)].

William Chavers enlisted for 12 months in Brevard's Company of the 3rd North Carolina Regiment in 1781 and left the service on 12 April 1782 [Clark, *The State Records of North Carolina*, XVI:1036]. He was head of a Wake County household of 6 "other free" in 1800.

Robert Cook enlisted in Blount's 10th North Carolina Regiment for 9 months on 20 July 1778 [Clark, *The State Records of North Carolina*, XVI:1034]. He was a "free negro" taxable in the undated Bertie County tax list of Humphrey Hardy, about 1772, with his wife Penny and Elizabeth James: 2 Molattos and 1 Black tithe [CR 10.702.1, Box 13]. He died before 15 February 1780 when administration on his estate was granted to (his father) Caesar Cook. No inventory was recorded, apparently because his father died soon after. On 9 August 1792 Humphrey Hardy was granted administration on the estate on £500 surety, but Hardy reported that no goods or chattels had come into his hands other than a certificate from the army accounts at Hillsborough for the wages that were due the deceased in the amount of $94.69 [North Carolina Estate Files, 1663-1979, Bertie County, Cone, Thomas-Davidson, James, frames 201-3, 228-231 of 1881; http://familysearch.org/search/collection/1911121].

Francis Coley/ Cooley, born in Charles City County, Virginia, enlisted there in the militia in 1777, and moved to Halifax County, North Carolina, in 1779. He volunteered for six months in Halifax County and then settled in Brunswick County, Virginia, as an overseer for one Othen Myrick. He moved to Smith County, Tennessee, from where he petitioned for a pension on 28 November 1833 [NARA, S.3197, M804, Roll 609, frame 465 of 618; http://fold3.com/image/12745128]. He was listed in the state census for North Carolina in the 6th District in 1786. He was probably related to George, Charles, Thomas and George Coley, Jr., who were "Mulattos" convicted by the Charles City County court in 1758 for not listing their wives as tithables [Orders 1758-62, 56, 78].

James Coley, born in Charles City County, served in the Revolution in Virginia and then enlisted in Halifax County, North Carolina. He lived in Montgomery County, Tennessee, about 12 years and then moved to Humphreys County, Tennessee, where he appeared in court to apply for a pension on 18 September 1833 [NARA, S.3188, M804, Roll 643, frame 218 of 651; http://fold3.com/image/13181016]. He was head of a Halifax County, North Carolina household of 7 whites in 1790 [NC:62].

Jeffrey Cooley enlisted in Montfort's Company of the 10th North Carolina Regiment on 20 July 1778, deserted the next day and then mustered in the 5th Regiment in January 1779 [Clark, *The State Records of North Carolina*, XVI:1034]. Jeffrey Coley was head of a Halifax County, North Carolina household of 5 whites in 1790 [NC:62]. Robin 18 months was head of a Halifax County, North Carolina household of 6 "free colored" in 1830. He was called Robin Coley when he appeared in Halifax County court on 17 February 1844 and testified that his sister Sally Coley, widow of Jeffrey Coley a Revolutionary War pensioner, died in Halifax County on 26 December 1843 and he was her heir [NARA, W.4160, M804, Roll 609, frame 494 of 618; http://fold3.com/image/12743960].

James Conner received voucher no. 2153 on 22 March 1782 in Wilmington, New Hanover County, for £1 specie for service in the militia [North Carolina Revolutionary Pay Vouchers, 1779-1782, http://familysearch.org/ark:/61903/1:1:Q2WT-G9KD, Conner, James]. He was head of a New Hanover County household of 5 "other free" in 1800 [NC:311].

Docias Conner received voucher nos. 2749 and 2823 for £10 specie on 30 March 1782 from Wilmington District for service in the militia [North Carolina Revolutionary Pay Vouchers, 1779-1782, http://familysearch.org/ark:/61903/1:1:Q2WT-5RNP, Conner, Docias].

Cato Copeland was head of a Craven County household of 1 "other free" in 1790 [NC:134] and 2 in Halifax County in 1810 [NC:12]. While a resident of Halifax County he applied for and was granted a pension for three years service in the 2nd North Carolina Regiment. He stated in his application that he was in the Battles of Monmouth and Stony Point and was taken prisoner at Charleston [NARA, W.17665, M804, Roll 650, frame 294 of 579; http://fold3.com/image/15200960].

Byrd Cornet enlisted in the 10th Regiment of the North Carolina Continental Line for 9 months on 20 July 1778 [Clark, *The State Records of North Carolina*, XVI:1034]. He was listed in the roll of Lieutenant William Davidson's North Carolina Company on 23 April 1779 [NARA M246, Roll 79, frame 142 of 323; http://fold3.com/image/10200387]. H. Montfort received his final pay of £27 [Clark, *The State Records of North Carolina*, XVII:198]. He was head of a Northampton County household of 8 "other free" and 3 slaves in 1790 [NC:75] and 7 "other free" in Chatham County in 1800, called "Hew Bird Cornet" [NC:196].

Jack Cotance was a "Mullatto" who brought an unsuccessful suit for his freedom from Simon Whitehurst in Princess Anne County, Virginia court on 21 July 1747 [Minutes 1744-53, 98, 105]. He was probably the John Cotanch who was listed in Child's Company of soldiers in the North Carolina Continental Line on 20 July 1778, listed as dead in Lytle's Company in 1782 [Clark, *The State Records of North Carolina*, XVI: 1035].

Cannon Cumbo received voucher no. 2592 on 12 September 1783 in Wilmington District on his claim for £3 for services to the Revolution [North Carolina Revolutionary Pay Vouchers, 1779-1782, http://familysearch.org/ark:/61903/1:1:Q2WT-GMR4, Cumbo, Cannon]. He was head of a Robeson County household of 11 "other free" in 1790.

Gibson Cumbo received pay for serving in the Bladen County militia in 1785 [Haun, *North Carolina Revolutionary Army Accounts, Journal A*, I:9, VII: 931]. Gibby was head of a Robeson County household of 1 "other free" in 1790 [NC:50], 5 in 1800 [NC:372], and 6 in 1810 [NC:231].

Peter Cumbo received voucher no. 6772 for £10 from the Hillsboro Auditor's office on 4 August 1784 for services to the Revolution [North Carolina Revolutionary Pay Vouchers, 1779-1782, http://familysearch.org/ark:/61903/1:1:Q2WT-GWJG, Cumbo, Peter].

Richard Davis was head of a Brunswick County, North Carolina household of 8 "other free" in 1800 [NC:13] and 5 "other free" in 1810 [NC:236]. On 14 December 1791 he and his mother Grace Davis petitioned the North Carolina General Assembly that her children, born after her emancipation, be officially emancipated. Richard had served as an artilleryman in the Revolution [N.C. Archives, GASR Dec. 1791-Jan. 1792, Box 3, cited by Schweninger, Race, Slavery, and Free Blacks, Series 1, 63; petition no. 11279109].

John Day enlisted in Armstrong's Company of the 2nd North Carolina Regiment in 1777 and died at Valley Forge on 14 January 1778 [NARA, M246, Roll 79, frame 97 of 323; http://fold3.com/image/10199665; Clark, *The State Records of North Carolina*, XVI:1040]. His unnamed heirs were issued a warrant for 640 acres on 11 January 1822, assigned to Tignal Jones [North Carolina and Tennessee, Revolutionary War Land Warrants, 1783-1843, Roll 14: William Hill Warrants, 1811-1837 (Nos. 676-1131), 1064 (http://ancestry.com)]. His brother Jesse Day called himself a "man of Colour," when he made a 22 February 1822 power of attorney to Tignal Jones to receive the lands for him. Jesse Day's sons Reuben, James and Henderson Day sued Tignal and Westwood Jones for stealing the warrant and were awarded $650 and court costs [North Carolina, Wills and Probate Records, 1665-1998; Day, Jesse, 1838]. Jesse Day was head of a Granville county household of 10 "other free" in 1800, and his heirs were "Mulatto" heads of Granville County and Orange County households in 1850.

Allen Demery was a taxable "Black Male" in Matthew Moore's Bladen County household in 1770 [Byrd, *Bladen County Tax Lists*, I:50; II:174] and head of an Anson County household of 7 "other free" in 1790 [NC:35] and 5 in 1800 [NC:203]. He enlisted in Brevard's Company of the 10th North Carolina Regiment on 25 May 1781

95

and left the service on 25 May 1782 [Clark, Colonial and State Records, 16:1047].

John Demery was one of the "Black" members of the undated colonial muster of Captain James Fason's Northampton County militia [T.R., box 1, folder 3]. He sold his Northampton County land on 15 February 1778 [DB 6:227]. He received military land warrant no. 3901 of 640 acres for his service in the Revolution. He was called John Dimery of Liberty County, South Carolina, late of North Carolina and County Bladen, on 8 October 1795 when he made over his rights to the land warrant to Benjamin Fitzrandolph [North Carolina and Tennessee, Revolutionary War Land Warrants, 1783-1843, Roll 06: Revolutionary Warrants, frame 288 of 597 http://ancestry.com]. He was head of a Bladen County household of 9 "other free" in 1790 [NC:188].

___emiah (Jeremiah?) Dempsey received voucher no. 1646 for £9 on 20 May 1783 in Edenton District for military service in the Revolution [North Carolina Revolutionary Pay Vouchers, 1779-1782, http://familysearch.org/ark:/61903/1:1:Q2WT-5T8Y, Dempseys, *Miah].

Johnson Dempsey received voucher no. 2428 on 26 August 1783 for £7 specie pay in Edenton District for military service in the Revolution [North Carolina Revolutionary Pay Vouchers, 1779-1782, http://familysearch.org/ark:/61903/1:1:Q2WT-5MF1, Dempseys, Johnson]. He was head of a Bertie County household of 7 in 1800 [NC:40], 5 in Halifax County, North Carolina, in 1810 [NC:16], and 8 "free colored" in Halifax County in 1830.

Squire Demsey, the six-year-old son of Amy Demsey a "Free Mullattoe," was bound to Margaret Dukinfield to learn husbandry in Bertie County on 27 January 1756 [CR 010.101.7 by NCGSJ XIII:168, 169, 170]. He enlisted in Williams' Company in the 5th North Carolina Regiment in 1777 and died on 17 May 1778 [Clark, The State Records of North Carolina, XVI:1042].

William Dempsey enlisted as a private in Baker's Regiment for 9 months on 20 July 1778 and deserted on 30 August 1778 [Clark, The State Records of North Carolina, XVI:1046]. He received voucher no. 2228 for £11 specie in Edenton District on 26 August 1783 for military service in the Revolution [North Carolina Revolutionary Pay Vouchers, 1779-1782, http://familysearch.org/ark:/61903/1:1:Q2WT-GSLD, Demseys, William]. He was head of a Bertie County household of 8 "other free" in 1800 [NC:41] and 11 "free colored" in 1820 [NC:68].

David Dennum/ Denham was head of a Claiborne County, Tennessee household of 9 "free colored" in 1830. He was about 80 years old on 1 December 1834 when he appeared in Hawkins County, Tennessee court to apply for a pension for services in the Revolution. He stated that he was born in Louisa County, Virginia, enlisted in Guilford County, North Carolina, and was marched to the frontier of North Carolina where he was in a battle with the Indians [NARA, W.27540, M804, Roll 794, frame 255 of 626; http://fold3.com/image/20148333].

Harden Dennum/ Denham was head of a Harrison County, Indiana household of 10 "free colored" in 1830. He was about 73 when he appeared in Jackson County, Tennessee court on 11 November 1833 to apply for a pension for his service in the Revolution. He entered the service in Guilford and Washington counties, North Carolina, for several terms of 2-6 months and served as a substitute for his brother David Denham. He stated that he was born in Hanover County, Virginia, and was living in North Carolina when he entered the service [NARA, S.30985, M804, Roll 794, frame 324 of 626; http://fold3.com/image/20148444].

James Doyal/ Dial, born say 1740, purchased 100 acres near Ash Pole Swamp in Bladen County, North Carolina, on 19 July 1765 and sold this land on 20 February 1767 [DB 23:162]. He was taxable in Bladen County with his wife and Arthur Evans ("Mulatoes") in 1768 and taxable with his wife from 1769 to 1772 [Byrd, *Bladen County Tax Lists*, I:6, 15, 44, 61, 95]. He served in the Revolution and was living in Robeson County on 7 March 1786 when he assigned his right to military land warrant no. 756 in Davidson County, Tennessee, to James Robertson [N.C. Archives, S.S. Military Papers, Revolutionary War Army Accounts, Dyal, James, 19:82, 28:30; S.S., Land Office: Land Warrants, Tennessee, Davidson County, Dial, James, file no. 223, call no. S.108.351, http://archives.ncdcr.gov/doc/search-doc].

Nelson Donathan was sued jointly with William Donathan in Halifax County, Virginia court on 17 December 1773 for a debt of £2.12 [Pleas 1772-4, 322]. He received voucher nos. 1398 and 5049 in Salisbury District for a total of £23 specie for public claims on 8 August 1782 and 23 September 178 [North Carolina Revolutionary Pay Vouchers, 1779-1782, http://familysearch.org/ark:/61903/1:1:Q2WT-P12F]. He was counted as white in Wilkes County, North Carolina, in 1790 [NC:122]. (His father?) William Donathan was a "Mullatto" who petitioned the Spotsylvania County, Virginia court for his freedom in 1734 [Orders 1734-5, 285].

William Dove received £4 pay for 40 days service in the Craven County Militia under Major John Tillman in an expedition to Wilmington [Haun, Revolutionary Army Accounts, Journal "A", 141]. He enlisted for 3 years in Stevenson's Company of the 10th North Carolina Regiment on 14 Jun 1777 and was at White Plains on 9 September 1778 [Clark, *The State Records of North Carolina*, XVI:1045; XIII:516]. He assigned his rights to military land warrant no. 3202, issued 26 November 1789 for 264 acres, to John Craddock [N.C. Archives S.S. file 1526, call no. S.108.357; http://archives.ncdcr.gov/doc/search-doc]. He was head of a Craven County household of 9 "other free" in 1790 [NC:131].

Percival Dring was head of a Currituck County household of 4 "other free" in 1790 [NC:20]. He may have been the father of Thomas Dring who enlisted in Allen's Company of the 2nd North Carolina Regiment in the Revolutionary War and died 11 September 1777 [Clark, *The State Records of North Carolina*, XVI:1040]. His only brother and heir James Dring sold his right to military land warrant no. 3048 of 640 acres for £10 in Craven County, North Carolina, on 16 January 1786 [North Carolina and Tennessee, Revolutionary War Land Warrants, 1783-1843, Roll 04: Revolutionary Warrants, 1783-1799 (Nos. 1895-3085), frame 579 of 619, ancestry.com].

William Dunstan was one of the "Molatto Children of Patience Dunstan," bound apprentice to John Howell by the April 1757 Lunenburg County, Virginia court [Orders 1755-57, 278]. He was in the roster of enlistments for 9 months from Bute County on 3 September 1778: *Born Virg^a, 5'2", 24, Black Hair, Black Eyes* [T.R., Box 4, Folder 35]. He married Fanny **Bibby**, 11 July 1778 Bute County bond. He received £31.6 in Halifax District for service in the war [Revolutionary War Pay Vouchers, http://familysearch.org/search/collection/1498361, Dunston, William, image 242. Image 241 is for Charles Dunston as a substitute].

John Ellis was a "man of Colour" who made a declaration for a pension in Wake County court on 27 July 1820. He stated that he spent a year guarding the Legislature in Hillsborough and was later in skirmishes with the Tories [NARA, S.32233, M804, Roll 916, frame 0427; http://fold3.com/image/17122960]. He was head of a Wake County household of 3 "other free" in 1790 [NC:103].

Burwell Evans enlisted in Montfort's Company of the 10th North Carolina Regiment on 20 July 1778 for 9 months [Clark, *The State Records of North Carolina*, XVI:1053]. He married Mary Mitchell, 22 July 1779 Granville County bond with William Roberson bondsman. He was head of a Nash County household of 1 "other free" in 1790 [NC:70] and 2 "other free" in Halifax County in 1810 [NC:18].

Charles Evans enlisted in Baker's Company of the 10th North Carolina Regiment on 20 July 1778 for 9 months [Clark, *The State Records of North Carolina*, XVI:1053]. He received vouchers 101, 102, 177, and 178 for a total of £48 specie in Hillsboro on 1 May 1792 for military services in the Revolution [North Carolina Revolutionary Pay Vouchers, 1779-1782, http://familysearch.org/ark:/61903/1:1:Q2WT-PCTY, Evans, Charles]. He was head of an "other free" (number crossed out and counted as zero) Hillsboro, Orange County, North Carolina household in 1800 [NC:505].

John Evans died in the Revolutionary War after serving three years. Testimony in Wake County court on 10 August 1820 proved that his immediate heirs and brothers Morris, Gilbert and William Evans (all Sr.) who lived in Wake County, were entitled to 640 acres for John Evans's service, and warrant no. 507 was issued to his heirs on 29 August 1820 [North Carolina Archives SS Military papers, folio 355 cited by Martha Evans in email correspondence].

Morris Evans enlisted in Armstrong's Company of the North Carolina Line in 1781 and served until 1 October 1782. He assigned his final pay of £32 to Dan Hunter in Warrenton in 1786 [Clark, *The State Records of North Carolina*, XVI:1054, XVII:209; DAR, *Roster of Soldiers from North Carolina in the American Revolution*, 8, 206]. He received voucher no. 333 for £8 specie in Warrenton on 1 May 1792, being one fourth his pay [North Carolina Revolutionary Pay Vouchers, 1779-1782, http://familysearch.org/ark:/61903/1:1:Q2WT-5NSX]. He was counted as white in 1790, head of a Wake County household of 1 male over 16, 2 under 16, and 8 females [NC:103], 7 "other free" in 1800 [NC:761] and 7 "free colored" in 1830.

Reuben Evans enlisted in Captain Dixon's Company of the 10th North Carolina Regiment for 12 months and served from 12 May 1781 to 26 May 1782. He applied for a pension while resident in Wake County on 7 April 1831 at the age of 78 [NARA, S.41524, M804, roll 941, frame 401 of 798; http://fold3.com/image/17550453]. He was counted as white in the 1790 census for Wake County, listed near Morris Evans who was also counted as white, and was listed as white in the 1830 census. He was listed in the tax lists for Wake County in 1799 and 1802 [CR 099.701.1] but not listed in the census for 1800, perhaps living with Morris Evans who was head of an "other free" household in 1800.

Benjamin Flood was living in Halifax County on 4 August 1789 when he deposed that he had served as an 18 months soldier in the North Carolina Continental line and assigned all that was due to him for the service to John Eaton [*NCGSJ* IX:153]. He sold 640 acres in Davidson County, Tennessee, on the south side of the Cumberland River, a grant for his services in the Revolution, by Halifax County deed on 31 August 1801 [DB 18:806 & Franklin County DB 6:89]. He was head of a Halifax County household of 7 "other free" in 1800 [NC:308], 6 in 1810 [NC:19], and 7 "free colored" in 1820 [NC:148]. He married Lackey Underdue, 1790 Halifax County bond [CR 047.928.2].

Jesse Flood was head of a Halifax County household of 6 "other free" in 1800 [NC:308] and 6 in 1810 [NC:19]. He may have been the Jesse Flood whose final pay of £41 for serving in the North Carolina Continental Line was paid to J. Marshall for C. Dixon [Clark, *The State Records of North Carolina*, XVII:212].

Dempsy Underdew/ Underdue was counted as white in 1790, head of a Halifax County household of 1 male over 16, two under 16, and four females [NC:63]. He was a private in the Continental Line who assigned his right to 640 acres in Tennessee to Nicholas Long in Halifax County on 25 July 1795 [DB 17:810; http://fold3.com/image/10201165]. His widow may have been Polly Underdew, head of a Halifax County household of 5 "other free" in 1800 [NC:346].

Charles and Ambrose Franklin, sons of Martha **Walden**, wife of Micajah **Walden** of Northampton County, North Carolina, died while serving in the Revolutionary War. According to the testimony of Micajah **Walden**, administrator of their estate, their heirs were granted land warrants for 228 acres. They were also granted an additional 412 acres to be released when there was additional proof of their death. The additional land was released on 13 December 1805 when Micajah Walden presented the testimony of Samuel Parker, Henry Parker, and James Bradley, Captain of the North Carolina Regiment of Halifax [*NCGSJ* III]. Martha was counted as one of 5 "other free" persons in Micajah Walden's Northampton County household in 1790 and 8 "other free" and a slave in 1800, but in her 1807 Northampton County will she named her son Noah Franklin who was counted as white in the 1800 census for Northampton County. Sarah **Boon** was listed as the heir of Charles Franklin on 4 December 1806 when she assigned her right to his warrant for 412 acres of land to Darrell Young [North Carolina and Tennessee, Revolutionary War Land Warrants, 1783-1843, Roll 11: William White Warrants, (1800-1811), no. 128. (http://ancestry.com)].

Roger Freeman was a "Negro" man taxable in Bladen County in 1768 and 1770. He was head of a Bladen County household of two Blacks from 12 to 50 years old and six Blacks over 50 or under 12 years in 1786 [Byrd, *Bladen County Tax Lists*, I:12, 40, 51; II:169; 1784 Bladen County Tax List, 13]. He enlisted as a substitute from Bladen County in Lieutenant Wilkinson's Company of the 10th North Carolina Regiment of Colonel Abraham Sheppard on 19 February 1782 [NARA, M246, roll 79, frame 165 of 323; http://fold3.com/image/10200648. He was head of an Onslow County household of 7 "other free" in 1790 [NC:197], and 8 in 1800 [NC:14].

William Freeman was a "Black" taxable in Bladen County, called "free Will" in 1771 and called William Freeman when he was a "Mixt Blood" taxable on 1 male and 1 female in 1774. He enlisted as a substitute from Bladen County in Lieutenant Wilkinson's Company of the 10th North Carolina Regiment of Colonel Abraham Sheppard on 19 February 1782 [NARA, M246, roll 79, frame 165 of 323, http://fold3.com/image/10200648. He was head of a New Hanover County household of 2 "other free" in 1790 [NC:194].

Anthony Garnes enlisted in the Revolution for 3 years on 14 January 1777 and was listed in the 1st North Carolina Regiment in the roll of Captain Tilman Dixon's Company on 8 September 1778 [NARA M246, Roll 79, frame 70 of 323, http://fold3.com/image/10198780]. He was head of a Hertford County, North Carolina household of 2 "other free" in 1790 (called Anthony Garner) [NC:26]. He was a "free man of coler" who applied for a pension at the age of 59 while residing in Wilson County, Tennessee, on 27 October 1820. He stated that he enlisted for three years and was in Colonel James Hogan's Company of the 7th North Carolina Regiment, was in the Battles of Brandywine and Monmouth and was taken prisoner in Charleston [NARA, S.38723, M804, Roll 1050, frame 940; http://fold3.com/image/20879404]. He was one of the heirs of Jeffrey Garnes who received military land warrant no. 737 which was issued for 640 acres on 15 September 1787 [N.C. Archives S.S. file no. 375, call no. S.108.352; http://archives.ncdcr.gov/doc/search-doc].

Gabriel/ Gaby Garnes, son of Lucy Garnes, was bound out as an apprentice in Mecklenburg County in 1766 [Orders 1765-8, 173, 380]. Lucy was head of a Mecklenburg County, Virginia household of 4 "free colored" in 1820 [VA:153b]. Gaby enlisted in Dixon's Company of the 10th North Carolina Regiment on 25 May 1781 and was omitted in 1781 [Clark, *The State Records of North Carolina*, XVI:1069]. A warrant for 640 acres was issued to the trustees of the University of North Carolina on 17 February 1824 for Gabriel's service in the Revolution [North Carolina and Tennessee, Revolutionary War Land Warrants, 1783-1843, Roll 15: William Hill Warrants, 1811-1837 (Nos. 1132-4409), 1144 (http://ancestry.com)].

Jeffrey Garnes was a six-year-old bound by the Lunenburg County court to William Cocke to be a planter on 8 May 1765. In the 1778 Militia Returns for Captain Richard Taylor's Company of Granville County, North Carolina, he was listed as "a black man," twenty years old, (serving) in place of William Edwards Cock [T.R. box 4, folder 40]. He enlisted in Ely's Company of the 7th North Carolina Regiment in November 1777 and died on 22 January 1778 [Clark, *The State Records of North Carolina*, XVI:1066].

Thomas Garnes was a four-year-old son of Lucy Garnes bound by the Lunenburg County court to William Cocke on 8 May 1765 to be a planter. On 16 June 1783 he received £9 at Hillsborough for military service [N.C. Revolutionary Pay Vouchers, 1779-1782, http://familysearch.org/search/collection/1498361] and died before August court 1791 when his mother Lucy was granted administration on his Granville County estate [Minutes 1789-91]. She was head of a Mecklenburg County, Virginia household of 4 "free colored" in 1820.

Charles Gibson was "a Molata" taxable in Orange County, North Carolina in 1755 [N.C. Archives, T&C Box 1, p.19]. He was living in Wayne County, North Carolina, in August 1818 when he made a declaration to obtain a pension for Revolutionary War service. He claimed that he enlisted for 9 months in the Tenth Regiment at the courthouse in Northampton County, North Carolina. However, there was no record of his discharge or service. He applied for a pension from Hawkins County, Tennessee, stating that he was born in Louisa County, Virginia, on 19 January 1739 and entered into the service in Salisbury, North Carolina [NARA, R.3995, M805, Roll 355, frames 55, 62; http://fold3.com/image/21413416]. He was head of a Hawkins County Household of 6 "free colored" in 1830.

Joel Gibson was head of an Ashe County household of 2 "other free" in 1800 [NC:78]. He applied for a pension in Henderson County, Kentucky, stating that he served in the 1st North Carolina Regiment [NARA, S.35968, M805, Roll 355, frame 0162; http://fold3.com/image/21414198].

John Gibson was born in Orange County, North Carolina, on 16 September 1760 according to his father's family bible. He grew up in Guilford County, North Carolina, where he entered the service. He moved to Tennessee in 1805, and was living there on 16 July 1833 when he made his pension application. He was a horseman employed in collecting cattle for the use of the army [NARA, S.3395, M805, Roll 355, frame 0197; http://fold3.com/image/21420350].

Thomas Gibson was born in Randolph County, North Carolina, on 15 November 1763. When he was eighteen years old, he volunteered in Guilford County and served for two years during which he was in skirmishes with the Tories. He was allowed a pension while a resident of Randolph County [NARA, S.8560, M805, Roll 355, frame 0409; http://fold3.com/image/21420952].

Wilbourne Gibson was born in Guilford County in 1763, was drafted into the service in Randolph County in 1781 and was engaged in skirmishes with the Tories. He applied for a pension while residing in Ripley County, Indiana [NARA, S.4000, M805, Roll 355, frame 0411; http://fold3.com/image/21421413].

John Godett was in the List of Captain Bryan's Craven County Company in June 1778 [T.R., Box 3, folder 26]. He enlisted in Sharp's Company of the 10th North Carolina Regiment on 5 April 1781 and left the service on 5 April 1782 [Clark, *The State Records of North Carolina*, XVI:1069]. He was also paid £9 in New Bern District on 3 April 1786 for militia duty [North Carolina Revolutionary Pay Vouchers, 1779-1782, http://familysearch.org/ark:/61903/1:1:Q2WT-PJ8P]. He was head of a Craven County household of 2 "other free" in 1790 [NC:130].

Edward Going enlisted from Bute County in the North Carolina Continental Line for 9 months in September 1778: *Edward Going private, place of abode: Bute, born Virga, 5'7", 35 years of age, Black Hair; black eyes* [T.R., Box 4, Folder 35, http://digital.ncdcr.gov/cdm/compoundobject/collection/p16062coll26/id/648/rec/165]. In May 1792 he received voucher no. 300 for £6.12 specie, being one fourth of his pay and interest to August 1783 for military service [North Carolina Revolutionary Pay Vouchers, 1779-1782, http://familysearch.org/ark:/61903/1:1:Q2WT-GZKT]. He and Jenkins Goins sold their claims for Revolutionary War pay to John Hall of Hyco, Caswell County, on 27 April 1791 [*NCGSJ* IX:224]. He was head of a Person County household of 6 "other free" in 1800 [NC:599]. He gave his age as 90-100 years in August 1832 and on 30 January 1833 when he appeared in Granville County court and applied for a pension for his service in the Revolution. He stated that he was in the Battle of Guilford Courthouse [NARA, S.6899, M804, Roll 1087, frame 192 of 1089; http://fold3.com/image/22780909].

Jacob Going was head of a Stokes County household of 6 "other free" in 1800 [NC:495]. He was about 70 years of age and living in Vermillion County, Illinois, on 7 June 1832 when applied for a Revolutionary War pension, stating that he was born in Henry County, Virginia, that he lived in Kentucky for about 30 years, then lived for seven years in Vincennes, Indiana [NARA, S.32273, M805, reel 368, frame 115; http://fold3.com/image/21817288].

Jenkins Gowen was a seventeen-year-old "mullato" in 1778 when he enlisted in Captain John Rust's Company of Granville County militia [T.R., Box 4, folder 40]. C. Dixon received his final pay of £41 for service in the North Carolina Line [Clark, *The State Records of North Carolina*, XVII:214].

Reeps Gowen was taxable in his father Edward Gowen's Granville County household in the 1761 list of Robert Harris. He was called Rapes Gowing when he was listed as a private in the Payroll of the 2nd South Carolina Regiment on 1 November 1779 [NARA, M246, Roll 89, frame 107 of 389; http://fold3.com/image/9679368].

William Goin received £5 specie for military service on 1 November 178_ [North Carolina Revolutionary Pay Vouchers, 1779-1782, http://familysearch.org/ark:/61903/1:1:Q2WT-GDHN]. He was head of a Moore County household of 10 "other free" in 1790 [NC:43], 9 in 1800 [NC:60], and 6 in 1810 [NC:615].

Ezekiel Graves was taxable on a horse in Greensville County, Virginia, in 1787 [PPTL, 1782-1830] and head of a Northampton County household of 6 "other free" in 1790 (called Ezekiel Groves) [NC:72] and 3 in 1800 (called Ezekiel Graves) [NC:447]. On 22 November 1787 he applied for compensation for 12 months service as a soldier in Captain Troughton's North Carolina Company [*NCGSJ* V:161].

John Gregory was head of a Craven County, North Carolina household of 2 "other free" in 1790 [NC:130] and 2 "free colored" in 1820 [NC:65]. He was 74 years old on 15 August 1832 when he made a declaration in Craven County court to obtain a pension for his services in the Revolution. He stated that he was living in Brunswick County, North Carolina, when he was drafted, and had two severe cuts from a sword which extended from his eyelid to the crown of his head [*NCGSJ* XII:186 (CR 28.301.29)].

Edward Griffin, a man of "mixed blood," was promised his freedom when he was sold to William Kitchen to serve in his place in the Revolution. The North Carolina General Assembly passed a bill to give him his freedom on 15 May 1784 [NC Archives GASR Apr-June 1784, Box 3, location 3A-464]. He was a "Mulatto" head of an Edgecombe County household of 1 "other free" in 1790 and 1800 [NC:202].

David Hall was head of a Camden County household of 2 "other free" and a white woman in 1790 and 8 "free colored" in 1830 (age 55-99). He received a pension of $80 per annum from 3 March 1826 as a private in Major Hardy Murfree's Company of the 2 North Carolina Battalion commanded by Colonel John Patton. He was reported as being sick at Lancaster in the 9 September 1778 muster of Murfree's Company in White Plains. There are no papers in his pension file, only a letter from his heir David Hall, Jr., dated 14 March 1919 inquiring about bounty land. There is a note from the War Department that he received the pension and died on 31 August 1835 and that the paperwork was probably with the Treasury Department [NARA, 1828, M804, roll 1159, frame 732 of 1009; M246, roll 79, frame 115 of 323; http://fold3.com/image/21860617].

Joshua Hall was a "free man of color" living in Greene County, Tennessee, in 1817 when white residents of the county petitioned the legislature to allow him to prove his accounts in court by his own oath, he having paid taxes, performed military duty, and participated in the war with Britain [Schweninger, Race, Slavery, and Free Blacks, Series 1, 180].

Nathaniel Hall enlisted in the Revolution on 5 August 1779 in Blount's Company of the 10th North Carolina Regiment and died on 24 August the same year [Clark, *The State Records of North Carolina*, XVI:1081]. Micajah **Reed**, head of a Gates County household of 10 "other free" in 1810 and 11 "free colored" in 1820, proved to the Gates County court that he was the lawful heir of Nathaniel Hall, who died in Revolutionary War service. Nathaniel was apparently related to Nathaniel Hall, a "Molatto Boy," born about 1786, bound an apprentice cooper in Gates County in May 1806 [Fouts, *Minutes of Gates County*, IV:1001; III:499].

Isaac Hammond, "a man of color," was a fifer in the 10th North Carolina Regiment for 12 months. In 1849 William **Lomack** swore that they were in the Battle of Eutaw Springs [NARA, W.7654, M804, Reel 1175, frame 449 of 1053; http://fold3.com/image/21891935]. He was head of a Fayetteville, Cumberland County, household of 5 "other free" in 1790 [NC:42].

John Hammond was head of a Cumberland County household of 5 "other free" in 1800. He stated that he was about 98 years old on 24 May 1852 when he appeared in Robeson County court to petition for a pension for service in the Revolution. He stated that he enlisted in Cheraw District, South Carolina, and was in the Battles of Brier Creek, Camden, Cowpens, Bettis's Bridge and Eutaw Springs. He resided in Anson County after the war until 1807 and then moved to Robeson County. Levi **Locklier** and Elias **Paul** testified for him [NARA, S.8654, M804, Roll 1176, frame 681 of 902; http://fold3.com/image/22603188].

Benjamin Harden served in the militia in Wilmington District [DAR, *Roster of Soldiers from North Carolina in the American Revolution*, 339; N.C. Archives, State Treasurer Record Group, Military Papers, Revolutionary War Army Accounts, Harden, Benja., W-1:50; B:191]. He was head of a Sampson County household of 9 "other free" in 1800 [NC:510] and was counted as head of a household of 5 white males and 5 white females in 1810 [NC:486].

David Harden/ Harding enlisted as a substitute from Duplin County in Lieutenant Wilkinson's Company of the 10th North Carolina Regiment of Colonel Abraham Sheppard but was listed as a deserter on 19 February 1782 [NARA, M246, roll 79, frame 165 of 323; http://fold3.com/image/10200648]. He was head of a Sampson County household of 12 "other free" in 1800 [NC:501].

Solomon Harden/ Harding enlisted as a substitute from Duplin County in Lieutenant Wilkinson's Company of the 10th North Carolina Regiment of Colonel Abraham Sheppard but was listed as a deserter on 19 February 1782 [NARA, M246, roll 79, frame 165 of 323; http://fold3.com/image/10200648]. He was head of a Robeson County household of 6 "other free" in 1790 [NC:49], 10 in 1800 [NC:383] and 10 in 1810 [NC:239]. He was called a "yeoman of Richmond County, North Carolina, Husband of Delaney Order (alias Harden), wife of Peter Order, Deceased," on 25 October 1791 when he and his wife gave power of attorney to Robert Webb to receive the final settlement for Revolutionary War service of his wife's deceased husband [*NCGSJ* XIV:114].

Edward Harris died before 14 July 1792 when his brother Gibson, as "Eldest Brother & heir at law to Edward Harris decd.," gave power of attorney to Philemon Hodges to receive his pay for service in the Revolution. His brothers, Sherwood and Solomon Harris, made a similar deposition confirming Gibson's statement on 22 July 1792 [*NCGSJ* X:111]. Solomon was head of a Granville County, North Carolina household of 4 "other free" in 1800.

Gibson Harris was listed in the 1778 Granville County Militia Returns for Captain Abraham Potter's Company: *17-year-old "black man," occupation planter* [T.R., Box 4, folder 40]. J. Craven received his final pay of £41 for his service in the army [Clark, *The State Records of North Carolina*, XVII:216]. He was head of a Surry County, North Carolina household of 12 "other free" in 1810 [NC:684].

Jesse Harris was head of a Granville County household of 2 "other free" in 1800 and 4 in 1810 [NC:864]. He made a declaration in Wake County court to obtain a pension for service in the Revolution, stating that he enlisted for 18 months at Hillsborough in the 10th Regiment commanded by Captain William Lytle and was transferred to Captain Hadley's Company and served until the end of the war [NARA, W.1277, M804, Roll 1199, frame 861 of 947; http://fold3.com/image/22991228].

Sherwood Harris was head of a Wake County household of 6 "other free" in 1800 [NC:770] and 10 in Granville County in 1810 [NC:864]. George **Pettiford** testified for the pension application of his widow Patty Harris that he was acquainted with Sherwood when they both served in the Revolutionary War. Both settled in Granville County, and Sherwood died there. On 23 November 1797 a warrant for 228 acres was issued for Sherwood's 2-1/2 years of service [NARA, W.3984, M804, Roll 1202, frame 606 of 1071; http://fold3.com/image/21852568].

David Hatcher was a sixteen-year-old "half Indian" planter who enlisted in Captain Samuel Walker's Granville County, North Carolina Militia on 25 May 1778 [T.R., Box 4, folder 40]. He was listed as dead in the September 1779 muster of the 10th Regiment [Clark, *The State Records of North Carolina*, XVI:1085].

Aaron Hathcock enlisted in Quinn's Company of the 10th North Carolina Regiment for two years on 22 June 1779 and was allowed pay until 5 June 1781 for his services in the Revolution [Clark, *The State Records of North Carolina*, XVI:1080; Haun, *Revolutionary Army Accounts*, vol. II, Book 1, 273]. He was head of a Northampton County household of 5 "other free" in 1800 [NC:449] and 4 "other free" in 1810 [NC:728].

Amos Hathcock apparently died in the service as his heirs received bounty land warrant no. 2654 of 640 acres for his service as a private in the Continental Line. Ishum Hathcock was his heir [N.C. Archives S.S. 112, call no. S.108.388, http://archives.ncdcr.gov/doc/search-doc]. DNA testing indicates that all members of the Hathcock family from North Carolina and adjoining Virginia counties descend from an African male.

103

Edward Hathcock received voucher no. 560 for £19 specie at New Bern on 1 August 1792 with interest from 1 August 1783 as a late solder in the Continental Line of the State and voucher 737 for £6 on the same date [North Carolina Revolutionary Pay Vouchers, 1779-1782, http://familysearch.org/ark:/61903/1:1:Q2WT-GD26, Hathcock, Edward]. He died before November 1786 when the Johnston County court ordered his orphans Stephen, Amos, and Mary brought to court to be bound out [Haun, *Johnston County Court Minutes*, III:206, 336].

Frederick Haithcock enlisted in the Revolution for 2-1/2 years on 20 April 1776 and was listed in the Roll of Lieutenant Colonel Harney's Company of the 2nd North Carolina Battalion commanded by Colonel John Patten on 9 September 1778, in the same list as Zachariah Hathcock who enlisted in 1777 [NARA, M246, Roll 79, frame 108 of 323; http://fold3.com/image/10199832]. Ab. Thomas drew his final pay of £49 [Clark, *The State Records of North Carolina*, XIII: 518; XVII:216]. Frederick was head of a Halifax County household of 7 "other free" in 1790 [NC:61] and 5 "free colored" in 1820 [NC:151].

Isham Hathcock enlisted in Montfort's Company of the 10th North Carolina Regiment for 9 months on 20 July 1778. He received final pay of £27 for serving in the North Carolina Continental Line [Clark, *The State Records of North Carolina*, XVI:1079; XVII:217]. He was head of a Halifax County household of 5 "other free" and a white woman in 1790 [NC:61].

James Hathcock was counted as white in the 1830 Chatham County census. He was about ninety years old on 7 June 1833 when he applied for a pension while resident in Chatham County. He stated that he was drafted into the militia under Captain Peterson in Northampton County [NARA, S.2613, M804, reel 1245, frame 15 of 822; http://fold3.com/image/22591977].

John Hathcock was in the Northampton County return of troops on 15 March 1780 [T.R. Box 6, Folder 11]. He was head of a Halifax County, North Carolina household of 9 "other free" in 1800.

Joel Hathcock received voucher no. 5943 for £9 specie in Halifax District for military service in the Revolution [North Carolina Revolutionary Pay Vouchers, 1779-1782, http://familysearch.org/ark:/61903/1:1:Q2WT-PTXM, Hathcock, Joel].

John Hathcock received voucher no. 808 for £2 specie in Halifax District on 3 September 1781 for military service [North Carolina Revolutionary Pay Vouchers, 1779-1782, http://familysearch.org/ark:/61903/1:1:Q2WT-GZNL].

Holiday Haithcock served in the Revolution from North Carolina. His final pay of £25 for service in the North Carolina Continental Line was paid to John Sheppard [Clark, *The State Records of North Carolina*, XVII:219]. He was head of a Johnston County household of 6 "other free" in 1790 [NC:142] and 6 in Orange County in 1800 [NC:569]. He applied for a pension in 1836 [NARA, R.4812, M804, Roll 1263, frame 437 of 827; http://fold3.com/image/22996357].

William Hathcock, Jr., was on the roll of Lieutenant William Davidson's North Carolina Company on 23 April 1779 [NARA M246, Roll 79, frame 142 of 323; http://fold3.com/image/10200387]. He was called William Hethcock in 1790, head of a Halifax County household of 5 "other free" [NC:61] and 6 "other free" in 1810 [NC:26].

Zachariah Hathcock was paid $100 bounty at the completion of his enlistment in Lieutenant Colonel Harnegy's Company on 4 June 1780 [NARA, M246, Roll 79, frame 130 of 323; http://fold3.com/image/10199832].

Henry Hawkins enlisted in Ballard's Company of the 10th North Carolina Regiment for 9 months on 20 July 1778 [Clark, *The State Records of North Carolina*, XVI.1080]. He was head of a Halifax County household of 3 "other free" in 1790 [NC:61], 7 in 1800 [NC:318], 8 in 1810 [NC:23], and 9 "free colored" in 1820 [NC:151]. He made a deposition on 23 November 1812 that he was in the service with Nathan **Scott** and that **Scott** died in the hospital in Philadelphia [N.C. Archives, LP 262, by *NCGSJ* VI:15].

Joseph Hawkins was a saddler hired for 12 months in Halifax by Colonel Nicholas Long, deputy quartermaster general for North Carolina in the Revolution, according to his return for 23 August 1781 [Clark, *The State Records of North Carolina*, XV:620]. He was allowed voucher no. 8289, for £12 in Halifax District for military service on 16 June 1783, voucher no. 3149 for £11 on 8 March 1784, and voucher no. 4687 for £11 on 14 July 1781 [North Carolina Revolutionary Pay Vouchers, 1779-1782, http://familysearch.org/ark:/61903/1:1:Q2WT-GD8S, Hawkins, Joseph]. He was head of a Halifax County household of 9 "other free" in 1790 [NC:64], 5 in 1800, and 5 "other free" and 1 slave in 1810 [NC:27].

Benjamin Hawley was underage when he enlisted for 9 months in the Continental Line according to the deposition of his father Joseph Hawley who was living in Granville County on 7 June 1791 when he gave Thomas Beavan his power of attorney to collect wages due to Benjamin for service in the Revolution [*NCGSJ* X:112]. He mustered for the war in Lytle's Company of the 10th North Carolina Regiment in January 1782 [Clark, *The State Records of North Carolina*, XVI:1082]. Benjamin received voucher no 6809 on 4 June 1782 for £4 specie in Halifax District for military service in the Revolution [North Carolina Revolutionary Pay Vouchers, 1779-1782, http://familysearch.org/ark:/61903/1:1:Q2WT-GXYF, Hawley, Ben].

Jacob Hawley was listed in his father Joseph Hawley's Granville county household in 1764 in the list of Samuel Benton. He enlisted as a private in Captain Lytle's Company of the 10th North Carolina Regiment in 1781 [Clark, *The State Records of North Carolina*, XVI:1082]. He was the heir of Benjamin Hawley who received military bounty land warrant no. 1389, 640 acres entered 12 November 1784 and issued 20 December 1791, for Benjamin's service in the Continental Line [N.C. Archives S.S. file 96, call no. S.108.388; http://archives.ncdcr.gov/doc/search-doc]. He was head of a Granville County household of 8 "other free" in 1810 [NC:893]. He was a private in Captain Little's Company of the 10th North Carolina Regiment [NARA, W.21388, M804, Roll 1312, frame 110 of 1097; http://fold3.com/image/29344152].

Joseph Hawley was in the 8 October 1754 Granville County colonial muster of Colonel Eaton, called Joseph Halley, next to Lawrence Pettiford [Clark, *Colonial Soldiers of the South*, 728]. On 25 May 1791 he gave Thomas Bevan his power of attorney to receive the wages due him for three years service as a Continental soldier [*NCGSJ* X:112].

Joseph Hawley enlisted for 3 years as a private in Sharp's Company of the 1st North Carolina Regiment on 9 January 1777 and died on 1 September 1778 [Clark, *The State Records of North Carolina*, XVI:1072]. His heir Joseph Hawley received military bounty land of 640 acres, entered 1 November 1784 and issued 18 March 1794 [N.C. Archives, S.S. file no. 408, call no. S.108.389, http://archives.ncdcr.gov/doc/search-doc].

Peter Hedgepeth enlisted in Yarboro's Company in the 10th North Carolina Regiment as a musician in 1781 for 12 months and was discharged on 7 May 1782 [Clark, *The State Records of North Carolina*, XVI:1083]. He was head of a Wake County, North Carolina household of 5 "other free" in 1790. He was living in Wake County on 21 March when he gave William Fearel power of attorney to collect his final settlement for his service in the Revolution [*NCGSJ* X:235].

105

Micajah Hicks was head of a Chatham County household of 4 "other free" in 1800. He was about 70 years old on 29 October 1831 when he appeared in Guilford County court to apply for a pension for his service in the Revolution. He stated that he enlisted in Lewisburg, Franklin County, for three years, was placed in the 1st Regiment, sent to South Carolina and taken prisoner. He enlisted again when he returned to North Carolina [NARA, W.7738, M804, Roll 1269, frame 331 of 902; http://fold3.com/image/22772692].

Charles Hood, a "Man of Colour," enlisted in Caswell County in Captain Thomas Donoho's 6th Regiment in 1780 and served until the close of the war according to an affidavit from Donoho included in Charles' pension application in Orange County on 27 May 1820. Charles (signing) testified that he was in the Battle of Eutaw Springs and the Siege of Charleston but was not taken prisoner because he was marched onto Ashley Hill before the surrender [NARA, S.41659, M804, Roll 1320, frames 70-78; http://fold3.com/image/23390416]. He was head of an Orange County household of 5 "free colored" in 1820.

William Hood was a "remarkably smart" sixteen-year-old "Mulatto boy" who had been on two voyages to sea, ran away from Henry Minson of Charles City County on 23 September 1769 and was taken up in Halifax County, North Carolina, according to the 21 December 1769 issue of the *Virginia Gazette* [Purdie and Dixon edition, p 3, col. 3]. He was a "Mulatto" counted in the 1786 North Carolina State Census for the Caswell District of Caswell County, listed adjacent to "Mulattoes" Arthur **Toney** and John **Wright** and head of a Rockingham County, North Carolina household of 7 "other free" in 1800 [NC:491]. He was about 65 years old in 1818 and living in Jennings County, Indiana, when he applied for a pension. He stated that he enlisted in the 4th North Carolina Regiment for 18 months and was in the Battles of Sumpter and Ashley River [NARA, W.25781, M804, Roll 1320, frames 644-672; http://fold3.com/image/23390522].

Aaron Howell received voucher no 5961 for £9 specie in Halifax District in February 1782 for military service in the Revolution [North Carolina Revolutionary Pay Vouchers, 1779-1782, http://familysearch.org/ark:/61903/1:1:Q2WT-P66S, Howell, Jaron]. He was head of a Northampton County household of 6 "other free" in 1790 [NC:75] and 6 in 1800 [NC:449].

Jackson Hull enlisted for 3 years in the 3rd North Carolina Regiment in 1777 and was deceased by January 1778 [Clark, *The State Records of North Carolina*, XVI:1073]. He may have married a member of the **Chavis** family because Bartholomew **Chavis** was one of the heirs of Jackson Hull, a Continental soldier who died at Valley Forge [*NCGSJ* I:160].

David Hunt was "a black man" listed in the Militia Returns of Captain Samuel Walker of Granville County in 1778 [T.R., Box 4, folder 40]. He enlisted in Baker's Company for 9 months on 20 July 1778 [Clark, *The State Records of North Carolina*, XVI:1080]. His heir Samuel Hunt received military warrant no. 1619 for 640 acres for his service in the Revolution [N.C. Archives, SS file 208, John Marshall, Assignee of Heirs of David Hunt].

Elisha Hunt was listed in Darnal's Company of the 5th North Carolina Regiment in 1777, a "Coloured Man" or "Black Man" who lost his right arm at the Siege of Charleston and was awarded a pension of $5 on 4 March 1789 while a resident of Lenoir County, North Carolina. On 5 October 1821 he applied for a pension in Cumberland County, North Carolina [NARA, S.13486, M804, Roll 1370, frame 0091; http://fold3.com/image/24189015; http://fold3.com/image/10200866].

David Ivey, a "Coloured" musician, received warrant no. 456 for 154 acres for service in the North Carolina Continental Line which was escheated on 21 August 1820 because it was said he had died in the service without heirs [North Carolina and Tennessee, Revolutionary War Land Warrants, 1783-1843, Roll 13, William Hill Warrants, frame 197 of 568; ancestry.com]. He was 60 years old on 2 December 1820 when he appeared in Davidson County, Tennessee court to apply for a pension for his service in the Revolution. He enlisted for a 3-year term in 1777 in the company commanded by Captain James Wilson in Abraham Sheppard's 10th North Carolina Regiment and was transferred to the 1st Regiment at Valley Forge. He served as a drummer for a year and a wagoner until 1783 when he was discharged at Hillsborough, North Carolina [NARA, W.26156, M804-1396, frame 0486; http://fold3.com/image/24167148].

Ezekiah Jacobs enlisted as a private in Mill's Company of the 10th North Carolina Regiment on 18 December 1781 for 1 year [Clark, *The State Records of North Carolina*, XVI:1094]. He was head of a Brunswick County household of 4 "other free" in 1800 [NC:13], and 8 in 1810 [NC:236]. He recorded a certificate of his discharge from his service as a soldier in the North Carolina Line on 18 February 1788 in New Hanover County [*NCGSJ* XI:114].

Josiah Jacobs received voucher nos. 4995 and 6003 in Wilmington District on 2 October 1783 and 26 January 1785 each for £9 for his services in the militia during the Revolution, returned in the payrolls [North Carolina Revolutionary Pay Vouchers, 1779-1782, http://familysearch.org/ark:/61903/1:1:Q2WT-RMNF, Jacobs, Josiah]. He was head of a Robeson County household of 8 "other free" in 1800 and may have been the J. Jacobs, Sr., who was head of a Brunswick County household of 4 "other free" in 1810 [NC:234].

Matthew Jacobs received voucher no. 4998 in Wilmington District for £9 specie on 2 October 1783 for military service in the militia during the Revolution and voucher no. 6006 on 26 January 1785 for the same [North Carolina Revolutionary Pay Vouchers, 1779-1782, http://familysearch.org/ark:/61903/1:1:Q2WT-P735, Jacobs, Matthew]. He was head of a New Hanover County household of 8 "other free" in 1790 [NC:194].

Peter Jacobs enlisted in Hogg's Company of the 1st North Carolina Regiment for 3 years on 1 January 1777. T. Dixon received his final pay of £131 for service in the Revolution [Clark, *The State Records of North Carolina*, XVI:1088; XVII:222]. Tilman Dixon was assigned Peter's right to military land warrant no. 1405 for his service in the Continental Line: 640 acres entered 16 November 1784 [N.C. Archives, S.S. 2051, Land Warrants, Tennessee, http://archives.ncdcr.gov/doc/search-doc]. He was not counted in the 1790 census, deceased by 21 May 1792 when John Jacobs proved to the New Hanover County court that Zachariah Jacobs was his heir [Minutes 1792-98, 8].

Primus Jacobs was head of a New Hanover County household of 4 "other free" in 1790 [NC:194]. He enlisted in the Revolution in New Hanover County in the 1st Regiment commanded by Colonel Rhodes in August 1782 [NARA, S.41688, M804-1403, frame 0193; http://fold3.com/image/24013660].

William Jacobs served in the Revolution and died before 1796 when his heirs Hezekiah and Josiah Jacobs received a warrant for 640 acres for his service as a private in the Continental Line of North Carolina. They assigned their rights Duncan Stewart [N.C. Archives, S.S. file 2369, Duncan Stewart warrant no. 4012].

Zachariah Jacobs was a "Black" taxable in Brunswick County in 1772 [GA 11.1] and head of a New Hanover County household of 6 "other free" in 1790 [NC:194], 10 in 1800 [NC:313], 5 in Richland District, South Carolina, in 1810 [SC:175a] and 7 "free colored" in Richland District in 1830. He enlisted in October 1781 with Captain James Mills in the 8th Regiment from Brunswick County, North Carolina, and left the service about a year later. He was in a skirmish near Dorchester, South Carolina, and was

107

wounded in the leg at Guilford Courthouse [NARA, W.5304, BlWt.17037-160-55, M805, Roll 466, frame 0444; http://fold3.com/image/24013810]. He assigned his right to his final pay for 12 months service in the Continental Line to Isaac Cole in New Hanover County on 6 December 1791 [NCGSJ XI:114].

Benjamin James enlisted in Hall's Company of the 10th North Carolina Regiment in 1781 and left the service on 16 August 1782 [Clark, The State Records of North Carolina, XVI:1093]. He and his brother Jeremiah gave Seth Peebles of Northampton County power of attorney to obtain settlement of their Revolutionary War service pay [NCGSJ XI:114]. He was head of a Halifax County household of 6 "other free" in 1790 [NC:68], 7 in 1800 [NC:322], 7 in 1810 [NC:29], and 5 "free colored" in 1820 [NC:153].

David James was ordered bound as an apprentice to Arthur Williams by the Bertie County court on 2 June 1763. Sampson Hays received £27 as David's final pay for service in the North Carolina Continental Line [Clark, The State Records of North Carolina, XVII:222]. He was head of a Northampton County household of 3 "other free" and 2 slaves in 1790 [NC:73].

Elisha James was bound by the Bertie County court to Samuel Moore to be a cordwainer on 29 July 1757 [CR 10.101]. He was listed among the militiamen from Northampton County who were paroled by Lord Cornwallis in Halifax in 1781, probably captured during the events surrounding the Battle of Guilford Courthouse on 15 March 1781 [NCGSJ IV:149]. He was head of a Halifax County household of 6 "other free" in 1790 [NC:65], 7 in 1800 [NC:320], 4 in 1810 [NC:29], 6 "free colored" in 1820 [NC:152], and 9 "free colored" in 1830. He made a declaration in Halifax County court to obtain a Revolutionary War pension on 16 November 1824.

Frederick James was bound by the Bertie County court as an apprentice to John Norwood on 26 September 1768 [CR 10.101.7 by NCGSJ XIV:33]. He was listed among the militiamen from Bertie County who were paroled by Lord Cornwallis in 1781 in Halifax, probably captured during the events surrounding the Battle of Guilford Courthouse on 15 March 1781 [NCGSJ IV:150]. John Marshall received his final pay of £27 for service in the North Carolina Continental Line in 1786 [Clark, The State Records of North Carolina, XVII:223]. He was head of a Bertie County household of 9 "other free" in 1790 [NC:13], 5 in 1800 [NC:54], and 3 "other free" and 3 slaves in 1810 [NC:148].

Isaac James, "child of Ann," was bound by the Bertie County court to Edward Rasor to be a cordwainer on 29 July 1757 [CR 10.101]. He received voucher no. 1963 for £11 specie in Edenton District on 1 August 1783 for military service [North Carolina Revolutionary Pay Vouchers, 1779-1782, http://familysearch.org/ark:/61903/1:1:Q2WT-P34F, James Isaac]. He was head of a Hertford County household of 1 "other free" in 1800.

Jeremiah James was a "free Mulatto" taxable in John Norwood's household in the undated (1772?) Bertie County tax list of Humphrey Nichols [CR 10.702.1, box 13]. He was head of a Northampton County household of 3 "other free" in 1790 [NC:73] and 6 in 1800 [NC:453]. He entered the service in Bertie County in Captain Blount's Company of the 10th Regiment for 9 months on 20 July 1778 and again as a private in Captain Raiford's Company from 17 May 1781 to 15 April 1782 [NARA, M804, roll 1404, frame 605 of 781; http://fold3.com/image/23393053].

Jesse James was taxable in David and Elizabeth James' Bertie County household in the 1761 list of John Hill. He was called Jesse Andrews, son of Elizabeth James, and was 14 years old when he was apprenticed to John Perry on 23 February 1763 [CR 10.101.7]. He received voucher no. 4844 in Halifax District for £3 specie per the Board of Auditors of 26 January 1782 for military service in the Revolution [North Carolina

Revolutionary Pay Vouchers, 1779-1782,
http://familysearch.org/ark:/61903/1:1:Q2WT-RMCK, James, Jesse]. He was head of
a Northampton County household of 9 "other free" in 1790 [NC:73].

John James, 7 year old orphan of Easter James, was bound as an apprentice to John
Moore in Bertie County on 30 August 1763 [CR 10.101]. He received voucher nos.
4285 and 9483 in Halifax District for £1.16 specie on 18 February 1782 and no. 9483
for £5 on 16 December 1783 for military service in the Revolution [North Carolina
Revolutionary Pay Vouchers, 1779-1782,
http://familysearch.org/ark:/61903/1:1:Q2WT-P486, James, John]. He was head of a
Bertie County household of 8 "other free" in 1790 [NC:13], 11 in 1800 [NC:56], and
7 in 1810 [NC:149].

Solomon James, Jr., was a "Molato" head of household in Bladen County in 1776 [Byrd,
Bladen County Tax Lists, I:81; II:67, 183]. He served in the Revolution from
Wilmington District [DAR, *Roster of Soldiers from North Carolina in the American
Revolution*, 221]. He was head of a Robeson County household of 9 "other free" and a
white woman in 1790 [NC:49].

Thomas James was the six-year-old son of Betty James, a "Free Mulatoe," bound as an
apprentice by the Bertie County court in May 1763. Humphrey Hardy was granted
administration on his estate on 6 August 1792 on £500 security [Haun, *Bertie County
Court Minutes*, VI:957]. The administrator had a certificate from the Board of Army
Accounts that wages due were settled at Halifax in the amount of £69 [N.C. Archives,
Bertie County Estate Papers]. He enlisted in Blount's Company on 20 July 1778, the
same day as Jeremiah and David James [Clark, *The State Records of North Carolina*,
XVI:1092].

Edwin James enlisted in the Revolution for 3 years and was in the muster of Captain
Clement Hall's 1st North Carolina Regiment on 6 February 1778 at Springfield, sick at
the hospital, in the same list with Squire **Dempsey** [NARA, M246, roll 79, frame 102
of 323; U.S., Revolutionary War Rolls, 1775-1783, http://ancestry.com]. Ann Gardner
was granted administration on his and William James's Bertie County estate on 6
August 1792 [Haun, *Bertie County Court Minutes*, VI:697, 969;
http://familysearch.org/search/collection/1911121].

William James, "12 year old son of Elizabeth James," was ordered bound to Arthur
Williams by the 2 June 1763 Bertie court [Haun, *Bertie County Court Minutes*, III:621].
He received voucher no. 1778 for £12 specie in Edenton District on 20 May 1783 for
service in the Revolution [North Carolina Revolutionary Pay Vouchers, 1779-1782,
http://familysearch.org/ark:/61903/1:1:Q2WT-P9BQ, James, William]. He died before
May 1788 when the Bertie court ordered his children bound as apprentices. Ann
Gardner was granted administration on his Bertie County estate on 6 August 1792
[Haun, *Bertie County Court Minutes*, VI:697, 969;
http://familysearch.org/search/collection/1911121].

Jacob Jeffries enlisted in Donoho's Company of the 10th North Carolina Regiment on
25 May 1781 and left the service a year later. His final pay of £21 was received by
William King [Clark, *The State Records of North Carolina*, XVI:1093; XVII:222]. He
was head of an Orange County household of 9 "other free" in 1800 [NC:514]. He
recorded a certificate in Orange County on 24 July 1791 that he was the "Mulatto Jacob"
who received a discharge for 12 months service as a soldier in the Revolution [*NCGSJ*
XI:115]. His 14 July 1818 Orange County will left his wife Jane a bounty ticket worth
$3,000 due from Major Thomas Donoho (apparently for Revolutionary War service)
[North Carolina original will, D:543]. Jinncy was head of an Orange County, North
Carolina household of 7 "free colored" in 1820 [NC:344].

John Jeffries was listed as a volunteer Continental soldier from Bute County on 3 September 1778 for 9 months, to begin the 1 March 1779, in the same list and same description as Asa **Tyner**, Edmond **Bibby**, Charles **Row** and William **Dunston**: *born 1759 in N.C.: 5'6" tall, dark hair, dark eyes* [T.R., Box 4, Folder 41, http://digital.ncdcr.gov/cdm/compoundobject/collection/p16062coll26/id/648/rec/36]. He was probably the son of John Jeffries and his wife Mary who were "mulatto" taxables in the Cross Road District of Granville County, North Carolina, in James Paine's list in 1761 and 1762 [CR 44.701]. This part of Granville County became Bute County in 1769, and he and Joseph Jeffreys were insolvent taxpayers in Bute County in 1769 [Miscellaneous Tax Records in N.C. Genealogy, 2431]. He was taxable on only his own poll in Bute County in 1771 [N.C. Archives, Tax List CR.015.70001, p.12 of pamphlet].

Brutus Johnston enlisted as a musician in Major's Company of the 10th North Carolina Regiment, was mustered in January 1778 and died 15 February 1778 [Clark, *The State Records of North Carolina*, XVI:1092]. He was a drummer enlisted for 2-1/2 years in Benjamin Williams's Company of the 2nd North Carolina Battalion in January 1778 who died on 15 February 1778 [NARA, M246, roll 79, frames 122 of 323; http://fold3.com/image/10200094]. He was described by Charles Wood as a man of colour who died at Valley Forge while serving as a soldier in the North Carolina Line [*N.C. Genealogy* XVI:2580]. His estate descended to his brother David Johnson [*NCGSJ* IV:173].

David Jonston received voucher no. 1910 for £1.16 specie in Washington County in June 1782 for military service in the Revolution [North Carolina Revolutionary Pay Vouchers, 1779-1782, http://familysearch.org/ark:/61903/1:1:Q2WT-PM58, Jonston, David]. He was head of a Hyde County household of 10 "other free" in 1810 [NC:117].

Jeremiah Johnston "of Hyde County" received voucher no. 1435 on 20 January 1785 for £9 specie for his military service in the Revolution [North Carolina Revolutionary Pay Vouchers, 1779-1782, http://familysearch.org/ark:/61903/1:1:Q2WT-5GQ4, Johnston, Jeremiah]. He was head of a Hyde County household of 5 "other free" in 1790.

Joshua Johnston was in the list of men in the Beaufort County Regiment of Militia on 20 April 1781 [T. R., Box 7, folder 15, http://digital.ncdcr.gov/cdm/compoundobject/collection/p16062coll26/id/1107/rec/10]. He was taxed on an assessment of £101 and 4 polls in Beaufort County in 1779 [GA 30.1] and head of a Beaufort County household of 6 "other free" in 1790 [NC:126].

Abraham Jones was head of a household of 1 Black male and 1 Black female in the 1767 Granville County tax list of John Pope adjacent to Richard Jones. In 1768 he was listed in Pope's list with his wife Charity. In the 1778 Granville County Militia Returns he was listed in Captain John Rust's Company as a "mulatto," about 44 years old [T.R. Box 4, folder 40].

Francis Jones enlisted in Sharp's Company of the 10th North Carolina Regiment on 1 August 1782 and was transferred on 27 December 1782 [Clark, *The State Records of North Carolina*, XVI:1094]. He was about 50-60 years old when he appeared in Wake County court on 13 May 1818 to apply for a pension for his service in the Revolution. He stated that he volunteered for 18 months under Captain Sharp in the 10th North Carolina Regiment until the end of the war [NARA, S.36653, M804, Roll 1438, frame 915 of 1022; http://fold3.com/image/24155584]. He was head of a Wake County household of 5 "other free" in 1790 [NC:103] and 8 "free colored" in Caswell County in 1820 [NC:66] and a 75-year-old veteran in the household of Lemuel **Reed**, head of a household of 6 "free colored".

Hardy Jones was head of a Jones County household of 5 "other free" in 1790 [NC:144], 7 "other free" and a white woman over the age of 45 in Lenoir County in 1810 [NC:300] and 4 "free colored" in 1820 [NC:295]. He was residing in Lenoir County in 1818 when he appeared in the county court to apply for a pension. He stated that he enlisted in Jones County in 1778 in Captain John Taylor's Company of the 3rd North Carolina Regiment and served until 1783. He was in the Battle of Stono Creek and was taken prisoner in the Siege of Charleston. The records of the War Department confirmed that he had served five years [NARA, S.41699, M804, roll 1439, frame 351 of 1122; http://fold3.com/image/24156747].

James Jones was a "black" taxable in Craven County in 1769 [SS 837]. On 26 April 1780 he purchased 67 acres adjoining his land on Chinqapin Creek in Jones County from Jacob Jones, being the land where Jacob Jones, deceased, formerly lived, for £18 [DB 3:90]. He was called James Jones of Jones County when he received voucher no. 426 for serving in the militia under Captain Fred Hargess [North Carolina Revolutionary Pay Vouchers, 1779-1782, http://familysearch.org/ark:/61903/1:1:Q2WT-5VT9, Jones, James]. He was head of a Jones County household of 11 "other free" in 1790 [NC:144].

James Jones was head of a Halifax County household of 4 "other free" in 1790 [NC:65], 12 in 1810 [NC:29] and 10 "free colored" in 1820. He appeared in Halifax County court on 22 November 1821 to apply for a pension for his service in the Revolution. He enlisted in 1781 for a year in Captain Yarborough's Company of Colonel Blount's North Carolina Regiment and was in the Battle of Eutaw Springs. Isham **Scott** testified that they were both under the command of Colonel Hardy Murfree for a part of their time in the service [NARA, S.41701, M804, roll 1440, frame 314 of 991; http://fold3.com/image/24198243]. On 19 May 1823 he testified for Isham **Scott** in Halifax County court that he was in the service with him in Colonel Ashe's Regiment.

Jonathan Jones was a 17-year-old "mulatto" listed in Captain Rust's Granville County Militia Returns adjacent to Abraham Jones [T.R. Box 4, folder 40]. His final pay of £94 was received by Selby Harney [Clark, *The State Records of North Carolina*, XVII:222]. He was head of a Person County household of 7 "other free" in 1800 [NC:597] and 8 "free colored" in 1820 [NC:498].

Philip Jones was head of a Halifax County household of 7 "other free" in 1790 [NC:5] and 2 in 1800 (called Philip, Senr.) [NC:322]. He made a deposition in Northampton County court on 26 March 1791 that he enlisted and served as a soldier in the Continental Army [*NCGSJ* XI:118]. He may have been the Philip Jones who sometime before 7 September 1787 sold bounty land in Davidson County, Tennessee, which he received for his services in the War [Franklin County DB 6:89].

George Kersey was head of a Robeson County household of 5 "free colored" in 1820 [NC:310]. He was born in Bladen County where he enlisted under Captain Baker and Colonel Culp for 11 months in August 1777. His colonel was killed by the Tories commanded by Mike **Gowen** and Thomas **Gibson**. They found Mike **Gowen** in Robeson County. George lived for about five years in Marion District, South Carolina, the balance in Robeson County and Cumberland County where he then lived. James Kersey testified in Robeson County court on 24 November 1834 that both he and George served under General Francis Marion. James **Hunt** testified in Cumberland County court on 13 March 1834 that George served under General Marion [NARA, R.5801, M804, Roll, frame 1457, 437 of 1135; http://fold3.com/image/24631742].

James Kersey was listed in the militia returns for Bladen County in 1782: *5 feet 9 Inches, age 18, Dark Complexion, brown hair, hazel eyes, Captain Regan's Company, a planter* [T.R., Box 6, Folder 30]. He was living alone in Robeson County, counted as "other free" in 1800 [NC:388]. He made a declaration in Robeson County court to obtain a pension for his services in the Revolution. He stated that he volunteered in a company of militia on 1 August 1782 in what was then Bladen County in the town of Elizabeth. He marched to Charleston, South Carolina, to James Island, and received his discharge in Wilmington on 1 August 1783. He was never in any engagement "but once which was with a body of negroes above Charleston at a place called as he thinks the Quarter House." He was inscribed in the Roll of North Carolina on 4 March 1831 [NARA, S.8788, M804, Roll 1477; frame 16 of 1201; http://fold3.com/image/25012774].

Arthur Lamb was a "Mulato" taxable in Bladen County from 1768 to 1774, taxable with Meedy (Needham) Lamb in 1776 [Byrd, *Bladen County Tax Lists*, I:4, 15, 35, 81, 111, 130; II:68, 84, 182]. He received voucher no. 4465 on 4 September 1783 in Wilmington District for £10 specie for service in the militia [North Carolina Revolutionary Pay Vouchers, 1779-1782, http://familysearch.org/ark:/61903/1:1:Q2WT-PD2M, Lamb, Arthur]. He was head of a Robeson County household of 7 whites in 1790 and 5 "other free" in 1800 [NC:389a].

Needham Lamb was called Meedy Lamb when he who was taxable in the household of (his brother?) Arthur Lamb in 1776. Needy Lamb was allowed voucher no. 4814 for £9 specie in Wilmington District on 22 September 1783 for service in the militia [North Carolina Revolutionary Pay Vouchers, 1779-1782, http://familysearch.org/ark:/61903/1:1:Q2WT-5J5Y, Lamb, Needy]. Meedy was head of a Robeson County household of 9 whites in 1790 [NC:49].

Lemon /Lamentation Land was a waiter in the roll of Lieutenant William Davidson's North Carolina Company in the Revolution on 23 April 1779 [NARA M246, Roll 79, frame 142 of 323; http://fold3.com/image/10200387], head of Northampton County, North Carolina household of 6 "other free" and 1 white woman [NC:72] in 1790, called Lamentation Land in 1800 when he was head of a Northampton County household of 8 "other free" [NC:459], called Lemuel Land in 1810, head of a Halifax County household of 6 "other free" [NC:32] and called Lemon Lamb in 1820, head of a Halifax County household of 5 "free colored" [NC:156].

Charles Lewis enlisted as a private in Hogg's Company of the 10th Regiment on 20 July 1778 [Clark, *The State Records of North Carolina* XVI:1105]. He received voucher no. 7141 in Halifax District on 6 June 1782 for military service in the Revolution and received voucher no. 1026 for £20 for service in the Continental Line in September 1784 [North Carolina Revolutionary Pay Vouchers, 1779-1782, http://familysearch.org/ark:/61903/1:1:Q2WT-P8L4, Lewis, Charles].

Morgan Lewis made a declaration in Halifax County court to obtain a pension for his services as a private in the 10th North Carolina Regiment in the infantry commanded by Colonel Hogan in Captain G. Bradley's Company [NARA, S. 41766, M804, Roll 1558, frame 123 of 897; http://fold3.com/image/24789911]. He was head of a Halifax County household of 4 "other free" in 1790 [NC:62], 3 in 1800 [NC:324], and 4 in 1810 [NC:33].

Bennett Localear received voucher no. 605 for £139 specie as his pay to 1 August 1783 for military service in the Revolution [North Carolina Revolutionary Pay Vouchers, 1779-1782, http://familysearch.org/ark:/61903/1:1:Q2WT-5TF7, Localear, Bennett].

Robert Locklear received voucher no. 1740 on 1 May 1786 for £31 specie for his pay to January 1782 for service in the Continental Line. However, the words "Not Admitted" were written across the voucher. Some time after December 1785 he received voucher no. 554 for £10, being a fourth of his pay which he was entitled to receive for military service & interest to 1 August 1783 [North Carolina Revolutionary Pay Vouchers, 1779-1782, http://familysearch.org/ark:/61903/1:1:Q2WT-PJZ9, Localear, Robert]. He was in Captain Peter Tyler's Little Pee Dee Company of the South Carolina Loyal Militia from 1 September 1780 to 6 October 1782 [Clark, *Loyalists in the*

Southern Campaign of the Revolutionary War, 1:153, 189]. He was head of a Robeson County household of 9 "other free" in 1790 [NC:48].

Francis Locus(t) received voucher no. 1254 on 10 June 1783 for £9 specie at Hillsboro for military service in the Revolution [North Carolina Revolutionary Pay Vouchers, 1779-1782, http://familysearch.org/ark:/61903/1:1:Q2WT-PWZY, Loacust, Thomas]. He was head of a Nash County household of 8 "other free" in 1790 [NC:70].

John Locus received voucher no. 8845 in Halifax District on 29 August 1783 for service in the Revolution and was called John Locas of Nash County on 8 June 1786 when he received voucher no. 36 for £32 specie in Halifax District for military service in the Revolution [North Carolina Revolutionary Pay Vouchers, 1779-1782, http://familysearch.org/ark:/61903/1:1:Q2WT-PYVQ, Locus, John]. He was head of a Nash County household of 6 "other free" in 1790 [NC:70], 6 in 1800 [NC:109], and 4 in 1810 [NC:660].

Thomas Locus, born about 1748, "base born son of ____ Locus "a free Negro woman," was bound an apprentice shoemaker in Granville County, North Carolina [CR 44.101.2]. On 30 September 1785 the heirs of Thomas Locust received warrant no. 2670 of 640 acres for his service in the Revolution [N.C. Archives S.S. file 1137, call no. S.108.385, http://archives.ncdcr.gov/doc/search-doc; DAR, *Roster of Soldiers From North Carolina in the American Revolution,* 287]. All 9 Locus(t) households counted in the 1790 North Carolina census were "other free" persons.

Valentine Locus married Rachel **Pettiford,** 1780 Granville County bond. He was listed in th 9 September 1778 muster of Colonel John Patten's 2nd North Carolina Battalion with Zachariah and Frederick **Hathcock** [http://fold3.com/image/10199832]. He received 228 acres bounty land in 1784 for 2-1/2 years service, and Rachel received a pension for his service [NARA, W.20497, M805, Roll 533, frame 766; http://fold3.com/image/25841648]. He was head of a Wake County household of 8 "other free" in 1790 [NC:106] and 9 "other free" in 1800 [NC:778].

Billing Lucas, a "man of color," enlisted for 9 months in Blount's Company of the 10th North Carolina Regiment and died 5 September 1779 [Crow, *Black Experience in Revolutionary North Carolina,* 101; Clark, *The State Records of North Carolina,* XVI:1106]. Military land warrant no. 529 for 640 acres was issued to the Trustees of the University of North Carolina for his service [North Carolina and Tennessee, Revolutionary War Land Warrants, 1783-1843, Roll 13: William Hill Warrants, 1811-1837 (Nos. 364-675), frame 286 of 568, ancestry.com].

William Lomack enlisted in Blount's Company of the 10th North Carolina Regiment in 1779, was omitted in November 1779, enlisted in McRae's Company on 9 May 1781 and left the service a year later [Clark, *The State Records of North Carolina,* XVI:1106]. He stated that he enlisted with Captain James Curry as a private in the 2nd North Carolina Regiment in 1777 for five years. He was taken prisoner at the Battle of Charleston, made his escape from the British, and rejoined his regiment at Deep Run under General Gates. He received two wounds at the Battle of Eutaw Springs [NARA, S.41783, M804, Roll 1579, frame 397 of 1042; http://fold3.com/image/24697431]. He was head of a Robeson County household of 10 "other free" in 1810 [NC:240] and counted in the 1850 census for Fayetteville as a 95-year-old Black cooper, born in New Jersey.

William Lowry was head of a Bladen County household of 5 "other free" in 1800 [NC:9] and 9 "free colored" in Robeson County in 1820 [NC:304]. His widow Susan Loughry applied in Robeson County court for a pension for his service in the Revolution. She stated that her husband died at about 92 years of age on 26 May 1847, that her maiden name was Susan **Locklear,** that they were married in May 1803, and

113

that she was 70 years old in 1853. Jordan and Easter **Oxendine** and Aaron **Revells** testified on her behalf [NARA, W.8263, M804, Roll 1589, frame 455 of 904; http://fold3.com/image/27290621].

Robert Mackey was in the 3 September 1778 list of new levies from Hyde County who enlisted for 9 months from the following March: *place of abode Hyde, born do, 5'9", 22 years of age, Dark Hair, Black Eyes* [T. R., Box 4, Folder 42, http://digital.ncdcr.gov/cdm/compoundobject/collection/p16062coll26/id/699/rec/164]. He was head of a Hyde County household of 2 "other free" and a white woman in 1800 [NC:373].

Allen Manly was sized in the 3rd North Carolina Regiment at Halifax (no date): *age 16, 5', Black Complexion, enlisted for 3 years in No Hampton on Octr 10th 81, born in N Carolina, a planter, Enlisted a Servt* [T.R., box 6, folder 20; http://digital.ncdcr.gov/cdm/compoundobject/collection/p16062coll26/id/980/rec/2]. He was listed as a private in Armstrong's Company who enlisted in 1781 and left the service on 1 April 1782 [Clark, *The State Records of North Carolina*, XVI:1120].

Gabriel Manly, Jr., was taxable in his "Mulatto" father Gabriel Manly's Bertie County household in 1751. John Marshall received his final pay of £41 for service in the North Carolina Continental Line [Clark, *The State Records of North Carolina*, XVII:234]. He was head of a Hertford County household of 2 "other free" in 1790 [NC:25].

Littleton Manly was head of a Northampton of 5 "other free" in 1790 [NC:75]. He enlisted for 18 months in Captain Lytle's Company of the 10th North Carolina Regiment in 1782 [Clark, *The State Records of North Carolina*, XVI:1122].

Mark Manly was in a list of militia men drafted from Hertford County in the Third Division commanded by Major George Little between 1778 and 1780 [T.R., Box 5, Folder 20]. He served in the Revolution [DAR, *Roster of Soldiers from North Carolina in the American Revolution*, 192, 677]. In 1786 his heir Letitia **Archer** received military bounty land warrant no. 215 for his service [N.C. Archives S.S. file no. 254; http://archives.ncdcr.gov/doc/search-doc]. Letisha Manley was head of a Hertford County household of 4 "other free" in 1790.

Moses Manly enlisted with Colonel Lytle in the 10th North Carolina Regiment for 9 months in August 1781. He made a declaration in Hertford County court for a pension on 17 August 1819 [NARA, S.41796, M805, reel 549, frame 703; http://fold3.com/image/23400188]. He was head of a Bertie County household of 3 "other free" in 1790 [NC:14] and 5 in Halifax County in 1800 [NC:328], 7 in 1810 [NC:36], and 7 "free colored" in 1820 [NC:157].

Solomon Manly was taxable in Bertie County in 1751, in the same list with "Mulattos" Moses, Abel and Gabriel Manley [CCR 190], taxable in 1759 in the constable's list of William Witherington for Captain Benjamin Wynn's District, and taxable in Hertford County on 2 persons in 1768 and [1770 Fouts, *Tax Receipt Book*, 55]. His final pay of £28 for service in the Revolution was received by H. Murfree [Clark, *The State Records of North Carolina*, XVII:233]. His relict Anna Manley received 640 acres for his service which she assigned to Hardy Murfree [N.C. Archives, S.S. file 113, call no. S.108.350, http://archives.ncdcr.gov/doc/search-doc].

Southerland Manly was taxable in Hertford County on one person in 1768, two in 1769 and 1770 [Fouts, *Tax Receipt Book*, 54]. He enlisted as Southey Manley in the 10th North Carolina Regiment on 20 July 1778 [Clark, *The State Records of North Carolina*, XVI:1117], listed in the roll of Lieutenant William Davidson's North Carolina Company on 23 April 1779 [NARA, M246, Roll 79, frame 142 of 323; http://fold3.com/image/10200387]. H. Murfree received his final pay (and Moses

Manley's) [Clark, *The State Records of North Carolina*, XVII:233]. He was head of a Northampton County household of 9 "other free" in 1800 [NC:461].

William Manley was called "William Manley of Northampton County" when he received voucher no. 8999 for £9 specie on 30 August 1783 in Halifax District for military services in the Revolution [North Carolina Revolutionary Pay Vouchers, 1779-1782, http://familysearch.org/ark:/61903/1:1:Q2WT-5GF4, Manly, William]. He assigned his right to military warrant no. 148 for 274 acres to James Robertson in 1793 [N.C. Archives, S.S. file 1665]. He was called "William Munley Mulatto" in the state census for Northampton County in 1786, head of a Northampton County household of 4 "other free" in 1790 [NC:75], and a Halifax County household of 7 in 1800 [NC:330], 10 in 1810 [NC:38], and 7 "free colored" in 1820 (Billie Manly) [NC:157].

Aaron Emanuel served in the Revolution from North Carolina [N.C. Archives, State Treasurer Record Group, Military Papers, Revolutionary War Army Accounts, XI:84, folio 4].

Christopher Manuel was head of a Northampton County household of 8 "other free" in 1790 [NC:75], 11 in Sampson County in 1800 [NC:517] and 6 "free colored" in Sampson County in 1820 [NC:308]. He stated that he was born in Halifax County, North Carolina, moved to the part of Duplin County which became Sampson County before the war, and was at the Battle of Rockfish Creek [NARA, S.7182, M804, Roll 1627, frame 615 of 1040; http://fold3.com/image/23664291].

Ephraim Emanuel received pay in Wilmington, New Hanover County, for service in the militia during the Revolution [North Carolina Revolutionary Pay Vouchers, 1779-1782, http://familysearch.org/ark:/61903/1:1:Q2WT-PFRT, Manuel Ephraim]. He was head of a Sampson County household of 3 "other free" in 1790 [NC:51].

Jesse Manuel received his final settlement certificate as a 12 months soldier in the Revolution on 25 December 1787 [*NCGSJ* XIII:93]. He was head of a Sampson County household of 6 "other free" in 1790 [NC:51]. He enlisted in Bladen County in April 1782 and served in the 2nd North Carolina Regiment. Henry and Moses **Carter** testified on his behalf. Henry stated that he had been acquainted with him since they were boys, that they were near-neighbors in Duplin County, that they met while both were in the service, and that he could not be mistaken about Jesse because he was such a remarkably tall man [NARA, S.41808, M804, Roll 1627, fame 629 of 1040; http://fold3.com/image/23664315].

Levy Emanuel/ Manuel received voucher no. 487 for £12 specie on 22 December 1781 in Wilmington District for services in the militia [North Carolina Revolutionary Pay Vouchers, 1779-1782, http://familysearch.org/ark:/61903/1:1:Q2WT-RMRJ, Emanuel, Levi]. He was head of a Sampson County household of 5 "other free" in 1790 [NC:53].

Nicholas Manuel was head of a Sampson County household of 5 "other free" in 1790 [NC:51] and 9 in 1800. His widow applied for a pension for his service in the Revolution [NARA, R.6887, M804, Roll 1627, frame 648 of 1040; http://fold3.com/image/23664341].

Absalom Martin enlisted in the town of Beaufort, North Carolina, for 12 months in Captain William Dennis' Company in the 1st North Carolina Regiment in April 1781. He made a declaration in Carteret County court to obtain a pension on 22 August 1820 [NARA, S.41800, M805, reel 0555, frame 20; http://fold3.com/image/29347530]. He was head of a Carteret County household of 9 "other free" in 1790 [NC:128], 12 in 1800, 16 in 1810 [NC:443], and 7 "free colored" in 1820 [NC:121].

John Martin was head of a New Hanover County, North Carolina household of 6 "other free" in 1790 [NC:194] and 11 in 1800 [NC:310]. He gave power of attorney to Thomas Nuse to receive his final settlement for service in the Continental Line on 9 September 1791. John Williams, a justice of the peace for New Hanover County, attested that he served in 1782 [*NCGSJ* XIII:94].

Jesse Martin enlisted for 9 months in 1780 in Captain Arthur Gatling's regiment of the North Carolina Line commanded by Colonel Armstrong. He was discharged in Stono, South Carolina, in 1781 [NARA, R.6949, M805, reel 883, frame 836]. He was head of a Gates County household of 8 "other free" in 1790 [NC:23], 9 in 1800 [NC:273], 7 in 1810 [NC:842], and 7 "free colored" in 1820 [NC:162].

Patrick Mason was head of a Person County household of 6 "other free" in 1800 [NC:613] and 10 "free colored" in 1820 [NC:498]. He enlisted for 12 months on 1 April 1780 [NARA, S.41810, M804, Roll 1647, frame 241 of 768; http://fold3.com/image/23478388; *NCGSJ* XIV:172].

Thomas Mason was head of a Louisa County household of 6 "other free" persons in 1800 [*Louisa County Historical Society* (June 1972)] and was listed as a "Mulatto" shoemaker in a "List of free Negroes and Mulattoes" in Louisa County about 1801-3 [Abercrombie, *Free Blacks of Louisa County*, 20]. He enlisted in 1777 in Caswell County, North Carolina, served six months in a horse corps, enlisted again in 1780 and 1781 [NARA, R.6993, M804, Roll 1647, frame 636 of 768; http://fold3.com/image/23478607].

Isham Mitchel received a total of about £50 in pay for his service in the Revolution. He married Mary **Holly** (**Hawley**) in Granville County about 1768 and had 9 children [NARA, W.18510, M804, Roll 1742, frame 118 of 1124; http://fold3.com/image/24781248]. His children Josiah, Joab, Joel, Jo, and Isham Mitchell were listed as "other free" or "free colored" in the census.

Paul Mitcham enlisted in Montfort's Company of the 10th North Carolina Regiment on 20 July 1778 for 9 months [Clark, [*The State Records of North Carolina*, XVI:1117]. He was head of a Halifax County household of 5 "other free" in 1810 [NC:38] and 8 "free colored" in 1820 [NC:156].

Joseph Mitcham served in the Revolution in North Carolina [S.S., State Treasurer Record Group, Revolutionary Army Accounts, Mitcham, Joseph, XI:40, Folio 4; http://archives.ncdcr.gov/doc/search-doc]. He was head of a Halifax County household of 6 "other free" in 1800 [NC:330].

Giles Moore was in the list of men in the Beaufort County Regiment of Militia on 20 April 1781 [T.R., Box 7, folder 15, http://digital.ncdcr.gov/cdm/compoundobject/collection/p16062coll26/id/1107/rec/10]. He was head of a Beaufort County household of 6 "other free" as Giles Punch in 1800 [NC:15], 6 in 1810 (as Giles Moore) [NC:118], and head of a Beaufort County household of 5 "free colored" as Giles Moore in 1820 [NC:27].

John Punch Moore was head of a Beaufort County household of 5 "other free" in 1790 (called John P. Moore) [NC:126] and 9 in 1800 (called John Moore) [NC:9]. He may have been the John Moore who gave Thomas Armstrong his power of attorney to collect his pay due for 9 months service as a soldier in the Continental Line in Beaufort County on 5 June 1792 [*NCGSJ* XIII:236].

Joseph Moore, "a free born Negroe Boy Aged Sixteen Years," was bound an apprentice house carpenter to Nathaniel Scarbrough by the 17 June 1774 Craven County court [Minutes 1772-74, 18d]. He mustered in Fenner's Company of the 10th North Carolina

Regiment as a musician in January 1778 and died on 16 March 1778 [Clark, *The State Records of North Carolina*, XVI:1116].

Kuffie Moore, "free Negro," was a "Black" taxable in his own Beaufort County household in 1769 [S.S. 837]. He enlisted for 9 months in Captain Blount's Company of the 10th North Carolina Regiment on 1 July 1779 and died on 17 August 1779 [Clark, *The State Records of North Carolina*, XVI:1118].

Lemuel Moore was a fourteen-year-old "Free Negroe Boy" ordered bound apprentice to John Davis to be a house carpenter by the Craven County court on 14 December 1771 [Minutes 1767-75, 189b]. He enlisted in Alderson's Company as a private in November 1777, served as a musician in January and February 1778 and died on 26 April 1778 [Clark, *The State Records of North Carolina*, XVI:1112].

Simon Moore was living in Beaufort County when he and (his brother?) Abram, called "free Negroes," purchased 300 acres on the south side of Terts Swamp and Durham's Creek on 28 March 1758 [DB 3:383]. He was head of a Craven County household of 1 "Black" male and 2 "Black" females in 1769 and head of a Craven County household of 11 "other free" in 1790 [NC:134]. On 13 September 1782 he and Benajah Bogey were charged in Craven County court with having joined the British. They were released when they consented to join the Continental Army [Minutes 1779-84, 47b]. He enlisted for 18 months in Evans's Company of the 10th North Carolina Regiment [Clark, *The State Records of North Carolina*, XVI:1122]. He was head of a Jones County household of 5 "other free" in 1810 [NC:270]. He was about 78 years old on 12 June 1818 when he applied for a pension in Craven County, stating that he enlisted sometime in 1779 and served until Colonel Archibald Lytle's Company was disbanded near Charleston [NARA, S.41960, M804, roll 1759; http://fold3.com/image/27213692].

Isaac Morgan was a 16-year-old "Mulatto" listed in 1782 among the Drafts & Substitutes from Edgecombe County in the Revolutionary War: *½ year enrollment, age 16, 5'5³/⁴", Spears Company, substitute, dark complexion, dark hair, dark eyes, a farmer* [T.R., Box 6, folder 31]. He was a "Mulatto" head of an Edgecombe County household of 6 "other free" and a white woman in 1800 [NC:223].

William Morgan was a "Mulatto" head of an Edgecombe County household of 5 "other free" in 1800 [NC:223] and 2 "free colored" males in 1820 [NC:126]. He was about 68 years old in August 1832 when he appeared in Edgecombe County court to apply for a pension for his service in the Revolution. He was drafted from Edgecombe County in February 1781 into a company commanded by Captain Etheldred Philips in a regiment commanded by Colonel Linton and guarded prisoners [NARA, S.9034, M804, roll 1767, frame 489 of 787; http://fold3.com/image/25941923].

Mark Murray received voucher no. 6109 for £11 in Halifax District in 1782 for military service in the Revolution [North Carolina Revolutionary Pay Vouchers, 1779-1782, http://familysearch.org/ark:/61903/1:1:Q2WT-PJ16, Murrey, Mark]. He was head of Halifax County household of 9 "other free" in 1790 [NC:64]. On 23 October 1832 he testified in Halifax County court to obtain a pension for his services in the Revolution, stating that he was born and raised in Caroline County, Virginia, moved from there to Hanover County and from there to Halifax County, North Carolina, about 1792. He applied for a pension while living in Wilson County, Tennessee, stating that he enlisted in 1780 and that "his Great Grandmother came from Ireland and after serving out her passage had children by a Negro which accounts for his being mixed blooded" [NARA, R.7523, M804, Roll 1796, frames 1-57; http://fold3.com/image/25083223].

Booth Newsom was listed in the Colonial Muster Roll of Captain James Fason's Northampton County Militia [T.R., box 1, folder 3]. He enlisted for 9 months in Lieutenant Col's Company in the 10th North Carolina Regiment on 20 July 1778 [Clark, *The State Records of North Carolina*, XVI:1126]. He was listed as a "pioneer" in the roll of Lieutenant William Davidson's Company in the Revolution on 23 April 1779 [NARA, M246, Roll 79, frame 142 of 323; http://fold3.com/image/10200387]. Between 1 September 1784 and 1 February 1785 he received the final pay for his own and Robert Newsom's service in the North Carolina Continental Line [Clark, *The State Records of North Carolina*, XVII:235]. He was head of a Northampton County household of 3 "other free" in 1790 [NC:74] and 8 in 1800 [NC:463].

Ethelred Newsom enlisted in Quinn's Company of the 10th North Carolina Regiment on 24 June 1779 [Clark, *The State Records of North Carolina*, XVI:1126], called "Netheneldred Newsom of Robeson County" on 18 April 1792 when he appointed Jacob Rhodes his attorney to receive his final settlement for serving in the war [*NCGSJ* XIV:111]. He was head of a Robeson County household of 3 "other free" in 1790 [NC:50], 3 in 1800 [NC:408], and 4 in 1810 [NC:241].

James Newsom was a "Black" member of the undated Colonial Muster of Captain James Fason's Northampton County militia [T.R. box 1, folder 3]. He received voucher no. 2106 for £8 in Halifax District on 20 September 1781 and another voucher on 13 February 1782 for military service in the Revolution [North Carolina Revolutionary Pay Vouchers, 1779-1782, http://familysearch.org/ark:/61903/1:1:Q2WT-P2XV, Newsome, James]. He was head of a Northampton County household of 5 "Black" persons 12-50 years old and 5 "Black" persons less than 12 or over 50 years old in Dupree's District for the 1786 state census and 11 "other free" in 1790 [NC:74].

Moses Newsom received State of North Carolina warrant no. 3716 for 640 acres for serving in the Revolution [North Carolina and Tennessee, Revolutionary War Land Warrants, 1783-1843, N.C. Revolutionary Warrants, frame 429 of 456 http://ancestry.com]. It is not noted on the warrant, but this was probably for the service of one of his sons who died in the Revolution. (There is more information in the N.C. Archives, State Treasurer Record Group, Military Papers, Revolutionary War Army Accounts, A:61; B:236; K:90, 92; VII:68). On 15 January 1783 he received voucher no. 4717 in Halifax District for £2,000 for services to the military in the Revolution [North Carolina Revolutionary Pay Vouchers, 1779-1782, http://familysearch.org/ark:/61903/1:1:Q2WT-54R1, Newsom, Moses].

Robert Newsom enlisted in Quinn's Company in the North Carolina Line on 31 May 1779 for three years. Booth Newsom received his final pay [Clark, *The State Records of North Carolina*, XVII:235; DAR, *Roster of Soldiers from North Carolina in the American Revolution*, 150, 546]. His heirs received warrant no. 1074 for 274 acres on 21 February 1822 for his service in the Revolution [North Carolina and Tennessee, Revolutionary War Land Warrants, 1783-1843, Roll 14:William Hill Warrants, 1811-1837 frame 430 of 540; http://ancestry.com].

Simon Newsom received voucher nos. 5518, 5592, and 7743 for a total of £27 in Halifax District between 11 February and 23 July 1782 for military service in the Revolution and a fourth voucher for £9 on 24 July 1787 [North Carolina Revolutionary Pay Vouchers, 1779-1782, http://familysearch.org/ark:/61903/1:1:Q2WT-PKXC, Newsom, Simon]. He was head of a Northampton County household of 1 "other free" in 1810.

Carter Nickens was in a list of militia men drafted from Hertford County in the Third Division commanded by Major George Little between 1778 and 1780 [T.R., Box 5, Folder 20]. He was paid £11.12 for services to the Revolution on 1 August 1783 [Haun, *Revolutionary Army Accounts*, vol. I, Book 4:232; http://familysearch.org/ark:/61903/1:1:Q2WT-5RZP].

Edward Nickens enlisted in the 10th North Carolina Regiment for 3 years and was mustered in January 1779 [Clark, *The State Records of North Carolina*, XVI:1127]. He received pay for service in the 6th and 10th Regiments of $239 from 5 August 1777 to

118

1 August 1780 [NARA, U.S. Revolutionary War Miscellaneous Records (Manuscript File), 1775-1790s, Records Pertaining to Troops of particular States, 14403, frames 30-32 of 397; http://ancestry.com].

Edward Nickens was a soldier from North Carolina in the Revolutionary War who was deceased by 5 December 1792 when a petition by his son and heir Richard Nickens was placed before the North Carolina General Assembly [LP 117 by *NCGSJ* IV:174]. Warrant no. 4317 for 640 acres was issued to the heirs of Edward Nicken on 14 December 1797 for his services as a private in the Revolution. Richard Nickens, "heir of Edward Nickens," sold his right to the warrant for $500 on 11 March 1797 [North Carolina and Tennessee, Revolutionary War Land Warrants, 1783-1843, Roll 07: Revolutionary Warrants, frame 324-5 of 608, http://ancestry.com]. Richard was head of a Currituck County household of 3 "other free" in 1790 (called Richard Mekins) [NC:22] and 8 "other free" in Captain Lewis' District of Hertford County in 1800.

Malachi Nickens was living in Hertford County on 19 May 1781 when he enlisted Carter's Company of the 10th North Carolina Regiment for a year and was discharged on 19 May 1782 [Clark, *The State Records of North Carolina*, XVI:1127]. He was about 56 years old on 13 November 1821 when he testified in Hertford County court for his pension, stating that he was in the Battles of Eutaw Springs and Ninety-Six and in a battle with Indians on the Savannah River. James **Smith** testified on his behalf [NARA, S.41925, M805, frame 0198; http://fold3.com/image/25387342]. Malachi was head of a Hertford County household of 5 "other free" in 1790 [NC:26], 3 in 1800, and 3 "free colored" in 1820 [NC:190].

Jacob Norton enlisted in Hogg's Company of the 1st North Carolina Regiment as a musician in 1777 and died 28 July 1778 [Clark, *The State Records of North Carolina*, XVI:1123]. He was a "man of colour" who died in Revolutionary War service and left no heirs according to a deposition by Charles Wood in Orange County, North Carolina, in 1820 [The North Carolinian, p. 2578]. Jacob enlisted in Hogg's Company of the 1st North Carolina Regiment as a musician in 1777 and died 28 July 1778 [Clark, *The State Records of North Carolina*, XVI:1123]. His warrant for 640 acres for his service was given to the president and trustees of the University of North Carolina on 21 August 1820 [North Carolina and Tennessee, Revolutionary War Land Warrants, 1783-1843, Survey Orders (Nos. 1-3992), no. 460 (http://ancestry.com)].

William Norton enlisted as a musician in Bowman's Company of the 1st North Carolina Regiment in 1777 and died before September 1778 [Clark, *The State Records of North Carolina*, XVI:1123]. On 1 July 1801 his widow Winnie Norton received 640 acres for his service [N.C. Archives, S.S. file 1876, warrant 3062, call no. S.108358; http://archives.ncdcr /doc/search-doc; North Carolina and Tennessee, Revolutionary War Land Warrants, 1783-1843, Survey Orders (Nos. 1-3992), no. 41 (http://ancestry.com)].

Theophilus/ Foy Norwood, a six-year-old "Molato" boy of Nan Norwood, a "Molato" woman, was ordered bound as an apprentice to Keziah Shackleford in Carteret County court on 6 September 1759 [Minutes 1747-64, 251]. He enlisted for three years in Carteret County in September 1778: *place of abode: Straights, born: Straights, 5'8", 27 years of age, Mulatto* [T.R., Box 4, Folder 37, http://digital.ncdcr.gov/cdm/compoundobject/collection/p16062coll26/id/654/rec/163].

Obed Norwood, a "Molato" boy of Nan Norwood, was bound to Keziah Shackleford in Carteret County on 6 September 1759 [Minutes 1747-64, 259]. He was called Obid Norward when he enlisted for three years in Carteret County in September 1778 [T.R., Box 4, folder 37, http://digital.ncdcr.gov/cdm/compoundobject/collection/p16062coll26/id/651/rec/162].

William Orange was sized in the 3rd North Carolina Regiment at Halifax (no date): *age 36, 5'9", Black Complexion, enlisted for 12 months in Halifax County, born in N Carolina, a planter, servt to Lt Ashe* [T.R., box 6, folder 20; http://digital.ncdcr.gov/cdm/compoundobject/collection/p16062coll26/id/980/rec/2]. He received £12.14 specie in Halifax District per the Board of Auditors Report of 4 November 1782 [http://familysearch.org/ark:/61903/1:1:Q2WT-P2Q2]. His heirs received warrant no. 2056 for 640 acres in 1788 for 84 months service [North Carolina and Tennessee, Revolutionary War Land Warrants, 1783-1843, Roll 04, frames 105-6 of 619; http://ancestry.com]. He was probably related to Henry Orange who was head of a Hertford County household of 3 "other free" in 1790 [NC:26].

Caleb Overton enlisted in Moore's Company of the 10th North Carolina Regiment on 30 June 1777 and was discharged on 6 June 1778 [Clark, *The State Records of North Carolina*, XV:724; XVI:1130]. He was deceased by 10 July 1820 when his heirs received a 274 acre land warrant for his service as a private in Captain Moore's Company of the 10th North Carolina Line in the Revolution. They were Samuel, Lemuel, Rachel and Elizabeth Overton who assigned their rights to the land to James Freeman in Pasquotank County [North Carolina and Tennessee, Revolutionary War Land Warrants, 1783-1843, Roll 13: William Hill Warrants, 1811-1837, no. 408 (http://ancestry.com)].

Daniel Overton enlisted for three years as a private in Raiford's Company of the 10th North Carolina Regiment on 20 June 1779 [Clark, *The State Records of North Carolina*, XVI:1131]. His heirs Samuel, Lemuel, Rachel and Elizabeth Overton of Pasquotank County received 274 acres for his service in the Revolution [North Carolina and Tennessee, Revolutionary War Land Warrants, 1783-1843, Roll 13: William Hill Warrants, 1811-1837, no. 405 (http://ancestry.com)].

John Overton enlisted as a private in Mills' Company of the 10th North Carolina Regiment on 7 January 1782 and died on 9 September the same year [Clark, *The State Records of North Carolina*, XVI:1131]. His heirs Samuel, Lemuel, Rachel and Elizabeth Overton of Pasquotank County received 640 acres for his service in the Revolution [North Carolina and Tennessee, Revolutionary War Land Warrants, 1783-1843, Roll 13: William Hill Warrants, 1811-1837, no. 409 (http://ancestry.com)].

Jonathan Overton enlisted in Jones' Company of the 10th North Carolina Regiment on 17 November 1781 [Clark, *The State Records of North Carolina* XVI:1131]. He was the apprentice of John Bateman of Chowan County when he entered the service as a substitute for him under Colonel Lytle. He was at sea for a while and then returned to Edenton. He was about 79 years old on 19 December 1832 when he made a declaration in Chowan County court to obtain a pension for three years service [NARA, S.8915, M804, Roll 1854, frame 0788; http://fold3.com/image/25220765]. He was head of a Chowan County household of 5 "other free" in Edenton in 1790, 9 "other free" in 1810 [NC:535] and 7 "free colored" in 1820 [NC:129]. He was described in a 1849 newspaper account: *a colored man, a soldier in the Revolution...at the advanced age of 101 years* [Crow, Black Experience in Revolutionary North Carolina, 101].

Lemuel Overton was head of Perquimans County household of 2 "other free" in 1790 [NC:31], 4 in Pasquotank County in 1800, entry blank in Pasquotank County in 1810, and 13 "free colored" in 1820. He was the husband of a slave named Rose and children John and Burdock who were emancipated by order of the North Carolina General Assembly [Byrd, In Full Force and Virtue, 298]. He enlisted in Moore's Company of the 10th North Carolina Regiment on 30 June 1777 [Clark, *The State Records of North Carolina*, XVI:1130]. He was living in Pasquotank County on 10 July 1820 when he appointed James Freeman his attorney to obtain a land warrant of 274 acres for his services as a soldier in the 10th Regiment of the North Carolina Line [*NCGSJ* VII:93; North Carolina and Tennessee, Revolutionary War Land Warrants, 1783-1843, Roll 13: William Hill Warrants, 1811-1837, no. 413 (http://ancestry.com)].

Samuel Overton was a "Molatto" Perquimans County taxable in 1771 [CR 77.701.1], head of a Pasquotank County household of 3 "other free" in 1790 [NC:31], 4 in 1800 [NC:634], and 13 "free colored" in 1820 [NC:277]. He was called a "free man of Colour" on 8 March 1825 when he made a declaration in Pasquotank County court to obtain a Revolutionary War pension [NARA, S.41928, M804, Roll 1854, frame 0826; http://fold3.com/image/25220866].

Titus Overton was taxable with his wife in Bladen County in 1763, was taxable on 2 "Mulatto" tithes in Cumberland County in 1767, was taxable with his wife ("Mulatoes") in Bladen County from 1770 to 1776 [SS 837; N.C. Genealogy XXI:3136; Byrd, *Bladen County Tax Lists*, I:32, 89, 123; II:90, 146]. He received £2.2 for 21 days service in the Bladen County Militia between 1775 and 1776 under Captain James Council [Haun, *Revolutionary Army Accounts, Journal "A"*, 22]. He was head of a Cumberland County household of 11 "other free" in 1790 [NC:31], 7 in 1800, and 1 in 1810 [NC:600].

Elisha Parker, a "man of color," made a declaration in Gates County, North Carolina, to obtain a pension for his services in the Revolution. He stated that he was born in Nansemond County, Virginia, near the North Carolina line about 1752. He stated that he enlisted in Gates County about 1779 for 9 months under Captain Arthur Gatling, then enlisted as a substitute for Francis Speight, was in the Battle of Stono Ferry and the Siege of Charleston. He had been a resident of Nansemond County for the previous 45 years [NARA, S.11211, M804, Roll 1871, frame 0787]. He was head of a Gates County household of 4 "other free" in 1790 [NC:23] and 3 "free colored" in Nansemond County in 1820 [VA:79].

Abraham Pavey served in the Revolution in North Carolina according to the pension application of his children in Alabama [NARA, W.10880, M804, Roll 1899; frame 281 of 1237; http://fold3.com/image/25980528].

Nehemiah Peavy was head of a Brunswick County, North Carolina household of 2 "other free" in 1810 [NC:236], 15 "free colored" in 1830 and 7 "free colored" in 1840. He enlisted as a musician in Mill's Company of the 10th North Carolina Regiment on 6 February 1782 and completed his service in September 1782 [Clark, *The State Records of North Carolina*, XVI:1140]. On 12 October 1795 he received a military land warrant for 640 acres for 84 months service as a fifer [N.C. Archives, S.S. 2240, call no. S.108.360].

Thomas Peavey enlisted in Dixon's Company in the 1st North Carolina Regiment in 1777 for the war, was omitted in January 1778, and enlisted in Montfort's Company of the 10th North Carolina Regiment on 24 June 1779 for the war [Clark, *The State Records of North Carolina*, XVI:1132, 1138; NARA, M246, Roll 79, frame 184 of 323; http://fold3.com/image/10201106], head of a New Hanover County household of 1 "Molatto" 21-60 years old with 3 "Molatto" females for the state census in 1787, probably the T. Peavy who was head of a Brunswick County, North Carolina household of 4 "other free" in 1810 [NC:234].

Richard Pendergrass, born say 1750, was a "Mulatto man servant" (called Richard Pendergast) on 27 April 1767 when his master Gideon Patteson of Cumberland County, Virginia, warned buyers at the sale of Samuel Jones of Halifax County that the indenture of Richard Pendergast had been conveyed to him to secure a debt [*Virginia Gazette*, Purdie & Dixon edition, p.3, col.2]. Richard was called "Negro Richd Pendegrass" on 17 March 1781 when he was listed as one of General Cornwallis's prisoners at his Guilford Courthouse headquarters [*NCGSJ* V:81]. He was head of a Person County household of 3 "other free" in 1800 [NC:601].

Isaac Perkins was head of a Craven County household of 2 "other free" in 1790 [NC:131] and 2 "free colored" in Craven County in 1820 [NC:67]. He made a declaration in Craven County court to obtain a Revolutionary War pension on 13 May

1829. He testified that he enlisted for three years in May 1778, marched to Valley Forge and was taken prisoner at Charleston. He was granted pension certificate no. 4666 on 30 November 1818. His lawyer, Samuel Gerock, called him a "Negroe Man, and Old Soldier of the Revolutionary Army" when he appealed for the restoration of his pension [NARA, S.41953, M804, roll 1911, frame 174 of 1034; http://fold3.com/image/25570503].

Jacob Perkins served in the Revolution under General Marion according to testimony of his son Jacob Perkins that Jacob also served several tours against the Indians after coming to Carter County (then Washington County, North Carolina) [NARA, R.8105, M804, Roll 1911, frame 285 of 1034; http://fold3.com/image/25580287].

Aaron Peters was drafted from the Third Division of the Hertford County Militia between 1779 and 1780 [T.R., box 5, folder 20]. He was head of a Halifax County, North Carolina household of 11 "free colored" in 1820 [NC:161] and 14 in 1830 [NC:322].

Elias Pettiford was listed in the payroll of Captain Dudley's 2nd Virginia State Regiment commanded by Colonel Gregory Smith from August to December 1778 [NARA, M246, Roll 96, frame 547 of 736; http://fold3.com/image/10081826, 10081833, 10081847, 10081873]. He enlisted in Donoho's Company of the 10th North Carolina Regiment on 14 June 1781 and left the service in 1782 [Clark, *The State Records of North Carolina*, XVI:1138]. On 4 October 1832 William Whicker appeared in Fayette County, Ohio court and testified that "he got one Elias Pettiford, a Colored, to take his place in the Revolution [NARA, S.17194, M804, Roll 2547, frame 555 of 822; http://fold3.com/image/28017843].

George Pettiford was about 63 years old on 10 February 1821 when he made a declaration in Granville County court in order to obtain a Revolutionary War pension, stating that he had enlisted in the company of Captain Goodwin in the 4th North Carolina Regiment. Jesse Bass and Poledore Johnson testified that they were well acquainted with George and that he was in reduced circumstances. Richard Glasgow of Granville County and Abram Gregory of Person County testified on 12 June 1827 that they served with George Pettiford, a "free man of Color" [NARA, W.9223, M805, Roll 648; M804, Roll 1920, frame 76 of 1326; http://fold3.com/image/27179368].

Philip Pettiford was head of an Oxford District, Granville County household of 5 male and 3 female "Blacks" and one white male in 1786 for the state census and head of a Cumberland County household of 9 "other free" [NC:40]. He enlisted and served in Colonel Shephard's 10th North Carolina Regiment from 14 June 1781 to 14 June 1782 [NARA, S.41952, M804, roll 1920, frame 152 of 1326; http://fold3.com/image/27181971].

William Pettiford was listed in Captain William Gill's Granville County Company as a seventeen-year-old "black man" [T.R., box 4, folder 40]. He was head of an Orange County household of 14 "other free" in 1810 [NC:863] and 8 "free colored" in 1820 [NC:312]. He was about 58 years old on 19 February 1819 when he made a deposition before one of the justices of Orange County to obtain a pension for his services in the Revolution. He served as a musician in Colonel Shepard's 10th North Carolina Regiment from 14 June 1781 to 14 June 1782 [NARA, S.41948, M804, frame 169 of 1326; http://fold3.com/image/27182030].

Israel Pierce was a "free colored" head of a Tyrrell County household of 3 free males and 3 free females in 1790 [NC:34], 7 "other free" in Hyde County in 1800 [NC:374], 11 in Hyde County in 1810 [NC:119] and 8 "free colored" in Beaufort County in 1820 [NC:32]. He was in Tyrrell County on 21 June 1791 when he gave power of attorney to Samuel Warren, an attorney, to receive his final settlement due him as a soldier in the North Carolina Continental Line [Clark, *The State Records of North Carolina*,

XVII:241; *NCGSJ* XIV:230]. He appeared in Beaufort County court and applied for a pension for his service in the Revolution, stating that he was born in Tyrell County and enlisted there for 12 months in the naval service on board the ship Caswell and then enlisted in the army under the command of Colonel Mebane and was in the Battles of Eutaw Springs and Camden and the Siege of Charleston [NARA, S.3660, M804, Roll 1895, frame 290 of 1337; http://fold3.com/image/25879880].

Thomas Pierce was a "free colored" head of a Tyrrell County household of 4 free males and 4 free females in 1790 [NC:34]. On 13 June 1795 he was called "Thomas Pierce of Tyrrell County, administrator of William Pierce," when he gave power of attorney to Samuel Warren, an attorney, to receive the final settlement due to (his son?) William Pierce for his service in the North Carolina Continental Line [*NCGSJ* XIV:230].

Stephen Powell was granted administration on the Johnston County estate of Archibald **Artis** on a bond of £200 [Haun, *Johnston County Court Minutes*, III:232] and was taxable on 150 acres and 1 poll in Johnston County in 1784 [GA 64.1]. He was about 52 years old on 29 February 1792 when he made a deposition in Johnston County court that his son Stephen, aged about 18 or 19 years old, enlisted for 18 months and died in the service in 1783 [*NCGSJ* XIV:234]. He was granted administration on his son's Johnston County estate in November 1792 [Haun, *Johnston County Court Minutes*, IV:234]. He was head of a Johnston County household of 11 "other free" in 1790 [NC:142], 11 in 1800, and 4 in Chatham County in 1810 [NC:197].

Hardimon Poythress/ Portiss enlisted in Lieutenant Colonel William L. Davidson's Company on 20 July 1778 and was listed as "Left at the Hospital" in the 23 April 1779 muster. H. Montfort received his final pay [Clark, *The State Records of North Carolina*, XVI:1137, XVII:238; NARA, M246, roll 79, frame 142 of 323; http://fold3.com/image/10200387]. He was head of a Northampton County household of 5 "other free" in 1790 [NC:72].

John Poythress/ Portress enlisted in Eaton's Company of the 3rd North Carolina Regiment in 1777 and died on 1 May 1778 [Clark, *The State Records of North Carolina*, XVI:1133]. Administration on his estate was granted to Hardimon Poythress in Northampton County court on 4 June 1792 on a bond of £50 [Minutes 1792-6, 18, 36].

Odam Poythress was called Oadom Portess of Northampton County when he received voucher no. 9616 in Halifax District on 19 March 178_ for his military service in the Revolution [North Carolina Revolutionary Pay Vouchers, 1779-1782, http://familysearch.org/ark:/61903/1:1:Q2WT-P98Z, Portess, Aadam]. He was head of a Northampton County household of 9 "other free" in 1790 [NC:72], 12 in 1800 [NC:469], and 10 in 1810 [NC:742].

Arthur Pugh, a Mulatto bastard of Sarah Pugh, was bound as an apprentice cooper in Bertie County on 30 March 1767 [Haun, Bertie County Court Minutes, III:765]. He enlisted in Captain Tatum's 1st North Carolina Regiment from 20 February 1778 for 3 years [Clark, *The State Records of North Carolina*, XVI:1132] and was listed in Captain Howell Tatum's Company of the 1st North Carolina Regiment on 8 September 1778 [NARA, M246, roll 79, frame 68 of 323; http://fold3.com/image/10198776].

David Pugh was the two-year-old minor of Sarah Pugh, bound to James Jones in Bertie County on 26 July 1759 to be a cooper [*NCGSJ* XIII:169]. He was saddler hired for three months in Halifax by Colonel Nicholas Long, deputy quartermaster general for North Carolina in the Revolution according to his return for 23 August 1781 [Clark, *The State Records of North Carolina*, XV:620]. He was head of a Hertford County household of 6 "other free" in 1800.

Isaac Ransom, "of Craven County," received voucher no. 966 for £1. ___teen specie on 22 October 1782 for militia duty [North Carolina Revolutionary Pay Vouchers, 1779-1782, http://familysearch.org/ark:/61903/1:1:Q2WT-5B69]. He was head of a Craven County household of 7 "other free" in 1790 [NC:134].

Benjamin Reed enlisted with Colonel Murfree for the term of the war. He made a declaration in Gates County court to obtain a pension on 19 November 1821, stating that he entered the war in 1779 or 1780, was in the Battles of Monmouth, Brandywine and Eutaw Springs and had a stiff arm from a wound [NARA, S.41976, M805, reel 680, frame 89]. He was head of a Gates County household of 3 "other free" in 1790, 3 in 1810 [NC:842], and 3 "free colored" in 1820 [NC:154].

Dempsey Reed was listed in the Revolutionary War accounts, hired as a substitute by Nathaniel Harris in Mecklenburg County, North Carolina [Crow, Black Experience in Revolutionary North Carolina, 101; DAR, *Roster of Soldiers from North Carolina in the American Revolution*, 180]. He was head of a Warren County household of 8 "other free" in 1790 [NC:78], 13 in Mecklenburg County, North Carolina, in 1800 [NC:534], and 12 "free colored" in Cabarrus County in 1820 [NC:160].

Frederick Reed was head of a Franklin County, North Carolina household of 4 "other free" in 1790 [NC:60]. He was about 68 years old when he appeared in Orange County court on 7 February 1820 to apply for a pension for his service in the Revolution. The muster rolls indicated that he enlisted as a private in Captain Baker's Company of the 10th Regiment on 20 July 1778 but was not discharged. Elisha **Boon** testified that he served with him and left him at the hospital in Philadelphia in April 1779 [NARA, M804, R.8689, Roll 2014, frame 987 of 1018; http://fold3.com/image/13643092]. He may have been the Frederick Reed who received voucher no. 1030 for £20 specie for military service to 6 May 1779 [North Carolina Revolutionary War Pay Vouchers, http://familysearch.org/ark:/61903/1:1:Q2WT-P9PC].

Jacob Reed was 8 years old in April 1763 when the Chowan County court bound him to James Bond until the age of twenty-one. He served in the Revolutionary War and died before 23 May 1792 when the Gates County court appointed (his mother) Rachel Reid, administratrix of his estate. On 4 August 1792 in Gates County she gave her son Benjamin power of attorney to settle the balance of his army wages from 20 November 1778 to June 1779 [*NCGSJ* XV:103].

Jacob Reid was the son of Isaac Reed, a "Negro man" taxable with his wife Margaret from 1756 to 1769 in the part of Chowan County which became Gates County in 1779 [N.C. Archives file CR 24.701.2]. Isaac was head of a Gates County of 4 "other free," a white man and a white woman in 1790 and 2 "other free" and 3 white women in 1800. The Gates County court appointed him administrator of the estate of Jacob Reid on 22 May 1792 [Fouts, *Minutes of County Court of Pleas and Quarter Sessions* 1787-93, 110]. As administrator of the estate he appointed Samuel Smith attorney to settle the Continental Army accounts of (his son?) Jacob Reid, Jr., from 10 December 1778 to 10 April 1779. On 5 June 1792 Captain Arthur Gatling testified in Northampton County, North Carolina court that Jacob was a soldier in a company of new levies on the Continental Establishment which he marched from Hertford to South Carolina from November 1778 to March 1779, and Jacob died in the service in South Carolina [*NCGSJ* XV:102].

James Reed received military land warrant no. 406 of 274 acres for his service in the Revolution. His heir Shadrack Reed of Hertford County sold his right to the land for $100 on 1 August 1820 [North Carolina and Tennessee, Revolutionary War Land Warrants, 1783-1843, Roll 13: William Hill Warrants, 1811-1837 (Nos. 364-675), ancestry.com]. Shadrack was head of a Hertford County household of 6 "other free" in 1790 [NC:26], 3 in 1810 [NC:98], and 3 "free colored" in 1820.

Nathaniel Revell enlisted in Quinn's Company of the 10th North Carolina Regiment on 24 June 1779 for 18 months and deserted in September 1779 [Clark, *The State Records of North Carolina*, XVI:1149], listed as a substitute from Bladen County in Lieutenant Wilkinson's Company of the 10th North Carolina Regiment of Colonel Abraham Sheppard on 19 February 1782 as a deserter [NARA, M246, roll 79, frame 165 of 323; http://fold3.com/image/10200648]. He was head of a Sampson County household of 13 "other free" in 1790 and 10 "other free"' in 1800.

Benjamin Richardson "went out of Halifax and Warren Counties" and served as a militia soldier in the year 1780 and part of 1781 [NARA, W.4061, M804, Roll 2038, frame 0533; http://fold3.com/image/14161295]. He was head of a Halifax County household of 10 "other free" in 1800 [NC:338].

William Richardson received voucher no. 389 for £110 specie in Halifax District on 1 August 1783 as his pay as a soldier and wagoner in the Revolution [North Carolina Revolutionary Pay Vouchers, 1779-1782, http://familysearch.org/ark:/61903/1:1:Q2WT-PFHV]. He was head of a Halifax County household of 7 "other free" in 1790 [NC:63].

James Robbins received voucher no. 681 in Edenton for £6 specie on 8 April 1782 for military service in the Revolution [North Carolina Revolutionary Pay Vouchers, 1779-1782, http://familysearch.org/ark:/61903/1:1:Q2WT-G8BN, Robbins, James]. He was head of a Gates County household of 15 "other free" and a white woman in 1790 [NC:23].

Elias Roberts, "of Northampton County," received voucher nos. 569 and 9938 in Halifax District for a total of £19 specie on 22 July 1782 and 3 August 1784 for military service in the Revolution [North Carolina Revolutionary Pay Vouchers, 1779-1782, http://familysearch.org/ark:/61903/1:1:Q2WT-54DN, Roberts, Elias]. He was head of a Northampton County household of 4 "other free" in 1790 [NC:73], 11 in 1800 [NC:473], and 15 "other free" and 2 slaves in 1810 [NC:743].

Ishmael Roberts served in Shepherd's Company of the 10th North Carolina Regiment, enlisted on 3 June 1777 and was omitted as a casualty in June 1778 [NARA, M881, Roll 784; frame 486 of 837 http://fold3.com/image/21163844]. He received pay for Revolutionary War service from 3 June 1777 to 3 June 1778 as a private in Colonel Abraham Shepherd's Company. Colonel Shepherd gave him a certificate which stated, "he was furloughed at Head Quarters Valley Forge to come home with me who was Inlisted in my Regement for the Term of three years - and Returned Home with me" [*NCGSJ* XV:105]. He was head of a Robeson County household of 10 "other free" in 1790 [NC:50], 15 in 1800 [NC:415], and 14 in Chatham County in 1810 [NC:195].

James Roberts was in the roll of Major Hardy Murfree's Company in the 2nd North Carolina Battalion commanded by Colonel John Patton at White Plains on 9 September 1778. William Faircloth received his final pay of £25 [Clark, *The State Records of North Carolina*, XIII:521; XVII:244].

John Roberts served in the Revolution. H. Murfree received his final pay of £145 [Clark, *The State Records of North Carolina*, XVII:244]. He received military warrant no. 3961 of 640 acres for serving in the 1st North Carolina Regiment from July 1776 to July 1780 and assigned his rights to the warrant to Hardy Murfree on 18 May 1786 [North Carolina and Tennessee, Revolutionary War Land Warrants, 1783-1843, Roll 06: Revolutionary Warrants, 1783-1799 (Nos. 3716-4134), frames 346-7 of 597, ancestry.com]. He was head of a Northampton County household of 8 "other free" in 1790 [NC:73].

Jonathan Roberts received 18 shillings 8 pence pay for 7 days service in the Northampton County, North Carolina Militia under Colonel Allen Jones in 1775-1776 [Haun, Revolutionary Army Accounts, Journal "A", 20]. He was head of a Northampton County household of 5 "other free" in 1790 [NC:73], 10 in 1800 [NC:473], and 8 "other free" and a slave in 1810 [NC:743].

Kinchen Roberts enlisted in Brinkley's Company of the 3rd North Carolina Regiment in 1777 for 2-1/2 years and died on 10 March 1778. H. Montfort received his final pay of £31 [Clark, *The State Records of North Carolina*, XVI:1143; XVII:242]. On 29 September 1784 his heir Ishmael Roberts received 640 acres of military bounty land for his 84 months service in the Revolution [N.C. Archives, State Treasurer Record Group, Military Papers, Revolutionary War Army Accounts, Roberts, Kinchen; http://archives.ncdcr.gov/doc/search-doc; also abstracted in Haun, *North Carolina Revolutionary Army accounts*, pt. 15].

Richard Roberts was head of a Northampton County, North Carolina household of 2 "other free" in 1810 [NC:743] and 9 "free colored" in 1820 [NC:256], perhaps the Richard Roberts who enlisted in Hall's Company of the 2nd North Carolina Regiment in the Revolution for three years on 10 July 1777. He was a wagoner in the roll of Major Hardy Murfree's Company in the 2nd North Carolina Battalion commanded by Colonel John Patton at White Plains on 9 September 1778 and was a prisoner on 1 June 1779 [Clark, *The State Records of North Carolina*, XIII:522; XVI:1142].

Charles Randolph Rowe was one of the Continental soldiers who volunteered in Bute County in 1779: *Chas Row, born in Virga, 5'8" tall, dark hair and dark eyes* [T.R., Box 4, Folder 35, http://digital.ncdcr.gov/cdm/compoundobject/collection/p16062coll26/id/648/rec/36]. He enlisted in Ballard's Company of the 10th North Carolina Regiment in 1779 and was discharged on 9 December 1779. William Sanders received his final pay of £41 for his service in the North Carolina Continental Line between 1 September 1784 and 1 February 1785 [Clark, *The State Records of North Carolina*, XVI:1148; XVII:242]. He was head of a Wake County household of 2 "other free" in 1800 [NC:793], 5 in Chatham County in 1810 (called Randolf Roe) [NC:201], and 2 "free colored" in 1820 [NC:209]. He was a "man of Colour" who appeared in Chatham County court to apply for a pension, stating that he entered the service in Bute County and lost the sight of one of his eyes in a battle on the Savannah River [NARA, S.7416, M804, Roll 2072, frame 89 of 511; http://fold3.com/image/14130803].

Joseph Roberson received voucher no. 1371 on 22 August 1783 for £42 specie in Wilmington District for military service [North Carolina Revolutionary Pay Vouchers, 1779-1782, Roberson, Joseph http://familysearch.org/ark:/61903/1:1:Q2WT-GDKH], He was head of a New Hanover County household of 5 "other free" in 1800 [NC:311], and 1 "free colored" man over 45 years old in 1820 [NC:209].

Thomas Robison, received voucher no. 3095 on 21 March 1783 in the District of Wilmington for £5 specie for his service in the militia [North Carolina Revolutionary Pay Vouchers, 1779-1782, Robeson, Thomas, http://familysearch.org/ark:/61903/1:1:Q2WT-GNGV]. He was head of a "Molatto" New Hanover County household of 2 polls aged 21-60 years, 3 under 21 or over 60, and 5 females in 1786 in John Erwin's list for the North Carolina state census; called Thomas Roberson in 1800: head of a New Hanover County household of 7 "other free" [NC:311].

William Rudd was drafted in Halifax County in March 1779 [T.R., Box 3, Folder 40, http://digital.ncdcr.gov/cdm/compoundobject/collection/p16062coll26/id/510/rec/176]. He received voucher no. 532 for £5 specie in Halifax District on 4 March 1782 for military service in the Revolution [North Carolina Revolutionary Pay Vouchers, 1779-1782, http://familysearch.org/ark:/61903/1:1:Q2WT-5NZF, Rudd, William]. He was head of a Halifax County household of 8 "other free" in 1790 and 11 in 1800 [NC:338].

Caesar Santee, born say 1760, enlisted in the 3rd North Carolina Regiment in Eaton's Company on 22 February 1777 was at White Plains on 9 September 1778 [NARA, M246, roll 79, frame 130 of 323; http://fold3.com/image/10199799], reenlisted in Paramus on 12 March 1779, was in prison on 1 June 1779, and mustered for the war in 1781 [Clark, *The State Records of North Carolina*, XIII:528; XVI:1154]. He was issued a warrant for 640 acres for his service and was in Wake County when he assigned his rights to the land to William Hill in November 1818 [North Carolina and Tennessee, Revolutionary War Land Warrants, 1783-1843, Roll 2: Revolutionary Warrants, 1783-1799 (Nos. 399-1034), 904, frame 469 of 608].

Abraham Scott received voucher no. 3430 for £1.13 specie in January 1782 for military service in the Revolution [North Carolina Revolutionary Pay Vouchers, 1779-1782, http://familysearch.org/ark:/61903/1:1:Q2WT-GFG5, Scott, Abraham]. He was head of a Halifax County household of 6 "other free" in 1790 [NC:61].

David Scott was head of a Sumter District, South Carolina household of 15 "other free" in 1810 and 8 "free colored" and 2 female slaves in 1820. He appeared in Sumter District court on 12 June 1818 to apply for a pension, stating that he enlisted in Murfreesboro (Hertford County), North Carolina, on 25 September 1775 in Captain Hardy Murfree's Company of the 2nd North Carolina Regiment, served for a year, and then enlisted in the 5th South Carolina Regiment and served for three years. He stated that he was in the Siege of Charleston [NARA, S.9473, M804, roll 2135, frame 897 of 1004; http://fold3.com/image/14190486]. The inhabitants of Sumter District petitioned to release his descendants from paying the tax on free Blacks [S.C. Archives series S.108092, reel 131, frame 330].

Emanuel Scott enlisted for 12 months in Raiford's Company in the 10th North Carolina Regiment on 25 April 1781 and left the service on 25 April 1782 [Clark, *The State Records of North Carolina*, XVI:1162]. He made a deposition in Halifax County court on 22 August 1789 that he was a 12 months soldier in the Continental Line [*NCGSJ* XV:232]. He was head of a Halifax County household of 7 "other free" in 1790, 2 in 1800 [NC:342], and 6 in Cumberland County in 1810 [NC:599].

Exum Scott was head of a Halifax county household of 9 "other free" in 1790 [NC:63], and in 1800 he was called "Axiom" in Cumberland County, head of a household of 9 "other free" in 1810. He served 18 months in the Revolution under Colonel Nicholas Long and was paid £9 on 30 August 1783 and £23 in 1783 or 1784 [NARA, W.5994, M804, roll 2136, frame 172 of 850; http://fold3.com/image/14643308].

Isaac Scott was drafted from Northampton County during the Revolution [T.R., Box 5, folder 16]. He was head of a Northampton County household of 9 "other free" in 1790 [NC:73].

Isham Scott was head of a Halifax County household of 8 "other free" in 1800 [NC:342] and 8 in 1810 [NC:49]. He was a servant to Major Hogg and was at the skirmish at Halifax [NARA, S.42004, M804, Roll 2136, frame 0433; http://fold3.com/image/14643787].

Israel Scott was a "Mixt Blood/ Free Negro" taxable in Bladen County in 1776 [Byrd, *Bladen County Tax Lists*, II:94]. He enlisted in the 10th North Carolina Regiment on 20 July 1778 for 9 months [Clark, *The State Records of North Carolina*, XVI:1160]. He was head of an Edgecombe County household of 7 "other free" in 1790 [NC:55], 6 in 1800 (called "Free Negro"), 5 in 1810 [NC:776], and 2 "free colored" in 1820 [NC:94].

James Scott was head of a Sumter County, South Carolina household of 8 "other free" in 1810 and 5 "free colored" in 1820. He was residing in Claremont County when he appeared in Sumter District court on 12 June 1818 to apply for a pension for services in the Revolution. He stated that he enlisted in Northampton County, North Carolina, in 1776 and served in Captain William Barrett's 3rd Regiment commanded by Colonel Sumner for 2-1/2 years and was discharged at Halifax. After his discharge he moved to South Carolina, was in the Battle of Eutaw Springs and served in the militia [NARA, S.39064, M804, roll 2136, frame 626 of 850; http://fold3.com/image/14647967].

John Scott was called John Scott of Halifax County when he received voucher no. 9318 for £12 specie on 8 December 1783 for military service in the Revolution [North Carolina Revolutionary Pay Vouchers, 1779-1782, http://familysearch.org/ark:/61903/1:1:Q2WT-G62D, Scotte, John]. He was head of a Halifax County household of 7 "other free" in 1790 [NC:65], 6 in 1800 [NC:338], and 6 in 1810 [NC:50].

Nathaniel Scott enlisted in Ballard's Company of the 10th North Carolina Regiment on 20 July 1778 for 9 months [Clark, *The State Records of North Carolina*, XVI:1161]. Henry Hawkins enlisted the same day and made a deposition on 23 November 1812 that he was in the service with Nathan and that Nathan died in the hospital in Philadelphia [N.C. Archives L.P. 262, by *NCGSJ* VI:15].

Saul Scott received voucher no. 388 for £1 specie on 1 May 1792 for serving as a soldier in the Continental Line [North Carolina Revolutionary Pay Vouchers, 1779-1782, http://familysearch.org/ark:/61903/1:1:Q2WT-5HDD, Scott, Saul]. He was head of a Northampton County household of 1 "other free" in 1790 [NC:72].

Sterling Scott was a waiter listed in the roll of Lieutenant William Davidson's North Carolina Company in the Revolution on 23 April 1779 [NARA M246, Roll 79, frame 142 of 323; http://fold3.com/image/10200387] and head of a Northampton County household of 6 "other free" in 1790 [NC:72].

Abraham Shoecraft was head of a Hertford County household of 6 "other free" in 1800. His heirs received 640 acres of bounty land for his service in the Revolution [N.C. Archives, State Treasurer Record Group, Military Papers, Revolutionary War Army Accounts, http://archives.ncdcr.gov/doc/search-doc].

Lewis Sims was a "black man" listed in the militia returns for Granville County, North Carolina, in 1778 [T.R., box 4, folder 40].

Moses Skipper/ Scipper, received voucher no. 4726 in Wilmington District on 20 September 1783 for £14 specie for his service in the militia payroll no. 2733 [North Carolina Revolutionary Pay Vouchers, 1779-1782, Skipir, Moses http://familysearch.org/ark:/61903/1:1:Q2WT-GCSH]. He was a "Mulato" taxable in Bladen County in 1768 [Byrd, *Bladen County Tax Lists*, I:9], head of a Brunswick County, Wilmington District household of 4 males and 2 females in 1790 [NC:189] and 5 "other free" in 1800 [NC:14].

James Smith was head of a Hertford County household of 6 "other free" in 1790 [NC:25], 4 in Captain Moore's District in 1800, and 11 "free colored" in 1820. He may have been the James Smith who enlisted in the 10th North Carolina Regiment for three years on 17 June 1777 and reenlisted for 12 more months on 1 January 1782 [Clark, *The State Records of North Carolina*, XVI:1159, 1165]. He testified for Malachi **Nickens** and John **Weaver** in Hertford County court that he was a soldier with them.

128

Aaron Spelman was head of Craven County household of 3 "other free" in 1790 [NC:134]. He was called Aaron Spelmore when he enlisted in Sharp's Company of the 10th North Carolina Regiment on 5 May 1781 and served until 5 May 1782 [Clark, *The State Records of North Carolina*, XVI:1163]. On 18 January 1791 when he assigned his right to his final settlement for services in the "Twelve Months Draftees" in the Revolution [T&C, Box 22, by *NCGSJ* XVI:234]. He was called Aaron Spelmore on 12 September 1820 when he made a declaration in Craven County court to obtain a pension for his service under Captain Sharpe in the Tenth North Carolina Regiment, stating that he enlisted in May 1781 and was in the Battles of Ninety-Six and Eutaw Springs [NARA, S.42023, M804, Roll 2254, frame 590 of 818; http://fold3.com/image/13712617].

Asa Spelman was 11 years old when he was bound an apprentice in the April 1762 Craven County court. He was head of a Craven County household of 5 "other free" in 1790 [NC:134] and 4 "free colored" in 1820 [NC:72]. He was called Asa Spelmore alias Spelman on 13 September 1820 when he made a declaration in Craven County court to obtain a pension for service with Captain Quinn in the tenth North Carolina Regiment. He stated that during his 9 months service he was engaged in a skirmish at West Point and at Kings Ferry in Jersey. Isaac **Perkins** testified that he had seen Asa while they were both on duty in White Plains, New York. John **Carter** testified that Asa and he were in the same regiment [NARA, S.42022, M804, Roll 2254, frame 598 of 818; http://fold3.com/image/13712646].

Jacob Spelman, the 4-year-old son of Sarah Spelman, was bound out by the October 1760 Craven County court [Minutes 1758-61, 85a]. He enlisted in Carter's Company of the 10th North Carolina Regiment on 5 May and left the service on 5 May 1782. His final pay for service in the North Carolina Continental Line was received by F. Dixon [Clark, *The State Records of North Carolina*, XVI:1163; XVII:247]. A 5 May 1800 Fayetteville newspaper warned that a runaway slave might have changed his name to Jacob Spelman in order to pass as free [Fouts, *Newspapers of Edenton, Fayetteville, & Hillsborough*, 10].

Simon Spelman was a "free Negro" bound apprentice to Christopher Dawson in Craven County, North Carolina, on 13 March 1770 [Minutes 1766-75, 137]. He enlisted for the war in Bradley's Company of the 10th North Carolina Regiment on 28 June 1779 [Clark, *The State Records of North Carolina*, XVI:1161]. He assigned his right to military warrant no. 4264 for 640 acres to Howell Tatum and Henry Wiggin in 1797 [N.C. Archives, S.S. file 1365].

Tony Spelman, the two-year-old son of Sarah Spelman, was bound apprentice in Craven County on 10 October 1760 [CR 028.101.1]. He, Asa, and Jacob Spelman were in Captain John Bryan's Craven County Company in June 1778 [T.R., Box 3, folder 26, http://digital.ncdcr.gov/cdm/compoundobject/collection/p16062coll26/id/471/rec/161].

Dempsey Stewart enlisted in Evans's Company in the 10th North Carolina Regiment for 18 months while residing in Northampton County, North Carolina [Clark, *The State Records of North Carolina*, XVI:1166]. He registered in Petersburg on 9 November 1805: *a brown Free Negro man, five feet ten inches high, thin made, about forty one years old, Born free p. register from the Clk of Brunswick County* [Register of Free Negroes 1794-1819, no. 368]. He was head of a Free Town, Brunswick County household of 4 "other free" in 1810 [VA:770], 2 "free colored" over 45 years old in 1820 [VA:670], and 5 in 1830 [VA:249]. He made a declaration in Brunswick County court, stating that he had entered the service in 1782 [NARA, W.3734, M804, Roll 2290, frame 0162; http://fold3.com/image/17980389].

Peter Stewart received voucher no. 6821 for £3 specie in Halifax District on 4 June 1782 for military service in the Revolution [North Carolina Revolutionary Pay Vouchers, 1779-1782, http://familysearch.org/ark:/61903/1:1:Q2WT-GKPH, Stewart, Peter]. He was head of a Northampton County household of 2 "other free" and 5 slaves in 1790 [NC:73] and 4 "other free" in 1800 [NC:477] and 8 in 1810.

William Stewart was head of a Northampton County, North Carolina household of 7 "other free" in 1800 [NC:479]. He was "a Colored man...free born" about 1759 in Brunswick County, Virginia, according to his Revolutionary War pension file. He enlisted in 1777 under Major Hardy Murphy (Murfree) in Northampton County, North Carolina, and marched to West Point and Valley Forge, was in the Battles of Stony Point and Monmouth, and served three years. After the war he returned to Northampton County and then moved with his family to Westmoreland County, Pennsylvania, where he had been living from 1814 until 19 May 1835 when he made his pension application [NARA, R.10173, M805, Roll 773, frame 400; http://fold3.com/image/18492028].

Hezekiah Stringer enlisted for 12 months in Sharp's Company of the 10th North Carolina Regiment on 5 May 1781, left the service on 5 April 1782 and enlisted again in Coleman's Company for 18 months in 1782 [Clark, *The State Records of North Carolina*, XVI:1163]. He was in Craven County on 20 March 1787 when he registered his furlough papers before the justice of the peace. His papers, dated 26 May 1783, granted him a leave of absence from the 1st North Carolina Regiment until his final discharge [*NCGSJ* XVI:238]. He was called Kiah Stringer in 1800, head of a New Hanover County household of 5 "other free" [NC:316]

Mingo Stringer served in Sharp's Company of the 10th North Carolina Regiment between 5 May 1781 and 5 April 1782 [Clark, *The State Records of North Carolina*, XVI:1166]. He was head of a Craven County household of 2 "other free" in 1790 [NC:131].

Allen Sweat was head of a household of a free male and 2 free females in the state census in District 10 of Halifax County, North Carolina, in 1786. He married Nancy **Evans**, 7 January 1792 Wake County bond, Reuben **Evans** surety. He was taxable in Henry King's list for Wake County on 100 acres in 1794 and taxable on 1 poll in 1799 and 1802 [C.R. 099.701.1, microfilm frames 151, 228, 254]. He made a declaration in Wake County court to obtain a pension, stating that he enlisted in Halifax County about 1782. Exum **Scott** testified that he had known him since his infancy when he lived on Exum's plantation in Roanoke. Francis Jones testified that "he was well acquainted with Allen Swett, knows he served in the 15th Regiment...left the said Swett in the said service, who this deponent left the army in the capacity of Servant to an Officer." Allen later moved to McNairy County, Tennessee, where his wife received a survivor's pension [NARA, W.16, M804, Roll 2332, frame 15 of 1164; http://fold3.com/image/18323695]. He was counted as white in the 1840 Mcnairy County, Tennessee census.

Anthony Sweat was in the roll of Captain Bynum's Company of North Carolina Militia taken on 7 April 1781 [NARA, M246, Roll 79, frame 237 of 323; http://fold3.com/image/10202465].

Abraham Sweat served in Raiford's Company of the 10th North Carolina Regiment between 25 April 1781 and 25 April 1782 [Clark, State Records, XVI:1162]. He was head of a Halifax County household of 5 "other free" in 1790 [NC:62], 6 in 1800 [NC:344], and 4 in 1810 [NC:50].

Daniel Sweat served in the Revolution from North Carolina [N.C. Archives, State Treasurer Record Group, Military Papers, Revolutionary War Army Accounts, 19:288].

David Sweat enlisted in Shepard's Company of the 10th North Carolina Regiment on 12 July 1777 for three years [Clark, *The State Records of North Carolina*, XVI:1159; NARA, M246, http://fold3.com/image/10201146]. He was about 60 years old on 27 September 1820 when he appeared in Robeson County court and applied for a pension for his service in the Revolution. He testified that he enlisted for three years on 12 July 1777 in the company commanded by Captain Abraham Shepherd in the 10th Regiment, was in the Battles of Monmouth and Stony Point and the Seige of Charleston, and served his time [NARA, S.42031, M804, Roll 2329, frame 443 of 754; http://fold3.com/image/18467125].

George Sweat received £27 as his final pay for serving in the North Carolina Continental Line in the Revolution [Clark, *The State Records of North Carolina*, XVII:250]. He was head of a Halifax County household of 4 "other free" in 1790 [NC:62].

John Sweat served in the Revolution from North Carolina [N.C. Archives, State Treasurer Record Group, Military Papers, Revolutionary War Army Accounts, J:211; VI:15, Folio 2].

Leonard Sweat served in the Revolution from North Carolina [N.C. Archives, State Treasurer Record Group, Military Papers, Revolutionary War Army Accounts, J:211; VI:15, Folio 2].

William Sweat enlisted in Eaton's Company of the 3rd North Carolina Regiment on 20 April 1776 and was discharged on 20 October 1778. He was in the roll of Major Hardy Murfree's Company in the 2nd North Carolina Battalion commanded by Colonel John Patton at White Plains on 9 September 1778 [Clark, *The State Records of North Carolina*, XIII:522; XVI:1154; NARA, M246, Roll 79, frame 115 of 323; http://fold3.com/image/10199976]. He was head of a household of 1 free male and 3 females in District 8 of Halifax County for the 1786 state census. He received a 640 acre grant for his services in the Revolution [mentioned in Franklin County DB 6:89].

Allen Taborn enlisted in Baker's Company in the 10th North Carolina Regiment on 20 July 1778 but deserted three days later. John Bonds received his final pay of £27 for his service in the North Carolina Continental Line [Clark, *The State Records of North Carolina*, XVI:1173, XVII:252]. He was head of a Northampton County household of 7 "other free" in 1790 [NC:73] and 8 in 1810 [NC:748].

Burrell Taborn was a resident of Nash County in 1781 when he enlisted in Captain Lytle's Company for 12 months. He was head of a Nash County household of 7 "other free" in 1800 [NC:122], 10 in 1810 [NC:668], and 6 "free colored" in 1820 [NC:445]. His children were named in the survivor's pension application of his son Hardimon [NARA, S.7694, M804, Roll 2335, frame 744; http://fold3.com/image/20448044].

Joel Taborn was living in Nash County, North Carolina, in 1776 when he enlisted in the company of Captain Tarrent under Colonel Lytle. He was a resident of Wake County when he made his declaration in Granville County court in order to obtain a pension. "Being very young and a person of colour" he was first employed as a servant to the officers before being placed in the ranks a short time after his arrival in Charleston. He stated that he was in the Battles of Eutaw Springs and Ninety-Six and the Siege of Charleston [NARA, S.42037, M804, Roll 2335, frame 0772; http://fold3.com/image/20448700]. He was taxable in Meherrin Parish, Greensville County, Virginia, in 1788 [PPTL 1782-1807; 1809-50, frame 68] and taxable in St. Luke's Parish, Southampton County, from 1790 to 1805: a "M"(ullato) taxable in 1805 [PPTL 1782-92, frames 756, 826, 870, 885; 1792-1806, frames 51, 74, 155, 181, 280,

330, 392].

Nathan Taborn was listed in the North Carolina military accounts during the Revolution [N.C. Archives, State Treasurer Record Group, Military Papers, Revolutionary War Army Accounts, I:105, folio 4, Tabor, Nathan http://archives.ncdcr.gov/doc/search-doc]. He was head of a Northampton County household of 3 "other free" in 1790 and 15 in 1800 [NC:481].

William Taborn was living in Granville County in 1778 when Colonel William Taylor and Captain James Saunders requisitioned his wagon and team of horses for use as a baggage wagon for the soldiers. He made an agreement with John Davis to look after his crop in exchange for Davis looking after his wagon. He was later drafted as a soldier and received a pension. He served in South Carolina under Colonel Lytle, who placed him under guard for getting drunk and cursing him. One of the witnesses for his pension application testified that William served for a while as cook to General Butler. Another testified that he was a "Brother Soldier" with him in the expedition to the Savannah River. Jacob Anderson testified that he lived near him in Granville County when his wagon was requisitioned [NARA, W.18115, M804, Roll 2335, frame 0798; http://fold3.com/image/20448837]. He was listed in Captain Satterwhite's Company in the Granville County Militia Returns for 1778: *19 years old, 5 feet 8 inches high, Darkish coloured hair & complexion, planter* [T.R., box 4, folder 40]. He was head of a Granville County household of 8 "other free" in 1810 [NC:898].

Benjamin Tann was listed among the "Black" members of the undated colonial muster roll of Captain James Fason [T.R. box 1, folder 3]. He received £9 payment on certificate number 1859 from the North Carolina Army Accounts on 10 June 1783 and a further £14.18 on undated certificate no. 238 [N.C. Archives T&C, Rev. War Accounts, Vol I:45 folio 2; XI:48, folio 2]. He was head of a Nash County household of 5 "other free" in 1790 [NC:71] and 8 in 1800 [NC:122].

Drury Tann enlisted for 14 months as a private in Hadley's Company of the 2nd Regiment of the North Carolina Continental Line on 1 August 1782 according to the muster of 1 September 1782 [NARA, M256, http://fold3.com/image/10200698; Clark, *The State Records of North Carolina*, XVI:1175]. He was head of a Northampton County, North Carolina household 4 "other free" in 1790 [NC:74], 3 in Hertford County in 1800 [NC:722], and 2 "free colored" in Southampton County, Virginia, in 1820: a man and woman over 45 years of age. He made an application for a Revolutionary War pension in Southampton County court in which he stated that he was stolen from his parents as a small boy by persons who were going to sell him into slavery [NARA, S.19484, M804, Roll 2339, frame 986 of 1071; http://fold3.com/image/19565717].

Ephraim Tann was a private in Baker's Company who enlisted on 20 July 1778 for 9 months. He was deceased by 8 March 1785 when his heirs received 640 acres for 84 months service in the North Carolina Continental Line [Clark, *The State Records of North Carolina*, XVI:1173; T&C Rev. War Army Accts. Vol III:73, folio 3 & VII:108, folio 3; http://fold3.com/image/291770905].

James Tann was a soldier who died in the service in Philadelphia during the Revolutionary War. He enlisted on 20 July 1778 in Quinn's North Carolina Company but omitted in 1779 [Clark, *The State Records of North Carolina*, XVI:1173; http://fold3.com/image/291770905]. Jesse **Boothe**, executor of Benjamin Tann's Nash County will, deposed in Nash County on 20 June 1821 that James's rightful heir was Hannah Tann, daughter of his brother Jesse Tann [S.S. 460.1]. She received a land warrant for 640 acres for her uncle's service [S.S. 460.1, 460.2, 460.3, 460.12].

Joseph Tann died before 1792 when his heirs received 640 acres for his 84 months service in the Revolution [N.C. Archives, S.S., Land Warrants, Tennessee, file no. 117,

Micajah Thomas, Assignee of Joseph Tann (Military Warrant No. 1586), http://archives.ncdcr.gov/doc/search-doc].

Ross Thomas, born about 1759, was in the 3 September 1778 list of new levies from Hyde County who enlisted for 9 months from the following March: *place of abode Hyde, born Hyde, 5'7", 19 years of age, Black Hair, Black Eyes and skin* [T.R., Box 4, folder 42, http://digital.ncdcr.gov/cdm/compoundobject/collection/p16062coll26/id/699/rec/164]. He received voucher no. 770 for £6 specie on 1 May 1792, being a fourth of the pay and interest due him for military service in the Revolution [North Carolina Revolutionary Pay Vouchers, 1779-1782, http://familysearch.org/ark:/61903/1:1:Q2WT-GJ6Y]. He was head of a Hyde County household of 1 "other free" in 1790 and 1 in 1800 [NC:378].

Arthur Toney was born about 1764 in Dinwiddie County, Virginia. He lived there until he was 10 years old when he moved to Halifax County, North Carolina. He took the place of his brother John Toney in the Revolutionary War in Warren County and marched to Bacon's Bridge in South Carolina where he reenlisted. He was not involved in any battles since he was assigned to the baggage wagon. When he returned in 1782, he moved to Caswell County and made his declaration to obtain a pension in Caswell County court 50 years later on 9 October 1832 [NARA, W.4835, M805, Roll 807, frame 582]. He was a "Mulatto" counted in the 1786 State Census for the Caswell District of Caswell County and head of a Caswell County household of 10 "free colored" in 1820 [NC:90].

John Toney was a "Free Mulatto" added to Wood Jones' list of tithables for Amelia County on 27 November 1766 [Orders 1766-9, 24]. He enlisted in the 10th Regiment of the North Carolina Continental Line. He fought at the battle of Guilford Courthouse and "ran home and was taken and made to serve to the end of the war" [NARA, W.9859, M804, Roll 2399, frame 597 of 941; http://fold3.com/image/19362325]. He was head of a Halifax County household of 7 "other free" in 1790 [NC:62], 16 in 1800 [NC:344], 11 in 1810 [NC:51], and 11 "free colored" in 1820 [NC:167].

John Toney received voucher no. 589 for £22 specie in the counties of Anson, Montgomery and Richmond on 4 September 1782 for military service in the Revolution [North Carolina Revolutionary Pay Vouchers, 1779-1782, http://familysearch.org/ark:/61903/1:1:Q2WT-5N8M, Toney, John]. He was head of a household of 3 free males and 2 free females in District 5 of Halifax County, North Carolina, in 1786 for the state census (called John Toney, Jr.) and was head of a Fayetteville, Cumberland County household of 5 "other free" in 1790 [NC:42].

Charles Turner made a declaration in Pasquotank County court on 4 March 1834 to obtain a pension for his service in the North Carolina Continental Line [*NCGSJ* XVII:160]. He was head of a Pasquotank County household of 4 "other free" in 1790 [NC:29] and 9 in 1810 [NC:933].

Bartlet Tyler complained to the Granville County court on 5 August 1778 that he was forced into Revolutionary War service on the pretence that he was a vagrant [Owen, *Granville County Notes*, vol. V]. He served in the Revolution [N.C. Archives, State Treasurer Record Group, Military Papers, Revolutionary War Army Accounts, XI:35, Folio 4, Tyler, Bartlett]. He received voucher no. 178 at Hillsboro for £9 specie on 10 June 1783 for military service [North Carolina Revolutionary Pay Vouchers, 1779-1782, http://familysearch.org/ark:/61903/1:1:Q2WT-RHM5, Tyler, ___ lett]. He was head of a Warren County household of 5 "other free" a white woman 26-45 years, and a white boy under 10 years of age in 1800 [NC:836] and 5 "other free" and a white woman over 45 years old in 1810 [NC:738].

Asa Tyner, husband of Keziah Chavis, was brought into Granville County court as a vagrant and "delivered to a Continental Officer and to serve as the Law directs" on 10

November 1778 [Minutes 1773-83, 142]. He was listed among the volunteers for 9 months service as a Continental soldier from Bute County on 3 September 1778: *Asea Tyner, Place of Abode Bute County, born N.C., 5'8", 34 years of Age, Dark Fair, Dark Eyes* [T.R., Box 4, Folder 35].

Daniel Valentine was the brother of Peter Valentine according to the declaration of Polly's children on 21 May 1835 in Halifax County, North Carolina court. He enlisted in Captain Bradley's Company in the 10th North Carolina Regiment on 7 June 1779 for 18 months, but nothing more was said of him on the rolls [Clark, *The State Records of North Carolina*, XVI:1179]. A military land warrant was issued by a field officer to his heirs for 640 acres [NARA, R.10,820, M805, Roll 820, frame 0119; http://fold3.com/image/19915548].

Peter Valentine enlisted in the 10th North Carolina Regiment on 20 July 1778 for 9 months, but died at Philadelphia Hospital according to the 23 April muster roll of Lieutenant Colonel Wm L. Davidson's Company [NARA, M246, roll 79, frames 143 of 323; http://fold3.com/image/10200399]. A military warrant was issued to his heirs for 640 acres of bounty land by a field officer according to the application for a survivor's pension which his nephews Daniel and Sarah made while living in Halifax County, North Carolina [NARA, R.10,820, M805, Roll 820, frame 0119; http://fold3.com/image/19915548]. Between 1 September 1784 and 1 February 1785 C. Dixon received Peter's final pay of £41 for service in the North Carolina Continental Line [Clark, *The State Records of North Carolina*, XVI:1179; XVII:255].

Drury Walden was a Revolutionary War pensioner who served as a private [Clark, *The State Records of North Carolina*, XXII:91]. He was a private and musician who received $114.99 in Northampton County [DAR, *Roster of Soldiers from North Carolina in the American Revolution*, 448, 588]. He made a declaration (signing) in Northampton County court to obtain pension, stating that he was born in Surry County, Virginia, in 1762 and was living in Bute County in 1779 when he was called into the service. He served 5 months in Captain Allen's Company of the 4th North Carolina Regiment commanded by Colonel Eaton, then 3 months in the Commissary General's Department in Halifax and then as a private in Captain Kidd's North Carolina Militia as a substitute for Edward Jackson. He marched to Augusta on his first tour and was in the Battle of Brier Creek, and on his second tour made gun carriages for the cannon and canteens for the soldiers. Henry Hill testified for him that he was a musician on his first tour to Georgia [NARA, R.11014, M804, roll 2471, frame 456 of 1334; http://fold3.com/image/19780439]. He was in the Third Company detached from the Northampton County Regiment in the War of 1812 [N.C. Adjutant General, Muster Rolls of the War of 1812, 20]. He was head of a Northampton County household of 8 other free in 1790 [NC:73], 9 in 1800 [NC:483], 12 in 1810 [NC:752], 11 "free colored" in 1820 [NC:266], and 4 "free colored" in 1830.

John Walden was a taxable "Molato" in John Hutson's Bladen County household in 1770 [Byrd, *Bladen County Tax Lists*, I:34]. H. Montfort received his final pay of £20 for his service in the North Carolina Continental Line [Clark, *The State Records of North Carolina*, XVII:256]. He was head of a Northampton County, North Carolina household of 7 "other free" and a slave in 1790 [NC:73].

Micajah Walden was in the 15 March 1780 return of troops for Northampton County [T.R., Box 6, Folder 11] and received voucher no. 5909 for £6 specie in Halifax District for his military services to the Revolution [North Carolina Revolutionary Pay Vouchers, 1779-1782, http://familysearch.org/ark:/61903/1:1:Q2WT-GR5T, Walden, Micajah]. He was head of a Northampton County household of 5 "other free" in 1790.

John Warburton received voucher no. 374 in Halifax District for £10 specie on 8 January 1782 for military service in the Revolution [North Carolina Revolutionary Pay Vouchers, 1779-1782, http://familysearch.org/ark:/61903/1:1:Q2WT-5WH8,

Warburton, John]. John Wharburton was head of a Bertie County household of 4 "other free" in 1790.

Edward Weaver was head of a Hertford County, North Carolina household of 7 "other free" in 1790 [NC:25] and 7 in Captain Moore's District in 1800. He was in Hertford County when he appointed an attorney to receive his final settlement for service in the Revolution on 29 March 1791 [*NCGSJ* XVIII:92-3].

James Weaver received voucher no. 8299 in Halifax District for £18 specie on 19 June 1783 for military service in the Revolution [North Carolina Revolutionary Pay Vouchers, 1779-1782, http://familysearch.org/ark:/61903/1:1:Q2WT-5HTZ, Weaver, James]. He was head of a Halifax County household of 4 "other free" in 1790 [NC:63], 5 in 1800 [NC:350], 9 in 1810 [NC:54], and 10 "free colored" in 1820 [NC:170].

Jesse Weaver received voucher no. 2686 for £7 specie in Edenton District on 29 December 1783 for military service in the Revolution [North Carolina Revolutionary Pay Vouchers, 1779-1782, http://familysearch.org/ark:/61903/1:1:Q2WT-PKVC, Weaver, Jesse]. He was head of a Hertford County household of 6 "other free" in 1790 [NC:26], 5 in Captain Lewis' District in 1800, 3 in 1810 [NC:102], 13 "free colored" in 1820 [NC:182], and 6 "free colored" in 1830 [NC:404].

Samuel Webb enlisted in the Revolution from Bladen County for 18 months as a substitute on 20 August 1782: *5'10", age 38, black complexion, black hair, black eyes, in Duprie's Company, occupation carpenter* [T.R., Box 6, folder 30, http://digital.ncdcr.gov/cdm/compoundobject/collection/p16062coll26/id/1017/rec/320].

Jacob Wharton was a free "Mulatto" taxable in Bertie County in Martha Hinton's household in the list of Josiah Harrell in 1769 [CR 10.702.1, box 2]. He enlisted in Blount's Company on 20 July 1778 for 9 months [Clark, *The State Records of North Carolina*, XVI:1188]. His heirs received military warrant no. 132 for 640 acres on 12 December 1806 [North Carolina and Tennessee, Revolutionary War Land Warrants, 1783-1843, Roll 13: William Hill Warrants, 1811-1837 (Survey Orders: Nos. 1-3992) http://ancestry.com].

Charles Whitmore was head of an Orange County, North Carolina household of 4 "free colored" in 1820 [NC:A:412]. He appeared in Orange County court on 25 May 1836 to apply for a pension for his service in the Revolution. He stated that he entered the service in the militia of Greensville County, Virginia. He was at the time bound to one Parr and substituted for his son Thomas Parr when he was drafted in October 1781. He served in Captain Andrew Jeter's Company and Colonel James Moore's Regiment and helped guard Norfolk [NARA, S.11739, M804,Roll 2547, frame 424 of 822; http://fold3.com/image/28017759].

Arthur Wiggins enlisted for 18 months in Bailey's Company on 10 September 1782 [Clark, *The State Records of North Carolina*, XVI:1192]. He appeared in Bertie County court to make a declaration for a pension for his service in the Revolution, stating that he was living in Bertie County in 1779 when he was drafted in the town of Winton, Hertford County. He had served six months when he enlisted for 18 months under Captain Bailey and served until the end of the war. He marched to Charleston, South Carolina, where he was taken prisoner along with Captain Bailey. He had a brother Matthew Wiggins who was also in Charleston, but was then deceased [NARA, S.7952, M804, 2572, frame 0377; http://fold3.com/image/28464276]. He was head of a Bertie household of 5 "other free" in 1800 [NC:86], 4 in 1810 [NC:163], and 3 "free colored" in 1820 [NC:114].

Edward Wiggins enlisted in Blount's Company on 20 July 1778 [Clark, State Records, XVI:1188]. He was head of a Northampton County household of 3 "other free" in 1800 [NC:483].

Matthew Wiggins was a "free Mulatto" taxable in the Bertie County list of Cullen Pollock in 1769 and taxable as Matthias in the 1774 list of Samuel Granberry. He enlisted in Bailey's Company of the 10th North Carolina Regiment for 18 months on 10 September 1782 [Clark, *The State Records of North Carolina*, XVI:1191]. He was called Mathias Wiggins (a Mulatto) when he married Prissey Tabert (Taborn?), 3 January 1786 Bertie County bond. Matthew was head of an Edgecombe County household of 4 "other free" in 1790 [NC:55].

Michael Wiggins received voucher no. 2438 for £7 specie in Edenton District on 26 August 1783 for military service to the Revolution [North Carolina Revolutionary Pay Vouchers, 1779-1782, http://familysearch.org/ark:/61903/1:1:Q2WT-G56J, Wiggen?, Michael]. He was head of a Bertie County household of 4 "other free" in 1790 [NC:15].

Zachariah Winn received voucher no. 500 for £14 specie in the counties of Anson, Montgomery and Richmond on 3 September 1782 for military service in the Revolution [North Carolina Revolutionary Pay Vouchers, 1779-1782, http://familysearch.org/ark:/61903/1:1:Q2WT-GTYR, Winn, Zach]. He was head of an Anson County household of 1 "other free" in 1790 [NC:35].

Benjamin Wilkins, a "free man of colour," appeared in Edgecombe County, North Carolina court to apply for a pension for his services in the Revolution. He stated that he enlisted with Colonel Branch in the town of Halifax in the 2nd Regiment and served in a company commanded by Captain Levi Lane. He was in the Battle of Brier Creek and was a substitute for John Glover. William **Morgan** testified that Benjamin served as a substitute for Samuel Foreman for three months. His application was rejected [NARA, R.11545, M804, Roll 2580, frame 267 of 904; http://fold3.com/image/28318965].

John Wilkinson was head of a Northampton County, North Carolina household of 6 "other free" in 1800 [NC:485] and 6 "free colored" in Halifax County in 1820 [NC:169]. He was in Northampton County when he gave Presly Prichard his power of attorney to receive his final settlement certificate for his services in the Revolution [*NCGSJ* XVIII:99].

John Womble was a carpenter who enlisted in the 10th North Carolina Regiment on 1 June 1779 in Halifax County. He was captured in the siege of Charleston and remained on parole for the remainder of the war. He married his wife Catherine in Edgecombe County in 1798 [NARA, S.42083, M804, Roll 2624, frame 981 of 1118; http://fold3.com/image/28372447]. He was head of an Edgecombe County household of 1 "other free" in 1790 and 11 "free colored" in 1820.

Cubet enlisted as a drummer in Brown's Company of the 1st North Carolina Regiment in 1777. Mingo enlisted on 10 June 1776 and was an assistant armourer in Dixon's Company. Negro Benjamin enlisted as a musician in Armstrong's Company of the 2nd Regiment in 1777 and was discharged in December 1777 [Clark, *The State Records of North Carolina*, XVI:1025, 1108, 1123].

Ishmael Titus was a slave belonging to Lawrence Ross who served as a substitute for his master. He entered the service in Rowan County, North Carolina, in 1780 and applied for a pension while resident in Williamstown, Berkshire County, Massachusetts, on 6 August 1833 and 15 December 1851. After the war he lived in New Rochelle, Ballston and Troy, New York, from there moved to Bennington, Vermont and then to Williamston [NARA, R.10623, M804, roll 1293, frame 282 of 1114; http://fold3.com/image/18483999]. He was head of a Bennington household of 5 "free colored' in 1820 and a 104-year-old Black man in Williamston in 1850 with Lucy Titus.

Negroe Peter was allowed £5 specie for public claims by the auditors in Salisbury, Rowan County, on 7 April 1784 [North Carolina Revolutionary Pay Vouchers, 1779-1782, http://familysearch.org/ark:/61903/1:1:Q2WT-PCVK, Peter, Negroe].

OTHERS WHO MAY HAVE SERVED FROM NORTH CAROLINA

Jacob Burke, born about 1759, a four-year-old "Free Mulatto" boy, was bound by the Chowan County court to Lydia Herron to be a sawyer in January 1764. He was twelve years old on 29 January 1771 when the court bound him to William Topping to be a house carpenter and joiner [Minutes 1755-61, 26; 1761-6, 193; 1766-72, 605]. He may have been the Jacob Burk who enlisted in Stedman's Company of the 5th North Carolina Regiment in 1777 [Clark, State Records, XVI:1013]. He received voucher no. 419 for £26 specie, being one fourth his pay, on 1 May 1792 [North Carolina Revolutionary Pay Vouchers, 1779-1782, http://familysearch.org/ark:/61903/1:1:Q2WT-G4GN].

Stephen Arters enlisted for 12 months in Hall's Company of the North Carolina Line in 1781 and was discharged on 21 November 1782 [Clark, *The State Records of North Carolina*, XVI:1007].

John Tabor served in the Revolution from North Carolina [S.S., State Treasurer Record Group, Military Papers, Revolutionary Army Accounts, Tabor, John: IX, 118, Folio 4; 119, Folio 2; A:177, 200; I:92, Folio 2].

Thomas Tabor served in the Revolution from North Carolina [S.S., State Treasurer Record Group, Military Papers, Revolutionary Army Accounts, Tabor, Thomas: XI:34, Folio 3].

Melchar Tan served in the Revolution from North Carolina [S.S., State Treasurer Record Group, Military Papers, Revolutionary Army Accounts, Tan, Melchar, 54:222].

LOYALISTS

Talbot/Talbert Thompson entered into an agreement with Benjamin Waller to purchase his freedom after his master Alexander McKensie moved to England. He paid Waller £60 and then petitioned the governor and Council of Virginia for his freedom in November 1761. Eight years later he purchased his wife Jenny from the estate of Robert Tucker of Norfolk County and then successfully petitioned for her freedom [McIlwaine, *Executive Journals*, VI:200, 320]. He was a taxable "free negro" on the east side of the borough of Norfolk in 1767 with his slave Joseph, and in 1774 he was taxable on "negroes" Peter, Murray and Joe [Wingo, *Norfolk County Tithables 1766-80*, 39, 243]. On 18 May 1762 the Princess Anne County court bound Joseph and Peter Anderson to him to be sailmakers [Minutes 1753-62, 488]. He and his wife Jenny defected to Lord Dunmore after his property and sailmaking business was destroyed by the Virginia military in January 1776. He died in New York in April 1782 just before his family relocated to Nova Scotia. Jenny submitted a claim to the Loyalist Claims Commission for the loss of their house and sail loft burnt by Patriot forces as well as land and livestock confiscated and a slave killed while working for the British at Great Bridge. She included a copy of the original deed for the land and buildings Talbot purchased from Samuel Boush [Loyalist Claims Commission file A.O. 13/25/479, Archives of United Kingdom, Kew, London, cited by Professor Cassandra Pybus, University of Sydney, Australia].

Peter Anderson defected to the British in January 1776. He was captured at Great Bridge but escaped and hid out in the woods until 1777 when he joined the British fleet on its way to the Siege of Charleston. He was taken to England where he submitted a claim to the Loyalist Claims Commission in which he said that he still had a wife and three children who were enslaved in Norfolk and had lost four chests of clothes, 20 hogs and four beds and furniture [Loyalist Claims Commission, file AO 12/99/354 and AO 13/27/230, cited by Professor Cassandra Pybus, University of Sydney, Australia].

James Ashcroft (head of a Opelousas, Louisiana household of 11"other free"), Thomas Hathcock, Edmund Revells (head of a Robeson County, North Carolina household of 9 "other free" in 1790), Jeremiah Revells, Jacob Locklear (head of a Robeson County household of 6 "other free" in 1790), Joseph Locklear (6 "other free in Robeson in 1790), and Robert Locklear (9 "other free" in Robeson in 1790) received pay from 1 September 1780 to 6 October 1782 for serving in Captain Peter Tyler's Company of South Carolina Loyal Militia [Clark, *Loyalists in the Southern Campaign of the Revolutionary War*, 1:153, 189]. Joseph Locklear may have served on both sides of the conflict, or there may have been two by that name.

SOUTH CAROLINA

John Biddie was head of a Union District household of 4 "other free" in 1800 [SC:230]. He made a declaration in Union District court on 30 October 1832 to obtain a pension for his service in the Revolution. He stated that he was born in Lunenburg County, Virginia, on 17 July 1762 and lived in Union District when he volunteered. He moved to Marshall County, Alabama, by 26 December 1837 when he applied to have his pension paid there [NARA, S.10374, M805, Roll 85, frame 0372; http://fold3.com/image/11261593].

Spencer Bolton was head of a Georgetown District, Prince George's Parish, South Carolina household of 8 "other free" in 1790. He was about 70-80 years of age and living in Laurens District, South Carolina, when he appeared in court on 17 October 1832 to apply for a pension for his service in the Revolution. He stated that he was born on the Pee Dee River in South Carolina, was drafted into the militia while resident in Marion District in 1776, moved to Rafting Creek in Sumter District, then to Spartanburg, and had been living in Henderson County, North Carolina, about a year on 3 October 1845 when he renewed his pension application [NARA, R.995, M804, Roll 296, frame 732 of 809; http://fold3.com/image/10984504].

John Bunch was listed in the payroll of the 3rd South Carolina Regiment commanded by Colonel William Thomson and the payroll of the 7th South Carolina Regiment from the 17 March to 1 July 1779 and for March 1780 [NARA, M246, roll 89, frames 119, 176; http://fold3.com/image/9679449].

Jeremiah Bunch purchased land from John Bunch by deed recorded in Charleston District between 1800 and 1801 [Lucas, *Index to Deeds of South Carolina*, D-7:224]. He was about 72 years old and residing in St. George's, Dorchester, on 13 February 1832 when he appeared in the District Court in Charleston to apply for a pension. He stated that he entered the war at the age of 16 in Orangeburg. A minister and two men named John Bunch (signing) made an affidavit stating that he had been a member of the Methodist Church for 35 or 40 years [NARA, S.17867, M804, Roll 405, frame 162; http://fold3.com/image/12026748].

John Busby was head of a Barnwell District household of 2 "other free" in 1800 [SC:62] and 2 "free colored" in 1820 [SC:3a]. He enlisted in the 3rd South Carolina Regiment on 18 July 1778 and was discharged on 1 July 1781. He was nearly 80 years old on 23 October 1829 when he applied for a pension for his services in the Revolution while resident in Barnwell District, South Carolina. He stated that he entered the service in 1779 on the Savannah River under Captain Daniel Green until the end of the war, "being a colored man, the duty assigned him was to remain with and protect the baggage and provisions of the company." He received a pension on 5 June 1830 [NARA, M246, roll 89, frame 379; http://fold3.com/image/9679654].

138

Elisha Chavers was paid for serving in Captain Felix Warley's 3rd South Carolina Regiment commanded by Colonel William Thompson [NARA, M246, roll 89, frames 234, 237, 241 of 389; http://fold3.com/image/9679504].

John Chavis recorded a memorial for 100 acres on Neds Branch and Steel Creek near the Savannah River in Granville County, South Carolina, on 3 January 1771 [South Carolina Archives series S111001, 10:294]. He was called John Chavis, "a free black" when he petitioned the South Carolina Legislature for a pension in 1823 based on the wounds he had received in the Revolutionary War [South Carolina Archives series S108092, reel 22, frames 125, 128]. He was listed in the payroll of the 7th Company, 3rd South Carolina Regiment in March 1780 [NARA, M246, roll 89, frame 119; http://fold3.com/image/9679419].

Lazarus Chavis enlisted with Captain Moon in South Carolina for 14 months in 1778 under General Andrew Williamson. He was in the battles of Stono and Savannah [NARA, S.9316, M805, reel 180, frame 153; http://fold3.com/image/12039268]. He was head of an Orangeburg District household of 6 "other free" in 1790 [SC:100].

William Chavis was listed in the payroll of the 7th Company, 3rd South Carolina Regiment in August 1779 and March 1780 [NARA, M246, roll 89, frames 119, 149; http://fold3.com/image/9679383]. He was a soldier entitled to military bounty land in 1835 [Brumbaugh, *Revolutionary War Records*, 228].

Edward Coleman, born about 1764, a "coloured man," appeared in New York City on 19 June 1829 to apply for a pension for his service in the Revolution. He enlisted in South Carolina and went to sea after the war. Doctor Thomas Cock testified that Edward had wounds: in his knee apparently from a bullet and one in his abdomen, apparently from a bayonet. Jacob **Francis**, a "coloured man," about 60 years of age, testified that he was a servant in the French Army under Rochambeau and well remembered seeing Edward Coleman in the South Carolina Regiment at Little York in Virginia [NARA, M804, R.2160, http://fold3.com/image/12714044].

Josiah Combess was a fifer listed in the Payroll of the 6th South Carolina Regiment commanded by Lieutenant Colonel Henderson from 1 august to 1 December 1779 [NARA, M246, roll 89, frame 268; http://fold3.com/image/9679533].

Nathaniel Cumbo was listed in the roll of Captain Henry Hampton's Company of the 6th South Carolina Regiment commanded by Lieutenant Colonel Henderson from 1 August 1779 to January 1780 and in the 1st South Carolina Regiment for February 1780 [NARA, M246, roll 89, frames 44, 286, 289; http://fold3.com/image/9679302]. He was head of a Robeson County household of 4 "other free" in 1790 [NC:50].

Devorix Driggers enlisted in the Revolution in South Carolina on 15 June 1778 [NARA, M853, http://fold3.com/image/291771387].

Daniel Gibson was listed in the payroll of the 7th Company in the 3rd South Carolina Regiment commanded by Colonel William Thomason in August 1779 and March 1780 [NARA, M246, roll 89, frames 119, 149; http://fold3.com/image/9679416]. He was head of a Georgetown District, Prince Fredericks Parish, household of 6 "other free" in 1790.

Levy Goins was head of a Moore County household of 5 "other free" in 1800 [NC:62] and 8 in 1810 [NC:615], and 10 "free colored" in 1820 [NC:307]. He appeared in Moore County, North Carolina court to apply for a pension for his service in the Revolution, stating that he volunteered in Fairfield County, South Carolina, in Captain John Gray's Company, commanded by Colonel John Winn. He moved to Moore County soon after the war [NARA, R.3865, M804, Roll 1041, frame 330 of 881, http://fold3.com/image/22042789]. He was a 87-year-old "Mulatto" farmer counted in 1850 census for Moore County.

Morgan Griffin was head of a Richland District household of 4 "free colored" in 1830. On 25 November 1819 he petitioned (signing) while in Richland County for compensation for his service in the Revolution. He stated that he was a prisoner on Sullivan Island in the fall of Charleston [NARA, S.18844, M804, Roll 1132, frame 187 of 1028; http://fold3.com/image/21672823].

Gideon Griffin was head of a Richland District household of 7 "other free" in 1810 [SC:175a] and 6 "free colored" in 1830 [SC:409]. He was living in Richland District on 29 November 1826 when he petitioned the legislature for a pension for his services in the Revolution. He stated that he enlisted in Colonel Wm Mowson's 3rd South Carolina State Regiment and served a total of three years during which he was in several of the most important battles [S.C. Archives S108092, reel 61, frame 18 and NARA, W.8877, M804, Roll 1131, frame 466 of 1121; http://fold3.com/image/21834694].

Drury Harris was listed in the payroll of the 3rd South Carolina Regiment of Colonel William Thomson in August 1779, in the same list as Benjamin **Holly**, Berry **Jeffers**, Gideon Griffin, Osborn **Jeffers**, Allen **Jeffers** and John **Busby**, and in the payroll for March 1780 [NARA, M246, frames 119, 120, 124, 196; http://fold3.com/image/9679460]. He was head of a Abbeville District, South Carolina household of 3 "other free" in 1810 [SC:82], an over-45-year-old head of a Rutherford County, Tennessee household of 6 "free colored" in 1820, listed near John Rouse who was also in Abbeville in 1810 [SC:82].

Edward Harris was head of a Richland District, South Carolina household of 6 "other free" in 1810 [SC:175a]. His son Rowland Harris appeared in Richland County court in 1850 to make a declaration to obtain a survivor's pension for Edward's service in the Revolution. He stated that his father's comrades in the service from the same neighborhood were Gideon **Griffin**, Morgan **Griffin**, Berry **Jeffers**, Allen **Jeffers**, Osborne **Jeffers**, and Edward's cousin Drury Harris. James **Rawlinson** testified for him [NARA, R.4649, M804, Roll 1198, frame 1000; http://fold3.com/image/23206759].

Benjamin Holley was listed in the Payroll of the 3rd South Carolina Regiment commanded by Colonel William Thomson for the month of August 1779 and 1 November 1779, in the same list with Berry, Osborn and Allen **Jeffers**, Gideon and Morgan **Griffin**, and Drury **Harris** [NARA, M246, roll 89, frame 194, 196, 198; http://fold3.com/image/21741226]. He was a taxable "free negro" in the district between the Broad and Catawba rivers in South Carolina in 1784 [South Carolina Tax List, 1783-1800, frame 37]. He entered the war in what was then Orangeburg District near the homestead of Colonel William Thomson and enlisted until the end of the war with his comrades: Allen **Jeffers**, Osborne **Jeffers**, Benjamin **Jeffers**, Drury **Harris**, Morgan **Griffin**, Gideon **Griffin**, Arthur Jackson, and Benjamin Carter, many of whom lived not far from her father. His daughter Sarah Holley's application for a survivor's pension included a book with the birth dates of her family that was said to have been in the handwriting of Colonel Thomson [NARA, W.8941, M804, roll 1312, frame 54; http://fold3.com/image/29342628]. His widow Priscilla was head of a St. Matthews Parish, Orangeburg household of 8 "free colored" in 1820.

Adam Ivey was head of a Sumter District, South Carolina household of 8 "other free" in 1800 [SC:605] and 10 "free colored" in 1820 [SC:211], counted as white in Sumter District, South Carolina census in 1830. He appeared in Montgomery County, Alabama court to apply for a pension for services in the Revolution, stating that he was born in Lumberton, on Drowning Creek, in Robeson County, North Carolina, and moved to Marion District, South Carolina, near Marrs Bluff at the age of 9 or 10. At the age of 15 he entered the service as a volunteer and was taken prisoner at Charleston [NARA,

R.5507, M804, Roll 1396, frame 459 of 817; http://fold3.com/image/24167357].

Allen Jeffers enlisted in the Revolution in South Carolina on 13 August 1782 and was listed in the muster of the 1st Company of South Carolina Troops on 11 December 1782, on the payroll of the 3rd South Carolina Regiment in March 1780 and reenlisted on 13 August 1782, listed in the muster of March 1783 [NARA, M246, roll 89, frames 339, 341; http://fold3.com/image/967938]. He was head of a household of 4 "free colored" in the town of Columbia in 1820 [SC:16]. He made a declaration in Richland County court, stating that he was born in North Carolina and brought to South Carolina as a child to the fork of the Congaree and Wateree Rivers where he had lived ever since, and that he enlisted in the 3rd Regiment of Rangers in 1778. He stated that he was in the Battles of Stono Creek and Savannah and was taken prisoner at Charleston. Gideon and Morgan **Griffin** appeared in Richland County court to attest to his service [NARA, S1770, M804, 1408, frame 661 of 884; http://fold3.com/image/24147530].

George Jeffers enlisted in the Revolution in South Carolina on 8 August 1782, 5 days before Allen Jeffers, and was in the muster of the 5th Regiment of the 1st Company of South Carolina Troops on 11 December 1782 and was listed in the muster of March 1783 [NARA, M246, roll 89, frames 339, 341; http://fold3.com/image/9679608].

Osborne Jeffers enlisted in the Revolution in South Carolina on 25 May 1778 and served until 1 July 1781. He was listed in the payroll of the 3rd South Carolina Regiment in August 1779 and March 1780 [NARA, M246, roll 89, frames 120, 196, 379; http://fold3.com/image/9679452].

Berry Jeffers was listed in the payroll of the 3rd South Carolina Regiment in March 1780 [M246, Roll 89, frame 196 of 389; http://fold3.com/image/9679460]. He was head of Richland District household of 10 "other free" in 1810 [SC:176]. He served for 3 years with fellow soldiers Morgan and Gideon **Griffin** and Allen and Osborne **Jeffers**. His brother Osborne Jeffers died in the Battle of Charleston. James Rawlinson testified that Berry told him he was in the Battles of Savannah, Charleston, Brier Creek, King's Mountain and Eutaw Springs [NARA, W.10145, M804, Roll 1408, frame 696 of 884; http://fold3.com/image/24147596].

Moses Knight was head of a Frederick County, Maryland household of 5 "other free" in 1800 (Moses Night) [MD:788] and 10 in 1810 (M. Knight) [MD:635]. He was about 76 years old on 26 March 1831 when he appeared in Davis County, Indiana court and petitioned (signing) for a pension for his services in the Revolution. He stated that he enlisted in 1779 in South Carolina in the regiment commanded by Colonel Jack McIntosh. He was sometimes called Moses Sharper and Moses McIntosh because he was raised by Colonel Alexander McIntosh [NARA, W.10182, M804, Roll 1503, frame 624 of 1635; http://fold3.com/image/24655780].

Robert Locklear enlisted in the 6th South Carolina Regiment on 20 May 1776 [NARA, M853, http://fold3.com/image/291771927]. He was head of a Fairfield County, South Carolina household of 4 "other free" in 1800 [SC:226].

Joseph Locklear enlisted in the 6th South Carolina Regiment in the Revolution on 20 May 1776 [NARA, M853, http://fold3.com/image/291771927]. He was head of a Robeson County household of 6 "other free" in 1790 [NC:48], 9 in 1800 [NC:389], 7 in 1810 [NC:230], and 8 "free colored" in 1820 [NC:294].

George Perkins was born in Liberty County (present-day Marion County), South Carolina, according to his pension application. He applied for a pension while living in Lawrence County, Kentucky, on 15 March 1834. He was living in South Carolina when he entered the service in Charleston. He served four tours of ten days each in the militia under Lieutenant Richard Whittington in 1780 [NARA, R.8113, M804, roll 1911, frame

Uriah Portee was the son of John Portee, Sr., who was taxable on the female members of his household in Granville County, Granville County, North Carolina in the list of Phil. Pryor in 1762 [N.C. Archives CR 44.701.19]. He was listed in the payroll of Captain John Hennington's Company commanded by Colonel William Thompson in the 3rd South Carolina Regiment in the Revolution from 1 August to 1 November 1779 [NARA, M246, roll 89, frames 128, 131, http://fold3.com/image/22768213 and 9679392].

William Redman was head of Spartansburg, South Carolina household of 6 "other free" in 1790 [SC:33 (microfilm of original)], a Lincoln County, North Carolina household of 11 "other free" in 1800 [NC:900], and 4 "other free" and a white woman in Rutherford County in 1810 [NC:431]. He applied for a pension while resident in Buncombe County on 7 April 1820, stating that he enlisted in South Carolina in May 1775, was in the first battle at Sullivan's Island, was sent to the frontier, and was discharged in the Cherokee Nation after 15 months service [NARA, R.8645, M805, Roll 679, frame 0652; http://fold3.com/image/15172120].

Willis Reed was head of a South Orangeburg District household of 1 "other free" in 1790 [SC:99], paid a little over £35 for militia duty as a horseman from 15 April 1781 to 15 February 1782 [South Carolina Archives, Accounts Audited for Revolutionary War Service, AA 6309].

Cornelius Rouse was a "Molato" taxable in Bladen County, North Carolina, in 1771 [Byrd, *Bladen County Tax Lists*, I:61]. He was a "Negroe" head of a Cheraw District, South Carolina household of 2 "other free" males above the age of 16, 2 "other free" males under 16, and 7 "other free" females in 1790 [SC:358], 15 "other free" in Barnwell District in 1800 [SC:62], and 9 in Abbeville District in 1810 [SC:84]. He was called Neale Rous when he received pay for 30 days duty in the militia in 1782, perhaps identical to Cornelius Rose who was listed in the payroll of the 4th Company of the 3rd South Carolina Regiment commanded by Colonel William Thomson in July 1779 and March 1780, listed as waiting on Colonel Thomson in 1779 [NARA, M246, roll 89, frames 121, 246, 249; http://fold3.com/image/9679512].

Abraham Scott received partial payment for 163 days duty in Captain Joseph Johnston's and Captain Frederick Wommack's Company from 20 June to December 1781 and was in Winton County on 11 August 1787 when he assigned William Holmes his right to the remainder [Scott, Abraham, Account Audited (File No. 6818) of Claims Growing out of the American Revolution, S.C. Archives Series S108092, Reel 0131, frame 00294; http://archivesindex.sc.gov]. He was head of a South Orangeburg District household of 9 "other free" in 1790. He was a man of color who served in the Revolution [Moss, *Roster of South Carolina Patriots*, 1849].

Sampson Shoemaker made a claim in South Carolina for services in the Revolution [S.C. Archives, series S108092, reel 133, frame 328; http://archivesindex.sc.gov]. He was head of a Prince George Parish household of 6 "other free" in 1790 and 1 in Liberty County in 1800 [SC:806].

James Sweat was counted as white in 1790, head of a Beaufort District, South Carolina household of four males over 16, three under 16, three females, and a slave [SC:11]. He was listed in the payrolls of Captain Uriah Goodwyn's company of the 3rd South Carolina Regiment from March 1779 to March 1780 [M246, roll 89, frames 121, 138, 142, 147; http://fold3.com/image/9679406].

Nathan Sweat was listed in Captain Robert Lide's Company of Volunteer Militia who signed a petition to the Council of Safety of South Carolina on 9 October 1775 [*South Carolina Historical and Genealogical Magazine*, Vol. 2, No. 4 (1901): 265]. He was counted as white in 1790, head of a Beaufort District, South Carolina household of one male over 16, one under 16, and 4 females [SC:11].

Thomas Sweat was listed in the muster of Captain Alexander McKintosh's Company of Colonel Gabriel Powell's Battalion in the expedition against the Cherokees from 11 October 1759 to 15 January 1760, in the same list as Winslow Driggers [Clark, *Colonial Soldiers of the South*, 929]. He was a "Mulato" taxable in Bladen County, North Carolina, in 1768 and 1769 and taxable in the household of Ann Perkins in 1771 [Byrd, *Bladen County Tax Lists*, I:8, 17, 60]. He was in the list of Captain Robert Lide's Company of Volunteer Militia who signed a petition to the Council of Safety of South Carolina on 9 October 1775 [*South Carolina Historical and Genealogical Magazine*, Vol. 2, No. 4 (1901): 265].

William Sweat was listed in Captain Robert Lide's Company of Volunteer Militia who signed a petition to the Council of Safety of South Carolina on 9 October 1775 [*South Carolina Historical and Genealogical Magazine*, Vol. 2, No. 4 (1901): 265].. He was counted as white in 1790, head of a Beaufort District, South Carolina household of 1 male over 16, 3 under 16, and 2 females [SC:11].

John Tann was listed in the payroll of Captain Uriah Goodwyn's Company of the 3rd South Carolina Regiment commanded by Colonel William Thomson from March 1779 to March 1780, listed with James **Sweat** [NARA, M246, roll 89, frames 119, 141, 144, 147 of 389; http://fold3.com/image/9679405].

Jim Capers, a man of Color, aged 107 years, appeared in Pike County, Alabama, on 2 July 1849 to apply for a pension for his service in the Revolution. He enlisted in Christ Church Parish opposite Bull's Island in June 1775 in the 4th South Carolina Regiment under General Marion and Colonel John Browry in Captain John White's Company and also served under Colonel William Capers as a drum major. He served until October 1782. He was the freed slave of a Mr. Capers. His widow Milly was a slave, so her application for a pension was denied [NARA, R.1669, M804, roll 465, frame 513 of 607; http://fold3.com/image/12832563].

MARYLAND

Negro Absolom was drafted from Prince George's County in 1781 *[Archives of Maryland*, 18:382].

Adam Adams, a "free black citizen of Charles County," enlisted May 1777 in Captain Henry Gaither's Company of the 1st Maryland Regiment commanded by General William Smallwood. He received his discharge in November 1783. He received a pension and 50 acres of bounty land for his service [NARA, S.34623, M804, Roll 8, frame 599 of 967, http://fold3.com/image/10982341]. He was head of a Charles County household of 2 "other free" in 1790 and 2 in 1800 [MD:551] and 8 "free colored" in 1830.

John Adams was a "free Negro" head of a Prince George County household of 8 "other free" in 1800 [MD:268] and 8 in 1810 (called J. B. Adams) [MD:22]. He may have been one of four "Black Persons being Soldiers (of the Maryland Line), VIZT. Thomas Thompson, Leonard Turner, Valentine Murrin, and John Adams," who were arrested by the local authorities in Orange County, North Carolina, in December 1780 for breaking into someone's house. They were forcibly rescued by the Continental Army [Orange County Court Minutes 1777-8, Part I, Dec. 19 and 23, 1780]. John Adams was listed in the muster of Captain Henry Gaither's Company in August and September 1778, the same company as Charles **Proctor**, Adam Adams and John **Butler** of Charles County [NARA, M246, roll 33, frames 153, 159, 162 of 526; http://fold3.com/image/10108848].

John Allsop was in Captain Bayley's Maryland Regiment commanded by Colonel John Gumby at White Plains on 9 September 1778 [NARA, M246, roll 34, frames 240, 397 of 587; http://fold3.com/image/12005275]. He enlisted from Frederick County until 10 December 1781 [*Archives of Maryland*, 18:653]. John Allstep was head of an Anne Arundel County household of 4 "other free" in 1810.

William Anderson appeared in Lebanon, Ohio court, to apply for a pension. He stated that he enlisted in the 6th Maryland Regiment under Captain Carberry. His name did not appear on any roster, but Jeremiah Collins, a captain of horse of the French troops, testified that he knew William Anderson, a "black man," who was a servant to Captain West and served part of the time with the French troops and part with the Americans. He received a severe wound to his thigh [NARA, R.203, M804, roll 59, frame 104 of 693; http://fold3.com/image/11030088].

William Balentine, enlisted in the 2nd Maryland Regiment on 22 April 1782: *residence. Anne Arundel County, age 25, 5'8-3/4" height, complexion: Mulatto* [NARA, M246, roll 34, frame 434 of 587; http://fold3.com/image/12007228].

Thomas Batterson (Negro) enlisted in the Revolution as a substitute in Anne Arundel County [*Archives of Maryland*, 18:369]. Thomas was from the Island of Nevis in the Caribbean [*Virginia Gazette*, Rind edition, p.4, col. 1].

Edward Blake was a "molatto" who enlisted and served in the Revolutionary War [*Archives of Maryland* 47:460].

Jacob Blake applied for a pension in Worcester County court on 20 June 1818 and 28 February 1821 for his services in the Revolution. He stated that he enlisted at Snowhill in 1780, served in the Battles of Eutaw Springs, Ninety-Six, Cowpens, and Guilford Courthouse and was discharged at Annapolis in 1783 [NARA, S.34654, M804; Roll 259, frame 16 of 698; http://fold3.com/image/12710922]. He was head of a Worcester County, Maryland household of 7 "free colored" in 1820.

Oliver Blake was drafted into service in the 3rd Regiment from Worcester County on 7 May 1781 for 3 years, and was delinquent on 10 December [*Archives of Maryland* 18:425, 473; NARA, M246, roll 34, frame 450 of 587; http://fold3.com/image/12007533]. He was taxable in Mattopony Hundred of Worcester County in 1783. Michael Tarr was his surety [MSA S1161-11-8, 1/4/5/54, http://msa.maryland.gov/msa/stagser/s1400/s1437/html/1437wo.html].

Thomas Bowser, was head of a Kent County, Maryland household of 3 "other free" and 4 slaves in 1810 [MD:878]. He was deceased on 10 March 1846 when his only heir William Bowser provided testimony to the Anne Arundel County court that Thomas had served as a private in the Maryland Line during the Revolution [NARA, BlWt. 2385-100, M804, Roll 306, frame 0134; http://fold3.com/image/11411364]. He was listed in the muster of Captain John Hawkins' Company of the 5th Maryland Regiment, engaged to serve 3 years [NARA, M246, roll 34, frame 181 of 587; http://fold3.com/image/12004858].

Abram Brissington was a "Free Negro" who enlisted as a substitute in the Revolution in Maryland for 3 years on 18 May 1778, listed as dead or deserted in 1780 [*Archives of Maryland*, 18:82, 317].

Bristol (a free Negro) and Spindilow (a free Negro) were drafted in Talbot County on 30 August 1781 to serve until 10 December 1781 [Archives of Maryland, 18:387].

Major Brown was a "Negro" who was drafted in the Revolution from Cecil County in May 1781 but listed among those who absconded [NARA, M246, roll 34, frame 447 of 587; http://fold3.com/image/12007510].

Job Buley enlisted in the 3rd Maryland Regiment on 8 April 1782: *residence Cambridge, age 27 years, 5'7-1/2" high, stout, black complexion, form of hair: wool* [M246, roll 34, frame 433 of 587; http://fold3.com/image/12007204; NARA, M881, http://fold3.com/image/17229501;

George Buley, a "Mulatto" soldier who enlisted in the Revolution in Dorchester County, appeared in Dorchester County court at the age of 72 years on 9 April 1833 and applied for a pension for his services in the Revolution. He stated that he was born in Prince George's County about 1761 and was living in Dorchester County when he entered the service at East New Market for 9 months on 10 March 1781, was at Yorktown for the surrender of Cornwallis and later guarded prisoners [NARA, W.27576, M804, Roll 401, frame 142 of 1003; http://fold3.com/image/12028637].

Henry Butler was head of a Charles County household of 8 "other free" and 4 slaves in 1800 [MD:530] and 9 "other free" and a slave in 1810 [MD:342]. He was one of the drafts and substitutes from Charles County who were discharged from service in the Revolutionary War on 3 December 1781 [*Archives of Maryland* 48:10].

Ignatius/ Nace Butler died on 6 August 1809 according to testimony on 30 July 1840 by his widow Mary Butler, aged 76, who was residing in the 1st Election District of Anne Arundel County when she appeared in court to apply for a pension for his services as a musician in the Revolution. He was listed at the Land Office in Annapolis in an "Alphabetical list of the 2nd Regiment in 1782: Butler, Nace Fifer, entered 1776 for the War, dischd in 1783" [NARA, R.1549, M804, Roll 438, frame 236 of 703; http://fold3.com/image/12741094].

Thomas Carney, Jr., a man of color, was about 60 years old on 24 February 1818 when he appeared in Caroline County court to apply for a pension for his services in the Revolution. He stated that he enlisted in the 5th Maryland Regiment in June 1777 for three years and then for the war, was in the Battles of Brandywine, Germantown, White Plains, Monmouth, Camden, Guilford Courthouse, Ninety-Six and Eutaw Springs and was discharged at Annapolis [NARA, S.35203, M804, roll 473, frame 552; http://fold3.com/image/12831332]. He was head of a Duck Creek Hundred, Kent County, Delaware household of 6 "free colored" in 1820.

Isaac Carr enlisted in the 2nd Maryland Regiment on 6 April 1782: *residence: Montgomery County, age 24, 5'7" height, complexion: yellow Molato* [NARA, M246, roll 34, frame 430 of 587; http://fold3.com/image/17098774].

Edward Chambers, "a man of color," received arrears of pay for his service in the Revolution from 1 August 1780 to 15 November 1783. He appeared in Anne Arundel County court on 20 June 1818 and 21 April 1820 to make a declaration to obtain a pension for his service. He stated that he enlisted in the 3rd Maryland Regiment about July 1777 in New Town, Chester, served about 3-1/2 years, and was in the Battle of the High Hills of Santee [NARA, S.34684, M804, roll 509, frame 322; http://fold3.com/image/19897567]. He was head of a Anne Arundel County household of 1 "other free" in 1790.

Pompey Colless enlisted from Frederick County until 10 December 1781 [*Archives of Maryland*, 18:653].

Charles Cornish was listed as one of the recruits from Caroline County in the Revolution "to the 10th December on 14 August 1781 [*Archives of Maryland*, 18:385]. He was head of a Talbot County household of 3 "other free" in 1790 and 6 in Baltimore City in 1800 [MD:169].

145

Gustavus/ Travis D. Croston appeared in Hampshire County court to make a declaration to obtain a pension for his service in the Revolution. He stated that he enlisted in Alexandria and served for three years. He made a second declaration in court on 18 July 1820, stating that he enlisted in Newport (Charles County), Maryland, served as a private from 1778 to 1783 and was discharged in Alexandria, Virginia. He stated that he was in the Battles of Camden and Ninety-Six where he was taken prisoner [NARA, S.39379, M804, Roll 701, frame 728 of 810; http://fold3.com/image/13009229]. He was head of a Hampshire County household of 9 "other free" in 1810 [VA:833], 11 "free colored" in 1820 [VA:281] and 2 "free colored" in 1840 [VA:8].

Henry Dalton, the "mulatto" son of white woman, was bound to Samuel Pruitt until the age of 31 years in Frederick County, Maryland court in August 1750 [Rice, *Frederick County, Maryland Judgment Records 1748-65*, 49]. He was head of a Monongalia County household of 8 "free colored" in 1820 [VA:169] and 8 "free colored" in 1830 [VA:344]. He was granted a pension for his service in the Revolution, stating in his application on 31 November 1832 that he was born in Bladensburg, Maryland, in 1748, enlisted in 1777 at Redstone settlement near Brownsville, Pennsylvania, served on the Ohio River near Wheeling, resided in Prince George's County for nine years after the Revolution and then moved to Monongalia County [NARA, S.5362, M804, Roll 834, frame 579 of 620; http://fold3.com/image/16979121].

Charles Davis enlisted in the 2nd Maryland Regiment on 23 April 1782: *residence: Baltimore, age 19, 5'4-1/2" height, complexion: Negro* [NARA, M246, roll 34, frame 434 of 587; http://fold3.com/image/12007228].

Massam/ Marsham Dean enrolled in the first militia company organized for the Revolutionary War in the Elizabeth Town District of Frederick County on 6 January 1776 [Peden, *Revolutionary Patriots of Washington County, Maryland*]. He was head of an Allegany County, Maryland household of 9 "other free" in 1800 (called Marsham Dean) [MD:3]

James Dean enrolled in the first militia company organized for the Revolutionary War in the Elizabeth Town District of Frederick County on 6 January 1776 [Peden, *Revolutionary Patriots of Washington County, Maryland*]. He was head of a Washington County, Maryland household of 5 "other free" in 1790 and 5 in 1800 [MD:641].

George Dias/ Dice was a "man of Colour" residing in Lancaster County, Pennsylvania, on 5 May 1818 when he appeared in court to apply for a pension for his services in the Revolution (called George Dias). He stated that he enlisted in the 5th Maryland Regiment in Queen Anne's County, was in the Battle of Stony Point, was taken prisoner in Elizabethtown in 1779, and was discharged at James Island in South Carolina in 1783. He received a land warrant and pension [NARA, S.42,161, M804, Bounty Land Warrant no. 618-100, Roll 808, frame 518 of 876; http://fold3.com/image/15490549]. He was head of a Queen Anne's County household of 8 "other free" in 1790 (called George Dice) [MD:509] and 2 "free colored" males in the Middle Ward of Philadelphia in 1820 (called George Dies).

James Due was head of a Caroline County, Maryland household of 5 "other free" in 1790, 6 "other free," a white boy 10-15, and a white woman 26-44 in 1810 [MD:195]. He appeared in Caroline County court and stated that he enlisted in 1778 under Captain John Hawkins of Queen Anne's County in the 5th Virginia Regiment for 9 months and at the expiration of the term enlisted for the war. He was kept prisoner in Elizabethtown for 11 months. He received pension no. 5876 in November 1818. On 9 April 1821 he had a woman living with him named Elizabeth Cevil, a house keeper aged 40 years, a son Enoch aged 26 years, a son John aged 17 years, a daughter Rachel, 17, and a daughter Surrena who was 12 [NARA, S.34771, M804, roll 859, frame 35 of 775; http://fold3.com/image/13175424].

Charles Fenton enlisted in the Revolution on 20 July 1776 [*Archives of Maryland*, 18:41]. He was head of a Patapsco Hundred, Baltimore County household of 5 whites in 1790 and head of a Soldiers Delight Hundred, Baltimore County household of 4 "other free," a white woman 16-26 and 2 slaves in 1810. He was the son of a white woman named Margaret Fenton who was sold by the Anne Arundel County court for 21 years for having three "Molatto" children [Court Record, 1748-1751, Liber ISB#1, 65; 1751-54, Liber ISB#2, 85 (MSA)].

Francis Freeman, a "person of colour," was a resident of White Clay Creek when he appeared in New Castle County, Delaware court on 1 July 1818 to apply for a pension for his service in the Revolution. He enlisted in the 2nd Maryland Regiment in 1776, was discharged on 1 November 1780 and re-enlisted for the war [NARA, S.35951, M804, Roll 1022, frame of 379 of 738; http://fold3.com/image/22083198], perhaps the Francis Freeman who was head of a Montgomery County, Maryland household of 4 "other free" in 1810.

Ephraim Game was taxable in George Scott's Nanticoke Hundred, Somerset County household in 1759. He was a recruit from Dorchester County in the Revolutionary War on 25 July 1780 [*Archives of Maryland* 18:339].

William Grace who enlisted for 9 months in Lieutenant Hardman's Company of the 2nd Maryland Regiment on 25 May 1778 and was listed in the roll of December 1778 [NARA, M246, roll 33, frames 501, 504, 507, 510 of 526; http://fold3.com/image/10110363], perhaps the William Grace who was head of a Caroline County household of 6 "other free" in 1810 [MD:219].

Benjamin Grinnage served in the Revolution as a substitute from Queen Anne's County, and was described as "a poor man with children but never applied for his discharge" [*Archives of Maryland* 48:11; NARA, M246, roll 34, frame 446 of 587; http://fold3.com/image/12007501].

James Grinnage (Grindage) enlisted for 3 years and was in the roll of Captain Josias Johnson's Company in the 5th Maryland Regiment on 8 September 1778 [NARA, M246, roll 34, frame 183 of 587; http://fold3.com/image/12004890].

William Grinnage was paid £100 bounty on 7 March 1779 for enlisting in the 5th Maryland Regiment [NARA, M246, roll 34, frame 557 of 587; http://fold3.com/image/12008800].

Frederick Hall was head of a Montgomery County household of 1 "Free Negro or Mulatto" over 16, 3 under 16 and 2 female "Free Negroes or Mulattos" in 1790 [MD:235] and 4 "free colored," including a man and woman over 45, and a female slave over the age of 45 years in Fairfax Township, Fairfax County, Virginia, in 1820. He was born in Port Tobacco, Charles County. His name appeared on the muster rolls on 11 May 1777 but was listed as a deserter on 10 January 1778; enlisted again on 25 March 1779 and was on the rolls to April 1780, so his application was denied [NARA, R.7569, M804, roll 1160, frame 686 of 1020; http://fold3.com/image/22600211].

Lazarous Harmon served in the 6th Company of the 1st Maryland Regiment from 1 August 1780 to 15 November 1783 [*Archives of Maryland* 18:356, 539]. He was head of a Worcester County household of 6 "other free" in 1790 [MD:124], 9 in 1800 [MD:745] and 7 "other free" and a slave in 1810 [MD:623]. He made a declaration in Worcester County court on 10 April 1818 to obtain a pension for his service in the Revolution. He stated that he enlisted at Snowhill in 1780, was in the Battles of Guilford Courthouse and Camden (where he was wounded), and was discharged at the end of the war in Annapolis [NARA, S.34911, M805, Roll 399; M804, Roll 1192, frame 297 of 1046; http://fold3.com/image/22755486].

Solomon Haycock served in the Revolution from Queen Anne's County and was discharged on 3 December 1781 [*Archives of Maryland* 48:11]. He was head of a Queen Anne's County household of 6 "other free" in 1790, 6 in 1800 [MD:349] and 6 "free colored" in Harford County in 1830.

Baker Hazard, a "mulatto man," ran away from John Scott's plantation in Fauquier County on 17 June 1777 according to the 25 July 1777 issue of the *Virginia Gazette* [Purdie edition, p.3, col. 1]. He was described in the 19 July 1780 issue of the *Virginia Gazette*: *a mulatto man, almost white, about 5 feet 8 inches high, pitted with the smallpox, born in Virginia (where he is now supposed to be) and waited on Mr. Gill of the Maryland regiment of light dragoons until he was taken prisoner last summer* [Dixon & Nicholson edition].

Abednego Jackson, born in 1758 in St. Mary's County, was residing there when he enlisted for 9 months in the 2nd Maryland Regiment on 25 May 1778. He was discharged on 3 April 1779. After the war he moved to Georgetown where he was employed by and lived at the Catholic College. He was 76 on 29 August 1833 when he appeared in the District of Columbia court to apply for a pension [NARA, S.10909, M804, roll 1397, frame 662 of 1069; http://fold3.com/image/24142805]. He was a "Mulatto" head of a Charles County household of 4 "other free" in 1790 and apparently the A. Jackson who was head of a Washington, D.C. household of 2 "free colored" and 6 slaves in 1830.

Peter Jackson enlisted in the 5th Maryland Regiment on 2 April 1782: *residence: Cecil County, age 23, 5'6" height, complexion. black.* He was due $59 pay by the end of the year [NARA, M246, roll 34, frames 400, 433 of 587; http://fold3.com/image/12007204].

Valentine Murray enlisted in the Revolution for 3 years on 14 May 1778 and was discharged on 19 June 1781 [*Archives of Maryland*, 18:299, 545; http://fold3.com/image/17100257]. He was apparently identical to Valentine Murrin who was one of four "Black Persons being Soldiers (of the Maryland Line), VIZT. Thomas Thompson, Leonard Turner, Valentine Murrin, and John Adams," who were arrested by the local authorities in Orange County, North Carolina, in December 1780 for breaking into someone's house. They were forcibly rescued by the Continental Army [Orange County Court Minutes 1777-8, Part I, Dec. 19 and 23, 1780].

Bazabel Norman was in a list of "free Negroes" in Frederick County, Virginia, in 1802 frame [PPTL 1782-1802, frame 856] and head of a Frederick County, Virginia household of 7 "other free" in 1810 [VA:569]. He gave his age as 57 the 12th July last on 14 May 1818 in Washington County, Ohio court when he made a declaration to obtain a pension, stating that he enlisted in the 7th Maryland Regiment in 1777, was in the Battles of Monmouth, Camden, Cowpens, Guilford Courthouse and Eutaw Springs, and was discharged at the close of the war [NARA, W.5429, M804, Roll 1825, frame 447 of 834; http://fold3.com/image/25355603].

Matthew Oliver was a "Mulatto" drafted from Kent County, Maryland, on 10 December 1781 but had not reported for service [NARA, M246, roll 34, frame 444 of 587; http://fold3.com/image/12007483. He was a "Negro" head of a Kent County household of 2 "other free" in 1790.

Stephen Phillips, born before 1776, was head of a household of 2 "free colored" in Election District 3 of Caroline County in 1820. In 1843 Jacob **Charles** (counted in the 1820-1840 census for Election District 3 of Caroline County) received Stephen's pay of $13.33 for serving in the Revolution [*Archives of Maryland* Online 595:422].

Cupid Plummer enlisted as a private in Captain Lilburn Williams's Company of the 2nd Maryland Regiment on 27 April 1778 and was listed in the muster of September 1778 to March 1780 [NARA, M246, roll 33, frames 475, 478, 481, 483 of 526; http://fold3.com/image/10110235]. He was head of a Prince George's County, Maryland household of 6 "other free" in 1790 and 6 in 1800 [MD:281].

Obediah Plummer enlisted as a private in Captain Lilburn Williams' Company of the 2nd Maryland Regiment on 27 April 1778 and was listed in the muster of September and December 1778 (with Cupit Plummer), then transferred on 1 March 1780 [NARA, M246, roll 33, frames 475, 478 of 526; http://fold3.com/image/10110207]. He was head of an Erie County, Pennsylvania household of 1 "free colored" man over 45 years of age in 1820.

Charles Proctor died while serving in the Revolutionary War [*Archives of Maryland* 18:150]. He enlisted in the Revolution for 9 months on 5 July 1778 and was listed in the muster of Captain Henry Gaither's Company in August and at White Plains in September 1778, the same company as John and Adam **Adams**, Joshua and Charles **Scott**, Leonard **Gates** and Walter **Proctor** of Charles County [M246, roll 33, frames 153, 159, 162 of 526; http://fold3.com/image/10108823].

Henry Proctor was counted in the Constable's Census for Charles County in 1778 and was a "Mulatto" head of a Charles County household of 6 "other free" in 1790 and 11 in 1810 [MD:315]. He served in the Revolutionary War and was discharged on 3 December 1781 [*Archives of Maryland* 48:10].

Joseph Proctor was taxable in Luke Going's Loudoun County household in 1774 [Tithables 1758-99, 768] and a "F.N." taxable on a horse in Loudoun County in 1800 and 1803 [PPTL 1798-1812]. He was head of a Abrams Plains, Granville County, North Carolina household of 2 "free colored" men in 1820 [NC:24]. He was drafted from St. Mary's County, Maryland, where he was born and resident. Two of his older brothers died in the service quite young, under the age of twenty. He was placed in Pendergass's Company but spent most of his time in the hospital on account of the ague and fever. He was sent to Frederickstown sometime in the Winter and guarded the Hessian troops and the magazines. His claim was rejected because there was a record of a Joseph and James Proctor listed next to each other on a list of arrears paid, but there was no way to tell which of the two had been paid [NARA, R.8497, M804, roll 1980, frame 430 of 1041 and http://fold3.com/image/25933404].

Walter Proctor died while serving in the Revolutionary War [Archives of Maryland 18:150]. He enlisted in the Revolution for 9 months on 5 July 1778 and was listed in the muster of Captain Henry Gaither's Company in August and at White Plains in September 1778, the same company as Charles Proctor, John and Adam **Adams** of Charles County [NARA, M246, roll, frames 153, 159, 162 of 526; http://fold3.com/image/10108848].

David Randall enlisted as a substitute under the command of Captain Charles Williamson in the 2nd Maryland Regiment on 24 May 1778 and was discharged on 3 April 1779 [*Archives of Maryland*, 18:156, 327]. He was head of a Anne Arundel County household of 2 "other free" in 1790 and 1 "free colored" over the age of 55 in 1830.

Philip Savoy, a "Man of Colour," appeared in Anne Arundel County on 2 April 1818 and stated that he enlisted in Annapolis in the 1st Maryland Regiment in 1778, was at the Battles of Monmouth, White Plains, Elizabethtown (where he was taken prisoner) and Yorktown, and served until the end of the war. He had a wife and 10 children who were all slaves [NARA, S.35057, M804, roll 2125, frame 302; M246, roll 34, frame 177 of 526; http://fold3.com/image/15506157].

Charles Scott enlisted in Captain Henry Gaither's Company of the 1st Maryland Regiment on 28 May 1778, was sick in camp at White Plains on 2 September 1778, in Fish Kill Hospital later that month, present in March 1780, in the same list as John and Adam **Adams**, John **Butler**, Charles and Walter **Proctor** [NARA, M246, Roll 33, frames 162, 168 of 526; http://fold3.com/image/10108823]. He was head of a Frederick County household of 11 "other free" in 1800 [MD:798].

Joshua Scott enlisted in Captain Henry Gaither's Company of the 1st Maryland Regiment on 27 May 1778, was sick in camp at White Plains on 2 September 1778, in Fish Kill Hospital later that month, present in March 1780, in the same list as Charles Scott [NARA, M246, Roll 33, frames 162, 168 of 526; http://fold3.com/image/10108837]. He was a "Mulatto" head of a Charles County household of 3 "other free" in 1790 and 2 in 1800 [MD:513].

Alexander Shaw enlisted on 10 December 1776 in Captain Alexander Roxburgh's Company of 1st Maryland Regiment of foot. He was at White Plains on 2 September 1778 and at Middlebrook on 3 March 1779 [NARA, M246, Roll 33, frames 186, 195, of 526; http://fold3.com/image/10108954]. He was head of a Middlesex Hundred, Baltimore County household of 2 Free Negroes age 16 and upwards and 4 females 16 and upwards in 1776 [Carothers, *1776 Census of Maryland*, 163].

Randall Shly enlisted in the 2nd Maryland Regiment on 22 April 1782: *residence· Virginia, Arundel County, age 24, 5'10" height, complexion: Negro* [NARA, M246, roll 34, frame 434 of 587; http://fold3.com/image/1207228].

Salady Stanley was probably identical to the "Negro Boy named Salady" who still had seven years to serve when he was listed in the 7 June 1770 Dorchester County estate of Edward Smith [Prerogative Court (Inventories) 105:144 (MSA, SM 11-106)]. He was a "coloured man" who enlisted in the 4th Maryland Regiment on 4 September 1781 and was discharged at Frederickstown at the end of the war. He appeared in Dorchester County court on 4 April 1821 to apply for a pension, stating that he was about 67 and had served for three years [NARA, R.10057, M804, Roll 2269, frame 461 of 1077; http://fold3.com/image/16260520]. He was head of a Dorchester County household of 1 "Free Negro or Mulatto" over 16 and 5 slaves in 1790 [MD:439] and 5 "other free" in 1800 [MD:657].

William Taylor was a "Mulatto" head of a Charles County household of 5 "other free" in 1790, perhaps identical to William Taylor who was head of a Queen Anne's County household of 2 "other free" and 3 slaves in 1800 [MD:381]. He was described as "yellow (Mulatto) complexioned, aged 29, 5'7-3/4" high, born in Maryland, from Montgomery County, enlisted April 2, 1782," when he was listed in the Revolutionary War Maryland roll [NARA, M246, roll 34, frame 436 of 586, http://fold3.com/image/12007265].

Thomas Thompson was one of four "Black Persons being Soldiers" of the Maryland Line who were arrested by the local authorities in Orange County, North Carolina, for breaking into someone's house. They were forcibly rescued by the Continental Army [Orange County Court Minutes 1777-8, Part I, Dec. 19 and 23, 1780].

Negroe Tower was drafted in Harford County in 1781 but was discharged because he had a wife and children [*Archives of Maryland*, 18:400].

Leonard Turner was one of four "Black Persons being Soldiers (of the Maryland Line), VIZT. Thomas Thompson, Leonard Turner, Valentine Murrin, and John Adams," who were arrested by the local authorities in Orange County, North Carolina, in December 1780 for breaking into someone's house. They were forcibly rescued by the Continental

Army [Orange County Court Minutes 1777-8, Part I, Dec. 19 and 23, 1780].

York Waters, "a negro," was in the 2nd Maryland Regiment on 10 February 1780 when the Maryland Council ordered the commissary to deliver him cloth sufficient for a pair of breeches [*Archives of Maryland*, 43:82].

Samuel Wedge, born of a white servant woman in 1738, was bound out until the age of 30 in Prince George's County [Court Records 1738-40, Liber Y, 192 (MSA CR 34,713-2)]. He enlisted in the 3rd Maryland Regiment on 1 January 1782 and was due £45 on 16 November 1783 [NARA, M246, Roll 34, frames 403, 511 of 587; http://fold3.com/image/12008279].

Henry Williams was a "man of color" from Anne Arundel County who enlisted in the Revolution in Annapolis about 1777 and died in Baltimore on 5 January 1850 [NARA, W.3638, Bounty land warrant 6767F-160-55, M804, Roll 2588, frame 511 of 1183; http://fold3.com/image/28347880].

David Wilson, "a man of Colour," was about 64 years old when he appeared in Washington County, Maryland court on 1 August 1820 to apply for a pension for his service in the Revolution. He enlisted in June 1778 under Captain Josiah Johnson in the 5th Maryland Regiment in the 1st Brigade under General Smallwood, served until the end of the war and was discharged in Annapolis. Boston Medlar, a drummer and corporal, testified that David was in the Battles of Camden, Eutaw Springs, Guilford Courthouse and Ninety-Six [NARA, S.35119, M804, Roll 2605, frame 97 of 874; http://fold3.com/image/28357336].

DELAWARE

Peter Beckett, was a "Negro" about 25 years and seven months old on 27 January 1770 when Samuel Hanson of Kent County set him free [Historical Society of Pennsylvania, Duck Creek Monthly Meeting, Deed of Manumission of Slaves, 1774-1792, 21]. He served in the First Company of the Delaware Regiment in the Revolutionary War and received pay from 1 August 1780 to 4 November 1783 [DHS, MS Delaware Regiment Pay Records, 1778-1783, certificates 54,483; 54,830; 54,938; 55,184; Public Archives Commission, *Delaware Archives*, I:196, 607; NARA, M881, Roll 382, frame 1087 of 2309; http://fold3.com/image/16725573].

Mark Becket was a private in Hall's Delaware Regiment [http://fold3.com/image/7809667, 16725564].

William Butcher, Sr., enlisted in the Revolution on 24 April 1777 and was listed in the Muster of the Independent Company of Foot raised for the safe guard of the...persons...residing near the Town of Lewis and the Coast of Delaware Bay, commanded by Captain William Pary [NARA, M246, roll 31, frame 322 of 658; http://fold3.com/image/12448884]. He was a "Mulattoe taxable on 2 horses in Kent County in 1797.

Thomas Clark married Elizabeth **Morris** ("Mustees, free"), on 1 July 1773 in Sussex County [Records of the United Presbyterian Churches of Lewes, Indian River and Cool Spring, Delaware 1756-1855, 286]. He was a soldier in the Revolution from Sussex County who died before 13 August 1833 when his children Whittington Clark, Nathaniel Clark, John Clark and Comfort **Miller** applied for bounty land for his service. One of his fellow soldiers testified that they were marched to Philadelphia where they guarded British prisoners [NARA, B.L.Wt. 2047-100, M804, roll 566, frame 463 of 782; http://fold3.com/image/12832321]. Whittington and Nathaniel were "free colored" heads of Sussex County households in 1820.

James Driggers was listed in the payroll of Captain Matthew Manlove's Company in the Revolutionary War on 1 October 1776, having served a month and 17 days and paid £3.16 [Public Archives Commission, *Delaware Archives*, 70-1].

Henry Game was listed in Colonel Thomas Couch's 2nd Battalion of Delaware Militia in 1776 [NARA, M246, roll 29, frame 199 of 694; http://fold3.com/image/7809317]. He was head of a St. Mary's County, Maryland household of 3 "other free' in 1800 [MD:340].

Amindab Handzor was in the June 1777 payroll of Captain McLane's Company of Colonel John Patton's Company of Foot in the Revolution [http://fold3.com/10126482]. He married Hannah Pettyjohn on 13 November 1784 in Sussex County [*Records of the United Presbyterian Churches of Lewes, Indian River and Cool Spring, Delaware 1756-1855*, 298]. He was taxable in Indian River Hundred, Sussex County, in 1784 and 1789. Perhaps his widow was Hannah Hansor, head of an Indian River Hundred household of 4 "other free" in 1800 [DE:438]. The Hanzer family descended from Aminadab, a slave in Accomack County, Virginia, who had a child by a white woman [Deeds, Wills, 1663-66, fol. 91; 1664-71, fol. 20]. His son Aminadab Hanzer, moved to Sussex County, Delaware, by September 1688 when "Aminidab Hanger Negro" testified in court about moving cattle from Accomack County to Sussex County, Delaware [Sussex County Court Records 1680-99, 262]. He purchased land in Sussex County in 1696 [DB A-198]. On 2 February 1773 Thomas and William Handzer, "Mallatos," made a quit claim deed for 350 acres in Sussex County, Delaware, which had been granted to "Aminadab Handzer Malatto Deceasd" [DB D-4:225-7; F-6:220-2; H-1, 329-30; L-11, 314-5].

David Handzer served in the First Company of the Delaware Regiment and died before the February 1780 muster. His administrator received his pay from 1 August 1780 to 1 November 1782 [DHS, MS Delaware Regiment Pay Records, 1778-1783, certificates 54,358, 54,816, 54,479, 55,180; Public Archives Commission, *Delaware Archives*, I:196; also M246, roll 31, frame 496; http://fold3.com/image/12449345].

Edward Harman received pay from 1 August 1780 to 4 November 1783 for service in the Delaware Regiment in the Revolution [DHS, MS Delaware Regiment Pay Records, 1778-1783, certificates 54,359; 54,480; 54,860; 54,935; 55,181]. He was head of an Indian River, Sussex County household of 6 "other free" in 1800 [DE:438], 8 in 1810 [DE:437] and 5 "free colored" in Lewis and Rehoboth Hundred in 1820 [DE:308]. He was about 60 years old on 20 April 1818 when he appeared in Sussex County court to make a declaration to apply for a pension for his service in the Revolutionary War. Mitchell Kershaw testified that Edward was in the same regiment with him at Gates defeat [NARA, S.36000, microfilm M805, Roll 399; M804, Roll 1192, frame 514 of 1046; http://fold3.com/image/22756535].

Major Hitchens was listed in the Muster Roll of Recruits to the Delaware Regiment at the Port of Christiana Bridge on 20 June 1781 with Caleb Hitchens, Peter **Beckett**, Levin **Magee**, Presley/ Preston **Hutt**, George Lehea (a slave), Edward **Harmon** and David **Hanser** in an undated list of the 1st Delaware Company. Major and Caleb were paid for their services [NARA, M246, roll 30, frame 283 of 532, roll 31, frame 495 of 658; http://fold3.com/image/10110883; *Delaware Archives*, I:135]. Major was the son of Major Hitchens of Northampton County, Virginia, who was a "mulatoe man" indicted by the court on 12 May 1747 for intermarrying with a "mulatoe" woman [Orders 1742-8, 402-3, 422, 429, 445, 457]. He left a Worcester County, Maryland will, proved 18 June 1766, naming his sons Edward, Major, Edmond and Jard [WB JW-3, 1759-1769, 36]. Major was counted as white in the 1800 Delaware census.

Presley Hutt received pay for service in the Delaware Regiment in the Revolutionary War from 1 August 1780 to 4 November 1783 [DHS, MS Delaware Regiment Pay

Records, 1778-1783, certificates 54,361; 54,861; 55,018; 55,273; http://fold3.com/image/10110883], a delinquent "Negroe" taxable in Duck Creek Hundred in 1780, 1781, 1788, delinquent in 1789, a "Negro" taxable on a cow and a calf in 1797 [Levy List 1768-84, frame 425, 491; 1785-98, frames 104, 128, 174, 516], head of a Duck Creek Hundred, Kent County household of 4 "other free" in 1800 [DE:13].

John Hutt enlisted in the Revolution in Delaware on 17 March 1781 and died in June 1781 [NARA, M246, roll 31, frame 502; http://fold3.com/image/12449363]. He was the grandson of Hannah Hutt whose son John Hutt was sold by the Kent County, Delaware court for 31 years [Delaware State Archives, Record Group, 3815.031, 1722-1732, frames 65, 153, 206; Record Group, 3535, Levy Assessments 1743-67, frames 140, 169, 184, 198, 212, 228, 244, 264, 269, 305, 315, 383; Brewer, *Kent County Guardian Accounts*, Houston to McBride, 30; Record Group, 3535, Kent County Levy List, 1743-67, frame 529; 1768-84, frame 6].

George Lahea enlisted in Quenoult's Company of the Delaware Militia on 9 March 1781 and was discharged on 14 February 1782, "being a slave for a life and being claimed" [*Delaware Archives*, III:1150].

James Magee, born 28 July 1750, "otherwise James Game son of mullato Sue other wise Sue Magee or Game" [Wright, *Maryland Eastern Shore Vital Records*, Book 2:126; 3:42], enlisted in the 2nd Delaware Regiment on 9 March 1781, in the same list as Edward **Harmon** [NARA, M246, roll 31, frames 498, 504; http://fold3.com/image/12449368].

Levin Magee was taxable in Little Creek Hundred from 1777 to 1791. Levin McGee enlisted in the 1st Company of the 2nd Battalion of Colonel Williams' Delaware Regiment and was listed in the muster for July and August 1780, transferred in September, delivered a coat at Lewis Town in March 1780, delivered clothing in Dover on 13 June 1780 [NARA, M246, roll 29, frames 312, 393, 402, 495; http://fold3.com/image/12449735].

Stephen Puckham enlisted in Colonel David Hall's Company in the Delaware Regiment on 3 February 1776 and was listed in the muster in the barracks at Lewes Town on 11 April 1776 [Public Archives Commission, *Delaware Archives*, I:43-5]. The Puckhams descend from an Indian named John Puckham and Joan **Johnson**, the African American granddaughter of Anthony **Johnson** [Terrence, *Old Somerset*, 142-3]. George, Levin and John Puckham were "other free" heads of Somerset County, Maryland households.

James Songo was in the muster roll of Captain McLane's Delaware Company for March to June 1779 [*Delaware Archives*, *Military* I:539]. He enlisted again on 25 December 1781 and was sized in a Delaware muster roll on 28 January 1782: *age 25 years, 5'7", born in Delaware, a resident of Kent County, black hair, yellow complexion.* He was listed as a deserter who was taken up and deserted again on 28 July 1782 [NARA, M246, roll 30, frames 347 & 405 of 532; http://fold3.com/image/12448383; http://fold3.com/image/10111353]. He was advertised as a deserter in an ad placed in the *Pennsylvania Journal and the Weekly Advertiser* on 14 September 1782: *James Songo, a mulatto, born in Kent County, Delaware State, 25 years of age, 5 feet six inches high, has lost some of his toes* [Boyle, Joseph L, *He Loves a good deal of rum...Military Desertions during the American Revolution, 1775-1783*, Vol. 2, June 1777-1783, 249, 298-9]. He was head of a Worcester County household of 2 "other free" in 1800 [MD:786].

John Wilson enlisted in the Revolution in Delaware and was sized on 25 June 1782: *age 22, 5'5" high, a weaver, born in Maryland, residence: Sussex County, Delaware, hair black, complexion yellow, enlisted as a substitute for James Messix.* He deserted the following month [NARA, M246, roll 30, frames 347, 406;

http://fold3.com/image/10111353].

FRENCH AND INDIAN WARS, COLONIAL MILITIAS

VIRGINIA AND NORTH CAROLINA

William Allen was one of the "Black" members of the undated colonial muster roll of Captain James Fason's Northampton County, North Carolina Company [T. R., Box 1, folder 3].

Lewis Anderson was number 87 in the 8 October 1754 Muster Roll of the regiment of Colonel William Eaton, Granville County, Captain John Sallis's Company [T. R., Box 1, folder 37, p. 8; http://digital.ncdcr.gov/digital/collection/p16062coll26/id/146/rec/229].

Armstrong Archer was listed in his own Bertie County household in the 1756 constable's list of Edward Williams and an insolvent taxpayer in 1757. He mustered with Captain Benjamin Lane's Edgecombe County Militia in the 1750's [T.R., Box 1, folder 12, p.5]. He was head of a Hertford County household of 4 "other free" in 1790 [NC:25], 3 "other free" and a white woman in 1800, 6 "other free" in 1810 [NC:105], and 9 "free colored" in 1820 [NC:186].

Lewis Artist was a "Black" man listed in the undated colonial Northampton County, North Carolina Muster Roll of Captain James Fason's Company [T.R. box 1, folder 3].

James Black was a "free Negro" in the muster roll of Abner Neale's Craven County Company in 1754 and 1755 [T.R., box 2, folder 3].

Thomas Blango and Thomas Blango, Jr., were listed in the Beaufort County Militia under the command of Colonel William Brown prior to 1765 [Clark, *Colonial Soldiers of the South*, 781]. Thomas Blango was a "free Negro" head of a Beaufort County household in 1755 [N.C. Archives S.S. 837].

Randall Branch was listed among the "Black" members of the undated colonial muster of Captain James Fason's Northampton County, North Carolina Militia [T.R., box 1, folder 3]. In 1769 he was taxable in Dobbs County [SS 837], and in 1790 he was head of a Robeson County household of 11 "other free" [NC:49].

Nathaniel Branham was living in Louisa County on 14 February 1780 when he received a land office warrant for service in the French and Indian War as a soldier in Captain William Phillips' company of volunteer rangers in 1763 [Magazine of Virginia Genealogy, 31:199]. He was taxable in Louisa County from 1782 to 1814, listed as a "free Negro & Mulatto" in 1813 and 1814 [PPTL, 1782-1814].

Ephraim and Gideon Bunch were in the Berkeley County, South Carolina detachment under command of Captain Benjamin Elliot: drafted 8 November 1759, discharged 8 January 1760 [Clark, *Colonial Soldiers of the South*, 938].

Philip Byrd was listed among the "Black" members of the undated colonial muster roll of Captain James Fason's Company [T.R., box 1, folder 3]. He was head of a Northampton County household of 2 free males and 2 free females in Captain Winborne's District for the 1786 North Carolina State Census, 5 "other free" in 1790 [NC:76], and 7 in 1800 [NC:425].

Abel Carter was a "free Negro" with John Carter in Abner Neale's 1754 and 1755 Craven Muster Roll [T.R., box 2, folder 3].

154

Edward and Solomon Carter were in an undated colonial muster roll of a company of foot soldiers in the Dobbs County militia of Captain William Whitfield [Clark, *Colonial Soldiers of the South*, 641-2].

Isaac Carter was in the 25 October 1754 muster roll of Lewis Bryan's Craven County, North Carolina Company (not identified by race) [Clark, *Colonial Soldiers of the South*, 703].

John Carter was a "free Negro," listed in the 4 October 1754 and 4 October 1755 Muster Roll of Craven County, North Carolina, for the district between the head of Slocumb's Creek and the head of Turnagain Bay. This is near the Craven - Carteret County line. Listed in this same muster roll were "free Negro" Peter **George**, Abel Carter, and Jacob **Copes** who were also from Northampton County, Virginia [T.R., box 2, folder 3].

Benjamin Chavis was listed in the Edgecombe County, North Carolina muster of militia in the 1750s [T.R., box 1, folder 12, last page], taxable with his wife Jane in the 1757 Granville County list of Robert Harris and an insolvent taxpayer that year.

William Chavers was "Negro" in the 8 October 1754 Muster Roll of the Granville County Regiment of Colonel William Eaton [T.R., Box 1, folder 37, p. 1; http://digital.ncdcr.gov/digital/collection/p16062coll26/id/146/rec/229].

William Chavers, Jr., and Gilbert Chavers were listed as "Mulatto" in the 8 October 1754 Muster Roll of the Granville County Regiment of Colonel William Eaton [T.R., Box 1, folder 37, p. 1].

Joseph Cheavers was listed in the undated 1750's Edgecombe County muster of Captain William Haywood, the last person on the list after Cannon **Cumber (Cumbo)** and John **Sweet (Sweat)** [T.R., Box 1, folder 7].

William Combs was a 39-year-old James City County "Mulatto" planter, listed in the August 1757 Size Roll of Captain Thomas Waggener's Company at Fort Holland [Clark, *Colonial Soldiers of the South,* 463].

James Conner who was listed in the Beaufort County, North Carolina Militia under the command of Colonel William Brown prior to 1765, listed after Thomas Blango [Clark, *Colonial Soldiers of the South*, 781].

Robert Corn was living in Mecklenburg County, Virginia, on 8 May 1780 when he applied for bounty land in court stating on oath that he was recruited as a soldier in the French and Indian War before 7 October 1763 [Orders 1779-84, 36]. He was head of a Wake County household of 3 "other free" in 1790 [NC:106] and 1 in 1800 [NC:756].

Jacob Copes was a "free Negro" listed in the muster roll of Abner Neale's Craven County, North Carolina Company between the head of Slocomb's Creek and Turnagain Bay on 4 October 1754 and 1755 [T.R., box 2, folder 3].

Cannon Cumbo was listed in the Edgecombe County Muster Roll of Captain William Haywood in the 1750s [T.R., Box 1, folder 7].

Robert Davis was a "Mulatto" in the muster of Colonel William Eaton on 8 October 1754 [T.R., Box 1, folder 37, p. 3; http://digital.ncdcr.gov/digital/collection/p16062coll26/id/146/rec/229].

Caleb Driggers was in the 8 March 1754 muster roll of Captain Casson Brinson's Craven County Company, listed next to Johnston Drigers [Clark, *Colonial Soldiers of the South*, 701].

Isaiah Driggers was called Isaac Draghouse when he was listed among the soldiers who died on 9 June 1741 while serving aboard His Majesty's ship *Princess Caroline* [Clark, *Colonial Soldiers of the South*, 142]. Sarah Drighouse, a "free Negro," received £5 on 21 September 1744 for the services of her unnamed husband who died in the expedition against the Spanish [McIlwaine, *Journals of the House of Burgesses*, 87, 101].

Johnson Driggers was listed in the 8 March 1754 muster roll of Captain Casson Brinson's Craven County, North Carolina Company [Clark, *Colonial Soldiers of the South*, 701].

Winslow Driggers was in the Muster Roll of Captain Alexander McKintosh's Company of Colonel George Gabriel Powell's Battalion of South Carolina Militia "Serving in the Late Expedition Against the Cherokees from October 11, 1759 to January 15, 1760, inclusive ..." [Clark, *Colonial Soldiers of the South*, 892].

John Demery was one of the "Black" members of the undated colonial muster of Captain James Fason's Northampton County militia [T.R. box 1, folder 3].

Dudley Delks was listed as a deserter from the camp at Willamsburg on 31 July 1746 along with three other soldiers: *a Mulatto, born in North Carolina, about 5 feet 11 inches high, has a smooth Skin, Slender-made and seems weak in his Knees, aged about 24* [*Virginia Gazette*, p. 2, col. 3].

Ephraim Emanuel was listed in the muster roll of Captain Elisha Williams' Edgecombe County Militia in the 1750's [T.R. Box 1, folder 12, p.5] and head of a Sampson County household of 3 "other free" in 1790 [NC:51].

Peter George was listed in the 4 October 1754 muster of Abner Neale's Craven County, North Carolina Company between the head of Slocomb's Creek and the head of Turnagain Bay. In Neale's 4 October 1755 muster he was among five "free Negroes" including John and Abel **Carter**, Jacob **Copes**, James **Black** [T.R., box 2, folder 31; box 2, folder 3].

Daniel Gowen from Stafford County was listed in the 13 July 1756 size roll of Captain Thomas Cocke's Company of the Virginia Militia. He was called a hatter in the July 1757 size roll of Captain Joshua Lewis' Seventh Company of the Virginia Regiment [Clark, *Colonial Soldiers of the South*, 385, 449].

Edward, Michael and Thomas Gowen were all listed as "Mulatto" in the 8 October 1754 muster roll of Captain Osborne Jeffreys' Granville County Company [T.R., box 1, folder 37].

Moses Going testified in Henry County court on 27 April 1780 that he had served as a soldier in Captain James Gunn's Company in Colonel Byrd's Regiment in 1760 (in the French and Indian War) but had not received bounty land [Orders 1778-82, 86; 1782-5, 75].

William Gowen was in the 8 October 1754 muster of Captain John Sallis's Company in the Granville County Regiment of Colonel William Eaton [T.R., box 1, folder 37].

Edward Harris was a "negro" in the 8 October 1754 muster roll of the Granville County Regiment of Colonel William Eaton [T.R., box 1, folder 37, p.1].

Joseph Hawley was in the 8 October 1754 Granville County colonial muster of Colonel Eaton, called Joseph Halley, next to Lawrence **Pettiford** [Clark, *Colonial Soldiers of the South*, 728].

William Holmes was a "Mulatto" living in Henrico County in August 1744 when he complained to the court that he had not received payment for taking up a runaway Negro slave who belonged to Nicholas Davies of Goochland County [Orders 1737-46, 277]. On 28 February 1755 he was listed in the *Virginia Gazette* among soldiers from King William County in the French and Indian War who had deserted: *a Mullatoe, Age 45 Years, about 6 Feet* [Hunter edition, p. 4, col. 2].

Samuel Howell was a 25-year old "mulatto" sawyer from Charles City County, Virginia, listed in the 1757 size roll of Captain Robert Spotswood's Company in Fort Young [Clark, *Colonial Soldiers of the South*, 570].

Thomas Huelin was listed among the "Black" members of the undated colonial muster roll of Captain James Fason's Northampton County Militia [T.R. box 1, folder 3].

Edward Huelin/ Huling was listed as a "Black" member of Fason's Muster [T.R. box 1, folder 3].

Adam Ivey was listed in the Edgecombe County, North Carolina militia in the 1750s [Clark, *Colonial Soldiers of the South*, 672].

Francis Jones was a "Black" member of Captain James Fason's colonial Northampton County, North Carolina Militia [T.R., box 1, folder 3].

James Jones, born say 1716, was a soldier who enlisted in the expedition against the Spaniards at Carthagena and died in Jamaica. His "Mulatto" widow Rebecca Jones petitioned the Virginia House of Burgesses for a pension and was granted an allowance of £5 on 26 May 1742 [McIlwaine, *Journals of the House of Burgesses*, 21, 37].

George Kersey was listed in Captain Hardy Cone's Company of Edgecombe County Militia in the 1750s adjacent to Thomas Kersey [Clark, *Colonial Soldiers of the South*, 667].

Thomas Kersey was in Captain Hardy Cone's Edgecombe County militia in the 1750's [Clark, *Colonial Soldiers of the South*, 667]. He was a "Molato" taxable in Bladen County in 1768 and taxable on 2 "Molatoes" (himself and William **Horn**) and two slaves (Dick and Quash) in 1776 [Byrd, *Bladen County Tax Lists*, I:9, 71, 83, 124, 135; II:66, 76].

Benjamin Knight was listed in the muster roll of Colonel Richard Richardson's Battalion of South Carolina Militia in the 1759 Cherokee Expedition from 18 October 1759 to 10 January 1760 [Clark, *Colonial Soldiers of the South*, 898]. He was called Ben Night, "Mulatto," head of a 96 District, South Carolina household of 1 "other free" in 1790.

Randall Locklear was in the muster roll of Captain Smith's Company of the Edgecombe County Militia in the 1750's [Clark, *Colonial Soldiers of the South*, 672]. In 1765 he and wife Sarah were "Black" tithables in Granville County, North Carolina [CR 44.701.20].

James Longo was a delinquent Accomack County militiaman in January 1685 [W&Co 1682-97, 57, 119a, 142a].

Thomas Morgan was a soldier from Suffolk, Virginia, in the French and Indian War who deserted from the Virginia Regiment on 2 September 1757 and was described as: age 26, 5'7", mulatto [*Virginia Gazette*, Hunter edition, p. 4, col. 2].

Booth Newsom was listed in the Colonial Muster Roll of Captain James Fason's Northampton County Militia [T.R., box 1, folder 3].

James Newsom was a "Black" member of the undated Colonial Muster of Captain James Fason's Northampton County militia [T.R. box 1, folder 3]. He was head of a Northampton County household of 11 "other free" in 1790 [NC:74] and 10 in 1800 [NC:463].

John Newsom was a "Black" member of Captain Fason's Northampton County militia [T.R. box 1, folder 3].

Moses Newsom was listed among the "Black" members of the undated Colonial Muster Roll of Captain Fason's Northampton County Militia [T.R. box 1, folder 3]. He was head of a Northampton County household of 14 "other free" in 1790 [NC:74], and 10 in 1800 [NC:463].

Richard Nickens and Simon **Shewcraft** were in the muster roll of Major William Shergold's Regiment of Currituck County, North Carolina Militia in the 1750's [Clark, *Colonial Soldiers of the South*, 657-8].

Joshua Pavey was listed in the 27 November 1752 muster of the Wilmington, North Carolina Company commanded by Captain George Merrick [Clark, *Colonial Soldiers of the South*, 683]. He was called "Pavey" in the 1755 New Hanover List of Taxables in which he was taxable on 4 "Negro Males" [N.C. Archives File T.O. 105].

George Pettiford was a "Black" taxable in the 1754 Granville County, North Carolina tax list of Robert Harris [CR 44.701.19], and he was listed in the muster roll of Colonel William Eaton's Granville County Militia [T.R., box 1, folder 37, p.8].

Lawrence Pettiford was in the 8 October 1754 Granville County muster of Colonel Eaton [T.R., box 1, folder 37, p.12].

George Perkis (Perkins) was in the Berkeley County, South Carolina Detachment of Captain Benjamin Elliot, drafted November 1759 and discharged January 8, 1760, in the same list with "Carter, a free Negro," Gideon **Bunch**, Ephraim **Bunch**, James **Bunch**, and Jacob **Bunch** [Clark, *Colonial Soldiers of the South*, 939]. He was a taxable head of his own "Black" Craven County, North Carolina household in 1769 [SS 837].

James Pompey was a "Negro planter" from Sussex County, Virginia, listed in the Size Roll of Captain Thomas Waggener's Company at Fort Holland in August 1757: *22 years old, 5 feet 4 inches tall* [Clark, *Colonial Soldiers of the South*, 463]. He, Amos Newsom, John **Muns**, and Samuel **Santee** were paid by the Sussex County court on 21 June 1757 for 2 to 6 days diet as county soldiers and guards [Court Papers, 1757, frame 747, LVA microfilm no. 39].

Peter Rouse was listed in the muster of Captain Paul Demere's Company of Independent Foot on duty in South Carolina and Georgia, "stationed on the spot," from 25 August 1756 to 24 October 1756 [Clark, *Colonial Soldiers of the South*, 989].

Francis and Abraham Scott were listed (consecutively) in the Edgecombe County, North Carolina muster of militia with members of the **Chavis** and **Evans** families in the 1750s: *Willm Allen, Francess Scoot, James Evens, Benjamine Cheavers, Abraham Scoot* [T.R, box 1, folder 12, last page].

Simon Shoecraft was in North Carolina in the 1750s when he and Richard **Nickens** were listed in the Muster Roll of Captain Thomas Davis's Company in the Currituck County Militia [Clark, *Colonial Soldiers of the South*, 657-8]. Members of the Shoecraft family were counted as "other free" persons near the **Nickens** and **Weaver** families in Hertford County from 1790 to 1810.

James Shoemaker and his wife Mary were "Black" taxables in Fishing Creek District, Granville County, North Carolina, in 1762 [CR 044.701.19]. He was a "Black" member of the undated colonial muster roll of Captain James Fason's Northampton County militia [T.R. box 1, folder 3] and was head of a Georgetown District, Prince George's Parish, South Carolina household of 7 "other free" in 1790.

Anthony Sweat was listed in the Muster Roll of Captain John McCant's Company of Colonel Gabriel Powell's Battalion of South Carolina Militia from 11 October 1759 to 15 January 1760 in the Cherokee Expedition [Clark, *Colonial Soldiers of the South*, 895, 925].

Barnet Sweat was listed in the 8 October 1759 to 10 January 1760 muster roll of Captain James McGirrt's Company in the South Carolina Regiment in the Cherokee Expedition [Clark, *Colonial Soldiers of the South*, 883]. He was listed among the "Black" members of the undated colonial muster roll of Captain James Fason's Company of Northampton County, North Carolina [T.R., box 1, folder 3].

Thomas Sweat was listed in the Muster Roll of Captain Alexander McKintosh's Company of Colonel Gabriel Powell's Battalion in the expedition against the Cherokees from 11 October 1759 to 15 January 1760, in the same list as Winslow Driggers [Clark, *Colonial Soldiers of the South*, 929].

Benjamin Tann was listed among the "Black" members of the undated colonial muster roll of Captain James Fason's Northampton County Militia [T.R., box 1, folder 3].

John Tiller was in the Size Roll of Captain Robert McKenzie's Company in 1757-1758: *age 28, 6 feet high, Charles City, Va., no trade, Mulatto* [Clark, *Colonial Soldiers of the South*].

Jacob Warwick/ Warrick was listed among the soldiers in King George's War who failed to report to their camp at Williamsburg in July 1746: *a whitish mulatto, age 25, 5'10"* [*Virginia Gazette*, Hunter edition, p. 3, cols. 1-2].

Jacob Warrick, Job Warrick, and Moses Warrick were "Black" members of the undated colonial muster of Captain James Fason's Company of Northampton County Militia [T.R. box 1, folder 3].

George Williams was a soldier from Richmond County in the French and Indian War, age 26, a mulatto, 6'1", when he was listed as a deserter on 2 September 1757 [*Virginia Gazette*, Hunter edition, p. 4, col. 2].

William Williams was a 33-year-old, 5'6" Virginia "Negro" planter who was listed in the 13 July 1756 roll of Captain Henry Harrison's Company, drafted in Surry County, Virginia [Clark, *Colonial Soldiers of the South*, 390].

DELAWARE COLONIAL

Bede Beckett was a 21-year-old, born in Maryland, who was listed in the 11 May 1759 muster of Captain John Wright's Company in the French and Indian War (abstracted as "Bedy Bullett," in the same list with Samuel and Thomas **Hanzer** of Sussex County, that included mostly men born in Sussex County [Montgomery, *Pennsylvania Archives, Fifth Series*, 278-9].

Samuel Hansor was a 24-year-old listed in the muster of Captain John Wright's Company of Delaware recruits in the French and Indian War on 11 May 1759 [Public Archives *Commission, Delaware*, 25]. He was married to Comfort Hanzer before 15

April 1770 when their "Melatto" daughter Ann was baptized at St. George's Chapel, Indian River Hundred [Wright, *Vital Records of Kent and Sussex Counties*, 99].

Thomas Hanzer was a 19-year-old listed in the muster of Captain John Wright's Company of Delaware recruits in the French and Indian War on 11 May 1759 [Public Archives *Commission, Delaware*, 25]. He was head of an Indian River Hundred, Sussex County household of 3 "other free" in 1800 [DE:437].

Daniel Norwood was a 19-year-old farmer born in Angola Hundred who enlisted in the French and Indian War on 19 April 1758 and was listed in the 17 May 1758 muster of Captain McClughan's Company for the campaign in the Lower Counties [Montgomery, *Pennsylvania Archives, Fifth Series*, 142-3].

Nathaniel Norwood was a 23-year-old planter born in Indian River Hundred who enlisted in the French and Indian War on 19 April 1758 and was listed in the 17 May 1758 muster of Captain McClughan's Company for the campaign in the Lower Counties [Montgomery, *Pennsylvania Archives, Fifth Series*, 142-4]. He and his wife, Jemimy, registered the 17 June 1769 birth of their "Melatto" son, Bowen, and their son Nathan at St. George's Protestant Episcopal Church, Indian River Hundred, Sussex County [Wright, *Vital Records of Kent and Sussex Counties*, 99, 103].

Southy Pride was a 21-year-old, born in Sussex County, who enlisted in Captain John Wright's Company in the French and Indian War on 11 May 1759 [Public Archives Commission, *Delaware Archives*, 18, 25]. He married Eunice **Hermon (Harmon)**, "Melattoes," on 13 May 1772 in Sussex County [Records of the United Presbyterian Churches of Lewes, Indian River and Cool Spring, Delaware 1756-1855, 284].

David Street was a 23-year-old, born in Sussex County, who was listed in the 11 May 1759 muster of Captain John Wright's Company in the French and Indian War, in the same list with Samuel and Thomas **Hanzer** of Sussex County and Andrew McGill, an Indian born in Maryland [Montgomery, *Pennsylvania Archives, Fifth Series*, 278-9].

SOURCES

VIRGINIA

Virginia county court records and personal property tax lists were taken from the microfilms of the originals at the Library of Virginia (on interlibrary loan).

The court order books for each county are listed under the Library of Virginia site https://www.lva.virginia gov/public/local The personal property tax lists for each county are listed under the Library of Virgina site http://www lva virginia.gov/public/guides/pptax htm.

However, the court records and personal property tax lists are now available in on-line pdf files on http://famhysearch.org For example, Amelia County Court Order Books 1735-1746 and 1746-1751 are available on-line at
https://www.familysearch.org/ark:/61903/3 1.3Q9M-CS4H-C9Z5-9?cat=275453
(Catalog, Virginia U.S.A., place within Virginia [county], Court records, Order Books.)
And Orange County, North Carolina County Court Minutes are available at
https://www.familysearch.org/ark:/61903/3.1:3Q9M-CS35-4SMB-S?mode=g&cat=474816

VIRGINIA COUNTIES

Accomack
MS Court Orders 1764-5, 1828-36. LVA films 83, 99-100. PPTL 1782-1814, film 1.

Albemarle
Court Orders 1801-1803; 1810-1811.

Amelia
MS Court Orders 1735-1782; Family History Department microfilm no. 30459

Amherst
MS Court Orders 1782-1787. LVA microfilm reels 27-30, 37. PPTL 1782-1823. LVA microfilm reels 18, 19

Bedford County
MS Register of Free Negroes, 1803-1820, 1820-1860, LVA film 102a.

Botetourt County
MS Register of Free Negroes,

Brunswick
MS Orders 1784-88, LVA film 34. PPTL 1782-1826. LVA films 60-61.

Campbell
MS Court Orders 1782-1792 LVA reel no. 25. PPTL 1785-1814. LVA reel no. 66.

Caroline
MS Court Orders 1755-1758, LVA microfilm reels 19-22, 6, 62. PPTL 1783-1811, microfilm reels 71-2

Charles City
MS Orders 1737-1762. PPTL 1783, 1788-1807, 1809-23, LVA microfilm reels 1, 2, 3, 8, 9, 23, 47, 78.

Charlotte
MS Register of Free Negroes 1794-1865. LVA microfilm reels 3, 16, 22-26, 136-140, 146, 155, 156. PPTL 1782-1813, LVA microfilm no. 80.

Chesterfield
MS Court Orders 1749-1778; Register of Free Negroes 1804-1830 LVA microfilm reels 38-40, 351 PPTL 1786-1811, 1812-1827, reels 84-5

Culpeper
PPTL 1782-1802, 1803-23; LVA reels 78, 89, 90.

Cumberland
MS Order Books 1752-1787. LVA reel nos. 17, 23-28. PPTL 1782-1816, LVA microfilm no. 93.

Dinwiddie
PPTL 1782-1819; LVA microfilm nos 96-7.

Elizabeth City
PPTL 1782-1844. LVA microfilm reel no 101.

Essex
PPTL 1782-1819. LVA microfilm no. 103

Fauquier
MS Minute Book 1768-1784, LVA microfilm reels 47-52, 115 PPTL 1782-1819, LVA microfilm reels 110-112.

Fluvanna
List of Free Negroes photocopied by the Court Clerk of Fluvanna County.
PPTL 1782-1826 LVA microfilm no. 118.

Franklin
MS Minutes 1806-9, LVA film 28.
PPTL 1804-1821. LVA microfilm no 121.

Frederick
PPTL 1782-1802. LVA film no. 124.

Gloucester
MS PPTL 1782-1820. LVA microfilm nos 132-3.

Goochland
MS Court Orders 1737-1746, Register of Free Negroes 1804-1857 LVA microfilm reels 21-29, 43, 77-79. PPTL 1782-1832 LVA microfilm reels 136-7.

Greensville
MS Registry of Free Negroes. LVA microfilm reel 25.

Halifax
MS Registers of Free Negroes 1802-1830, LVA microfilm 83a. PPTL, 1782-1832. LVA reels 147-150

Hardy
PPTL 1786-1806, LVA reel no. 163.

Henrico
MS Court Orders 1755-62, 1781-4, 1787-91, Register of Free Negroes 1831-1844. LVA microfilm reels 67, 69, 70 PPTL 1782-1814; LVA microfilm nos 171

Henry
MS Court Orders 1778-1785; LVA reel no. 20. PPTL, 1782-1830, LVA reel no. 175.

James City
PPTL 1782-1824, LVA microfilm no. 183.
Bruton Parish Register, 1732-1792, Family History Library film 34219.

King George
MS Court Orders 1766-1790, Register of Free Person 1785-1799, LVA microfilm reels 26, 58 PPTL 1782-1830. LVA reel no 196

Lancaster
MS Court Orders 1762-1841, LVA microfilm nos 29, 30, 33, 41
Burkett, Brigette 1999. *Lancaster County, Virginia, Register of Free Negroes* Iberian Publishing

Loudoun County
MS List of Tithables, 1758-1799 LVA film 99. PPTL 1782-1825 LVA reels 207-210

Lunenburg
MS Court Orders 1746-84; 1796-1805, LVA microfilm reels 19-20, 25-30, 32
PPTL 1782-1807. LVA microfilm no 217.

Mecklenburg
MS Orders 1765-1784, LVA microfilm reels 1-5, 23, 34-40. PPTL, 1782-1828, LVA reel 230-1

Middlesex County
MS Court Order Books, 1781-4, 1784-6, LVA microfilm reel no. 69.
National Society of the Colonial Dames of America 1964. *The Parish Register of Christ Church,*

Middlesex County, Virginia from 1653 to 1812. Baltimore.

Norfolk
MS Orders 1753-1810; Minutes 1820-55; Register of Free Negroes and Mulattoes, 1809-1852. LVA microfilm reels 11, 13-20, 46-7, 49-50, 53-60, 67-70, 133, 281. PPTL 1813-24. LVA microfilm reels 247, 249, 250
Wingo, Elizabeth B and W. Bruce Wingo 1979-1985. *Norfolk County, Virginia, Tithables 1730-1750, 1751-1765, 1766-1780.*

Northampton
MS Court Order Books, 1742-8, 1765-71, 1787-9, 1789-95, 1771-7, LVA microfilm reels 48, 50, 52. PPTL 1782-1823. LVA reel no. 254.

Northumberland
MS Court Order Books, 1762-1766, LVA microfilm 53
PPTL 1782-1849 LVA microfilm reels 256-7

Petersburg
Register of Free Negroes & Mulattos, 1794-1819; LVA microfilm nos. 1, 24, 25, 337

Pittsylvania
MS Court Records 1767-1809, Judgments, 1767-1778 LVA microfilm reels 47-51, 115-126, 148-50
PPTL 1782-1823, LVA film no 271-3.

Powhatan
MS Orders 1777-1804, Deeds & Wills 1809-1898; Register of Free Negroes 1820-65 LVA microfilm reels 1, 22-4, 45.
PPTL 1782-1825 LVA microfilm reels 277-8.

Prince Edward
MS PPTL 1782-1831 LVA microfilm nos 281-2.

Princess Anne
MS Court Orders/ Minutes 1744-1792; Register of Free Negroes 1830-1862. LVA Microfilm reels 38-41, 43, 75. PPTL, 1790-1822, LVA microfilm reel no. 292.

Richmond City
PPTL 1787-1834, LVA film nos. 363, 364

Richmond County
MS Court Order Books 1746-1752, LVA microfilm no 35

Southampton
MS Orders 1749-89; Minutes 1816-1819. Register of Free Negroes 1794-1832. LVA reels 25-7, 29, 33.
PPTL 1782-1830. LVA reels 320-3.

Spotsylvania
MS Court Orders/ Minutes 1734-5, 1738-95, LVA microfilm reels 26-8, 38, 44-7 PPTL 1782-1813
LVA microfilm reel 327.

Surry
MS Orders 1764-1774. LVA microfilms 28-34, 61
MS PPTL, 1782-1790, 1791-1816, LVA microfilms 329, 331.
Registry of Free Negroes at back of book. LVA Microfilm no. 49
Hudgins, Dennis 1995. *Surry County, Virginia Register of Free Negroes.* Virginia Genealogical Society.

Warwick
MS Minute Book 1748-1762, LVA microfilm reel no. 1. PPTL 1782-1820, LVA microfilm reel no 338.

Westmoreland
PPTL, 1782-1815 LVA reel no. 344

York
MS Orders 1746-1787, Register of Free Negroes 1798-1831, 1831-1850 LVA reels 29, 30, 32, 33, 42, 51. PPTL 1782-1841 LVA reel 353.

Other microfilm and internet sources
MS Virginia Census: 1810 and 1820. M252·66-71, M33:130, 140.
MS *The Virginia Gazette*, photocopied by Prince William County Genealogical Society, Manassas,

Virginia 22110-0812. And on-line Virginia Gazette Colonial Williamsburg
http://research.colonialwilliamsburg.org/DigitalLibrary/va.gazettes/

Runaway Slave advertisements from 18th-century Virginia newspapers Compiled by Professor Thomas Costa, Associate Professor of History, University of Virginia's College at Wise .
http://etext.lib.virginia.edu/subjects/runaways/allrecords.html

MS Revolutionary War Pension Files. National Archives microfilm series M804, M805.

"The Chesterfield Supplement" or *Size Roll of Troops at Chesterfield Court House since September 1st 1780, Capt[t] Joseph Scott*. On the title page· "This book is a supplement to Papers concerning the Army of the Revolution, vol 1 Executive Department and in order precedes Benjamin Harrison's mission to Philadelphia by Assembly, 1781." Manuscript accession number 23816, Library of Virginia, Richmond. Published on-line by Southern Campaigns Revolutionary War Pension Statements & Rosters: http·//revwarapps.org/b81.pdf

Register and description of Noncommissioned Officers & Privates at Chesterfield Court House, Powhatan Court House, Carter's Ferry, Albemarle Old Court House, Cumberland Old Court House& at Winchester Barracks. Enlisted at different times from 1777 to 1783, spine title· *Revolutionary Army, vol I, Register 1777 to 1783*. Manuscript accession number 24296, Library of Virginia, Richmond. Published on-line by Southern Campaigns Revolutionary War Pension Statements & Rosters· http://revwarapps.orgb69.pdf.

United States Government Printing Office. 2005. Naval Documents of the American Revolution, Volume 11, part 5 of 5, Washington, Electronically published by the American Naval Records Society, Bolton Landing, New York 2012, http://ibiblio.org/anrs//docs/E/E3/ndar_v11p05.pdf.

Printed sources
Abercrombie, Janice 1994. *Free Blacks of Louisa County, Virginia*. Iberian Publishing Athens, Georgia
Brumbaugh, Gaius Marcus. 1936. *Revolutionary War Records, Volume 1, Virginia*, Washington, D.C , viewed on-line at http //archive org
Bureau of the Census 1966 [1908]. *Heads of Families at the First Census of the United States Taken in the Year 1790 - Records of the State Enumerations 1782 to 1785, Virginia*. Baltimore
Burkett, Brigette. 1999. *Lancaster County, Virginia, Register of Free Negroes*. Iberian Publishing.
Chamberlayne, Churchill G. 1937. *The Vestry Book & Register of St Peter's Parish, New Kent & James City Counties, Virginia 1684-1786* Richmond: Library Board
Clark, Murtie June. 1983. *Colonial Soldiers of the South, 1732-1774* Baltimore, Md . Genealogical Publishing Co., Inc.
Eckenrode, H. J. (Hamilton James) , Eckenrode, H J. (Hamilton James)., Virginia State Library and Archives. (1989). *Virginia soldiers of the American Revolution*. Richmond. Virginia State Library and Archives.
Gwathmey, John H. 2010. *Historical register of Virginians in the Revolution: soldiers, sailors, marines, 1775-1783* Baltimore, Md : Genealogical Publishing Co., Inc
Jones, W. Mac. 1966. *The Douglas Register, Being a Detailed Record of Births Marriages and Deaths, Kept by Rev William Douglas 1750-1797*. Baltimore.
Library of Virginia, African American Digital Narrative,
https·//www.virginiamemory.com/collections/aan/
Hening, William W., ed 1809-23. *The Statutes at Large Being a Collection of all the Laws of Virginia* Richmond
Hillman, Benjamin J , ed. 1966 *Executive Journals of the Council of Colonial Virginia, Vol VI , June 20, 1754 - May 3, 1775* Virginia State Library
Jackson, Luther Porter. 1944 *Virginia Negro Soldiers and Seamen in the Revolutionary War*. Norfolk,Virginia.
McIlwaine, H. B., ed. 1925. *Executive Journals of the Council of Colonial Virginia, Vol I, June 11, 1680 - June 22, 1699 .Vol IV* Virginia State Library.
McIlwaine, H B , ed. 1908 *Journals of the House of Burgesses of Virginia, 1619-1658/9 1761-1765*. Richmond.
McIlwaine, H.B., ed. 1979 (second edition) *Minutes of the Council and General Court of Virginia*, Richmond: Virginia State Library
Madden, T.O. 1993. *We Were Always Free*. Vintage Books.
Rice, Millard Milburn. 1979. *This Was the Life Excerpts From the Judgment Records of Frederick County, Maryland, 1748-1765* Redwood City. Monocacy Book Company
Schweninger, Loren, *Race, Slavery and Free Black Petitions to Southern Legislatures, Race And Slavery Petitions Project*, http·//library uncg.edu/slavery_petitions
Torrence, Clayton. 1973 [1935]. *Old Somerset on the Eastern Shore of Maryland A Study in Foundations and Founders*. Baltimore. Regional Publishing Company.
Virginia Genealogist, Volumes 1-33. Washington D.C.
United States Government Printing Office. 2005. Naval Documents of the American Revolution, Volume 11, part 5 of 5, Washington, Electronically published by the American Naval Records Society, Bolton Landing, New York 2012   http://ibiblio.org/anrs//docs/E/E3/ndar_v11p05.pdf.

Bertie
Haun, Weynette Parks. 1976-1984. *Bertie County North Carolina County Court Minutes (Court of Pleas & Quarter Sessions)*, Book III, 1763-1771, IV, 1772-1780, VI, 1788-1792. Durham, N C.

Bladen
Byrd, William L. 1998. *Bladen County, North Carolina Tax Lists, 1768 through 1774, Volume I* Privately printed.
Byrd, William L. 1998. *Bladen County, North Carolina Tax Lists, 1775 through 1789, Volume II* Heritage Books, Inc. Maryland.

Bute
Holcolm, Brent Howard 1988. *Court of Pleas and Quarter Sessions, Minutes 1767-1779*. Columbia, S.C.

Carteret
MS County Court Minutes 1723-1747, 1747-1777. N.C. Archives Microfilms C 019.30001-2.

Chowan
Minutes, Court of Pleas and Quarter Sessions, 1755-1772, N.C. Archives Microfilm C.024.30001

Craven
MS County Court Minutes, 1758-1766, 1764-1775, 1772-1784, 1784-87 N.C. Archives Microfilms C.028.30004-7.

Cumberland
MS County Court Minutes, Minutes 1755-1844 N C. Archives Microfilms C.029 30001-5.

Edgecombe
MS County Court Minutes, 1757-1800 N C. Archives Microfilm reels 1&2.

Gates
Fouts, Raymond Parker. Minutes of County Court of Pleas and Quarter Sessions, Gates County, N.C , 1779-1786; 1787-1793; Vols. I-IV· 1794-1799 Cocoa, Fl.

Granville
MS County Court Minutes, 1766-1795 N.C. Archives Microfilm reel 3.
Owen, Thomas McAdory 190_. *Granville County, North Carolina, Notes*. Montgomery, Alabama Library of Congress Microfilm Shelf No. 28037, call no. F262.G85087. (Minutes 1746-1759, 1767-1772, transcribed in 1895 - now missing).

Hertford
Tax Lists. N.C. Archives General Assembly Papers GA 30.1 and GA. 64 1.
Fouts, Raymond Parker. 1993 *William Murfree Tax Receipt Book, Hertford County, North Carolina* Cocoa, Fl.

Johnston
Haun, Weynette Parks 1980-1988. *Johnston County, North Carolina, County Court Minutes (Court of Pleas & Quarter Sessions), Book III (1778-1786), Book IV (1787-1792)*. Durham, N C.

Northampton
MS Court of Pleas and Quarter Sessions Minutes 1792-96. N C. Archives Microfilm reel 2.

Person
MS Court of Pleas & Quarter Sessions Minutes 1792-1802. N.C Archives Microfilm C.078 30001.

Other microfilm sources
MS North Carolina Governor's Office Census of 1784-87 N.C. Archives Microfilm S.51 567.
MS North Carolina Census. 1800, 1810, 1820, and 1830. Microfilms M32·29-34; M252·38-43; M33:80-85, M19·121,123

Printed sources
Bureau of the Census. 1978 [1908]. *Heads of Families at the First Census of the United States Taken in the Year 1790: North Carolina* Baltimore
Byrd, William L 1998 *Bladen County, North Carolina Tax Lists, 1768 through 1774, Volume I* Privately printed.
Byrd, William L. 1998. *Bladen County, North Carolina Tax Lists, 1775 through 1789, Volume II* Heritage Books, Inc. Maryland.
Clark, Walter, ed. 1895-1907. *The State Records of North Carolina*. 16 vols numbered XI-XXVI

Winston and Goldsboro, N.C.. State of North Carolina
Crow, Jeffrey J. 1983. *The Black Experience in Revolutionary North Carolina* Raleigh.
Fouts, Raymond Parker. 1984 *Abstracts from Newspapers of Edenton, Fayetteville, & Hillsborough, North Carolina 1785-1800.* Cocoa, Fl.
Haun, Weynette Parks. 1990. *North Carolina Revolutionary Army Accounts Secretary of State Treasurer's & Comptroller's Papers, Vol I & II, Part II* Durham, N.C
Haun, Weynette Parks. 1989. *North Carolina Revolutionary Army Accounts Secretary of State Treasurer's & Comptroller's Papers, Journal "A", (Public Accounts) 1775-1776* Durham, N C.
McBride, Ransom. *Revolutionary War Service Records and Settlements*, published in the *North Carolina Genealogical Society Journal.*
North Carolina Daughters of the American Revolution. *Roster of Soldiers from North Carolina in the American Revolution* Durham· North Carolina DAR, 1932 reprinted. Baltimore· Genealogical Publishing Co., 1984.

SOUTH CAROLINA SOURCES

MS South Carolina Tax Returns 1783-1800, South Carolina Archives microfilm AD-941 and AD-942.
MS South Carolina Census. 1790, 1800, 1810, and 1820. Microfilms M637-11; M32:47-50; M252 60-62
Bureau of the Census 1978 [1908]. *Heads of Families at the First Census of the United States Taken in the Year 1790 South Carolina* Baltimore

MARYLAND AND DELAWARE SOURCES

Manuscript and Microfilmed Manuscript Documents
Delaware Archives, Sussex County Assessments, Levy Lists 1770-1796, microfilm RG2535.
Delaware Archives, Kent County Assessments, Levy Lists 1727-1850, microfilm RG3535.
Delaware Census Records, 1800 Census. microfilm M32-4, 1810 Census: M252-4; 1820 Census: M33-5.
Records of the United Presbyterian Churches of Lewes, Indian River and Cool Spring, Delaware 1756-1855. Micro-reproduction of original records at the Genealogical Society of Pennsylvania Family History, http.//familysearch com/search/catalog, film number 0441441.
Census Records, 1800 Census: microfilm M32-9, 10, 11, 12. 1810 Census: M252-13, 14, 15.

Printed Sources·
Brown, William Hand, ed., et.al., 68 vols 1883-. Archives of Maryland. Baltimore
Bureau of the Census. 1965 [1908]. *Heads of Families at the First Census of the United States Taken in the Year 1790. Maryland* Baltimore
Boyle, Joseph L, *He Loves a good deal of rum Military Desertions during the American Revolution, 1775-1783,* Vol. 2, June 1777-1783, 249, 298-9].
Carothers, Bettie Stirling. 1910 *1776 Census of Maryland.* Lutherville, Maryland.
Public Archives Commission of Delaware, *Delaware Archives,* Revolutionary War, Volumes I-V, Wilmington, Delaware (1911-1916).
Windley, Lathan A. 1983. *Runaway Slave Advertisements A documentary History from the 1730s to 1790 Volume 2* Greenwood Press. Westport Connecticut.

169

171

172

173

CPSIA information can be obtained
at www.ICGtesting.com
Printed in the USA
FSHW020056291221
87163FS